Computational Intelligence
and Healthcare Informatics

Scrivener Publishing
100 Cummings Center, Suite 541J
Beverly MA, 01915-6106

Machine Learning in Biomedical Science and Healthcare Informatics

Series Editors: Vishal Jain and Jyotir Moy Chatterjee

In this series, the focus centres on the various applications of machine learning in the biomedical engineering and healthcare fields, with a special emphasis on the most representative learning techniques, namely deep learning-based approaches. Machine learning tasks typically classified into two broad categories depending on whether there is a learning "label" or "feedback" available to a learning system: supervised learning and unsupervised learning. This series also introduces various types of machine learning tasks in the biomedical engineering field from classification (supervised learning) to clustering (unsupervised learning). The objective of the series is to compile all aspects of biomedical science and healthcare informatics, from fundamental principles to current advanced concepts.

Submission to the series: Please send book proposals to **drvishaljain83@gmail.com** and/or **jyotirchatterjee@gmail.com**

Publishers at Scrivener
Martin Scrivener (martin@scrivenerpublishing.com)
Phillip Carmical (pcarmical@scrivenerpublishing.com)

Computational Intelligence and Healthcare Informatics

Edited by

**Om Prakash Jena, Alok Ranjan Tripathy,
Ahmed A. Elngar and Zdzislaw Polkowski**

Scrivener
Publishing

WILEY

This edition first published 2021 by John Wiley & Sons, Inc., 111 River Street, Hoboken, NJ 07030, USA and Scrivener Publishing LLC, 100 Cummings Center, Suite 541J, Beverly, MA 01915, USA
© 2021 Scrivener Publishing LLC
For more information about Scrivener publications please visit www.scrivenerpublishing.com.

Wiley Global Headquarters
111 River Street, Hoboken, NJ 07030, USA

For details of our global editorial offices, customer services, and more information about Wiley products visit us at www.wiley.com.

Limit of Liability/Disclaimer of Warranty
While the publisher and authors have used their best efforts in preparing this work, they make no representations or warranties with respect to the accuracy or completeness of the contents of this work and specifically disclaim all warranties, including without limitation any implied warranties of merchant-ability or fitness for a particular purpose. No warranty may be created or extended by sales representatives, written sales materials, or promotional statements for this work. The fact that an organization, website, or product is referred to in this work as a citation and/or potential source of further information does not mean that the publisher and authors endorse the information or services the organization, website, or product may provide or recommendations it may make. This work is sold with the understanding that the publisher is not engaged in rendering professional services. The advice and strategies contained herein may not be suitable for your situation. You should consult with a specialist where appropriate. Neither the publisher nor authors shall be liable for any loss of profit or any other commercial damages, including but not limited to special, incidental, consequential, or other damages. Further, readers should be aware that websites listed in this work may have changed or disappeared between when this work was written and when it is read.

Library of Congress Cataloging-in-Publication Data

ISBN 978-1-119-81868-7

Cover image: Pixabay.Com
Cover design by Russell Richadson

Set in size of 11pt and Minion Pro by Manila Typesetting Company, Makati, Philippines

10 9 8 7 6 5 4 3 2 1

Contents

Preface

Computational intelligence (CI) refers to the ability of computers to accomplish tasks that are normally completed by intelligent beings such as humans and animals. With the rapid advance of technology, artificial intelligence (AI) techniques are being effectively used in the fields of health to improve the efficiency of treatments, avoid the risk of false diagnoses, make therapeutic decisions, and predict the outcome in many clinical scenarios. Modern health treatments are faced with the challenge of acquiring, analysing and applying the large amount of knowledge necessary to solve complex problems. Computational intelligence in healthcare mainly uses computer techniques to perform clinical diagnoses and suggest treatments. In the present scenario of computing, CI tools present adaptive mechanisms that permit the understanding of data in difficult and changing environments. The desired results of CI technologies profit medical fields by assembling patients with the same types of diseases or fitness problems so that healthcare facilities can provide effectual treatments.

This book starts with the fundamentals of computer intelligence and the techniques and procedures associated with it. Contained in this book are state-of-the-art methods of computational intelligence and other allied techniques used in the healthcare system, as well as advances in different CI methods that will confront the problem of effective data analysis and storage faced by healthcare institutions. The objective of this book is to provide researchers with a platform encompassing state-of-the-art innovations; research and design; implementation of methodological and algorithmic solutions to data processing problems; and the design and analysis of evolving trends in health informatics, intelligent disease prediction and computer-aided diagnosis.

The book aims to integrate several aspects of CI, like machine learning and deep learning, from diversified perspectives involving recent research trends and advanced topics in the field which will be of interest to academicians and researchers working in this area. The purpose of the book is to endow different communities with innovative advances in theory, analytical approaches, numerical simulation, statistical analysis, modeling, advanced deployment, case studies, analytical results, computational structuring and significance progress in the field of machine learning and deep learning in healthcare applications. This book is targeted towards scientists, application doctors, health professionals, professors, researchers and students. Different dimensions of CI applications will be revealed and its use as a solution for assorted real-world biomedical and healthcare problems is illustrated. Following is a brief description of the subjects covered in each chapter.

- Chapter 1 is a systematic review of better options in the field of healthcare using machine learning and big data. The use of machine learning (ML) and big data in several application areas in healthcare services are identified which can further improve the unresolved challenges. Technologies such as ML will greatly transform traditional healthcare services and improve the relationship between service users and providers, providing better service in less time. Moreover, ML will help in keeping an eye on critical patients in real time, diagnose their disease, and recommend further treatment.

- Chapter 2 provides a critical analysis of the deep learning techniques utilized for thoracic image analysis and the respective accuracy achieved by it. Various deep learning techniques are described along with dataset, activation function and model used, number and types of layers used, learning rate, training time, epoch, performance metric, hardware used and type of abnormality detected. Moreover, a comparative analysis of existing deep learning models based on accuracy, precision and recall is also presented with an emphasis on the future direction of research.

- Chapter 3 discusses various application domains in need of feature selection techniques and also the way to deal with feature reduction problems occurring in large, voluminous datasets.

- Chapter 4 presents a detailed analysis of the available ML and ANN models conducted vis-à-vis the data considered, and the best one is applied for training and testing the neural networks developed for the present work to detect and predict a disease based on the symptoms described.

- Chapter 5 presents an approach for heart sound classification using the time-frequency image texture feature and support vector machine classifier.

- Chapter 6 proposes a novel approach for selecting a prototype without dropout for the accuracy of the multi-label classification algorithm.

- Chapter 7 introduces an intelligent computational predictive system for the identification and diagnosis of diabetes. Here, eight machine learning classification hypotheses are examined for the identification and diagnosis of diabetes. Numerous performance measuring metrics, such as accuracy, sensitivity, specificity, AUC, F1-score, MCC, and ROC curve, are applied to inspect the effectiveness and stability of the proposed model.

- Chapter 8 proposes hyperparameter optimization for ensemble learners as it has a lot of hyperparameters. The optimized ensemble learning model can be built by tuning the hyperparameters of ensemble learners. This chapter applies a grid search and random search algorithms for tuning the hyperparameters of ensemble learners. Three ensemble learners are used in this proposed work: two boosting models (AdaBoost and Gradient boosting algorithms) and one bagging model (Random Forest algorithm).

- Chapter 9 presents a detailed analysis of the different types of healthcare simulations—from discrete event simulation (DES) and agent-based methods (ABM) to system dynamics (SD).

- Chapter 10 focuses on the application of Wolfram's cellular automata (CA) model in different domains of health informatics, medical informatics and bioinformatics. It also reports on the analysis of medical imaging for breast cancer, heart disease, tumor detection and other diseases using CA. Augmenting the machine learning mechanism with CA is also discussed, which provides higher accuracy, precision, security, speed, etc.

– Chapter 11 considers the global dataset of 204 countries for the period of December 31st 2019 to May 19th 2020 from the Worldometer website for study purpose and data from May 20th to June 8th is considered to predict the evaluation of the outbreak, i.e., three weeks ahead. Three of the most prominent data mining techniques—linear regression (LR), association rule mining (ARM) and back propagation neural network (BPNN)—are utilized to predict and analyze the COVID-19 dataset.

– Chapter 12 proposes a hybrid support vector machine (SVM) with chicken swarm optimization (CSO) algorithm for efficient sentiment analysis. Part-of-speech (POS) tagged text is used in this algorithm for extracting the potential features.

– Chapter 13 discusses the primary healthcare model for remote areas using a self-organizing map network.

– Chapter 14 proposes a real-time face mask detection approach using VGG19 from the video stream recorded using a webcam that achieved 100 percent training accuracy with logloss 0.00 and a validation accuracy of 99.63 percent with logloss 0.01 in just 20 epochs.

– Chapter 15 focuses on different types of machine and deep learning algorithms like CNN and SVM for skin disease classification. The methods are very helpful in identifying skin diseases very easily and in fewer time periods.

– Chapter 16 discusses a program developed for collecting heart rhythm, pulse rate, body temperature, and inclination data from patients.

– Chapter 17 describes a proposed automatic COVID-19 detection system that can be used as an alternative diagnostic medium for the virus.

– Chapter 18 presents an innovative approach for deriving interesting patterns using machine learning and graph database models to incorporate the preventive measures in an earlier state. A graph-based statistical analysis (GSA) model to study the COVID-19 pandemic outbreak's impact is also proposed.

– Chapter 19 discusses the conceptualization of tomorrow's healthcare through digitization. The objective of this chapter is to utilize the latest resources available at hand to design the case studies.

– Chapter 20 provides a systematic procedure for the development of the POS tagger trained on general domain corpus and the development of biomedical corpus in Hindi.

– Chapter 21 studies the concepts of neuro-linguistic programming (NLP) used in healthcare applications, and also examines the NLP system and the resources which are used in healthcare. Along with the challenges of NLP, different aspects of NLP are studied as well as clinical methods.

Finally, we would like to sincerely thank all the chapter authors who contributed their time and expertise and for helping to reach a successful completion of the book. Second, the editors wish to acknowledge the valuable contributions of the reviewers regarding the improvement of quality, coherence, and content presentation of chapters.

The Editors
July 2021

Part I
INTRODUCTION

Machine Learning and Big Data: An Approach Toward Better Healthcare Services

Nahid Sami* and Asfia Aziz

School of Engineering Science and Technology, Jamia Hamdard, New Delhi, India

Abstract

Artificial Intelligence has been considered the biggest technology in transforming society. The transformation is highly influenced by the tools and techniques provided by Machine Learning and Deep Learning. One latest discovery is Robotic Surgical Tools like Da Vinci robot which helps surgeons to perform surgeries more accurately and detect distances of particular body parts to perform surgery precisely over them using computer vision assisted by machine learning. The maintenance of health records is a tedious process and ML in association with Big Data has greatly saved the effort, money and time required while processing such records. MIT is working on intelligent smart health record learning method using machine learning techniques to give suggestions regarding diagnosis and medication. Deep mining techniques are used in medical image analysis for the detection of tissue in radiotherapy. Outbreak of several chronic diseases can also be predicted using data gathered through satellite, online information and social media updates. Big Data provides a major part by maintaining the EHR which is in form of complex unstructured data. Another major challenging area is related to the infrastructure of the hospital. Moving toward more advance technologies, the infrastructure need to be updated which is time consuming and costly.

Keywords: Machine learning, deep learning, healthcare, electronic medical records (EMRs), big data

1.1 Introduction

Machine Learning (ML) is a computer program that learns from experience with respect to a particular task assigned and gives result accordingly. The performance of such computational algorithm improves with experience. Health is a major area of concern for everyone and to provide the best healthcare service is becoming one of the major goals of almost every country. But doing that is not an easy task as collecting the medical data and providing it to leverage knowledge so that the best possible treatment can be provided is itself very challenging. So, data plays a crucial part in extracting information and addressing problems related to health. ML has the ability to extract information

*Corresponding author: nahidsami187@gmail.com

Om Prakash Jena, Alok Ranjan Tripathy, Ahmed A. Elngar and Zdzislaw Polkowski (eds.) Computational Intelligence and Healthcare Informatics, (3–14) © 2021 Scrivener Publishing LLC

from the data being provided and further helps in resolving this fundamental issue to some extent.

The huge medical data need to be interpreted and processed by epidemiologists. The input of healthcare providers has been expanded and also created new opportunities due to the availability of huge amount of data related to patients and facility being provided which will further help in achieving the necessary approaches related to prevention and treatment [1]. Due to the complexity of medical data and also lack of technology, the collection was completely ignored in the past. ML algorithm has proved to overcome such difficulties by collecting the medical data securely and further applying it for diagnosis and prognosis. ML has improved several domains like Automatic Speech Recognition (ASR), Natural Language Processing (NLP), and computer vision by using the data. Creating the correct model for maintaining the electronic medical records (EMRs) is a challenging issue due to its availability, quality, and heterogeneity.

Big data is going to play a major role in revolutionizing the healthcare services in the coming future by using algorithm to detect and treat diseases [2]. Its impact on the practice of medicine is fundamentally going to transform the physician ability to personalize care directly to the people. The way to achieve this goal is by collecting data through handheld and wearable devices. This data will be compared with the genetic profile of people and further used for decision-making. The vast medical data needs to be integrated and accessed intelligently to support better healthcare delivery. Big data can create new networks of sharing knowledge by measuring and monitoring processes digitally [3]. Data comparison will be easier which will facilitate streamlined workflows greater efficiencies and improved patient care. Systematic analysis of extensive data can help to detect patterns so that clinicians can provide treatment to individuals and project health outcomes. Digital networks can bring together partners and knowledge sharing delivering context relevant clinical information enables more holistic decision-making. Healthcare can only benefit from big data when it is made structured relevant smart and accessible.

Figure 1.1 shows the how ML and big data analytics plays an important role in different fields associated with healthcare services. There are five major modules associated with ML algorithm and their contribution. The physician unstructured data is provided to ML algorithm and, in return, gets better clinical decision support. Also, the radiologist provides data in form of MRI/images and receives diagnostics from ML. It provides the patient a better lifestyle advice and treatment option. Patients are complex module with different genetic back ground so the risks associated with them are different over time. The drug makers get patients medical records for development of necessary drugs. The clinical research and development module provides bio illustration to the algorithm and gets predictive analysis.

1.2 Machine Learning in Healthcare

In recent years, artificial intelligence (AI) has shown tremendous growth in transforming every aspect of life due to its wide range of tools which help in decision-making by analyzing

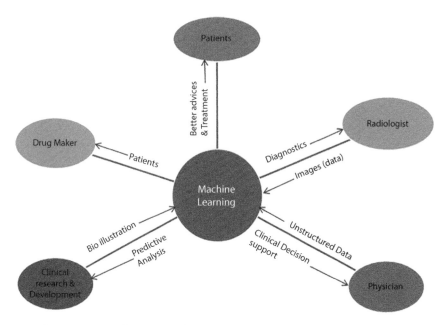

Figure 1.1 Machine learning and big data analysis in healthcare.

data and integrating information. In terms of technology, AI has stolen spotlight and its advancements are quicker than our prediction [4]. ML being a subset of AI is transforming the world and raising its importance for the society. ML is defined as the study of methods and tools which help in identifying patterns within data and make computer learn without being programmed explicitly. ML can further be used to extend our knowledge regarding current scenario as well as for future prediction by allowing program to learn through experience. It uses the concept of AI for data optimization. Analyzing the best model to make the machine intelligent for data explanation is the goal. We will be discussing here its development in the field of medicine.

Figure 1.2 shows the different areas where ML algorithm is playing a major role to provide better healthcare services. Applying such technology will help in proving personalized treatment which will improve the health condition of patients. Drug discovery and research will be highly benefited as the structured data will be available. Further support will be provided to clinical decision-making and early detection of diseases will be possible to make the services better for individual. The use of Deep Learning (DL) and neural network will be highly helpful in improving the imaging and diagnostic techniques. By proving all the essential services in medical, the fraud related to medical insurance will minimized to the least.

ML can transform the healthcare services by making us better providers of correct medical facility at the patient level. We can gather information on how different environmental exposure and lifestyle will vary the symptoms of disease. The intervention and history will help us decide treatment and decision-making. We can further understand the health and disease trajectory which will help in prepare us before arrival of the pandemics in

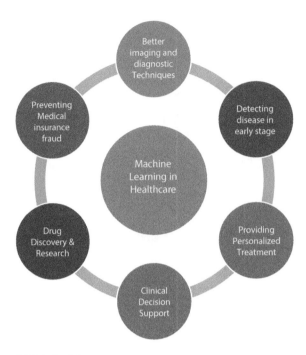

Figure 1.2 Application of ML in healthcare.

worst possible situation. The resources available to us can be utilized in more efficient way with reduced costs. Also, the public health policies can be transformed in a way benefiting the people.

1.3 Machine Learning Algorithms

Depending upon the problem and approach to be applied, it has been categorized into various types among which major application lie into supervised, unsupervised, semi-supervised, reinforcement, and DL. The various types and its contribution to healthcare sector are shown in Figure 1.3.

1.3.1 Supervised Learning

This ML algorithm works under supervision, i.e., machine is trained with data which is well labeled and helps the model to predict with the help of dataset. Furthermore, supervised learning is divided into classification and regression. When the resultant variable is categorical, i.e., with two or more classes (yes/no, true/false, disease/no disease), we make use of classification. Whereas, when the resultant variable is a real and uninterrupted value, the problem is regression, here, a change in one variable is linked with a change in other variable (e.g., weight based on height). Some common examples of supervised ML in medicine is to perform pattern recognition over selected set of diagnosis by a

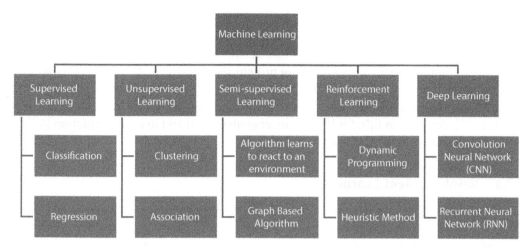

Figure 1.3 The types of machine learning algorithm.

cardiologist by interpretation of EKG and also from a chest X ray detection of lung module can be determined [5]. In medicine, for detection of risk in coronary heart disease, the best possible method adopted for analysis is Framingham Risk Score which is an example of supervised ML [6]. Risk models like above in medicine can guide in antithrombotic therapy in atrial fibrillation [7] and in hypertrophic cardiomyopathy for the implantation of electronic defibrillators [8].

1.3.2 Unsupervised Learning

Such type of ML algorithm does not work upon labeled data and the machine learns from the dataset given and finds out the hidden pattern to make prediction about the output. It is further grouped into clustering and association; in clustering, the machine forms groups based on the behavior of the data, whereas association is a rule-based ML to discover relation between variables of large datasets. Precision medicine initiative is used to perform unsupervised learning problems in medicine [9]. How unsupervised learning can be applied in pathophysiologic mechanism to redefine the inherent heterogeneity in complex multi-factorial diseases, for instance, in cardiac disease like myocarditis. To apply the mechanism, inexplicable acute systolic heart failure is required and performed with myocardial biopsies to identify similar pattern between cellular compositions which will, in return, guide the therapist accordingly. Albiet the same technique to identify a subtype of asthma which responded to IL-13 [10, 11] is adopted.

1.3.3 Semi-Supervised Learning

It is a combination of supervised and unsupervised learning. It uses a combination of small portion of labeled data and massive collection of unlabeled to improve the prediction.

The algorithm has ability to learn how to react on a particular situation based on the environment. The main aim of this method is to improve classification performance. This method is highly applicable in the healthcare sector when labeled data is not sufficiently available. It is applicable for classification of protein sequence typically due to the large size of DNA strands. Consistency enforcing strategy is mostly followed by this method [12]. It has been widely used for classification of medical images to reduce effort over labeling data [13–15]. Apart from this, for breast cancer analysis [16] and liver segmentation [17], a co-training mechanism has been applied.

1.3.4   Reinforcement Learning

This category of algorithm has no predefined data and the input depends upon the action taken by the agent and these actions are then recorded in the form of matrices so that it can serve as the memory to the agent. The agent explores the environment and collects data which is further used to get the output. In medicine, there are several instances of reinforcement learning (RL) application like for the development of therapy plan for lung cancer [18] and epilepsy [19]. Deep RL approach has been recently proposed for the therapy plan development on medical registry data [20] and also to learn treatment strategies for sepsis [21].

1.3.5   Deep Learning

Such algorithms has been widely used in the field of science for solving and analyzing problems related to healthcare by using different techniques for image analysis for obtaining information effectively. DL requires data to get information but, when combined with the medicinal data, makes the work complex for the researcher. Once the data is obtained, it can be applied accordingly in different field of medicine like prognosis, diagnosis, treatment, and clinical workflow. DL concept is used to build tool for skin cancer detection in dermatology [22]. Neural network training using DL method is applied for the computation of diabetic retinopathy severity by using the strength of pixels in fundus image [23].

1.4   Big Data in Healthcare

Sebastian Thrum, a computer scientist, once said, "Just as machines made human muscles a thousand times stronger, machines will make the human brain a thousand times more powerful." This statement is the seed of what big data and ML is doing to healthcare today impacting human lives like never before opening new doors of possibilities and for much good.

In this digital era, massive amounts of data are being generated every moment, the digital universe which was about 130 exabytes (EB) in 2005 has expanded to about 40,000 EB in 2020 [24]. Such huge amount of data, known as big data, is a storehouse of critical information which can transform the way we provide healthcare services.

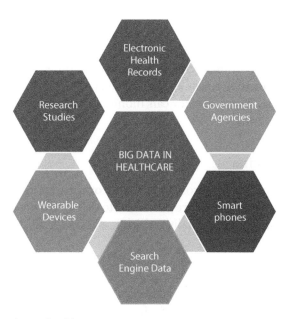

Figure 1.4 Sources of big data in healthcare.

Large amounts of data are generated in healthcare services, and these are from sources (Figure 1.4) as diverse as government agencies, patient portals, research studies, generic databases, electronic health records, public health records, wearable devices, smart phones, and many more. All these sources generate data in different formats which need to be not just merged but also made available instantly when needed; this is where big data and ML together empower healthcare services.

1.5   Application of Big Data in Healthcare

1.5.1   Electronic Health Records

This is one aspect of healthcare where the biggest challenge was assimilating data generated in different forms and different sources and to be able to replicate it instantly for analysis. This helps not just the healthcare provider by keeping record of medical history, tests, and allergies but also keeps the patient informed of any tests or appointments due.

1.5.2   Helping in Diagnostics

With medicine moving toward a more preventive and predictive science and also generalized toward a more individualized science, big data analytics has assumed a more integral role. Use of large volumes of data in fields like radiology, pathology, and oncology helps in arriving at an early diagnosis with computer-assisted devices increasing the accuracy of diagnosis and helping in early intervention thereby improving outcomes.

1.5.3 Preventive Medicine

Wearable devices are the new healthcare providers in today's times and they have an increasingly important role to play in medicine in the times to come. These devices are the new physicians which continue to monitor an individual at all times having not just diagnostic but also predictive value. These devices can monitor many parameters and can connect with physicians even far away.

1.5.4 Precision Medicine

In robotic surgeries especially neurosurgeries and oncosurgeries where precision is of utmost importance, big data and ML are combined to deliver results that lead to better outcomes with lesser morbidity and mortality, which is a boon for all stakeholders.

1.5.5 Medical Research

Advancements in medical research have gathered pace with the availability of big data and ML. With all the data at hand, researchers are forever trying to find better cures. Varied data available for analysis helps in understanding why a particular treatment modality worked in a population group while it failed to bring the desired response in another, blood thinners working in one patient population and not working in another is an example. Researchers are using genetic information to personalise drug treatments [25].

Using algorithms, scientists have been able to identify molecules that activate a particular protein which is relevant to symptoms of Alzheimer's disease and schizophrenia; this could lead to early development of drugs for the treatment of these as yet incurable diseases [26].

1.5.6 Cost Reduction

With the availability of medical data, the healthcare provider gets all the background information of his patient helping him to make decisions with less errors, resulting in lower costs for the patient and the healthcare system. Analysis of data from a particular patient population helps in deciding disease management strategies improving preventive care, thereby minimizing costs.

1.5.7 Population Health

Big data availability leads to optimal use of the available resources for the entire community. It provides insights as to which patient population is especially vulnerable to a particular illness, so that measures can be taken to lessen the impact of a disease whether communicable or non-communicable by scaling up the facilities needed for its management so that the impact of the disease can be contained.

1.5.8 Telemedicine

Doctors recommend telemedicine to patients for personalized treatment solutions to prevent readmissions, and data analytics can then be used to make assessments and predictions of the course and associated management adjustments.

1.5.9   Equipment Maintenance

With connectivity between healthcare infrastructures for seamless real-time operations, its maintenance to prevent breakdowns becomes the backbone of the entire system.

1.5.10   Improved Operational Efficiency

The big data helps us understand the admission, diagnosis, and records of utilization of resources, helping to understand the efficiency and productivity of the hospital facilities.

1.5.11   Outbreak Prediction

With the availability of data like temperature and rainfall, reported cases reasonable predictions can be made about the outbreak of vector borne diseases like malaria and encephalitis, saving lives.

1.6   Challenges for Big Data

The volumes of data generated from diverse sources need to be sorted into a cohesive format and then be constantly updated so that it can be shared between healthcare service providers addressing the relevant security concerns, which is the biggest challenge. Insights gained from big data help us in understanding the pooled data better, thereby helping in improving the outcomes and benefitting insurance providers by reducing fraud and false claims.

The healthcare industry needs skilled data analysts who can sift out relevant data, analyze it, and communicate it to the relevant decision makers.

1.7   Conclusion

This chapter provides an overview regarding better healthcare services with the help of ML and big data technology. It presents big data approaches to gather valuable medical records

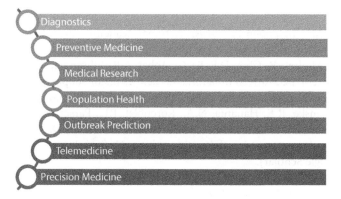

Figure 1.5 Applications of big data in healthcare.

and further the application of ML algorithm. The implementation of ML tool in medicine shows more accurate result with less processing time. Big data will surely help in collecting and maintaining EHR (electronic health records) for better decision-making in future. This paper provides a systematic review to the researchers about better options in the field of healthcare using ML and big data (Figure 1.5). This paper has identified several application areas in healthcare services using ML and big data which can further improve the unresolved challenges. The traditional healthcare services will be greatly transformed by such technologies. ML will help in improving the relationship between the locals and service provider by providing better service in less time. It will help in keeping an eye on critical patients in real time and help them diagnose the disease and recommend further treatment.

References

1. James, M., Michael, C., Brad, B., Jacques, B., *Big Data: The Next Frontier for Innovation, Competition, and Productivity*, McKinsey Global Institute, New York, NY, 2011.
2. Al-Jarrah, O.Y., Yoo, P.D., Muhaidat, S., Karagiannidis, G.K., Taha, K., Efficient machine learning for big data: A review. *Big Data Res.*, 2, 3, 87–93, Sep. 2015.
3. Beyer, M.A. and Laney, D., *The importance of 'big data': A definition*, Gartner Research, Stamford, CT, USA, Tech. Rep. G00235055, 2012.
4. Xing, L., Krupinski, E.A., Cai, J., Artificial intelligence will soon change the landscape of medical physics research and practice. *Med. Phys.*, 45, 5, 1791–1793, 2018.
5. Deo, R.C., Machine Learning in Medicine. *Circulation*, 132, 20, 1920–1930, 2015.
6. Kannel, W.B., Doyle, J.T., McNamara, P.M., Quickenton, P., Gordon, T., Precursors of sudden coronary death. Factors related to the incidence of sudden death. *Circulation*, 51, 606–613, 1975, [PubMed] [Google Scholar].
7. Lip, G.Y.H., Nieuwlaat, R., Pisters, R., Lane, D.A., Crijns, H.J.G.M., Refining clinical risk stratification for predicting stroke and thromboembolism in atrial fibrillation using a novel risk factor-based approach: the euro heart survey on atrial fibrillation. *Chest*, 137, 263–272, 2010, [PubMed] [Google Scholar].
8. O'Mahony, C., Jichi, F., Pavlou, M., Monserrat, L., Anastasakis, A., Rapezzi, C., Biagini, E., Gimeno, J.R., Limongelli, G., McKenna, W.J., Omar, R.Z., Elliott, P.M., A novel clinical risk prediction model for sudden cardiac death in hypertrophic cardiomyopathy (HCM risk-SCD). *Eur. Heart J.*, 35, 2010–2020, 2014, [PubMed] [Google Scholar].
9. National Research Council (US), Committee on A Framework for Developing a New Taxonomy of Disease, in: *Toward Precision Medicine: Building a Knowledge Network for Biomedical Research and a New Taxonomy of Disease*, National Academies Press (US), Washington (DC), 2011, [PubMed] [Google Scholar].
10. Woodruff, P.G., Modrek, B., Choy, D.F., Jia, G., Abbas, A.R., Ellwanger, A., Koth, L.L., Arron, J.R., Fahy, J.V., T-helper type 2-driven inflammation defines major subphenotypes of asthma. *Am. J. Respir. Crit. Care Med.*, 180, 388–395, 2009, [PMC free article] [PubMed] [Google Scholar].
11. Corren, J., Lemanske, R.F., Hanania, N.A., Korenblat, P.E., Parsey, M.V., Arron, J.R., Harris, J.M., Scheerens, H., Wu, L.C., Su, Z., Mosesova, S., Eisner, M.D., Bohen, S.P., Matthews, J.G., Lebrikizumab treatment in adults with asthma. *N. Engl. J. Med.*, 365, 1088–1098, 2011, [PubMed] [Google Scholar].
12. Laine, S. and Aila, T., Temporal ensembling for semi-supervised learning, in: *International Conference on Learning Representations*, 2017.

13. Cheplygina, V., d. Bruijne, M., Pluim, J.P.W., Not-so-supervised: a survey of semi-supervised, multi-instance, and transfer learning in medical image analysis. *Medical Image Analysis*, 54, 280–296, 2019.

14. Bai, W., Oktay, O., Sinclair, M., Suzuki, H., Rajchl, M., Tarroni, G., Glocker, B., King, A., Matthews, P.M., Rueckert, D., Semisupervised learning for network-based cardiac mr image segmentation, in: *Medical Image Computing and Comput.-Assisted Intervention*, pp. 253–260, Springer, Heidelberg, 2017.

15. Zhang, Y., Yang, L., Chen, J., Fredericksen, M., Hughes, D.P., Chen, D.Z., Deep adversarial networks for biomedical image segmentation utilizing unannotated images, in: *Medical Image Computing and Comput.-Assisted Intervention*, pp. 408–416, Springer, 2017.

16. Sun, W., Tseng, T.B., Zhang, J., Qian, W., Computerized breast cancer analysis system using three stage semi-supervised learning method. *Comput. Methods Programs Biomed.*, 135, 77–88, 2016.

17. Xia, Y., Liu, F., Yang, D., Cai, J., Yu, L., Zhu, Z., Xu, D., Yuille, A., Roth, H., 3d semi-supervised learning with uncertainty-aware multiview co-training, in: *IEEE Winter Conf. Appl. Comput. Vis.*, 2020.

18. Zhao, Y., Zeng, D., Socinski, M.A., Kosorok, M.R., Reinforcement learning strategies for clinical trials in nonsmall cell lung cancer. *Biometrics*, 67, 4, 1422–33, 2011 Dec.

19. Pineau, J., Guez, A., Vincent, R., Panuccio, G., Avoli, M., Treating epilepsy via adaptive neurostimulation: a reinforcement learning approach. *Int. J. Neural Syst.*, 19, 4, 227–40, 2009.

20. Liu, Y., Logan, B., Liu, N., Xu, Z., Tang, J., Wang, Y., Deep reinforcement learning for dynamic treatment regimes on medical registry data. *2017 IEEE International Conference on Healthcare Informatics (ICHI)*, 2017 Aug., pp. 380–5.

21. Raghu, A., Komorowski, M., Ahmed, I., Celi, L.A., Szolovits, P., Ghassemi, M., Deep reinforcement learning for sepsis treatment. *CoRR*, 2017, abs/1711.09602.

22. https://news.stanford.edu/2017/01/25/artificial-intelligence-used-identify-skin-cancer (dated: 13-09-2020)

23. Gulshan, V., Peng, L., Coram, M. *et al.*, Development and Validation of a Deep Learning Algorithm for Detection of Diabetic Retinopathy in Retinal Fundus Photographs. *JAMA*, 316, 22, 2402–2410, 2016.

24. Dash, S.S., Big data in healthcare: management, analysis and future prospects. *J. Big Data*, 6, 54, 2019.

25. Johnston, L.R. and P.L., Suboptimal response to clopidogrel and the effect of prasugrel in acute coronary syndromes. *Int. J. Cardiol.*, 995–999, 2013.

26. Sean Chia, J.H., SAR by kinetics for drug discovery in protein misfolding diseases. *PNAS*, 2018.

Part II

MEDICAL DATA PROCESSING AND ANALYSIS

Thoracic Image Analysis Using Deep Learning

Rakhi Wajgi[1]*, Jitendra V. Tembhurne[2] and Dipak Wajgi[2]

[1]Department of Computer Technology, Yeshwantrao Chavan College of Engineering, Nagpur, India
[2]Department of Computer Science & Engineering, Indian Institute of Information Technology, Nagpur, India

Abstract

Thoracic diseases are caused due to ill condition of heart, lungs, mediastinum, diaphragm, and great vessels. Basically, it is a disorder of organs in thoracic region (*rib cage*). Thoracic diseases create severe burden on the overall health of a person and ignorance to them may lead to the sudden death of patients. Lung tuberculosis is one of the thoracic diseases which is accepted as worldwide pandemic. Prevalence of thoracic diseases is rising day by day due to various environmental factors and COVID-19 has trigged it at higher level. Chest radiography is the only omnipresent solution utilized to capture the abnormalities in the chest. It requires periodic visits by patient and timely tracking of findings and observations from the chest radiographic reports. These thoracic disorders are classified under various classes such as Atelectasis, Pneumonia, Hernia, Edema, Emphysema, Cardiomegaly, Fibrosis, Pneumothorax, Consolidation, Pleural Thickening, Effusion, Infiltration, Nodules, and Mass. Precise and reliable detection of these disorders required experienced radiologist. The major area of research in this domain is accurate localization and classification of affected region. In order to make accurate prognosis of chest diseases, research community has developed various automated models using deep learning. Deep learning has created a massive impact in terms of analysis in the domain of medical imaging where unprecedented amount of data is generated daily. There are various challenges faced by the community prior to model building. These challenges include orientation, data augmentation, colour space augmentation, and feature space augmentation of image but are pragmatically handle by various parameters and functions in deep learning models by maintaining their accuracies.

This chapter aims to analyse critically the deep learning techniques utilized for thoracic image analysis with respective accuracy achieved by them. The various deep learning techniques are described along with dataset, activation function and model used, number and types of layers used, learning rate, training time, epoch, performance metric, hardware used, and type of abnormality detected. Moreover, a comparative analysis of existing deep learning models based on accuracy, precision, and recall is also presented with emphasize on the future direction of research.

Keywords: Accuracy, classification, deep learning, localization, precision, recall, radiography, thoracic disorder

---

**Corresponding author*: wajgi.rakhi@gmail.com

Om Prakash Jena, Alok Ranjan Tripathy, Ahmed A. Elngar and Zdzislaw Polkowski (eds.) Computational Intelligence and Healthcare Informatics, (17–42) © 2021 Scrivener Publishing LLC

2.1   Introduction

Identification of pathologies from chest x-ray (CXR) images plays a crucial role in planning of threptic strategies for diagnosis of thoracic diseases because thoracic diseases create severe burden on the overall health of a person and ignorance to them may lead to the sudden death of patients. Tuberculosis (TB) continues to remain major health threat worldwide and people continue to fall sick due to TB every year. According to WHO report of 2019 [24], 1.4 million people died due to TB in 2019. When a person suffers with TB, it takes time for symptoms to express prominently. Till then, the infection transfers from person to person results in increase in prevalence of infection and mortality rate. Moreover, Pneumonia is also creating major burden in many countries. Since December 2019, people all over the world were suddenly suffered with Pneumonia with unknown etiology which results in COVID-19 Pandemic. TB, Pneumonia and other disorders are located in the thoracic region are known as thoracic disorders and location of Thoracic pathology is captured through x-ray of thoracic region. There are 14 different classes of thoracic pathologies such as Atelectasis, Pneumonia, Hernia, Edema, Emphysema, Cardiomegaly, Fibrosis, Pneumothorax, Consolidation, Pleural Thickening, Effusion, Infiltration, Nodules, and Mass. CXR is the most preferable screening tool used by radiologist for prediction of abnormalities in thorax region. To understand the exact location and type of pathology, expert radiologists are needed who have enough experience in the field of detecting pathologies from the chest radiology x-ray and are seldom available.

Furthermore, economically less developed countries lack with experienced radiologist and growing air pollution is badly impacting human lungs for which x-ray is the only reasonable tool to detect abnormalities in them. Recent pandemic of COVID-19 motivates researchers to design deep learning models which can predict the impact of SARS CoV-2 virus on human lungs at early stages as well as to identify post COVID effect on lungs. Patients suffering with thoracic abnormalities are associated with major change in their mental, social, and health-related quality of life. For some of them, early chest radiography can save their life and prevent them from undergoing unnecessary exposure to x-rays radiations. Thus, this motivates to explore new findings from it. Therefore, to make accurate prognosis of chest pathologies, researchers have automated the process of localization using Deep Leaning (DL) techniques. These models will act as an assistant to less experienced radiologist with the help of which prediction can be tallied. Due to significant contribution of deep learning in medical field in terms of object detection and classification, researchers have developed many models of DL for classification and localization of thoracic pathologies and compared their efficacy with other models on the basis of various evaluation parameters. This automated system of thoracic pathology detection helps radiologists in faster asses to patients and their prioritization as per the severity.

The overall outline of the chapter is presented as follows: Section 2.2 consists of broad view of existing research employed by various researchers, challenges in detecting thoracic pathology, datasets used by researchers, thoracic pathologies, and parameters used for comparison of models. Section 2.3 details the models implemented by researchers using deep learning and demonstrates the comparison of models on various parameters. Section 2.4 present the conclusion and future directions.

2.2   Broad Overview of Research

Though ample number of models has been implemented for localization and classification of thoracic pathologies, the broad view of research carried out till date (i.e., December 2020) is represented using Figure 2.1.

It is observed that researchers have either designed their own ensemble models using existing pretrained models or use pre-trained models like GoogleNet, AlexNet, ResNet, and DenseNet for localization of yCXR. In ensemble models, either weights of neural networks are trained on widely available ImageNet dataset or averaging outputs of existing models were used for building new models. Input to these models could be either radiography CXR images or radiologist report in text form. One of the most regular and cost-effective medical imaging tests available is chest x-ray exams. Chest x-ray clinical diagnosis is however more complex and difficult than chest CT imaging diagnosis. The lack of publicly accessible databases with annotations makes clinically valid computer-aided diagnosis of chest pathologies more difficult but not impossible. Therefore, annotation of CXR images is done manually by researchers and is made available publicly to test the accuracy of novel models. These datasets include ChestX-ray14, ChestX-ray8, Indiana, JSRT, and Shenzhen dataset. The final output of existing models is identifying one or more than one pathology out of fourteen located in either x-ray image or radiologist report. DL models devised by researchers are compared on the basis of various metric such as Receiver Operating Characteristic (ROC), Area Under Curve (AUC), and F1-score, which are listed in Figure 2.1. While designing deep learning models for detection of thoracic pathologies various challenges are faced by researchers which are discussed in next section.

2.2.1   Challenges

There are various challenges while implementing deep learning models for analysis of thoracic images and these challenges are listed below. They could be in terms of availability of dataset and nature of images.

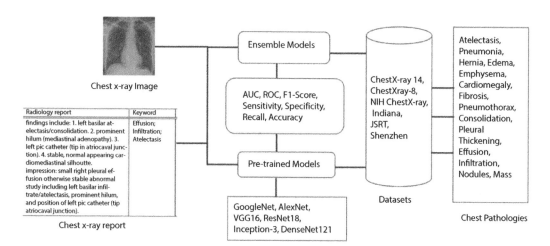

Figure 2.1 Broad view of existing research.

1. Non-availability of large number of labeled dataset [16].
2. Due to use of weights of neural nets trained on ImageNet dataset for ensemble model, overfitting problem occurs. Theses pre-trained models are computationally intensive and are less likely to generalize for comparatively smaller dataset [7].
3. Presence of lesions at different location in x-ray and varying proportion of images of each pathology might hinders performance of models [41].
4. X-ray images contain large amount of noise (healthy region) surrounding to lesion area which is very small. These large numbers of safe regions make it impossible for deep networks to concentrate on the lesion region of chest pathology, and the location of disease regions is often unpredictable. This problem is somewhat different from the classification of generic images [67], where the object of interest is normally located in the center of the image.
5. Due to the broad inter-class similarity of chest x-ray images, it is difficult for deep networks to capture the subtle differences in the entire images of different classes, particularly in one entire image.
6. CXR images suffer from distortion or misalignment due to variations in the capture state, e.g., the patient's pose or the small size of the child's body.
7. Sometimes, recapturing of images is not possible due to which computer-aided system has to do prediction on the basis of existing images only. Therefore, model should be vigorous to quality of x-ray image.
8. For localization of pathologies, images should be labeled or annotated with bounding boxes and for segmentation pixel-level mask is needed in the image. Both these processes are expensive and time consuming process.
9. Output of CNN is not shift invariant meaning that if input image is shifted then output of CNN also shifted which should not happen in the domain of medical imaging.
10. Imbalance between availability of number of normal class images and images with disorders and disproportion of availability of annotated and unannotated images.
11. Most of the models are trained for ImageNet data set which has altogether different features as compared to medical images [5].
12. Confounding variables in the x-ray images ruin the performance of models therefore there is a need of pre-processing [72].

To overcome these issues, following strategies can be deployed.

1. 2-D or 3-D image patches are taken as an input rather than full sized image [11, 14, 36, 50, 56–58, 63].
2. Annotate existing images using affine transformation and expand existing dataset by adding annotated image with existing images, and then, network will be trained from scratch on expanded dataset [11, 50, 56, 57].
3. Use of deep models trained on off-the shelf dataset for feature extraction and then use final classifier at last layer for classification by fine tuning the model with target dataset [14, 36, 58].
4. Initialize parameters of new models with value of parameters of pre-trained models applied on ImageNet dataset [60] and then fine tune the network with task specific dataset.

2.2.2   Performance Measuring Parameters

There are various parameters used by researchers to evaluate performance of their models, namely, ROC, AUC, F1-score, recall, accuracy, specificity, and sensitivity. Use of metric varies from application to application, and sometimes, single parameter does not justify the working of models. In such cases, subset of parameters are used to evaluate performance of model. For testing the accuracy of classification models, accuracy, precision, recall, F1-score, sensitivity, specificity, ROC curve, and AUC curve are utilized on the basis of which comparison is performed in the existing research. These parameters are discussed as follows.

1. *Accuracy:* It is defined as the ratio of number of correctly classified chest pathologies to the number of available samples. If the dataset has 1,000 images having some pathology or no-pathology and the model has correctly classified 820 pathologies and 10 as normal cases, then accuracy will be $830 \times 100/1,000 = 83\%$.

2. *Precision:* When there is imbalance in dataset with respect to availability of class-wise images, then accuracy is not an acceptable parameter. In such cases, model is tuned to major class only which does not make sense. For example, if in CXR dataset, images belonging to class nodule are more, then predicting maximum images of most frequent class will not solve the purpose. Therefore, class specific metric is needed known as precision.

3. *Recall:* It is also a class specific parameter. It is a fraction of images correctly classified for given class.

4. *F1-Score:* For critical application, F1-score is needed which will guide which parameter is more appropriate, i.e., precision or recall. Sometime, both metrics are equally important. Therefore, F1-score is a combination of both which is calculated as:

5. *Sensitivity and Specificity:* These metrics are generally used for medical application which are calculated as follows.

6. *ROC Curve:* It is a Receiver Operating Characteristic curve generally used to measure the performance of binary classifier model. This curve is plotted as True-Positive Rate against False-Positive Rate. It depicts overall performance of model and helps in selecting good cut-off threshold for the model.

7. *AUC Curve:* Area Under Curve (AUC) is a binary classifier's aggregated output metric for all possible threshold values (and therefore it is threshold invariant). Under the ROC curve, AUC calculates the field, and hence, it is between 0 and 1. One way to view AUC is as the likelihood that a random positive example is ranked more highly by the model than a random negative example.

2.2.3   Availability of Datasets

Mostly, deep learning models used for identification of chest radiography pathologies and training processes are carried out on the basis of available CXR datasets, of which the most famous datasets are the Indiana dataset [15], KIT dataset [54], MC dataset [29], Japanese Society of Radiological Technology (JSRT) dataset [59], ChestX-ray14 dataset [19], NIH

Tuberculosis Chest X-ray [17], and Belarus Tuberculosis [6]. There are major limitations to each cited dataset, some of which are addressed in a survey published in August 2018 [48]. The ChestX-ray14 is recognized as one of the most widespread CXR datasets among the available datasets, which contains 108,948 x-ray images obtained from 32,717 patients. These images are labeled by means of natural language processing with one or more diagnostic labels. A number of recent AI reports, such as Wang *et al.* [70], Yao *et al.* [71], Rajpurkar *et al.* [49], and Guan *et al.* [4], have used ChestX-ray14 dataset. All of these studies are trained and tested on ChestX-ray14 dataset accompanied with annotation for 14 different types of chest pathologies. Details of availability of number of each type of pathology in ChestX-ray14 dataset are shown in Table 2.1 [7].

It is observed that there is a presence of disproportion in the number of available images among 14 chest pathologies. This is one of the factors affecting performance of different deep models. Before analyzing existing models, 14 chest pathologies are described as follows in Figure 2.2.

1. *Atelectasis:* It is a disorder where there is no space for normal expansion of lung due to malfunctioning of air sacs in it.
2. *Cardiomegaly:* It is a disorder related to heart where heart enlarged due to stress or some medical condition.
3. *Consolidation:* When the small airways in lungs are filled with fluids like pus, water, or blood instead of air, then consolidation occurs.
4. *Edema:* It occurs due to deposition of excess fluid in lungs.
5. *Effusion:* In this disorder excess fluid filled in between chest wall and lungs.
6. *Emphysema:* Alveoli which are known as air sacs of lungs when damaged or get weak then person suffers with Emphysema.
7. *Fibrosis:* When lung tissues get thickened or stiff, then it becomes difficult for lungs to work normally. This condition is known as fibrosis.

Table 2.1 Details of ChestX-ray14 dataset.

Type of pathology	No. of images with label	Type of pathology	No. of images with label
Atelectasis	11559	Consolidation	4,667
Cardiomegaly	2776	Edema	2,303
Effusion	13317	Emphysema	2,516
Infiltration	19894	Fibrosis	1,686
Mass	5782	Pleural thickening	3,385
Nodule	6331	Hernia	227
Pneumonia	1431	Normal chest x-ray	60,412
Pneumothorax	5302		

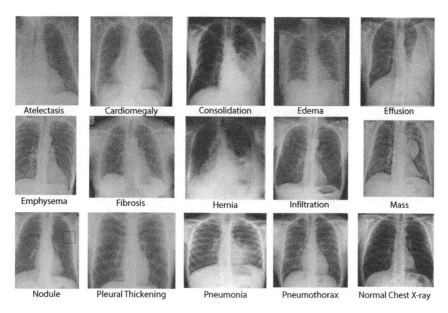

Figure 2.2 Types of chest pathologies.

8. *Hernia:* protuberance of thoracic contents outside their defined location in thorax region is known as thoracic hernia.
9. *Infiltration:* When there is a trail of denser substance such as pus, blood, or protein occurs within the parenchyma of the lungs, then it is known as a pulmonary infiltration.
10. *Mass*: It is a tumor that grows in mediastinum region of chest that separates the lungs is termed as Mass.
11. *Nodule:* A small masses of tissue in the lung are known as lung nodules.
12. *Pleural Thickening:* When the lung is exposed to asbestos, it causes lungs tissue to scar. This condition is known as pleural thickening.
13. *Pneumonia:* When there is an infection in air sacs of either or both lungs, then its results in Pneumonia.
14. *Pneumothorax:* When air leaks from lungs into the chest wall then this condition is known as Pneumothorax disorder.

Detection of Cardiomegaly is done by many researchers as it is a spatially spread disorder across large region and therefore easy to detect.

2.3 Existing Models

Models proposed in the past are mainly classified into two types: ensemble models and hybrid and pretrained models. Ensemble models either focused on classifying all fourteen pathologies or limited abnormalities like cardiomegaly, Edema, Pneumonia, or COVID-19. In pretrained models, initialization of parameters of deep learning models is done from ImageNet dataset, and then, the network is fine-tuned as per the pathologies targeted. This section deals with discussion on various existing models implemented in the literature along with issues they have addressed related to x-ray images, datasets used for training, and the type of pathologies detected by the model in chronological order of their implementation.

In [4], the deep learning model named Decaf trained on non-medical ImageNet dataset for detection of pathologies in medical CXR dataset is applied. Image is considered as Bag of Visual Words (BoVW). The model is created using CNN, GIST descriptor, and BoVW for feature extraction on ImageNet dataset and then it was applied for feature extraction from medical images. Once the model is trained, SVM is utilized for pathology classification of CXR and the AUC is obtained in the range of 0.87 to 0.97. The results of feature extraction can be further improved by using fusion of Decafs model such as Decaf5, Decaf6, and GIST is presented by the authors. In [41], pre-trained model GoogleNet is employed to classify chest radiograph report into normal and five chest pathologies namely, pleural effusion, consolidation, pulmonary edema, pneumothorax, and cardiomegaly through natural language processing techniques. The sentences were separated from the report into keywords such as "inclusion" and "exclusion" and report is classified into one of the six classes including normal class.

Considering popularity of deep learning, four different models of AlexNet [34] and GoogleNet [65] are applied for thoracic image analysis wherein two of them are trained from ImageNet and two are trained from scratch. Then, these models are used for detecting TB from CXR radiography images. Parameters of AlexNet-T and GoogleNet-T are initialized from ImageNet, whereas AlexNet-U and GoogleNet-U parameters are trained from scratch. The performance of all four models are compared and it is observed that trained versions are having better accuracy than the untrained versions [35].

In another model, focus was given only on eight pathologies of thoracic diseases [70]. Weakly supervised DCNN is applied for large set of images which might have more than one pathology in same image. The pre-trained model is adopted on ImageNet by excluding fully connected and final classification layer. In place of these layers, a transition layer, a global pooling layer, a prediction layer, and a loss layer are inserted in the end after last convolution layer. Weights are obtained from the pre-trained models except transition, and prediction layers were trained from scratch. These two layers help in finding plausible location of disease. Also, instead of conventional softmax function, three different loss functions are utilized, namely, Hinge loss, Euclidean loss, and Cross Entropy loss due to disproportion of number of images having pathologies and without pathology. Global pooling layer and prediction layer help in generating heatmap to map presence of pathology with maximum probability. Moreover, Cardiomegaly and Pneumothorax have been well recognized using the model based on ResNet50 [21] as compared to other pathologies.

In [28], three different datasets, namely, Indiana, JSRT, and Shenzhen dataset, were utilized for the experimentation of proposed deep model. Indiana dataset consists of 7,284 CXR images of both frontal and lateral region of chest annotated for pathologies Cardiomegaly, Pulmonary Edema, Opacity, and Effusion. JSRT consists of 247 CXR having 154 lung nodule and 94 with no nodule. Shenzhen dataset consists of 662 frontal CXR images with 336 TB cases and remaining normal cases. Features of one of the layers from pre-defined models are extracted and used with binary classifier layer to detect abnormality and features are extracted from second fully connected layer in AlexNet, VGG16, and VGG19 network. It is observed that, dropout benefits shallow networks in terms of accuracy but it hampers the performance of deeper networks. Shallow DCN are generally used for detecting small objects in the image. Ensemble models perform better for spatially spread out abnormalities such as Cardiomegaly and Pulmonary Edema, whereas pointed small features like nodules cannot be easily located through ensemble models.

Subsequently, three branch attention guided CNN (AG-CNN) is proposed based on the two facts. First fact is that though the thoracic pathologies are located in a small region, complete CXR image is given as an input for training which add irrelevant noise in the network. Second fact is that the irregular border arises due to poor alignment of CXR, obstruct the performance of network [19]. ResNet50 and DenseNet121 have been used as backbone for two different version of AG-CNN in which global CNN uses complete image and a mask is created to crop disease specific region from the generated heat map of global CNN. The local CNN is then trained on disease specific part of the image and last pooling layers of both the CNNs are concatenated to fine tune the amalgamated branch. For classifying chest pathologies, conventional and deep learning approaches are used and are compared on the basis of error rate, accuracy, and training time [2]. Conventional models include Back Propagation Neural Network (BPNN) and Competitive Neural Network (CpNN) and deep learning model includes simple CNN. Deep CNN has better generalization ability than BPNN and CpNN but requires more iteration due to extraction of features at different layers.

A pre-defined CNN for binary classification of chest radiographs which assess their ability on live customized dataset obtained from U.S. National Institutes of Health is presented in [18]. Before applying deep learning models, the dataset is separated into different categories and labeled manually with two different radiologist. Their labels are tallied and conflicting images are discarded. Normal images without any pathology were removed and 200,000 images were finally used for training purpose. Out of those images, models were trained on different number of images and performance of models noted in terms of AUC score. It is observed that modestly size images achieve better accuracy for binary classification into normal and abnormal chest radiograph. This automated image analysis will be useful in poor resource areas.

The CheXNet deep learning algorithm is used to detect 14 pathologies in chest radiographs where the 121-layer DenseNet architecture is densely connected [49]. Ensemble network is generated by allowing multiple network to get trained on training set and networks which has less average prediction error are selected to become the part of ensemble network. The parameters of each ensemble network are initialized using the ImageNet pre-trained network. The image input size is 512×512 and the optimization of Adams was used to train the NN parameter with batch size of 8 and learning rate of 0.0001. To prevent dropouts and decay, network was saved after every epoch. To deal with overfitting, early stopping of iteration was done.

Considering the severity of TB which is classified as the fifth leading cause of death worldwide, with 10 million new cases and 1.5 million deaths per year, DL models are proposed to detect it from CXR. Being one of the world's biggest threats and being rather easy to cure, the World Health Organization (WHO) recommends systematic and broad use of screening to extirpate the disease. Posteroanterior chest radiography, in spite its low specificity and difficulty in interpretation, is still unfortunately one of the preferred TB screening methods. Since TB is primarily a disease of poor countries, the clinical officers trained to interpret these CXRs are often rare in number. In such circumstances, an automated algorithm for TB diagnosis could be an inexpensive and effective method to make widespread TB screening a reality. As a consequence, this has attracted the attention of the machine learning community [9, 27, 28, 30, 33, 35, 38, 40 , 42, 68] which has tackled the problem with methods ranging from hand-crafted algorithm to support vector machines and convolutional neural networks. Considering the rank of TB in the list of cause of death worldwide, deep learning models are implemented for fast screening of TB [46]. The results are encouraging, as some of these methods achieve nearly-human sensitivities and specificities. Considering the limitation of availability of powerful and costly hardware and large number learning parameters, a simple Deep CNN model has been proposed for CXR TB screening rather than using complex machine learning pipelining as used in [30, 40, 42, 68]. The saliency maps and the grad-CAMs have been used for the first time to provide better visualization effects. As radiologist is having deeper perspective of the chest abnormalities, this model is helpful in providing second opinion to them. The architecture of model consists of five blocks of convolution followed by global average pooling layer and fully connected softmax layer. In between each convolutional block, a max pooling layer is inserted moreover, the overall arrangement is similar to AlexNet. Batch normalization is used by each convolution layer to avoid problem of overfitting. After training of network, silency-maps and grad-CAM are used for better visualization. Silency-maps help generating heat map with same resolution as input image and grad-CAM helps in better localization with poor resolution due to pooling. NIH Tuberculosis Chest X-ray dataset [29] and Belarus Tuberculosis portal dataset [6] are used for experimentation. It is observed that model facilitates better visualization of presence or absence of TB for clinical practitioners. Subsequently, by considering the severity of Pneumonia, a novel model which is ensemble of two models RetinaNet and Mask R-CNN is proposed in [61] and is tested on Kaggle pneumonia detection competition dataset consisting of 26,684 images. Transfer learning is applied for weight initialization from models trained on Microsoft COCO challenge. To detect the object, RetinaNet is utilized first and then Mask R-CNN is employed as a supplementary model. Both these models are allowed to individually predict pneumonia region. If bounding box of predicted region from both models overlapped then averaged was taken on the basis of weight ratio 3:1, otherwise it was used in the dataset without any change for detection by ensemble model. In addition, Recall score is obtained by the ensemble model is 0.734.

A model, namely, ChestNet, is proposed for detection of consolidation, a kind of lung opacity in pediatric CXR images [5]. Consolidation is one of the critical abnormalities whose detection helps in early prediction of pneumonia. Before applying model, three-step pre-processing is done to deal with the issues, namely, checking the presence of confounding variables in the image, searching for consolidation patterns instead of using histogram features, and learning is used to detect sharp edges such as ribs and spines instead of directly detecting pattern of consolidation by the CNN. ChestNet models consist of convolutional layers, batch normalization layers embedded after each convolutional layer, and two classifier layers at the last. Only two max-pooling layers were used in contrast to five layers of VGG16, and DenseNet121 in order to preserve the region of image where the consolidation pattern is spread out. Smaller size convolutional layer such as 3×3 learns undesirable features, so to avoid this author used 7×7 size convolutional layer to learn largely spread consolidation pattern.

A multi-attention framework to deal with issues like class imbalance, shortage of annotated images, and diversity of lesion areas is developed in [41] and ChestX-ray14 dataset is used for experimental purpose. Three modules which are implemented by the authors are feature attention module, space attention module, and hard example attention module.

In feature attention module, interdependencies of pathologies are detected considering structure of ResNet101 model as base. Because of the ability of Squeeze and Excitation (SE) block [35] to model channel interdependencies of modules, one SE block is inserted into each ResNet block. The feature map generated by this module contains lots of noise and is learnt from global information rather than concentrating on small diseases related region. To avoid this, space attention module is introduced. In this module, global average pooling is applied on feature map obtained from ResNet101 [39]. This help in carrying out global information of image in each pixel which benefits classification and localization task. In hard attention modules, positive and negative images are separated into two different sets and model is trained on these individual sets to obtain threshold value of predicted score for each set. Then, set C is created which is combination of both sets and contained increased proportions of positive samples. The models is retrained on set C to distinguish 14 classes of thoracic diseases. This helps in resolving issue of presence of large gap in positive and negative samples.

Multiple feature extraction technique was used by author in paper [23] for the classification of thoracic pathologies. Various classifiers such as Gaussian discriminant analysis (GDA), KNN, Naïve Bayes, SVM, Adaptive Boosting (AdaBoost), Random forest, and ELM were compared with pretrained DenseNet121 which was used for localization by generating CAM (Class Activation Map) and integrated results of different shallow and deep feature extraction algorithms such as Scale Invariant Feature Transform (SIFT), Gradient-based (GIST), Local Binary Pattern (LBP), and Histogram Oriented Gradient–based (HOG) with different classifiers have been used for final classification of various lung abnormalities. It is observed that ELM is having better F1-score than the DenseNet121.

Two asymmetric networks ResNet and DenseNet which extract complementary unique features from input image were used to design new ensemble model known as DualCheXNet [10]. It has been the first attempt to use complementarity of dual asymmetric subnetworks developed in the field of thoracic disease classification. Two networks, i.e., ResNet and DenseNet are allowed to work simultaneously in Feature Level Fusion (FLF) module and selected features from both networks are combined in Decision Level fusion (DLF) on which two auxiliary classifiers are applied for classifying image into one of the pathologies.

The problem of poor alignment and noise in non-lesion area of CXR images which hinders the performance of network is overcome by building three branch attention guided CNN which is discussed in [20]. It helps to identify thorax diseases. Here, AGCNN is explored which works in the same manner as radiologist wherein ResNet50 is the backbone of AGCNN. Radiologist first browse the complete image and then gradually narrows down the focus on small lesion specific region. AGCNN mainly focus on small local region which is disease specific such as in case of Nodule. AGCNN has three branches local branch, global branch, and fusion branch. If lesion region is distributed throughout the image, then the pathologies which were missed by local branch in terms of loss of information such as in case of pneumonia were captured by global branch. Global and local branches are then fuse together to fine tune the CNN before drawing final conclusion. The training of AGCNN is done in different training orders. G_LF (Global branch then Local and Fusion together), GL_F (Global and Local together followed by Fusion), GLF all together, and then G_L_F (Global, Local and Fusion separately) one after another.

Lack of availability of annotated images majorly hinders the performance of deep learning model designed for localization or segmentation [53]. To deal with this issue, a novel loss function is proposed and the conditional random field layer is included in the backbone model of ResNet50 [22] whose last two layers are excluded and weights initialized on ImageNet have been used. In order to make CNN shift invariant, a low pass antialiasing filter as proposed by [73] is inserted prior to down sampling of network. This supports in achieving better accuracy across many models. NIH ChestX-ray14 has been used by the author which have very limited annotated images. Only 984 images with bounding boxes are used for detecting 8 chest pathologies and 11,240 images are having only labels associated with them. Furthermore, chest x-ray dataset is investigated which has many images with uncertain labels. To dispense this issue, a label smoothing regularization [44, 66] is adopted in the ensemble models proposed in [47] which performs averaging of output generated by the pre-trained models, i.e., DenseNet-121, DenseNet-169, DenseNet-201 [25], Inception-ResNet-v2 [64], Xception [12], and NASNetLarge [74]. Instead of ReLU, sigmoid function is utilized as an activation. In addition, label smoothing is applied on uncertain sample images which helped in improving AUC score.

A multiple instance learning (MEL) assures good performance of localization and multi-classification albeit in case of availability of less number of annotated images is discussed in [37]. Latest version of residual network pre-act-ResNet [22] has been employed to correctly locate site of disease. Initially, model is allowed to learn information of all images, namely, class and location. Later, input annotated image is divided into four patches and model is allowed to train for each patch. The learning task becomes a completely supervised problem for an image with bounding box annotation, since the disease mark for each patch can be calculated by the overlap between the patch and the bounding box. The task is formulated as a multiple-instance learning (MIL) problem where at least one patch in the image belongs to that disease. All patches have to be disease-free if there is no illness in the picture.

Considering orientation, rotation and tilting problems of images, hybrid deep learning framework, i.e., VDSNet by combining VGG, data augmentation, and spatial transformer network (STN) with CNN for detection of lung diseases such as asthma, TB, and pneumonia from NIH CXR dataset is presented in [7]. The comparison is performed with CapsNet, vanilla RGB, vanilla gray, and hybrid CNN VGG and result shows that the VDSNet achieved better accuracy of 73% than other models but is time consuming. In [67], a technique of using predefined deep CNN, namely, AlexNet, VGG16, ResNet18, Inception-v3, DenseNet121 with weights either initialized from ImageNet dataset or initialized with random values from scratch is adopted for classification of chest radiographs into normal and abnormal class. Pretrained weights of ImageNet performed better than random initialized weights from scratch. Deeper CNN works better for detection or segmentation kind of task rather than binary classification. ResNet outperformed training from scratch for moderate sized dataset (example, 8,500 rather than 18,000).

A customized U-NET–based CNN model is developed in [8] for the detection and localization of cardiomegaly which is one of the 14 pathologies of thorax region. To perform the experimentation ChestX-ray8 database was used which consist of 1,010 images of cardiomegaly. Modified (Low Contrast) Adaptive Histogram Equalization (LC-AHE) was applied to enhance the feature of image or sharpen the image. Brightness of low intensity pixel of small selected region is amplified from the intensities of all neighbouring pixels which sharpens the low intensity regions of given image. Considering the medical fact that the Cardiomegaly can be easily located just by observing significant thickening of cardiac ventricular walls, authors developed their own customized mask to locate it and separated out that infected region as image. This helped in achieving an accuracy of 93% which is better than VGG16, VGG19, and ResNet models.

Thoracic pathology detection not only restricted from CXR images but can also be done from video data of lung sonography. Deep learning approach for detection of COVID-19–related pathologies from Lung Ultrasonography is developed in [51]. By applying the facts that the augmented Lung Ultrasound (LUS) images improve the performance of network [62] in detecting healthy and ill patient and keeping consistencies in perturbed and original images, hence robust and more generalized network can be constructed [52, 55]. To do so, Regularized Spatial Transformer Network (Reg-STN) is developed. Later, CNN and spatial transformer network (STN) are jointly trained using ADAMS optimizer. Network lung sonography videos of 35 patients from various clinical centers from Italy were captured and then divided into 58,924 frames. The localization of COVID-19 pathologies were detected through STN which is based on the concept that the pathologies are located in a very small portion of image therefore no need to consider complete image.

A three-layer Fusion High Resolution Network (FHRNet) has been applied for feature extraction and fusion CNN is adopted for classifying pathologies in CXR is presented in [26]. FHRNet helped in reducing noise and highlighting lung region. Moreover, FHRN has three branches: local feature extraction, global feature extraction, and feature fusion module wherein local and global feature extraction network finds probabilities of one of the 14 classes. Input given to local feature extractor is a small lung region obtained by applying mask generated from global feature extractor. Two HRNets are adjusted to obtain prominent feature from lung region and whole image. HRNet is connected to global feature extraction layer through feature fusion layer having SoftMax classifier at the end which helps in classifying input image into one of the 14 pathologies. Another deep CNN consisting of 121 layer is developed to detect 5 different chest pathologies: Consolidation, Mass, Pneumonia, Nodule, and Atelectasis [43] entropy, as a loss function is utilized and achieved better AUC-ROC values for Pneumonia, Nodule, and Atelactasis than the model by Wang *et al.* [70].

Recently, due to cataclysmic outbreak of COVID-19, it is found by researchers that, as time passes, the lesions due to infection of virus spread more and more. The biggest challenge at such situations, however, is that it takes a lot of valuable time and the presence of medical specialists in the field to analyse each X-ray picture and extract important findings. Software assistance is therefore necessary for medical practitioners to help identify COVID-19 cases with X-ray images. Therefore, researchers have tried their expertise to design deep learning models on the data shared word wide to identify different perspective of spread of this virus in the chest. Many authors have created augmented data due to unavailability of enough CXRs images and applied deep learning models for detecting pneumonia caused due to COVID virus and other virus induced pneumonia. Author designed a new two-stage based deep learning model to detect COVID-induced pneumonia [31]. At the first stage, clinical CXR are given as input to ResNet50 deep network architecture for classification into virus induced pneumonia, bacterial pneumonia and normal cases. In addition, as COVID-19–induced pneumonia is due to virus, all identified cases of viral pneumonia are therefore differentiated with ResNet101 deep network architecture in the second stage, thus classifying the input image into COVID-19–induced pneumonia and other viral pneumonia. This two-stage strategy is intended to provide a fast, rational, and consistent computer-aided solution. A binary classifier model is proposed for classifying CXR image into COVID and non-COVID category along with multiclass model for COVID, non-COVID, and pneumonia classes in [45]. Authors adopted

DarkNet model as a base and proposed an ensemble model known as DarkCovidNet with 17 convolutional layers, 5 Maxpool layers with different varying size filters such as 8, 16, and 32. Each convolutional layer is followed by BatchNorm and LeakyReLU operations here LeakyReLU prohibits neurons from dying. Adams optimizer was used for weight updates with cross entropy loss function. Same model was used for binary as well multiclass classification and the binary class accuracy of 98.08% and multiclass accuracy of 87.02% is reported. Another CNN with softmax classifier model is implemented for classification of ChexNet dataset into COVID-19, Normal, and Pneumonia class and is compared with Inception Net v3, Xception Net, and ResNext models [32]. In order to handle irregularities in x-ray images, a *DeTraC* (Decompose-Transfer-Compose) model is proposed [1] which consists of three phases, namely, deep local feature extraction, training based on gradient descent optimization and class refinement layer for final classification into COVID-19, and normal class. *DeTraC* achieved accuracy of 98.23 with use of VGG19 pretrained ImageNet CNN model.

2.4   Comparison of Existing Models

In this section, existing models are compared on many different parameters as listed in Table 2.2.

1. Model parameters: type of model used, input image size, number of layers epoch, loss function used, and accuracy.
2. Accuracy achieved for all 14 different pathologies and dataset used for experimentation.
3. Other metrics: model used, specificity, sensitivity, F1-score, precision, and type of pathology detected.
4. On the basis of hardware and software used and input image size.

Table 2.2 shows datasets and pathologies detected by various DL models. It is observed that ChestX-ray14 is the most preferred dataset which can be used for training and testing of newly implemented models in the future. Cardiomegaly and Edema are easy to detect as compared to other pathologies because of their spatially spread out symptom. In addition, Table 2.3 shows comparison among different models on the basis of AUC score for 14 different chest pathologies. It is observed that cardiomegaly is having the highest value of AUC score obtained by most ensemble models. Edema, Emphysema, and Hernia are the pathologies following cardiomegaly which are having better AUC. CheXNext [59] is able to detect Mass, Pneumothorax, and Edema more accurately which other models cannot detect.

Table 2.4 highlights the comparison between various models on the basis of other performance measure. Most of the models have used accuracy, F1-score, specificity, sensitivity, and PPV and NPV parameters for comparison with other models. Pre-trained networks like AlexNet, VGG16, VGG19, DenseNet, and ResNet121 trained from scratch achieved better accuracy than those whose parameters are initialized from ImageNet because ImageNet has altogether different features than CXR images.

Table 2.5 shows hardware used by different models along with size of input image in terms of pixels and datasets used. Due to computationally intensive task, high definition hardware of NVIDIA card with larger size RAM has been used.

Table 2.2 Comparison of different deep learning models.

Ref.	Model used	Dataset	No. layers	Epoch	Activation function	Iterations	Pathology detected
[23]	DenseNet-121	ChestX-ray14	121	-	Softmax	50,000	14 chest pathologies
[67]	Pretrained CNNs:	ChestX-ray14	-	50	-	-	14 chest pathologies
[7]	VDSNet	ChestX-ray8	-	-	ReLU	-	Pulmonary diseases
[10]	DualCheXNet	ChestX-ray14	169	-	ReLU	-	14 chest pathologies
[2]	CNN	ChestX-ray8	5	1,000–4,000	ReLU	40,000	12 chest pathologies out of 14
	BPNN		3		-	5,000	
	CpNN		2		-	1,000	
[8]	Customized U-Net	ChestX-ray8	35	100–200	ReLU	20	Cardiomegaly
[47]	Ensemble of DesnSeNet-121, DenseNet-169, DenseNet-201, Inception-ResNet-v2 Xception, NASNetLarge	CheXpert	5		Sigmoid	50,000	Only 5 pathologies: Atelactasis, Cardiomegaly, Pleural, Effusion, and Edema
[51]	STN based CNN	Lung ultrasonography videos	-	-	ReLU	-	COVID-19 Pneumonia
[46]	Ensemble with AlexNet	NIH Tuberculosis Chest X-ray dataset [10.31] and Belarus Tuberculosis Portal dataset [10.32]	-	-	ReLU	-	Tuberculosis

(Continued)

Table 2.2 Comparison of different deep learning models. (*Continued*)

Ref.	Model used	Dataset	No. layers	Epoch	Activation function	Iterations	Pathology detected
[26]	FHRNet	ChestX-ray14 dataset	-	50	Sigmoid	-	14 chest pathologies
[20]	AG-CNN	ChestX-ray14		50	Sigmoid	-	14 chest pathologies
[53]	preact-ResNet [39_chp7_14]	ChestX-ray14	-	-	Sigmoid	-	8 chest pathologies out of 14
[70]	Unified DCNN	ChestX-ray8	-	-	Sigmoid	-	8 chest pathologies out of 14
[28]	Ensemble of AlexNet, VGG-16, VGG-19, ResNet-50, ResNet-101 and ResNet-152	Indiana dataset	-	-	-	-	Cardiomegaly, Edema, and Tuberculosis
[5]	ChestNet CNN	ChestX-ray14	14	30			Consolidation
[49]	CheXNeXt CNN	ChestX-ray14					14 chest pathologies
[46]	Customized CNN	NIH Tuberculosis Chest X-ray, Belarus Tuberculosis	23		ReLU		Tuberculosis
[61]	Ensemble of RetinaNet and Mask R-CNN	Kaggle dataset RSNA	-	-	ReLU	-	Pneumonia

(*Continued*)

Table 2.2 Comparison of different deep learning models. (*Continued*)

Ref.	Model used	Dataset	No. layers	Epoch	Activation function	Iterations	Pathology detected
[45]	DarkCovid-Net	COVID Chest x-ray Kaggle	17		ReLU	-	COVID, Normal and Pneumonia
[65]	GoogLeNet	St. Michael's Hospital chest x-ray	-	60	ReLU	-	5 pathologies: Cardiomegaly, Edema, Pleural effusion, pneumothorax, and consolidation
[35]	Ensemble of AlexNet and GoogleNet	NIH Tuberculosis Chest X-ray, Belarus Tuberculosis	-	-	-	-	Tuberculosis
[31]	ResNet101	Cohen and Kaggle [3]	-	-	-	-	COVID-19–induced pneumonia

Table 2.3 Comparison of models on the basis of AUC score for 14 chest pathologies.

Ref.	Atel	Card	Effu	Infi	Mass	Nodu	Pnel	Pnet	Cons	Edem	Emph	Fibr	PT	Hern
[10]	0.784	0.888	0.831	0.705	0.838	0.796	0.727	0.876	0.746	0.852	0.942	0.837	0.796	0.912
[23]	0.795	0.887	0.875	0.703	0.835	0.716	0.742	0.863	0.786	0.892	0.875	0.756	0.774	0.836
[70]	0.716	0.807	0.784	0.609	0.706	0.671	0.633	0.806	0.708	0.835	0.815	0.769	0.708	0.767
[69]	0.743	0.875	0.811	0.677	0.783	0.698	0.696	0.81	0.723	0.833	0.822	0.804	0.751	0.899
[8]	-	0.940	-	-	-	-	-	-	-	-	-	-	-	-
[47]	0.909	0.910	0.964	-	-	-	-	-	0.957	0.958	-	-	-	-
[26]	0.794	0902	0.839	0.714	0.827	0.727	0.703	0.848	0.773	0.834	0.911	0.824	0.752	0.916
[20]	0.853	0.939	0.903	0.754	0.902	0.828	0.774	0.921	0.842	0.924	0.932	0.964	0.837	0.921
[74] AlexNet	0.645	0.692	0.664	0.604	0.564	0.648	0.549	0.742	-	-	-	-	-	-
GoogleNet	0.631	0.706	0.688	0.609	0.536	0.558	0.599	0.782	-	-	-	-	-	-
VGGNet-16	0.628	0.708	0.650	0.589	0.510	0.656	0.510	0.751	-	-	-	-	-	-
ResNet50	0.707	0.814	0.736	0.613	0.561	0.716	0.63	0.789	-	-	-	-	-	-
[41]	0.762	0.883	0.816	0.679	0.801	0.729	0.709	0.838	0.744	0.841	0.884	0.800	0.754	0.876
[49]	0.862	0.831	0.901	0.721	0.909	0.894	0.851	0.944	0.893	0.924	0.704	0.806	0.798	0.851
[13]	-	0.875	0.962	-	-	-	-	0.861	0.850	0.868	-	-	-	-

Table 2.4 Comparison of DL models on the basis of different performance metrics.

Ref.	Model	Accuracy	F1-Score	Specificity	Sensitivity	PPV	NPV	AUC	Recall	Precision
[23]	DenseNet121	0.572–0.842	0.574–0.942	-	-	-	-	-	-	-
[67]	AlexNet (S)	0.9684	0.9023	87.99	92.65	87.94	90.68	-	-	-
	VGG16 (S)	0.9742	0.9228	91.46	93.42	91.18	93.63	-	-	-
	VGG19 (S)	0.9757	0.9161	88.86	94.49	88.90	94.46	-	-	-
	DenseNet121(S)	0.9801	0.9248	90.01	95.10	90.00	95.11	-	-	-
	ResNet18 (S)	0.9766	0.9099	85.09	96.63	85.97	96.52	-	-	-
	Inceptionv3(S)	0.9796	0.9225	89.58	95.08	89.58	95.08	-	-	-
	ResNet50 (S)	0.9775	0.9233	90.59	94.32	90.43	94.42	-	-	-
[7]	VDSNet	0.73	0.68	-	-	-	-	0.74	0.63	0.69
[10]	DualCheXNet	-	-	-	-	-	-	0.823	-	-
[2]	CNN	0.9240	-	-	-	-	-	-	-	-
	BPNN	0.8004	-	-	-	-	-	-	-	-
	CpNN	0.8957	-	-	-	-	-	-	-	-
[8]	U-Net	0.94	-	-	-	-	-	-	-	-
[47]	Ensemble CNN							0.940		
[51]	STN based CNN	0.96	0.651	-	-	-	-	-	0.60	0.70
[46]	Ensemble with AlexNet	0.862						0.925		

(Continued)

Table 2.4 Comparison of DL models on the basis of different performance metrics. (*Continued*)

Ref.		Model	Accuracy	F1-Score	Specificity	Sensitivity	PPV	NPV	AUC	Recall	Precision
[26]		FHRNet	-	-	-	-	-	-	0.812	-	-
[20]		AG-CNN	-	-	-	-	-	-	0.871	-	-
[28]		Ensemble DCNN (for Cardiomegaly)	0.93	-	92.00	94.00	-	-	0.97	-	-
		Ensemble DCNN (for Tuberculosis)	0.90	-	92.00	88.00	-	-	0.94	-	-
[41]		MA-DCNN	-	-	-	-	-	-	0.794	-	-
[5]		ChestNet	0.932	-	-	97.13	85.85	-	0.984	-	-
[46]	CNN	Maryland (MC) dataset	0.79	-	-	-	-	-	0.811	-	-
		Shenzhen (SZ)	0.844	-	-	-	-	-	0.900	-	-
		Combined (CB)	0.862	-	-	-	-	-	0.925	-	-
[61]		Kaggle PSNA	-	0.755	-	-	-	-	-	0.793	0.758
[45]		DarkCovidNet	0.981	94.17	99.61	90.65	-	-	-	-	0.979
[13]		GoogleNet (for normal class)	-	-	91.00	91.00	-	-	0.964	-	-
[4]		DecafCNN [78]	-	-	78.00	84.00	-	-	87.00	-	-
[35]		Ensemble DCNN	-	-	-	-	-	-	0.99	-	-
[31]		ResNet101	0.989	98.15	98.66	98.93	-	-	-	-	0.964

Table 2.5 Models with hardware used and time required for training.

Ref.	Dataset	Hardware and software platform used	Input image size	Time required for training
[47]	CheXpert	NVIDIA Geforce RTX 2080 Ti with 11GB memory. Python with Keras and TensorFlow	224×224 pixels	-
[51]	Lung ultrasonography videos from Italy	RTX-2080 NVIDIA GPU	1,005 frames	11 hours
[46]	NIH Tuberculosis Chest X-ray dataset [18] and Belarus Tuberculosis Portal dataset [21]	Nvidia GeForce GTX 1050 Ti	512×512	5–6 ms
[26]	ChestX-ray14 dataset	8-core CPU and four TITAN V GPUs Pytorch 1.0 framework in Python 3.6 on an Ubuntu 16.04 server	224×224	-
[20]	ChestX-ray14 dataset	NVIDIA TITAN Xp GPUs Pytorch	224×224	6 hours
[70]	ChestX-ray14 dataset	Dev-Box linux server with 4 Titan X GPUs	224×224	-
[5]	ChestX-ray14 dataset	Intel Core(TM) i7-6850k CPU 3.60GHz processor, 4TB of hard disk space, 7889 MB of RAM, and a CUDA-enabled NVidia Titan 11 GB graphics processing unit with python and Keras library on TensorFlow	224×224	-
[49]	ChestX-ray8	NVIDIA GeForce GTX TITAN and PyTorch	512×512	20 hours
[46]	NIH Tuberculosis Chest X-ray [18], Belarus Tuberculosis [A6]	Nvidia GeForce GTX 1050 Ti	512×512	1 hour
[61]	Kaggle PSNA	Nvidia Tesla V100 and Nvidia K80 and Keras library of Python	512×512	7 hours
[13]	St. Michael's Hospital chest x-ray	3 NVIDIA Titan X 12GB GPUs	256×256	1 hour
[35]	NIH Tuberculosis Chest X-ray [18], Belarus Tuberculosis [A6]	Intel i5 processor with 32 GB of RAM, and a CUDA-enabled Nvidia Titan 312 GB GPU	256×256	-

2.5   Summary

Considering scarcity of radiologists in less economically developed countries, deep learning models are used for medical imaging for detecting abnormalities in CXR images. There are 14 pathologies whose severity leads to mortality; therefore, many researchers try to detect all 14 pathologies. Generally, DL models are classified into two categories, namely, ensemble and non-ensemble models. Many researchers deployed parameters initialized from ImageNet dataset and then fine tune their proposed network as per the task. In order to deal with different issue, different pre-processing techniques are employed by the authors. The ChestX-ray14 dataset is the popular dataset which is experimented mostly as it contains large number of images with annotation. Cardiomegaly is the major chest pathology detected by many authors due to its spatially spread nature. We have also discussed factors affecting performance of models along with their significance. Finally, we have compared existing models on the basis of different parameters so that it will be easy to carry out future research to develop more robust and accurate model for the thoracic image analysis using deep models.

2.6   Conclusion and Future Scope

We found that it is tedious to obtain a good AUC score for all the diseases using single CNN. Doctors used to rely on a broad range of additional data such as patient age, gender, medical history, clinical symptoms, and possibly CXRs from different views. These additional information should also be incorporated into the model training. For the identification of diseases which have small and complex structures on CXRs, a finer resolution such as 512×512 or $1,024 \times 1,024$ may be advantageous. However, for preparation and inference, this investigation needs far more computational resources. In addition, another concern is CXR image consistency. When taking a deeper look at the CheXpert, it is observed that a considerable rate of samples have low quality (e.g., *rotated image, low-resolution, samples with texts,* and *noise*) that definitely deteriorate the model performance. Spatially spread abnormalities such as cardiomegaly and Edema can be localized more accurately. Due to shift variant nature of CNN, antialiasing filters are needed to improve the performance of CNN model.

Deep learning models should be able to integrate and interpret data from various imaging sources to obtain a better perspective on the anatomy of the patient in order to allow efficient analysis of patient scans. This could produce deeper insights into the nature and development of the disease, thereby offering a greater degree of understanding of the condition of patients by radiologists. Along with x-ray images other parameters such as heredity, age, and diabetes status, parameters can also be added to improve accuracy. Rather than going for ensemble and pre-trained models, pathology specific and data specific models can be implemented in future by combining good characteristics of existing models. Same models can also be used for detecting abnormalities in other region of body such as brain tumor, mouth cancer, and head-neck cancer. Novel deep learning models can be implemented for detecting post COVID impact on chest.

References

1. Abbas, A., Abdelsamea, M.M., Gaber, M.M., Classification of COVID-19 in chest X-ray images using DeTraC deep convolutional neural network. *Applied Intelligence, arXiv preprint arXiv:2003.13815.*, 51, 2, 854–864 2020.

2. Abiyev, R.H. and Ma'aitah, M.K.S., Deep convolutional neural networks for chest diseases detection. *J. Healthcare Eng., 2018*, 1–11, 2018.

3. Apostolopoulos, I.D., Aznaouridis, S.I., Tzani, M.A., Extracting possibly representative COVID-19 Biomarkers from X-Ray images with Deep Learning approach and image data related to Pulmonary Diseases. *J. Med. Biol. Eng.*, 1, 40, 462–469, 2020.

4. Bar, Y., Diamant, I., Wolf, L., Lieberman, S., Konen, E., Greenspan, H., Chest pathology detection using deep learning with non-medical training, in: *2015 IEEE 12th international symposium on biomedical imaging (ISBI)*, 2015, April, IEEE, pp. 294–297.

5. Behzadi-khormouji, H., Rostami, H., Salehi, S., Derakhshande-Rishehri, T., Masoumi, M., Salemi, S., Batouli, A., Deep learning, reusable and problem-based architectures for detection of consolidation on chest X-ray images. *Comput. Methods Programs Biomed.*, 185, 105162, 2020.

6. Belarus tuberculosis portal. Available at: http://tuberculosis.by.

7. Bharati, S., Podder, P., Mondal, M.R.H., Hybrid deep learning for detecting lung diseases from X-ray images. *Inf. Med. Unlocked*, 20, 100391, 2020.

8. Bouslama, A., Laaziz, Y., Tali, A., Diagnosis and precise localization of cardiomegaly disease using U-NET. *Inf. Med. Unlocked*, 19, 100306, 2020.

9. Chauhan, A., Chauhan, D., Rout, C., Role of gist and PHOG features in computer-aided diagnosis of tuberculosis without segmentation. *PLoS One*, 9, 11, e112980, 2014.

10. Chen, B., Li, J., Guo, X., Lu, G., DualCheXNet: dual asymmetric feature learning for thoracic disease classification in chest X-rays. *Biomed. Signal Process. Control*, 53, 101554, 2019.

11. Cheng, J.Z., Ni, D., Chou, Y.H., Qin, J., Tiu, C.M., Chang, Y.C., Chen, C.M., Computer-aided diagnosis with deep learning architecture: applications to breast lesions in US images and pulmonary nodules in CT scans. *Sci. Rep.*, 6, 1, 1–13, 2016.

12. Chollet, F., Xception: Deep learning with depthwise separable convolutions, in: *Proceedings of the IEEE conference on computer vision and pattern recognition*, pp. 1251–1258, 2017.

13. Cicero, M., Bilbily, A., Colak, E., Dowdell, T., Gray, B., Perampaladas, K., Barfett, J., Training and validating a deep convolutional neural network for computer-aided detection and classification of abnormalities on frontal chest radiographs. *Invest. Radiol.*, 52, 5, 281–287, 2017.

14. Ciompi, F., de Hoop, B., van Riel, S.J., Chung, K., Scholten, E.T., Oudkerk, M., van Ginneken, B., Automatic classification of pulmonary peri-fissural nodules in computed tomography using an ensemble of 2D views and a convolutional neural network out-of-the-box. *Med. Image Anal.*, 26, 1, 195–202, 2015.

15. Demner-Fushman, D., Kohli, M.D., Rosenman, M.B., Shooshan, S.E., Rodriguez, L., Antani, S., McDonald, C.J., Preparing a collection of radiology examinations for distribution and retrieval. *J. Am. Med. Inf. Assoc.*, 23, 2, 304–310, 2016.

16. Deng, J., Dong, W., Socher, R., Li, L.J., Li, K., Fei-Fei, L., Imagenet: A large-scale hierarchical image database, in: *2009 IEEE conference on computer vision and pattern recognition*, 2009, June, IEEE, pp. 248–255.

17. Donahue, J., Jia, Y., Vinyals, O., Hoffman, J., Zhang, N., Tzeng, E., Darrell, T., Decaf: A deep convolutional activation feature for generic visual recognition, in: *International conference on machine learning*, 2014, January, pp. 647–655.

18. Dunnmon, J.A., Yi, D., Langlotz, C.P., Ré, C., Rubin, D.L., Lungren, M.P., Assessment of convolutional neural networks for automated classification of chest radiographs. *Radiology*, 290, 2, 537–544, 2019.

19. Guan, Q., Huang, Y., Zhong, Z., Zheng, Z., Zheng, L., Yang, Y., Diagnose like a radiologist: Attention guided convolutional neural network for thorax disease classification. *arXiv preprint arXiv:1801.09927*, 1–10, 2018.

20. Guan, Q., Huang, Y., Zhong, Z., Zheng, Z., Zheng, L., Yang, Y., Diagnose like a radiologist: Attention guided convolutional neural network for thorax disease classification. *Pattern Recognition Letters, arXiv preprintarXiv:1801.09927*, 131, 38–45, 2018.

21. He, K., Zhang, X., Ren, S., Sun, J., Deep residual learning for image recognition, in: *Proceedings of the IEEE conference on computer vision and pattern recognition*, pp. 770–778, 2016.

22. He, K., Zhang, X., Ren, S., Sun, J., Identity mappings in deep residual networks, in: *European conference on computer vision*, 2016, October, Springer, Cham, pp. 630–645.

23. Ho, T.K.K. and Gwak, J., Multiple feature integration for classification of thoracic disease in chest radiography. *Appl. Sci.*, 9, 19, 4130, 2019.

24. https://www.who.int/news-room/fact-sheets/detail/tuberculosis [accessed on 24 Nov. 2020]

25. Huang, G., Liu, Z., Van Der Maaten, L., Weinberger, K.Q., Densely connected convolutional networks, in: *Proceedings of the IEEE conference on computer vision and pattern recognition*, pp. 4700–4708, 2017.

26. Huang, Z., Lin, J., Xu, L., Wang, H., Bai, T., Pang, Y., Meen, T.H., Fusion High-Resolution Network for Diagnosing ChestX-ray Images. *Electronics*, 9, 1, 190, 2020.

27. Hwang, S., Kim, H.E., Jeong, J., Kim, H.J., A novel approach for tuberculosis screening based on deep convolutional neural networks, in: *Medical imaging 2016: computer-aided diagnosis*, vol. 9785, pp. 97852W, International Society for Optics and Photonics, 2016 March.

28. Islam, M.T., Aowal, M.A., Minhaz, A.T., Ashraf, K., Abnormality detection and localization in chest x-rays using deep convolutional neural networks. *arXiv preprint arXiv:1705.09850*, 1–16, 2017.

29. Jaeger, S., Candemir, S., Antani, S., Wáng, Y.X.J., Lu, P.X., Thoma, G., Two public chest X-ray datasets for computer-aided screening of pulmonary diseases. *Quant. Imaging Med. Surg.*, 4, 6, 475, 2014.

30. Jaeger, S., Karargyris, A., Candemir, S., Folio, L., Siegelman, J., Callaghan, F., Thoma, G., Automatic tuberculosis screening using chest radiographs. *IEEE Trans. Med. Imaging*, 33, 2, 233–245, 2013.

31. Jain, G., Mittal, D., Thakur, D., Mittal, M.K., A deep learning approach to detect Covid-19 coronavirus with X-Ray images. *Biocybern. Biomed. Eng.*, 40, 4, 1391–1405, 2020.

32. Jain, R., Gupta, M., Taneja, S., Hemanth, D.J., Deep learning based detection and analysis of COVID-19 on chest X-ray images. *Appl. Intell.*, 51, 3, 1690–1700, 2020.

33. Karargyris, A., Siegelman, J., Tzortzis, D., Jaeger, S., Candemir, S., Xue, Z., Thoma, G.R., Combination of texture and shape features to detect pulmonary abnormalities in digital chest X-rays. *Int. J. Comput. Assist. Radiol. Surg.*, 11, 1, 99–106, 2016.

34. Krizhevsky, A., Sutskever, I., Hinton, G.E., Imagenet classification with deep convolutional neural networks. *Commun. ACM*, 60, 6, 84–90, 2017.

35. Lakhani, P. and Sundaram, B., Deep learning at chest radiography: automated classification of pulmonary tuberculosis by using convolutional neural networks. *Radiology*, 284, 2, 574–582, 2017.

36. Li, R., Zhang, W., Suk, H.I., Wang, L., Li, J., Shen, D., Ji, S., Deep learning based imaging data completion for improved brain disease diagnosis, in: *International Conference on Medical Image Computing and Computer-Assisted Intervention*, 2014, September, Springer, Cham, pp. 305–312.

37. Li, Z., Wang, C., Han, M., Xue, Y., Wei, W., Li, L.J., Fei-Fei, L., Thoracic disease identification and localization with limited supervision, in: *Proceedings of the IEEE Conference on Computer Vision and Pattern Recognition*, pp. 8290–8299, 2018.

38. Litjens, G., Kooi, T., Bejnordi, B.E., Setio, A.A.A., Ciompi, F., Ghafoorian, M., Sánchez, C.I., A survey on deep learning in medical image analysis. *Med. Image Anal.*, 42, 60–88, 2017.

39. Liu, W., Rabinovich, A., Berg, A.C., Parsenet: Looking wider to see better. *arXiv preprint arXiv:1506.04579*, Workshop track - ICLR 2016, 1–11, 2015.

40. Lopes, U.K. and Valiati, J.F., Pre-trained convolutional neural networks as feature extractors for tuberculosis detection. *Comput. Biol. Med.*, 89, 135–143, 2017.

41. Ma, Y., Zhou, Q., Chen, X., Lu, H., Zhao, Y., Multi-attention network for thoracic disease classification and localization, in: *ICASSP 2019-2019 IEEE International Conference on Acoustics, Speech and Signal Processing (ICASSP)*, 2019, May, IEEE, pp. 1378–1382.

42. Melendez, J., Sánchez, C.I., Philipsen, R.H., Maduskar, P., Dawson, R., Theron, G., Van Ginneken, B., An automated tuberculosis screening strategy combining X-ray-based computer-aided detection and clinical information. *Sci. Rep.*, 6, 25265, 2016.

43. Mukherjee, A., Feature Engineering for Cardio-Thoracic Disease Detection from NIH Chest Radiographs, in: *Computational Intelligence in Pattern Recognition*, pp. 277–284, Springer, Singapore, 2020.

44. Müller, R., Kornblith, S., Hinton, G.E., When does label smoothing help?, in: *Advances in Neural Information Processing Systems*, pp. 4694–4703, 2019.

45. Ozturk, T., Talo, M., Yildirim, E.A., Baloglu, U.B., Yildirim, O., Acharya, U.R., Automated detection of COVID-19 cases using deep neural networks with X-ray images. *Comput. Biol. Med.*, 121, 103792, 2020.

46. Pasa, F., Golkov, V., Pfeiffer, F., Cremers, D., Pfeiffer, D., Efficient deep network architectures for fast chest X-ray tuberculosis screening and visualization. *Sci. Rep.*, 9, 1, 1–9, 2019.

47. Pham, H.H., Le, T.T., Tran, D.Q., Ngo, D.T., Nguyen, H.Q., Interpreting chest X-rays via CNNs that exploit disease dependencies and uncertainty labels. *medRxiv*, 19013342, 1–27, 2019.

48. Qin, C., Yao, D., Shi, Y., Song, Z., Computer-aided detection in chest radiography based on artificial intelligence: a survey. *Biomed. Eng. Online*, 17, 1, 113, 2018.

49. Rajpurkar, P., Irvin, J., Zhu, K., Yang, B., Mehta, H., Duan, T., Lungren, M.P., Chexnet: Radiologist-level pneumonia detection on chest x-rays with deep learning. *arXiv preprint arXiv:1711.05225*, 05225, 1–6, 2017.

50. Roth, H.R., Lu, L., Liu, J., Yao, J., Seff, A., Cherry, K., Summers, R.M., Improving computer-aided detection using convolutional neural networks and random view aggregation. *IEEE Trans. Med. Imaging*, 35, 5, 1170–1181, 2015.

51. Roy, S., Menapace, W., Oei, S., Luijten, B., Fini, E., Saltori, C., Peschiera, E., Deep learning for classification and localization of COVID-19 markers in point-of-care lung ultrasound. *IEEE Trans. Med. Imaging*, 39, 8, 2676–2687, 2020.

52. Roy, S., Siarohin, A., Sangineto, E., Bulo, S.R., Sebe, N., Ricci, E., Unsupervised domain adaptation using feature-whitening and consensus loss, in: *Proceedings of the IEEE Conference on Computer Vision and Pattern Recognition*, pp. 9471–9480, 2019.

53. Rozenberg, E., Freedman, D., Bronstein, A., Localization with Limited Annotation for Chest X-rays, in: *Machine Learning for Health Workshop*, 2020, April, PMLR, pp. 52–65.

54. Ryoo, S. and Kim, H.J., Activities of the Korean institute of tuberculosis. *Osong Public Health Res. Perspect.*, 5, S43–S49, 2014.

55. Sajjadi, M., Javanmardi, M., Tasdizen, T., Regularization with stochastic transformations and perturbations for deep semi-supervised learning. *Adv. Neural Inf. Process. Syst.*, 29, 1163–1171, 2016.

56. Setio, A.A.A., Ciompi, F., Litjens, G., Gerke, P., Jacobs, C., Van Riel, S.J., van Ginneken, B., Pulmonary nodule detection in CT images: false positive reduction using multi-view convolutional networks. *IEEE Trans. Med. Imaging*, 35, 5, 1160–1169, 2016.

57. Shen, W., Zhou, M., Yang, F., Yang, C., Tian, J., Multi-scale convolutional neural networks for lung nodule classification, in: *International Conference on Information Processing in Medical Imaging*, 2015, June, Springer, Cham, pp. 588–599.

58. Shin, H.C., Roth, H.R., Gao, M., Lu, L., Xu, Z., Nogues, I., Summers, R.M., Deep convolutional neural networks for computer-aided detection: CNN architectures, dataset characteristics and transfer learning. *IEEE Trans. Med. Imaging*, 35, 5, 1285–1298, 2016.

59. Shiraishi, J., Katsuragawa, S., Ikezoe, J., Matsumoto, T., Kobayashi, T., Komatsu, K.I., Doi, K., Development of a digital image database for chest radiographs with and without a lung nodule: receiver operating characteristic analysis of radiologists' detection of pulmonary nodules. *Am. J. Roentgenol.*, *174*, 1, 71–74, 2000.

60. Simonyan, K. and Zisserman, A., Very deep convolutional networks for large-scale image recognition. *arXiv preprint arXiv:1409.1556*, ICLR 2015, 1–14, 2014.

61. Sirazitdinov, I., Kholiavchenko, M., Mustafaev, T., Yixuan, Y., Kuleev, R., Ibragimov, B., Deep neural network ensemble for pneumonia localization from a large-scale chest x-ray database. *Comput. Electr. Eng.*, *78*, 388–399, 2019.

62. Soldati, G., Smargiassi, A., Inchingolo, R., Buonsenso, D., Perrone, T., Briganti, D.F., Tursi, F., Proposal for international standardization of the use of lung ultrasound for COVID-19 patients; a simple, quantitative, reproducible method. *J. Ultrasound Med.*, *10*, 39, 7, 1413–1419, 2020.

63. Suk, H.I., Lee, S.W., Shen, D., Alzheimer's Disease Neuroimaging Initiative. Hierarchical feature representation and multimodal fusion with deep learning for AD/MCI diagnosis. *NeuroImage*, *101*, 569–582, 2014.

64. Szegedy, C., Ioffe, S., Vanhoucke, V., Alemi, A., Inception-v4, inception-resnet and the impact of residual connections on learning, in: *Proceedings of the AAAI Conference on Artificial Intelligence*, Vol. 31, No. 1, 2016.

65. Szegedy, C., Liu, W., Jia, Y., Sermanet, P., Reed, S., Anguelov, D., Rabinovich, A., Going deeper with convolutions, in: *Proceedings of the IEEE conference on computer vision and pattern recognition*, pp. 1–9, 2015.

66. Szegedy, C., Vanhoucke, V., Ioffe, S., Shlens, J., Wojna, Z., Rethinking the inception architecture for computer vision, in: *Proceedings of the IEEE conference on computer vision and pattern recognition*, pp. 2818–2826, 2016.

67. Tang, Y.X., Tang, Y.B., Peng, Y., Yan, K., Bagheri, M., Redd, B.A., Summers, R.M., Automated abnormality classification of chest radiographs using deep convolutional neural networks. *NPJ Digital Med.*, *3*, 1, 1–8, 2020.

68. Vajda, S., Karargyris, A., Jaeger, S., Santosh, K.C., Candemir, S., Xue, Z., Thoma, G., Feature selection for automatic tuberculosis screening in frontal chest radiographs. *J. Med. Syst.*, *42*, 8, 146, 2018.

69. Wang, H. and Xia, Y., Chestnet: A deep neural network for classification of thoracic diseases on chest radiography. *arXiv preprint arXiv:1807.03058*, 1–8, 2018.

70. Wang, X., Peng, Y., Lu, L., Lu, Z., Bagheri, M., Summers, R.M., Chestx-ray8: Hospital-scale chest x-ray database and benchmarks on weakly-supervised classification and localization of common thorax diseases, in: *Proceedings of the IEEE conference on computer vision and pattern recognition*, pp. 2097–2106, 2017.

71. Yao, L., Poblenz, E., Dagunts, D., Covington, B., Bernard, D., Lyman, K., Learning to diagnose from scratch by exploiting dependencies among labels. *arXiv preprint arXiv:1710.10501*, 1–12, 2017.

72. Zech, J.R., Badgeley, M.A., Liu, M., Costa, A.B., Titano, J.J., Oermann, E.K., Confounding variables can degrade generalization performance of radiological deep learning models. *arXiv preprint arXiv:1807.00431*, 1–15, 2018.

73. Zhang, R., Making convolutional networks shift-invariant again. *arXiv preprint arXiv:1904.11486*, In *International Conference on Machine Learning*, pp. 7324–7334, PMLR, 1–11, 2019.

74. Zoph, B., Vasudevan, V., Shlens, J., Le, Q.V., Learning transferable architectures for scalable image recognition, in: *Proceedings of the IEEE conference on computer vision and pattern recognition*, pp. 8697–8710, 2018.

3

Feature Selection and Machine Learning Models for High-Dimensional Data: State-of-the-Art

G. Manikandan[1]* and S. Abirami[2]

[1]Department of Computer Science & Engineering, College of Engineering Guindy, Anna University, Chennai, Tamil Nadu, India
[2]Department of Information Science and Technology, College of Engineering Guindy, Anna University, Chennai, India

Abstract

The technology developments in various domains generate the large amount data with millions of samples/instances and features. Some of the data are from many areas such as bio-informatics, text mining, and microarray data, which are commonly represented in high-dimensional feature vector, and prediction process is difficult task in this kind of data in field of pattern recognition, bioinformatics, statistical analysis, and machine learning. High dimensionality data increases the computational time as well as the space complexity while processing data. In general, most of the pattern recognition and machine learning techniques are available for processing the low-dimensional data; this will not solve the issues of high-dimensional data. To solve this issue, feature selection (FS) plays a vital role which is modeled to select the feature set from the greater number of features from the high-dimensional data; thereby, it builds the simpler model and gives the higher classification accuracy. Also, the FS process focuses on reducing and eliminating the dimensionality nature of the data by removing the irrelevant and redundant data and helps to improve the predictive modeling with the better visualization and understanding capabilities of the data. By considering the issues mentioned above, this chapter aims to provide the detailed introduction on FS techniques and gives the state-of-the-art methods, concerning machine learning and deep learning methods. At last, this chapter provides the various application domains which being in need of FS techniques, and also, further, this chapter also gives the directions to deal with the feature reduction problems occurring in the large voluminous dataset.

Keywords: Feature selection, deep learning, feature extraction, microarray, autoencoder, recurrent neural networks, dimensionality reduction

3.1 Introduction

In machine learning, designing the feature selection (FS) algorithms and creating the better model for classifying the high-dimensional data are major challenging tasks in many

---

*Corresponding author: manitamilm@gmail.com

Om Prakash Jena, Alok Ranjan Tripathy, Ahmed A. Elngar and Zdzislaw Polkowski (eds.) Computational Intelligence and Healthcare Informatics, (43–64) © 2021 Scrivener Publishing LLC

application areas such as image processing, video processing, text analytics, medical, and microarray [1, 2]. In traditional approach, the FS techniques are categorized as filter, wrapper, hybrid, ensemble, and embedded methods. Filter approaches select the feature subset by analyzing the internal characteristics and nature of the features supported on the evaluation criteria such as correlation, information gain, dependency, distance measure, and consistency; also, this filter method is independent of the learning algorithm unlike the other methods. Wrapper methods consider the performance measure, accuracy, or the error rate from the classifier as the evaluation criteria. This is an improvement over the filter approach since it uses the dependencies and bias in the learning algorithm. The main demerit of the wrapper approach is overfitting because of the repeated evaluation of each subset. Embedded approach selects the most relevant features with help of classifiers or machine learning algorithm and is more similar in results with the wrapper methods. Hybrid technique is the combination of any two approaches of the FS with the same criterion, thus making use of advantages of the both. Ensemble method creates a subset of features and then makes the aggregate result out of the group, thus making it the most flexible and robust method. The nature of the high-dimensional data may be supervised, semi-supervised, or unsupervised. The FS process for these types of data varies accordingly based on the machine learning approaches. The process of the FS is carried out by centralized or distributed manner. Due to the evolution of big data, some of the techniques of the centralized methods were failed to process the massive high-dimensional data. For this issue, many frameworks and techniques are evolved to help the machine learning programmers to design new algorithms and strategies to overcome the challenges in distributing the data over the clusters for better processing. The basic tool introduced by Google is the MapReduce which is then replaced by Apache Spark which is considered to be the superset of MapReduce. The modern approach of dividing the dataset into a number of partitions and processing each of them separately is the distributed way of FS carried out with help of programming model in Apache Spark. This is a far better improvement on the subject of efficiency, accuracy, and execution time while compared to the centralized one. One type of approach to the distributed one lies in the method of partitioning the dataset. The datasets can be partitioned both in the horizontal and in the vertical manner. The traditional correlation algorithm can be applied after the partition. Distributed approach is one of the techniques which performs the sequence of rounds to identify the predominant features based on partitioning the data. After the different rounds, the portioned data are consolidated into one subset based on the complexity measure of the data. The results obtained from the distributed approach results good classification accuracy as well as it saves run time of the algorithm among the original set of datasets.

Due to advancement of technologies in various fields, selecting the features from the high-dimensional microarray data is considered as a major research area in the field of biological computational intelligence. Various application domains for the FS includes healthcare, bio-informatics, government sectors, network analysis, and link prediction. In the perspective of the high-dimensional data, the data objects consist of more features in those situations it is difficult to process, select, and extract the most predominant feature which is going to optimize the classification problem. From the mathematical point of view, the statisticians talk this problem as "Big p Small n" which is explained in Section 3.1.1. It means that the total number of variables p present in the training data feature set exceeds the total number of samples n, and in this situation, it influences and affects the classification and processing capability. This is termed as the "curse of dimensionality" problem [3]. With the high-dimensional data spaces, the "curse of dimensionality" is one of the important that is to be considered in learning and classification task for the better results are not used for the predictive purposes. Also, as the number features/dimensions increases, it suffers not only in the complexity of the data but also in classification errors, irrelevant noise, and redundant data, which may also increase.

Nevertheless, the traditional algorithms which are used in the data mining, pattern recognition, computational intelligence, and machine learning applications are still susceptible to the "curse of dimensionality"; it indicates about the degradation of the performance and accuracy of the learning algorithm due to increasing number of the features. For solving this issue, many dimensionality reduction [32] approaches have been applied as a data pre-processing technique for simplifying the data analysis and model. The main objective is to identification/selection of the low-dimensional data from the whole set of high-dimensional datasets. By doing this considerable task, we yield better results in both clustering and classification.

3.1.1   Motivation of the Dimensionality Reduction

A very common statistical analysis problem to model the relationship between the target variables Y and their associated features $x_1, x_2, x_3, \ldots, x_p$ is based on the sample size of the input "n". In certain scenario, dimensionality of "p" is very large while potentially compared to the "n", so the dimensionality and the interaction of the features grow rapidly.

Figure 3.1a shows the normal case where number features are less and number samples are more; for this case, selecting features is simple, but Figure 3.1b shows that the total number of samples from the training data has the more features with smaller samples; for this case, extracting inference from the data is often difficult. But in the case of selecting the features from these kinds of high-dimensional data, making inference about the data is difficult because the dimension "n" of the data has to minimum when comparing to total number of features "p". For solving this problem with well-known example, we have discussed the two real-word scenarios in the application domains of bioinformatics and text mining.

Scenario 1: In the field of bioinformatics, microarray domain, gene expressions, coefficients, and measures corresponding to the large numbers of the mRNA samples are represented by the features [32]. The sample size of these types of datasets is small but the

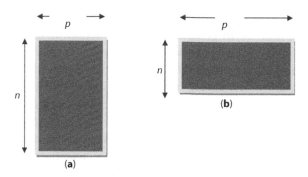

Figure 3.1 (a) This what the normal data looks like. (b) "Big p and small n" problem.

number of features is often more which may range from 6,000 to 60,000. For example, from [41], the breast cancer dataset consists of only 118 instances and 2 classes, but it is having 22,215 features, and to classify the positive and negative result from this dataset is difficult one. Furthermore, these datasets consist of systematic errors, human errors, and also large number of irrelevant and redundant data.

Scenario 2: Let us consider the text mining datasets; the representation of the text based on the features is extremely large and also the number of terms across the documents/ samples varies widely. Also, usually, the text document consists of much noisy and irrelevant information Meanwhile, the text documents normally contain redundant and irrelevant information which leads the classifier complexity. The text dataset from [1] consists of 12,897 instances and two classes with 7,495 features; because of large number of feature, the classifier suffers the learning task. To solve this issue, we need some novel computational intelligence based algorithms, to handling this voluminous data. The motivations behind the dimensionality reduction are as follows:

a. It aids to find out the reduced sets of features with better predictive power in the perspective of knowledge discovery.
b. It speeds up the classification or clustering algorithm while performing the experimental analysis because many machine learning algorithms suffers in the time complexity.
c. It provides better visualization and modeling mechanisms for the high-dimensional data.
d. It removes the noisy or irrelevant data which is not impact the classification accuracy.

The research on the dimensionality reduction has two dimensions: one is FS and other is feature extraction. In the process of FS, it selects the features with predominant feature set/subsets that contain the most relevant information with respect to resolving the high-dimensional problem, whereas the feature extraction is the more general method which converts the original high-dimensional data space into the low-dimensional space with keeping the relevant information.

3.1.2 Feature Selection and Feature Extraction

As discussed before, dimensionality reduction method has been categorized into two types i.e., feature extraction and FS. In general, feature extraction methods transform original features into various forms of the feature set with the lesser number of features. During this process, the new features are built from the original feature set based on the combinations of linear or nonlinear functions. Linear Discriminant Analysis [49] and Principal Component Analysis [6] are best examples of such algorithms. In FS process, it does not modify or alter the data rather than it selects the most predominant feature subsets with maximum classification performance. Many application areas such as machine learning, statistical analysis, data mining, image processing, bioinformatics, anomaly detection in social networks, and natural language processing (NLP). FS strategies will be used as pre-processing step [21, 31]. In general, FS is often used as a pre-processing stage before the training process and tuning the classifier. This technique is also called as feature reduction, attribute selection, and variable subset selection. In the upcoming section, we have discussed various objectives of the FS, process of selecting features, and types of FS in detail.

3.1.3   Objectives of the Feature Selection

The main motivation of the FS process is to identify and select best feature subset from the input samples which can effectively represent the input data by ignoring the issues from the noisy and irrelevant data with good prediction results [21, 37], which have been mentioned with the following few advantages of FS. (1) Dimensionality of the feature is reduced, thereby it increases computation speed of the algorithm and also reduces the requirement of storage space. (2) It ignores the irrelevant, noisy, and redundant features from the whole feature set. (3) It increases the performance of the predictive model and also gives the better visualizing capability of the data.

One of the applications domains is gene microarray analysis [16, 30]. The standardized gene expression data would contain hundreds and thousands of variables, in that many of features are highly correlated with the other features. For example, when the two features are perfectly correlated, it means that only few features are more than enough to describe the data, i.e., the dependent variables do not provide more information about the target classes and thus provide as noise for learner and the predictor.

3.1.4   Feature Selection Process

The FS process is categorized into four main steps [36], generating the subset, evaluation of the subset, stopping criteria, and validating the results. The systematic representation of the process of selecting the features is shown in Figure 3.2. Feature generation is the first stage which involves the searching process of all the features in samples. In any dataset, the number of combinations of feature subsets is 2^n, where n is the total number of the features; in this scenario, considering all attributes/features becomes costly and also it increases the

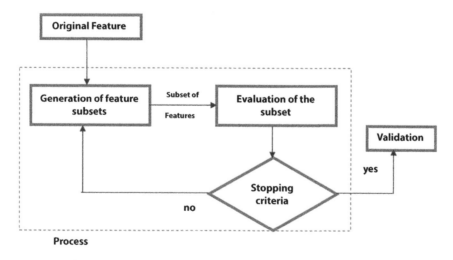

Figure 3.2 Feature selection process.

data dimensionality. In order to minimizing the search cost, many techniques [14] have been proposed to get the required optimal subset.

Among those, Sequential Forward Selection (SFS) and the Backward Elimination methods are considered common techniques which are used to traverse the sample space. The Sequential Forward Selection begins with the empty sets and adds the features by one at a time. On other hand, Backward Elimination starts with whole set of the attributes and elimination process will continue until stopping criterion met [46]. In evaluation step, the goodness of the features subset is evaluated. Evaluation criteria can be the learning algorithm accuracy or it can be done by internal characteristics of the training data without using classifier algorithms [36]. Filters, wrapper, and embedded are three common methods which are currently being used in many application fields which is explained in following sections. Stopping criterion identifies about when the process of selecting features should stop. There are numerous ways to stop the feature search process. The process of selecting the features may be quit when obtained new feature set could not have improved the classification accuracy. Another stopping criterion based on the ranking can be used for when to stop the process. Validation is final step is which evaluates the obtained subset against the classification accuracy.

The reminder of the chapter is structured as follows: Section 3.2 provides various types of FS techniques and also summarizes with the various state-of-the-art FS approaches based on centralized techniques such as filter methods, wrapper methods, embedded methods, and ensemble and hybrid methods for high-dimensional data, whereas Section 3.3 discusses the supervised learning, unsupervised learning, and semi-supervised learning methods and also the taxonomy of deep learning models. Section 3.4 aims to provide various computational intelligence and evolutionary-based FS on the high-dimensional data. Section 3.4 presents the application domains of the FS and feature reduction algorithms.

3.2   Types of Feature Selection

With respect to the recent review in the topic of FS, it is classified into two categories in the terms of evaluation strategy: the first one is classifier-dependent method like wrapper and embedded methods, and the another one is classifier-independent methods ("filter" methods) which shown in Figure 3.3.

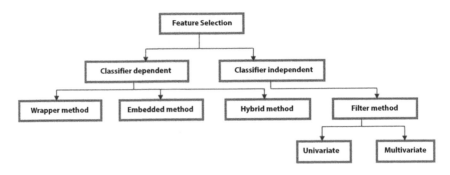

Figure 3.3 Taxonomy of feature selection.

3.2.1   Filter Methods

Filter methods use the statistical characteristics and functions of the data as the primary principle for the selection of predominant features from the vast samples. The well-suited criteria and functions are selected and applied for ranking the features, and after that, based on the applied threshold it selects the predominant subset. Filter techniques measure the features importance without consideration of the any learning algorithm, so the filter method is very popular in high-dimensional data [5, 7, 23]. Some of the standard filter methods are based on Mutual information [55, 64], minimum redundancy maximum relevance (mRMR) [47], Fast Correlation–Based Filter (FCBF) [58, 71], interaction capping (ICAP) [65], Trace-Oriented Feature Analysis (TOFA) [25, 68], ReliefF, and Ant Colony Optimization (ACO) [25]. Further, filter approaches can be categorized into two major divisions: univariate and multivariate methods [29, 56]. In the univariate methods, the importance of the feature is evaluated by individually with help of various function of evaluation criterion, whereas in the multivariate techniques, the feature importance is observed from the dependencies between the features. The most popular ever using univariate filter methods are Gain ratio, Information gain, Symmetrical uncertainty (SU), Laplacian score, Term variance (TV), Gini index, Improved Gini index (GINI) [39], and Fisher score. Also, the well-known multivariate filter-based methods which are used in most of the fields for selecting the features are mRMR [47], Mutual correlation-based FS, Random subspace method (RSM), Information Gain, and Relevance-redundancy FS.

In the high-dimensional microarray data, filter approaches measure the originality of the feature subsets by the observation of the internal properties of the data using the statistical dependencies measures; thereby, single features or a collection of features are extracted and evaluated against class labels. In the following section, we have discussed some important optimal filter methods that are implemented to the microarray data in the domain of bioinformatics. We brief some of the important filter based FS in the following subsection.

3.2.1.1   Correlation-Based Feature Selection

Correlation-based FS (CFS) [50] is one of the standard multivariate FS filter-based technique which ranks the feature subsets by using correlation-based measures and the evaluation function [15, 18]. The bias of the selected evaluation function will evaluate the feature subsets which contains the features with most correlated values with target. Based on the evaluated correlation function, the relevant features are identified and the irrelevant features are removed or ignored because based on the correlation measure. Also, the redundant features may be highlighted because those features are also highly correlated among the one or more features [9, 13]. The final selection of a feature will be based on prediction of classes in which the particular instance is not been predicted already by some other features. In general, the CFS measures the feature subsets based on the hypothesis. The following equation from [50] provides merits of the feature subset S which consisting of the k features:

$$Merits_{s_k} = \frac{k\overline{r_{cf}}}{\sqrt{k+k(k-1)\overline{r_{ff}}}} \tag{3.1}$$

where

$\overline{r_{cf}}$ is the average values of all the features to the classification correlations.

$\overline{r_{ff}}$ is the average values of all the feature to the feature correlations.

Then, the CFS criterion is expressed by

$$CFS = \max_{s_k} \frac{r_{cf1} + r_{cf2} + \cdots + r_{cfk}}{\sqrt{k + 2(r_{f1f2} + \cdots r_{fifj} + \cdots + r_{fkf1})}} \tag{3.2}$$

where r_{cf_i} and $r_{f_if_j}$ are variables which represent the correlations coefficient.

Pearson's correlation coefficient, Kendall Correlation, SU, Mutual Information, Spearman's coefficient, minimum description length (MDL), and relief are some optimally used evaluation methods in filter techniques.

3.2.1.2   The Fast Correlation-Based Filter

Fast Correlation–Based Filter [48] technique is one of the standard multivariate approaches which measure the dependency between the feature-feature interaction and also the feature-feature correlation. This approach selects the feature subsets based on the correlation values which are highly correlated among the class by using the common measure which is called SU. SU is expressed in terms of inter relation and the ratio between information gain and entropy among the features. In general, redundancy is expressed by the feature correlation if the two the features are correlated. However, in some cases, the linear correlations functions are will not able to find the non-linear dependencies among the features. For this purpose, in literature [36], the authors concentrated and proposed the technique to detect the non-linear dependences called SU. The SU is expressed by

$$SU(fi, C) = 2\left[\frac{IG(f_i, C)}{H(f_i) + H(C)}\right] \tag{3.3}$$

The information gain is the ratio between the ith feature f_i and the target class label C which is expressed by

$$IG(f_i, C) = H(f_i) - H(f_i/C)$$

where $H(f_i)$ be the entropy of the feature f_i, $H(f_i/C)$ is represented as entropy of the feature f_i after observation of the class C, and it is expressed below:

$$H(f_i) = -\sum_j p(x_j) \log_2 p(x_j)$$

$$H(f_i/C) = -\sum_k p(c_k) \sum_j p(x_j/c_k) \log_2 p(x_j/c_k)$$

Based on the above expression, it is simple to find out the dependence and independence of the variables. At present, in many high-dimensional analytical domains such as text mining, pattern recognition, and microarray domains, FCBF approach is used for removing the irrelevant and redundant features.

3.2.1.3   The INTERACT Algorithm

The INTERACT approach uses the same procedure and evaluation criteria which is indicated in the SU as the FCBF filter [20], but it includes some contribution regarding the consistency of the features. In this regard, INTERACT algorithm indicates the feature significance and also it shows how much effect will comes after the elimination of a features. The algorithm is made up off following steps.

Step 1: In the phase one, all the features in the data are processed and ranked based on the function, after that ranked features are to be sorted based on the descending order with respective SU values from the previous section.

Step 2: In the second phase, the evaluation is done among all the features starting from one by one till all the features in the index are ranked.

Step 3: If the consistency value among the features less than from the threshold which means the feature is not predominant, then it is removed from the set; otherwise, the feature is selected. The authors [9] indicated that this approach will perform the FS and feature interaction well and also it selects the predominant features efficiently.

3.2.1.4   ReliefF

ReliefF algorithm is extension of Relief technique. Initially, the Relief algorithm starts by sampling the instances randomly, and then, it locates the same and opposite class by nearest neighbor approach. After that, the attribute values of the nearest neighbors in the feature set are calculated and compared against the samples which are required to update relevance scores of each feature value. ReliefF has capable to deal with the multiclass problem and also it can solve issues of noisy and inconsistent data. This algorithm is used in many situations such as low bias, interaction among features, and local dependencies. In general, this algorithm starts by identifying the K nearest samples (nearest hits) of the similar target class and the K closest samples of the opposite class (nearest misses) of each training samples xi. Then, by considering the jth feature, i.e., the sum of distances between samples and respective nearest misses are compared to sum of distances of nearest samples is expressed by

$$C(X_j) = \frac{\sum_{i=1}^{N} \sum_{k=1}^{K} |x_i^j - x_{M_k(i)}^j|}{\sum_{i=1}^{N} \sum_{k=1}^{K} |x_i^j - x_{H(i)}^j|} \tag{3.4}$$

where $M_{k(i)}$ is the k the nearest miss and $H_{k(i)}$ is nearest hit of the feature pattern x_i. Based on this, features which are having highest scores go to the same class and features with for away goes to different classes.

3.2.1.5   Minimum Redundancy Maximum Relevance

mRMR method is also like SU, Mutual Information, and Information Gain–based approach, but it selects the features based on highest relevance criterion [47]. It is one of the approximation technique to maximize the dependencies between the join distributions of the particular features and classification variable which are selected for the classification and also it minimizes the redundancies present in the feature space. While minimizing the redundancy between the features differs in discrete and continuous variables [11]. For discrete function, the minimum redundancy (min R_d) and maximum relevance is expressed below.

For discrete features, its minimum redundancy of the feature i, j is expressed by $min\ R_d$, where

$$R_d = \frac{1}{|S|^2} \sum_{t,j \in S} MI(i,j) \tag{3.5}$$

$MI(i,j)$ is the mutual information
For discrete features, its maximum relevance is expressed by $max\ R_d$, where

$$R_e = \frac{1}{|S|^2} \sum_{t,j \in S} MI(h,j) \tag{3.6}$$

$MI(i,j)$ is the mutual information where h is the target class.
For continuous features, its minimum redundancy of the feature i, j is expressed by $min\ R_c$, where

$$R_c = \frac{1}{|S|^2} \sum_{t,j \in S} |cor(i,j)| \tag{3.7}$$

$cor(i,j)$ is correlation meaure between the features i, j.
For continuous features, its maximum relevance of the feature i, j is expressed by $max\ R_{ce}$, where

$$R_{ce} = \frac{1}{|S|^2} \sum_{t} F(i,h) \tag{3.8}$$

where $F(i,h)$ is the measure of F-Statistic.
Filter methods basically uses the statistical measure for assigning the score value to each feature. Afterward, the features are considered and removed based on the score. Some of the other filter methods which are efficiently used are information gain, Chi square, and correlation coefficient scores.

3.2.2   Wrapper Methods

Wrapper methods for the FS process uses machine learning algorithms for selecting and evaluating the features in the dataset. The wrapper method conducts search throughout the entire feature space and then it selects the feature subset based on the evaluation results from the classifier. Thus, the wrapper approaches [27] evaluate the selected feature subset by using the learning techniques. Sequential search and the random search are the two search techniques which are used in wrapper methods [7]. Sequential search approach selects the features sequentially, whereas the random search technique applies the randomness procedures in search strategy to ignore the local optimum solutions. Some of the popular strategies that are using in high-dimensional data are forward selection and the backward elimination, genetic search, and simulated annealing. These strategies have been exploited to conduct effective search mechanism in the past few years. Also, the goodness of the feature selected is assessed by the above strategies. The forward selection algorithm starts with empty feature subset and evaluates with all the conditions with a feature, and then, it selects the best subset among all the features and the backward elimination begins with selecting all the features and selects the best feature by removing irrelevant features. Genetic Search strategy is modeled by the genetic algorithm techniques to search entire space in all the feature sets. Each state is defined by the genetic algorithm operation such as selection, crossover, mutation, and evaluation. The simulated annealing is one of the alternative stochastic search approaches which is used in the genetic algorithm [44].

As we know, the wrapper algorithm finds the optimal feature subset with involvement of both learning model and classification model. Initially, the wrapper algorithms will utilize the full searching techniques to find predominant feature subsets in feature space. The feature subsets are evaluated by the complete searching mechanism will be reliable but it not applicable for handling the high-dimensional datasets.

For dealing the high-dimensional dataset, the exhaustive search methods like branch and bound have been used which starts from the entire subset with consideration of entire attribute and ends up by removing the irrelevant features by using the depth first strategy [52]. Beam Search is the method falls in this category, which sorts the features in the queue based on best cases. In each of the execution steps, it measures all the possible cases features, and then it adds the best feature in the queue. One of the drawbacks of this exhaustive search approach is cost, because it is computationally expensive. For solving this issue, heuristic approach has been proposed. Some of the heuristic approaches in [43] gives the solutions to identify the predominant subset of the features are Sequential Backward Selection (SBS), Sequential Forward Selection (SFS), genetic algorithms, ant colony optimization, neural network, etc.

3.2.3 Embedded Methods

Embedded techniques use the classification model to select the feature subset in such a way that it links a particular classifier to accomplish the FS process. Also, the algorithm itself determines which attribute is most predominant and which attribute not predominant one [43]. Support vector machine [7], Naïve Bayes classifiers, and the decision tree algorithm are the well-known algorithms which are used commonly to perform the FS in the embedded algorithms. These methods use entire dataset for selecting the features and for classification phase; meanwhile, the dataset will not be divided into the training sets and testing sets. Also, the optimal subset of the features is will obtained earlier when compared to the wrapper approaches, since embedded methods will not perform of the evaluation measure in each of the selected subset [45]. The main advantages of these methods are, it interacts among the classification algorithm and it is less computational cost when comparing with the wrapper methods [22].

AdaBoost approach for FS [56] works on methods based on the regularization techniques like random forests and decision trees that are the optimal techniques which being currently using in microarray and text mining domain to deal with the high-dimensional datasets. The operator called LASSO (least absolute shrinkage and selection operator) will eliminate the features with the less informative and predictive power in the least squares multiple linear regression process. This approach is used in many fields such as bioinformatics, text mining, and image processing. The authors from [22] proposed the simplified LASSO strategy to select the subsets of informative features using the linear regression principles. In this approach, the predominant features will be selected based on the induction of the classifier.

The authors from [17] give Support Vector Machine which supports on the Recursive Feature Elimination technique for selecting the gene in the microarray data for the cancer classification. Their proposed algorithm is based on the embedded method that selects the feature by training the support vector machine classifier iteratively with the present set of featured and by eliminating the less important features [9]. Some the approaches which are being currently used for dealing the high-dimensional data are kernel density estimation [20], self-organizing map [25], graph theory, logistic regression, information theory measures, and regularization techniques [19].

Approaches based on the regularization methods are the important embedded strategies [28], which gives better performance, and also, this method provides additional constraints to the objective function.

3.2.4 Hybrid Methods

The hybrid strategy is combination (hybrid) of filter and the wrapper methods. This approach consists of two stages [34]; in the first stage, the feature ranking is carried to ranking the features; meanwhile, it removes the noisy, irrelevant features in the dataset. In the second stage, the weighted features are feed in to the wrapper methods to select the predominant features. Meanwhile, rank search algorithm is one of the hybrid approaches for selecting the features from the large-dimensional data. The other searching algorithms based on the ranking mechanism, which are applied on the high-dimensional data (microarray, text mining, image processing) based on the hybrid FS method, are Sequential Forward search and Sequential Backward Search [35]. During the wrapper phase, the features may be added or deleted; the final optimal subset is evaluated by using SFS or SBS. Other than these two approaches, Linear Forward Selection (LFS) is one of the approaches similar to the SFS but it selects the final subset in filter phase itself without considering the wrapper phase.

Incremental Wrapper Subset Selection (IWSS) algorithm [8] is one of the method which currently being used to dealing the high-dimensional dataset particularly in gene selection and medical image classification. After completion of the feature weighting in the filter phase, it orders the features into descending order, and then, in the wrapper phase, IWSS algorithm uses the incremental searching mechanism to find the optimal feature subset. Initially, this algorithm starts by selecting the empty subset and it adds the most weighted feature in the subset. At the second step, the subset which is selected in previous step and the existing training dataset are feed to a classifier and the results obtained from the classifier is saved. In each step of the iteration, the feature with highest weight is selected and added, and then, it is given to the classifier for determining the accuracy. If the performance or accuracies of the classifier is improved, the added feature subset is selected as best subset; otherwise, it will be removed and next feature is evaluated.

The GRASP algorithm is one of the iterative meta-heuristic technique which is mostly used in solving the optimization problems. Each and every step of the iteration, it undergoes two phases, namely, construction and improving phase. Hybrid FS technique proposed by [8] is based on the GRASP technique, the SU is measured in the filter phase, and in wrapper phase, the GRASP approach is executed. In construction phase, the weights and the features are selected and saved, and then, IWSS algorithm is applied for removing the redundant features in the subset. In improving phase, it uses some FS techniques such as Best Agglomerative Ranked Subset (BARS), SFS, IWSSr, and Hill-Climbing approaches used to select the final subset [43, 60].

3.3   Machine Learning and Deep Learning Models

In FS domain, there are three types of the machine learning models, supervised learning, and unsupervised and semi-supervised learning. Supervised method is a traditional technique which is widely used approach learns the model from the labeled data. In this technique, the input features and an output class are known and an algorithm finds the output for unknown data by using the mapping function. Supervised FS technique uses the training dataset for the FS and then evaluates the relevancies among the features and classes. In unsupervised FS [51], there is no labeled data, and it uses some properties and measures of the nature of the data like variance, and locality measures to predict the importance of the feature. Semi-supervised FS techniques use both labeled and the unlabeled dataset to evaluate the relevancies of the features [61]. It contains a minimal number labeled training samples and large number of unlabeled samples. Apart from the machine learning models, the following discussions provide the various deep learning models which are being used currently in various domains, which are shown in Figure 3.4.

3.3.1   Restricted Boltzmann Machine

Nowadays, deep learning techniques have been used in various application fields such as image processing [10], computer vision, online learning approaches, and bioinformatics.

Also, these deep learning methods have more capabilities in performing feature mapping in image segmentation and image classification technique; in this way, it outperforms in some way from the machine learning techniques. Deep neural networks work based on the stochastic gradient descent approach and back propagation algorithm [11]. Deep belief network is considered as one of the standard approaches in deep learning method which consist of restricted Boltzmann machine which highly capable for extracting the features from the given data. It consists of two layers to represents the neurons and performs the process, namely, visible layer and the hidden layer. In hidden layer, neurons represent feature vector of the given input data. In RBM, the classification accuracy mainly depends on the structure of the network formed in the deep model and also the number of hidden layers which is formed in the neural network structures plays the important role in the selecting features.

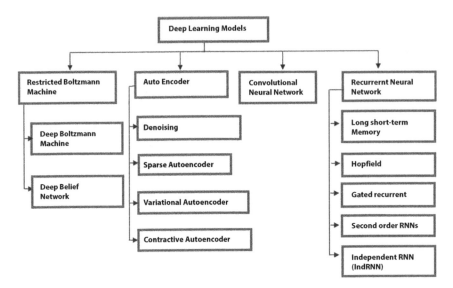

Figure 3.4 Taxonomy of deep learning models.

An extended version called high-order Boltzmann machine is proposed [11] based on the gating technique by using stochastic switch unit for selecting the feature from the raw input data. This model mainly depends on selecting and extracting the features with less computational cost [12].

3.3.2   Autoencoder

An autoencoder is one of the artificial neural network (ANN) which learns the data in efficient way by unsupervised manner. The autoencoder technique gives the most predominant features/attributes from the unlabeled data and also it projects the data by the low-dimensional space by help of encoding and decoding units [12]. The encoder unit transforms the data input into the hidden units which are reconstructed using by the decoding units. After the learning of reconstructing side, the autoencoder tries to generate the model from the reduced encoding which is close as possible to the original input. Recently, the autoencoder techniques perform better in many areas and it is become more popular and widely used method for learning the generative models of the data. Basically, an autoencoder is mainly a neural network which tries to reconstruct the given input data with the minimum number of features. Authors from [12] proposed the framework based on the encoders which performs the feature learning on data. The implemented framework provides the unified foundation for the construction and training of the autoencoders on top of the TensorFlow and Keras, and also, it allows for easy access and better functionalities with full customization.

A regularized autoencoder with the three variants were introduced in [4]. The first variant is the unsupervised mechanism based, whereas the second variant is mainly tailored for the clustering mechanism by incorporating the subspace clustering by the autoencoder generation. The third one is the supervised label consistent autoencoder will be used for classifying the single label as well as multi-label problems. Each of these proposed techniques has been compared with the standard existing methods against the benchmark datasets and the proposed method gives better performance than the existing techniques. The problems addressed by authors are image denoising, classification, and clustering.

Since the autoencoder is a form of the ANN which start performing the dimensionality reduction by nonlinear fashion and it learns the unlabeled data from the hidden representation. In linear transfer function, the autoencoder performs similar function like principal component analysis. Both linear and nonlinear methods use the weight vectors for the linear transformations. Authors from [66] proposed novel autoencoder node saliency methods for ranking the autoencoder hidden nodes by considering the performance of the learning task and also it examines the features which are constructed by the autoencoders. Normalized entropy difference (NED) based on the learning task is coupled to check the top nodes based on the ranking mechanisms. This method was applied on the real datasets and also it shows the better performance [59].

Akshay *et al.* [3] proposed a new strategy formulation of autoencoder called as R–Codean autoencoder for facial feature/attribute prediction. This approach incorporates with the Euclidean distance and cosine similarity for an initial step. The loss function incorporates both magnitude and the direction of the vectors of the image while learning the features. For the better performance, the extended the R–Codean formulation with the residual cross and the symmetric shortcut connections were used. The implemented techniques and the results achieved are compared with the state-of-the-art algorithms.

Yanan Liu *et al.* [69] presented two-stage framework for the multi-model video analysis by building the Stacked Contractive Autoencoder (SCAE) and Multimodal SCAE (MSCAE). This technique works based on the stacked contractive autoencoders which consist of two phases: the first phase incorporates with single modal pre-training, whereas the second phase is multi-modal fine tuning. The proposed algorithms give the better performance compared with the existing methods.

Denoising autoencoder considers a partly corrupted input against training set to recover the original input. This technique mainly focuses on good representation of inputs from the corrupted input. Sparse autoencoder is another approach to learn features from unlabeled data. This technique a type with sparsity enforcer working with the principle of directing the single layer network and then learns the code dictionary with minimal reconstruction error meanwhile minimizing the reconstruction of code-words [11]. The task of classification is to sparsify the algorithm, thereby reducing the input to a single class value by minimizing prediction error. A contractive autoencoder is also an unsupervised learning technique in the deep learning which helps a neural network to encode the unlabeled training data. A contractive autoencoder is less sensitive to small variations in its training dataset by adding an explicit regularizer in the objective function which involves the model to learn a function with the small variation of the input variables. Variational Autoencoders (VAEs) have one unique property by making strong assumptions among the distribution of the variables. It uses the variational approach with additional loss function and estimator for the training algorithm termed as Stochastic Gradient Variational Bayes (SGVB) estimator.

3.3.3 Convolutional Neural Networks

Convolutional Neural Networks (CNNs) are mostly used in processing of images and classification of videos; later, it is widely adopted in the domains text mining and the action recognition. The CNN starts with the convolution layer, which aims to extract the common patterns from the training data. The pre-processing needed in CNN before processing the entire datasets in the various layers. CNN consists of multiple kernel filters, input layer, and the output layer and also with multiple hidden layers (which is present in the network structure). The hidden layers of the CNNs [72] consist of Kernel matrix, convolutional layers, activation function and the pooling layers, normalization layers, and the fully connected layers. After obtaining the features from the input, the features are ready for the activation; later, the convolutional layer process is comes after with the non-linear activation function which allows to learn the boundaries of non-linear functions. Then, the outputs of the activation function come from the convolution layer that is given to pooling layers for aggregating and reducing the representation of features. Pooling layer takes average value (average pooling) or maximum values (maximum pooling) from its input. In general, maximum pooling is advisable since it will reduce the overfitting problems. CNN is used in many applications such as natural language processing, image processing, video analytics, and recommender systems.

3.3.4 Recurrent Neural Network

Recurrent Neural Network (RNN) is mainly framed to represent and model the sequence data and it has the wide range of application such as machine translation, text generation, video captioning, and speech recognition. RNN gives output from the preceding step as input to the current step since the memory cells are chained as the sequence. It direct learns from the input and output sequence. Traditional RNN tolerates from the issue of exploding or gradient vanishing. For solving this issue, Long Short-Term Memory is used; here, the memory cells/blocks are chained to perform the learning process of the long-term dependency in the data. Each memory cell is consisting of three types of non-linear gates to regulate the signals; they are input gate, forget gate, and the output gate. Gated Recurrent Unit is another alternative of Long Short-Term Memory network without the memory cells but still it works better for vanishing gradient problem and also it is faster to train. It is also having only two types of gates, namely, update gate and reset gate. Update gate finds the memory needed to keep, whereas the reset gate finds the quantum of information taken from the previous states. Hopfield, Second-order RNN, and Independent RNN [11] are the other best variant of RNN which are used widely in various application domains.

3.4 Real-World Applications and Scenario of Feature Selection

The applications of the FS include many fields; some of the real-world applications are intrusion detection [1], text categorization [64], DNA microarray analysis [26], music audio information retrieval [53], image processing [70], information processing and retrieval [42], customer relationship analytics and management [67], genomic data analysis [40], and remote sensing [24, 38]. Some of the illustrative scenarios and application with respect to high-dimensional data are discussed below.

3.4.1 Microarray

Microarray technology is one of the most developing technologies which are used to study of the gene expressions based on the measurement and evaluation of mRNA levels in one particular gene in the tissues [63]. The application includes understanding patterns of biological mechanisms, examining of drug response, and classifying the patients' base disease group, gene selection, disease identification (cancer identification from genes), etc. But as we discussed earlier, one of the issues presents over the microarray dataset [54] is "curse of dimensionality", i.e., each object of the microarray dataset consist of thousands of genes [26]. So, it is very hard to process and handle, in the sense the FS techniques plays much role in selecting the predominant genes from the high-dimensional datasets.

3.4.2 Intrusion Detection

With the tremendous growth of Internet and high-dimensional data, providing the security to the networks from the network intruders is a main research area focusing today. The intrusion detection system (IDS) [57] that identifies threats on computers by monitoring the network nodes system logs files, system calls, and events in networks. For detecting the abnormal activities from the network, we need to analyze the large datasets; it consists of anomalies, redundancy, noise, etc. Also, the dataset may be in the different forms, for doing analysis over the high-dimensional data; we need computational intelligence based algorithm for extracting/selecting the features from the data. For example, intrusion detection dataset (NSL-KDD) consists 125,973 instances/records in training set and the 22,544 instances in testing set [62] but it contains only 41 attributes (includes mixed types of attributes as binary, nominal, and numeric) with four categories. When the attributes are increased means again, it is problem to do the analytics over the datasets.

3.4.3 Text Categorization

Text categorization [62] is one of the major research areas in view of the big data, because more than 80% of data is stored in the form of text [33]; hence, it important to organize this massive information. Normally, the feature space of the text data will contain large number of features, performing the classification from those high-dimensional feature spaces is difficult process, and also the text data contains irrelevant and noisy features [32]. Hence, FS techniques help to identify the features from the text. Many FS techniques [15] are proposed in the field of text categorization in up to date manner to reduce the dimensionality of the text data and for selecting the informative features.

3.5 Conclusion

This chapter provides the detailed introduction on the FS process and methods with help of real-time examples and gives the detailed differentiation between the FS and feature extraction. Also, we have given the taxonomy of FS in diagrammatic way with explanation of filter, wrapper, embedded, and hybrid techniques with the state-of-the-art algorithms. We have discussed machine learning and the deep learning models with respect to FS. Further, this chapter provides the taxonomy of deep learning methods with the detailed explanation of the current methods for the various application domains. Finally, this chapter concludes with the real-world applications of the FS with respect to the high-dimensional data.

References

1. Eesa, A.S., Orma, Z., Brifcani, A.M.A., A novel feature-selection approach based on the cuttle-fish optimization algorithm for intrusion detection systems. *Expert Syst. Appl.*, 42, 2670–2679, 2015.

2. Hinrichs, A., Prochno, J., Ullrich, M., The curse of dimensionality for numerical integration on general domain. *J. Complexity*, 50, 25–42, 2019.

3. Sethi, A., Singh, M., Singh, R., Vatsa., M., Residual Codean autoencoder for facial attribute analysis. *Pattern Recogn. Lett.*, 119, 157–165, 2019.

4. Majumdar, A., Graph structured autoencoder. *Neural Networks*, 106, 271–280, 2018.

5. Bajwa, I., Naweed, M., Asif, M., Hyder, S., Feature based image classification by using principal component analysis. *ICGST Int. J. Graphics Vision Image Process.*, 9, 11–17, 2009.

6. Bardsley, W.E., Vetrova, V., Liu, S., Toward creating simpler hydrological models: A LASSO subset selection approach. *Environ. Modell. Software*, 72, 33–43, 2015.

7. Dadaneh, B.Z., Markid, H.Y., Zakerolhosseini, A., Unsupervised probabilistic feature selection using ant colony Optimization. *Expert Syst. Appl.*, 53, 27–42, 2016.

8. Bermejo, P., Gámez, J.A., Puerta, J.M.A., GRASP algorithm for fast hybrid (filter-wrapper) feature subset selection in high-dimensional datasets. *Pattern Recognit. Lett.*, 32, 701–711, 2016.

9. Bolon-Canedo, V., Sanchez-Marono, N., Alonso-Betanzos, A., Benitez, J.M., Herrera, F., A review of microarray datasets and applied feature selection methods. *Inf. Sci.*, 282, 111–135, 2014.

10. Cernuda, C., Lughofer, E., Hintenaus, P., Märzinger, W., Enhanced waveband selection inn NIR spectra using enhanced genetic operators. *J. Chemom.*, 28, 3, 123–136, 2014.

11. Taherkhani, A., Cosma, G., McGinnitya, T.M., Deep-FS: A feature selection algorithm for Deep Boltzmann Machines. *Neurocomputing*, 322, 22–37, 2018.

12. Pirmoradi, S., Teshnehlab, M., Zarghami, N., Sharif, A., The Self-Organizing Restricted Boltzmann Machine for Deep Representation with the Application on Classification Problems. *Experts Syst. Appl.*, 149, 1–11, 2020.

13. Fan, Du, L., Ren, D., Du, L., Ren, D., Efficient sequential feature selection based on adaptive eigenspace model. *Neurocomputing*, 161, 199–209, 2015.

14. Ghareb, A., Bakar, A., Hamdan, A.R., Saeed, A., Hybrid feature selection based on enhanced genetic algorithm for text categorization. *Expert Syst. Appl.*, 49, 31–47, 2016.

15. Chandrashekar, G. and Sahin, F., A survey on feature selection methods. *Comput. Electr. Eng.*, 40, 16–28, 2014.

16. Guyon, I., Weston, J., Barnhill, S., Vapnik, V., Gene selection for cancer classification using support vector machines. *Mach. Learn.*, 46, 1–3, 389–422, 2002.

17. Hall, M.A. and Holmes, G., Benchmarking attribute selection techniques fordiscrete class data mining. *IEEE Trans. Knowl. Data Eng.*, 15, 6, 1437–1447, 2003.

18. Savitha, R., Ambikapathi, A.M., Rajaraman, K., Online RBM: Growing Restricted Boltzmann Machine on the fly for unsupervised representation. *Appl. Soft Comput. J.*, 92, 1–10, 2020.

19. Zhang, Zhang, X., Gao, X.-Z., Song, S., Self-organizing multiobjective optimization based on decomposition with neighborhood ensemble. *Neurocomputing*, 173, 1868–1884, 2016.

20. Zhao, Z. and Liu, H., Searching for interacting features, in: *Proceedings of the 20th International Joint Conference on Artifical Intelligence*, Morgan Kaufmann Publishers Inc., pp. 1156–1161, 2007.

21. Hoque, N., Bhattacharyya, D.K., Kalita, J.K., MIFS-ND: a mutual information based feature selection method. *Expert Syst. Appl.*, 41, 14, 6371–6385, 2014.

22. Hsu, H.H., Hsieh, C.W., Lu, M.D., Hybrid feature selection by combining filters and wrappers. *Expert Syst. Appl.*, 38, 7, 8144–8150, 2011.

23. Huang, J., Horowitz, J.L., Ma, S., Asymptotic properties of bridge estimators in sparse high-dimensional regression models. *Ann. Stat.*, 36, 2, 587–613, 2008.

24. Yang, J.F., Zhang, Y., Siam, J., Alternating direction algorithms for L1-problems in compressive sensing. *SIAM J. Sci. Comput.*, 38, 250–278, 2011.

25. Janaki Meena, M., Chandran, K., Karthik, A., Vijay Samuel, A., An enhancedACO algorithm to select features for text categorization and its parallelization. *Expert Syst. Appl.*, 39, 5861–5871, 2012.

26. Krawczuk, J. and Łukaszuk, T., The feature selection bias problem in relation to high-dimensional gene data. *Artif. Intell. Med.*, 66, 63–71, 2016.

27. González, J., Ortega, J., Damas, M., Martín-Smith, P., Gan, J.Q., A new multi-objective wrapper method for feature selection – Accuracy and stability analysis for BCI. *Neurocomputing*, 333, 407–418, 2019.

28. Qin, J., Hu, Y., Xua, F., Yalamanchilia, H.K., Wang, J., Inferring gene regulatory networks by integrating ChIP-seq/chip and transcriptome data via LASSO-type regularization methods. *Methods*, 67, 294–303, 2014.

29. Li, J., Cheng, K., Wang, S., Morstatter, F., Trevino, R.P., Tang, J., Liu, H., Feature Selection: A Data Perspective. *ACM Comput. Surv. (CSUR)*, 50, 6, 1–45, 2017.

30. Zhang, J., Liu, Y., shi, G., Gene microarray analysis of expression profiles in Suberoyllanilide hyroxamic acid-treated Dendritic cells. *Biochem. Biophys. Res. Commun.*, 508, 2, 392–397, 2019.

31. Gajamannage, K., Paffenroth, R., Bollt, E.M., The nonlinear dimensionality reduction framework using smooth geodesics. *Pattern Recognit.*, 87, 226–236, 2019.

32. Khorsheed, M.S. and Al-Thubaity, A.O., Comparative evaluation of text classification techniques using a large diverse Arabic dataset. *Lang. Resour. Eval.*, 47, 2, 513–538, 2013.

33. Korde, V. and Mahender, C.N., Text classification and classifiers: a survey. *Int. J. Artif. Intell. Appl.*, 3, 2, 85–99, 2012.

34. Bharti, K.K. and Singh, P.K., Hybrid dimension reduction by integrating feature selection with feature extraction method for text clustering. *Expert Syst. Appl.*, 42, 3105–311, 2015.

35. Lazar, C., Taminau, J., Meganck, S., Steenhoff, D., Coletta, A., Molter, C., de Schaetzen, V., Duque, R., Bersini, H., Nowe, A., A survey on filter techniques for featureselection in gene expression microarray analysis. *IEEE/ACM Trans. Comput. Biol. Bioinform.*, 9, 4, 1106–1119, 2012.

36. Liu, H. and Yu, L., Toward integrating feature selection algorithms for classification and clustering. *IEEE Trans. Knowl. Data Eng.*, 17, 4, 491–592, 2005.

37. Maldonado, S., Weber, R., Basak, J., Simultaneous feature selection and classification using kernel-penalized support vector machines. *Inf. Sci.*, 181, 1, 115–128, 2011.

38. Imani, M. and Ghassemian, H., Binary coding based feature extraction in remote sensing high dimensional data. *Inf. Sci.*, 342, 191–208, 2016.

39. Mengle, S.S. and Goharian, N., Ambiguity measure feature-selectionalgorithm. *J. Am. Soc. Inf. Sci. Technol.*, 60, 1037–1050, 2009.

40. Garcia-Torres, M., Gomez-Vela, F., Melian-Batista, B., Marcos Moreno-Vega, J., High-dimensional feature selection via feature grouping: A Variable Neighborhood Search approach. *Inf. Sci.*, 326, 102–118, 2016.

41. Zhao, Z. and Liu, H., Searching for interacting features, in: *Proceedings of the 20th International Joint Conference on Artifical Intelligence*, Morgan Kaufmann Publishers Inc., pp. 1156–1161, 2007.

42. Bouadjenek, M.R., Hacid, H., Bouzeghoub, M., Social networks and information retrieval, how are they converging? A survey, a taxonomy and an analysis of social information retrieval approaches and platforms. *Inf. Syst.*, 56, 1–18, 2016.

43. Moradkhania, M., Amiria, A., Javaherian, M., Safari, H., A hybrid algorithm for feature subset selection in high-dimensional datasets using FICA and IWSSr algorithm. *Appl. Soft Comput.*, 35, 123–135, 2015.

44. Verbiest, N., Derrac, J., Cornelisa, C., Garcíac, S., Herrerac, F., Evolutionary wrapper approaches for training set selection as pre-processing mechanism for support vector machines: Experimental evaluation and support vector analysis. *Appl. Soft Comput.*, 38, 10–22, 2016.

45. Tran, N.M., Burdejova, P., Ospienko, M., Hardle, W.K., Principal Component analysis in an asymmetric norm. *J. Multivar. Anal.*, 171, 1–21, 2019.

46. Villacampa, O., *Feature Selection and Classification Methods for Decision Making: A Comparative Analysis*. Doctoral dissertation, Nova Southeastern University. Retrieved from NSUWorks, College of Engineering and Computing. Nova Southeastern University, Florida, http://nsu-works.nova.edu/gscis_etd/63, 20142014.

47. Peng, H., Long, F., Ding, C., Feature selection based on mutual information criteria of max-dependency, max-relevance, and min-redundancy. *IEEE Trans. Pattern Anal. Mach. Intell.*, 27, 8, 1226–1238, 2005.

48. Zhang, P., Guo, Q., Feng, W., Fast and object-adaptive spatial regularization for correlation filters based tracking. *Neurocomputing*, 337, 129–143, 2019.

49. Deng, P., Wang, H., Li, T., Horng, S.-J., Zhu, X., Linear Discriminant Analysis guided by unsupervised ensemble learning. *Inf. Sci.*, 480, 211–221, 2019.

50. Palma-Mendoza, R.-J., de-Marcos, L., Rodriguez, D., Alonso-Betanzos, A., Distributed correlation-based feature selection in spark. *Inf. Sci.*, 496, 287–299, 2018.

51. Sheikhpour, R., Sarram, M.A., Gharaghani, S., Chahooki, M.A.Z., A Survey on semi-supervised feature selection methods. *Pattern Recognit.*, 64, 141–158, 2017.

52. Ruiz, R., Riquelme, J.C., Aguilar-Ruiz, J.S., Incremental wrapper-based gene selection from microarray data for cancer classification. *Pattern Recognit.*, 39, 2383–2392, 2006.

53. Chithra, S., Sinith, M.S., Gayathri, A., Music Information Retrieval for Polyphonic Signals using Hidden Markov Model. *Proc. Comput. Sci.*, 46, 381–387, 2015.

54. Sayed, S., Nassef, M., Badr, A., Farag, I., A Nested Genetic Algorithm for feature selection in high-dimensional cancer Microarray datasets. *Expert Syst. Appl.*, 121, 233–243, 2019.

55. Sharmin, S., Shoyaib, M., Ali, A.A., Khan, M.A.H., Simultaneous Feature selection and discretization based on mutual information. *Pattern Recognit.*, 91, 162–174, 2019.

56. Saeys, Y., Inza, I., Larrañaga, P., A review of feature selection techniques in bioinformatics. *Bioinformatics*, 23, 19, 2507–2517, 2007.

57. Selvakumar, B. and Muneeswaran, K., Firefly algorithm based feature selection for network intrusion detection. *Comput. Secur.*, 81, 148–155, 2019.

58. Senliol, B., Fast Correlation Based Filter (FCBF) with a different search strategy. *Computer and Information Sciences, 2008.ISCIS'08.23rd International Symposium on IEEE*, 2008.

59. Zhang, S., Sun, Z., Long, J., Li, C., Bai, Y., Dynamic condition monitoring for 3D printers by using error fusion of multiple sparse autoencoders. *Comput. Ind.*, 105, 164–176, 2019.

60. Sivagaminathan, R.K. and Ramakrishnan, S., A hybrid approach for feature subsetselection using neural networks and ant colony optimization. *Expert Syst. Appl.*, 33, 49–60, 2007.

61. Song, Q., Ni, J., Wang, G., A fast clustering-based feature subset selection algorithm for high-dimensional data. *IEEE Trans. Knowl. Data Eng.*, 25, 1, 1–14, 2013.

62. Ji, S.-Y., Jeong, B.-K., Cho, S., Jeong, D.H., A multi-level intrusion detection method for abnormal network behaviors. *J. Netw. Comput. Appl.*, 62, 9–17, 2016.

63. Kasthurirathne, S.N., Dixon, B.E., Gichoya, J., Xu, H., Xia, Y., Mamlin, B., Grannis, S.J., Toward better public health reporting using existing off the shelf approaches: A comparison of alternative cancer detection approaches using plaintext medical data and non-dictionary based feature selection. *J. Biomed. Inf.*, 60, 145–152, 2016.

64. Zong, W., Wu, F., Chu, L.-K., Sculli, D., A discriminative and semantic feature selection method for text categorization. *Int. J. Prod. Econ.*, 165, 215–222, 2015.

65. Tang, X., dai, Y., Xiang, Y., Feature selection based on feature interaction with application to text categorization. *Expert Syst. Appl.*, 120, 207–216, 2019.

66. Fan, Y.J., Auto encoder node saliency: Selecting relevant latent representations. *Pattern Recognit.*, 88, 643–65, 2019.

67. Tu, Y. and Yang, Z., An enhanced Customer Relationship Management classification framework with Partial Focus Feature Reduction. *Expert Syst. Appl.*, 40, 2137–2146, 2013.

68. Yan, J., Liu, N., Yan, S., Yang, Q., Fan, W., Wei, Trace-oriented feature analysis for large-scale text data dimension reduction. *IEEE Trans. Knowl. Data Eng.*, 23, 1103–1117, 2011.

69. Liu, Y., Feng, X., Zhou, Z., Multimodal video classification with stacked contractive autoencoders. *Signal Process.*, 120, 761–766, 2016.

70. Yu, L. and Liu, H., Efficient feature selection via analysis of relevance and redundancy. *J. Mach. Learn. Res.*, 5, 1205–1224, 2004.

71. Wang, Y., Zhang, D., Liu, Y., Dai, B., Lee, L.H., Enhancing transportation systems via deep learning: A survey. *Transp. Res. Part C*, 99, 144–163, 2019.

72. Manbari, Z., AkhlaghianTab, F., Salavati, C., Hybrid fast unsupervised feature selection for high-dimensional data. *Expert Syst. Appl.*, 124, 97–118, 2019.

4

A Smart Web Application for Symptom-Based Disease Detection and Prediction Using State-of-the-Art ML and ANN Models

Parvej Reja Saleh* and Eeshankur Saikia

Department of Applied Sciences, Gauhati University, Guwahati, India

Abstract

Detection of diseases using symptoms might seem to be very normal in everyday life, but things get serious when symptoms increase in complexity and/or variety. With this increase in complexity or variety, we as human beings struggle to reliably diagnose any particular illness that may occur as a result of the observed symptoms. Various symptoms typically indicate different disease possibilities, that too with different levels of severity. An automatic generated database including diseases and its symptoms, based on textual discharge summaries of patients is used for the present work. The data includes 149 most common diseases along with symptoms on the basis of strength of association. Using this data, we have aimed at developing a Machine Learning model, based on Classification techniques to detect symptom-based diseases. Industry-standard classification methods, such as Multinomial Naïve Bayes, Logistic Regression, Decision Tree, K-nearest Neighbor, and Support Vector, and Random Forest Classifier are extensively used in this work. For accurate prediction, we have also implemented a Feedforward Neural Network using MLP for training purposes. In this work, we have proposed, for the first time, a smart and simple web-based application, integrated with our ML model to predict symptomatic diseases provided by the user, which, it is believed, would reduce the cost of the diagnosis process and save valuable time too.

Keywords: Machine learning, deep learning, multinomial Naïve Bayes classifier, support vector machine, random forest, logistic regression, multilayer perceptron

4.1 Introduction

Artificial Intelligence (AI) is the industrial science that uses computational abilities to exemplify smart actions with the limited entanglement of individuals, and Machine Learning (ML) is known to be a branch of AI routines. We usually recognize this intelligence as having developed with robotics inventions [1]. Computers are expected to exhibit intelligent behaviors comparable to human beings in the near future through rapidly increasing electronic and computational speeds and smarter programming languages/platforms, leading

---

*Corresponding author: prvzslh@gauhati.ac.in

Om Prakash Jena, Alok Ranjan Tripathy, Ahmed A. Elngar and Zdzislaw Polkowski (eds.) *Computational Intelligence and Healthcare Informatics*, (65–80) © 2021 Scrivener Publishing LLC

to significant developments in the form of application of AI in many different current topics [2]. In 1956, John McCarthy introduced AI for the first time and consists of a computer which can carry out human intelligence-specific tasks. While this is broad, it encompasses such issues as preparation, language comprehension, artifacts, and sound recognition, as well as training and interpreting. We can have AI in two classes, namely, General AI and Narrow AI [3]. General AI will have all human intelligence properties, and Narrow AI has some aspects of human intelligence that can do very well, but it is absent in other fields. An example of narrow AI is a system that is great in recognizing pictures but nothing else. AI can be described as the human intelligence that machines carry out. In computer science, the capacity of the machine to simulate smart behavior, using ML alone, is defined as AI [4]. Health AI technologies are growing rapidly. In 2016, AI ventures associated with medicine were more speculative than other ventures about the global economy [5]. The use of automated diagnosis systems and devising a treatment plan for patients in medicine applies to AI. Improved use of prescription using AI would make it possible to automate a substantial amount of the job, opening the time for medical professionals to carry out activities that cannot be optimized and use it in more important tasks.

ML is a simple way of achieving AI. "The ability to learn without being explicitly programmed" was quoted by Arthur Samuel as a definition of AI. So, to perform a specific task, ML is a method of building an algorithm instead of hard coding routines and libraries. The training means that the algorithm is fed an enormous amount of data, and the algorithm will adapt itself and move to the next step. For instance, it has been used extensively to enhance Computer Vision significantly. We collect millions of images and annotate them manually. The algorithm then seeks to create a model which accurately labels an image that contains both a cat and a human. After the level of accuracy was sufficiently high, the machine has now learned to recognize a cat and a human. ML creates a computer system that can understand and adjust its actions according to the circumstances [6]. The methodology for ML relies on the training from input data as well as the assessment of model outcomes and the optimization of its performance [7]. It is also used to render data predictions in data analytics. Figure 4.1 shows an overview of building ML models.

ML consists of three fundamental approaches [8], namely, Supervised learning, Unsupervised learning, and Reinforcement learning. In case of Supervised learning, it involves a target to be predicted, which is a dependent variable, from a given set of independent variables. We create a function that matches inputs to appropriate outputs with these variable sets. The training cycle goes on until the model reaches the desired degree of precision with respect to the training data. Few illustrations of Supervised Learning are Linear Regression, Decision Tree, Random Forest, Logistic Regression, K-Nearest Neighbor (KNN), etc. In an Unsupervised learning algorithm, we do not have any target to predict. It is used to divide people into separate categories, which is commonly used

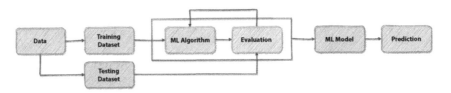

Figure 4.1 Overview of the processes involved in building ML models.

to divide consumers into similar groups. Few illustrations of Unsupervised Learning are Apriori algorithm, K-means, etc. Whereas the machine is schooled to execute strategic decisions in the Reinforcement algorithm. Here, the machine trains itself using trial and error methods continuously. It captures the best possible knowledge to make effective business decisions by learning from the past experiences. Few examples are Markov Decision Process, Q-learning, etc.

Deep learning is an integral part of ML, triggered by the arrangement and activity of the brain, which is the relation of many neurons. Figure 4.2 shows an overview of a Deep Learning workflow process in comparison with ML process. Artificial Neural Networks (ANNs) are methods that emulate the organic architecture of the brain. Neurons have distinct layers and connections to other neurons (or nodes) in ANNs. Each and every layer selects a particular feature to learn. This structuring gives deep learning its identity, where depth is constructed by using numerous layers. These interconnected nodes relay knowledge to each other imitating the human brain. The nodes communicate and exchange knowledge with each other. By taking an input, each node performs operations with each other before transferring it ahead. This operation is done by a function called as Activation Function. It transforms an input into an output in such a way that other nodes can use that output as an input. The weights between the nodes are revised to reflect the network performance. The weights are not adjusted if the accuracy is high enough. However, the weights are adjusted by particular estimation if the accuracy is low.

In Figure 4.3, the input layer is the initial layer of neurons and the output layer is the rightmost layer. The other layers within them are referred to as hidden layers. So, we can say that after taking input from the nodes, an Artificial Neuron applies an activation function

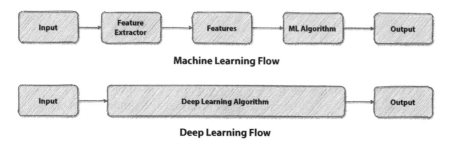

Figure 4.2 Machine Learning vs. Deep Learning workflow process.

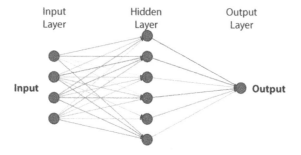

Figure 4.3 Overview of an Artificial Neural Network.

to the weighted sum of input, and then, the output is passed to the next neuron [9]. So as to avoid passing a null output, a threshold or a bias is added to the weighted sum. Through feedforward or feedback methods, numerous neural networks are connected to communicate information to each other. The simplest kind of ANN is Feedforward, where the connections do not have loops as they do not form a cycle. Through a series of weights, input is directly transmitted to the output in a single direction. Feedforward networks are widely used in pattern recognition today. Feedback, also known as recurrent, has connections that can pass in both directions. The output from the network is fed back into the network to enhance accuracy. Since feedback networks are dynamic, therefore they can become very much complex, though much more powerful than feedforward.

A human doctor today cannot come up with all required knowledge to make a precise diagnosis. No physician will master every aspect of healthcare and remember every single detail of comparable cases. Nevertheless, an AI-based program can be fed with the relevant information into the machine, and the computer can search through the vast database, rather than depending on the limited human knowledge, to reach a decision. Hence, disease detection was considered as the primary level in ML research in healthcare. The hunt for accurate diagnosis started, especially in areas of great need, such as oncology. The early recognition and effective diagnosis were achieved by ML applications in the healthcare and biomedical sector which has strengthened the patient care in recent years. Research shows that people use the internet to help them cope up with potential health issues. The disadvantage of this method is that the internet sites have bundled information, which is impossible to deduce in clustered format. Currently, many disease prediction systems are available which can predict disease of heart, skin, and also neurological disorders. However, a consistent symptomatic prediction is relatively rare. At a preliminary phase, diagnosis of disease based on symptoms is very useful for doctors. Probable diseases are indicated to the user with higher accuracy scores.

4.2 Literature Review

In recent times, many valuable contributions are made to predict diseases based on available symptoms. Zhang *et al.* (Y. Zhang, 2007) [10] trained and obtained successful results in a sentence-level semantic model to predict infectious diseases. Using the clinical data from New York's Presbyterian Hospital, Wang *et al.* (Wang X, 2008) [11] proposed an automated disease prediction system based on clinical terms. On the basis of the patient's specific text, and by analyzing symptoms, Sen *et al.* (Kumar Sen, 2013) [12] developed a program to predict coronary heart diseases. With the aid of patient's EHR data, Qian *et al.* (B. Qian, 2015) [13] developed an Alzheimer's risk prediction program. With structured and unstructured hospital data, Chen *et al.* (M. Chen, 2017) proposed [14] and introduced the new multimodal disease predictive algorithm based on Convolutional Neural Network (CNN). Three illnesses, such as diabetic disease, cerebral infarction, and heart disease, were considered to predict disease, where accuracy was around 94.8%. Kunjir *et al.* (Ajinkya Kunjir, 2017) [15] developed a disease prediction system based on the historical data of patients. Sharmila *et al.* (S. Leoni Sharmila, 2017) [16] achieved 91% accuracy in liver disease dataset by using Fuzzy Neural Network. Allen *et al.* (Allen Daniel Sunny1, 2018) [17] gave a conclusive study that Naïve Bayes and Apriori are very effective in predicting accurate disease using symptoms. However, they could not experiment it on a larger set of data. Using a large set of structured and unstructured data of hospital, Shirsath *et al.* (Shraddha Subhash Shirsath, 2018) [18] developed a disease prediction system using a CNN-MDRP algorithm.

4.3   Dataset, EDA, and Data Processing

One hundred forty-nine most frequent diseases with 405 various symptoms are collected from the discharge summaries of patients at New York Presbyterian Hospital admitted during 2004. The symptoms are categorized by the intensity of its correlation. The data includes the disease, number of discharge summaries, and the associated symptoms. The dataset is publicly available on the webpage of Columbia University and it can be scraped from the link, http://people.dbmi.columbia.edu/~friedma/Projects/DiseaseSymptomKB/index.html. Figure 4.4 shows the sample rows of the raw dataset.

An extensive data exploration is performed to understand the data, and then, it is processed and cleaned by removing the missing values. Forward fill methods have been used to replace the missing values. The data processing includes the removal of code words such as "UMLS" and "C0020538". Figure 4.5 shows the custom python function built for processing the dataset and its various attributes.

```
df.head()
```

	Disease	Count of Disease Occurence	Symptom
0	UMLS:C0020538_hypertensive disease	3363.0	UMLS:C0008031_pain chest
1	NaN	NaN	UMLS:C0392680_shortness of breath
2	NaN	NaN	UMLS:C0012833_dizziness
3	NaN	NaN	UMLS:C0004093_asthenia
4	NaN	NaN	UMLS:C0085639_fall

Figure 4.4 The description of the raw dataset showing the first five rows.

```
# Process Disease and Symptom Names
def process_data(data):
    data_list = []
    data_name = data.replace('^','_').split('_')
    n = 1
    for names in data_name:
        if (n % 2 == 0):
            data_list.append(names)
        n += 1
    return data_list

disease_list = []
disease_symptom_dict = defaultdict(list)
disease_symptom_count = {}
count = 0

for idx, row in data.iterrows():

    # Get the Disease Names
    if (row['Disease'] !="\xc2\xa0") and (row['Disease'] != ""):
        disease = row['Disease']
        disease_list = process_data(data=disease)
        count = row['Count of Disease Occurrence']

    # Get the Symptoms Corresponding to Diseases
    if (row['Symptom'] !="\xc2\xa0") and (row['Symptom'] != ""):
        symptom = row['Symptom']
        symptom_list = process_data(data=symptom)
        for d in disease_list:
            for s in symptom_list:
                disease_symptom_dict[d].append(s)
                disease_symptom_count[d] = count
```

Figure 4.5 The code snippet showing the data processing of the attributes such as diseases and symptoms.

Finally, a dictionary is created including disease and its respective symptoms based on the dataset. Sample rows of the cleaned dataset is shown in Figure 4.6.

Box plot method is applied to graphically depict the total number of occurrences of diseases through their quartiles. Figure 4.7 shows that there are few diseases which have high occurrences, i.e., 500. However, most of the disease occurrences count around ~200–300.

The highest occurrences of diseases and symptoms are also explored. Disease like "upper respiratory infection" and "bipolar disorder" has the highest counts. Whereas, "shortness of breath", "pain", and "fever" are the most common symptoms for the disease reported. Figures 4.8 and 4.9 show the counts of the highest ten diseases and symptoms, respectively.

Since the datasets also include the type of object data that must be converted into numeric, categorical variables are encoded by assigning a numerical value to each category.

In our dataset, the symptoms are transformed by using Label Encoder and One Hot Encoder as shown in Figure 4.10. The duplicate entries were then removed from the dataset and the processed data is exported in a new dataframe.

	disease	symptom	occurence_count
0	hypertensive disease	shortness of breath	3363.0
1	hypertensive disease	dizziness	3363.0
2	hypertensive disease	asthenia	3363.0
3	hypertensive disease	fall	3363.0
4	hypertensive disease	syncope	3363.0

Figure 4.6 The description of the cleaned and processed dataset showing the first five rows.

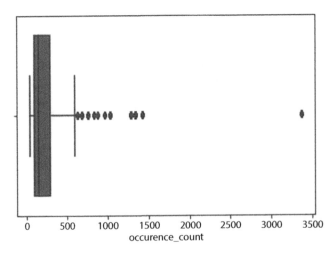

Figure 4.7 Boxplot showing number of disease occurrences.

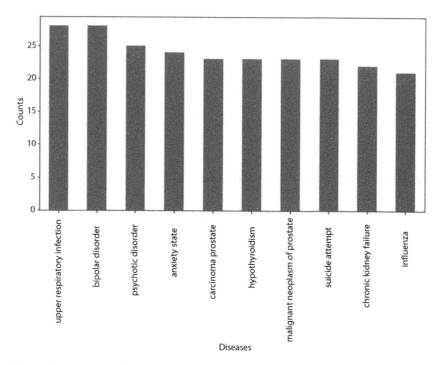

Figure 4.8 Ten highest reported diseases.

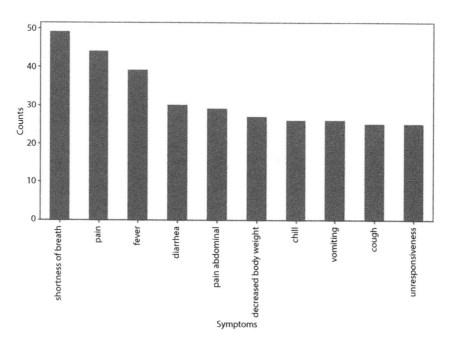

Figure 4.9 Ten highest reported symptoms.

```
# Label & OneHot Encoding
from sklearn.preprocessing import LabelEncoder
from sklearn.preprocessing import OneHotEncoder
label_encoder = LabelEncoder()
integer_encoded = label_encoder.fit_transform(df['symptom'].astype(str))

onehot_encoder = OneHotEncoder(sparse=False)
integer_encoded = integer_encoded.reshape(len(integer_encoded), 1)
onehot_encoded = onehot_encoder.fit_transform(integer_encoded)
print(onehot_encoded)
```

Figure 4.10 The code snippet of the label encoding and one hot encoding process used in the model building process.

4.4 Machine Learning Algorithms

Multiple ML and an ANN are trained on the dataset so as to classify the diseases with symptoms and hence generate accurate predictions. With a train-test split ratio of 80:20, Support Vector Machine (SVM), k-Nearest Neighbor, Random Forest, Multinomial Naïve Bayes, Decision Tree, Multilayer Perceptron (MLP), and Logistic Regression are used for training and testing. Scikit-learn, a ML package in Python, is extensively used to implement the algorithms. Below are the algorithms used in the present work, as discussed in detail.

4.4.1 Multinomial Naïve Bayes Classifier

Naïve Bayes classifiers have high interpretations between the features, based on Bayes' theorem. The multinomial classification of Naïve Bayes is ideal for classification with distinct characteristics. A multinomial $(p_1,...,p_n)$, where p_i is the probability that event i occurs, creates some events with feature vectors that describe the frequencies. With x_i being the amount of occurences i has occurred in a specific situation, a feature vector $\mathbf{x} = (x_1,...,x_n)$ can be described as a histogram. Mathematically, the likelihood of having a histogram $\mathbf{x}$ is given by $p(x \vee C_k) = \dfrac{\left(\sum_i x_i\right)!}{\prod_i x_i!} \prod_i p_{ki}^{xi}$. If represented with log, the multinomial Naïve Bayes classifier behave as a linear classifier as shown below:

$$logp(C_k \vee x) \infty log$$

$$= logp(C_k) + \sum_{i=1}^{n} x_i logp_{ki}$$

$$= b + w_k^T x$$

where $b = logp(C_k)$ and $w_{ki} = logp_{ki}$

Here, we have utilized the *MulitnomialNB* class in *naive_bayes* module of scikit-learn. By default, the additive smoothing parameter was set to 1.

4.4.2 Support Vector Machine Classifier

Even though SVMs were initially developed for binary classification, there are two methods available for multiclass SVM. Firstly is by building and merging numerous binary classifiers and another way is to take all data into account explicitly in one optimization formulation.

One-Versus-Rest (OVR) is probably one of the first methods to be implemented for multi-class SVM classification. With k as the number of classes, OVR builds k SVM models. The mth SVM gets trained with both examples of positive and negative labeling in the class. With l training data $(x_1, y_1),...,(x_l, y_l)$, where $x_i \in R^n$, $i = 1,...,l$ and $y_i \in \{1,...,k\}$ is the class of x_i, the mth SVM provides a solution to the below problem:

$$min(w^m, b^m, \xi^m) \frac{1}{2}(w^m)^T w^m + C \sum_{i=1}^{l} \xi_i^m$$

$$(w^m)^T \phi(x_i) + b^m \geq 1 - \xi_i^m, \text{if } y_i = m,$$

$$(w^m)^T \phi(x_i) + b^m \leq -1 + \xi_i^m, \text{if } y_i \neq m,$$

$$\xi_i^m \geq 0, i = 1,...,l,$$

where using the function ϕ, the training data x_i are mapped to a greater magnitude and C is the liability factor.

One-Versus-One (OVO) method develops $k(k-1)/2$ classifiers where data from two groups are trained on each. From the ith and the jth classes of the training data, the solution of the below binary classification problem is as follows:

$$min(w^{ij}, b^{ij}, \xi^{ij}) \frac{1}{2}(w^{ij})^T w^{ij} + C \sum_{t} \xi_t^{ij}$$

$$(w^{ij})^T \phi(x_t) + b^{ij} \geq 1 - \xi_t^{ij}, \text{if } y_t = i,$$

$$(w^{ij})^T \phi(x_t) + b^{ij} \leq -1 + \xi_t^{ij}, \text{if } y_t = j,$$

$$\xi_i^m \geq 0, i = 1,...,l,$$

C-Support Vector Classification (*SVC*) class in the SVM function is used with default positive regularization parameter as 1. The radial basis function kernel is considered in the algorithm for building the model.

4.4.3   Random Forest Classifier

Another Supervised learning method which can be utilized for both regression and classification problems is Random Forest, though extensively used for classification issues mostly. It establishes decision trees on datasets and then predicts each sample and selects the appropriate approach by choosing. Averaging reduces the over-fitting which eventually enhances the predictive accuracy, hence better than a single decision tree. Mathematically, a random forest is a reliable indicator dwelling a collection of distributed regression trees $\{r_n(x, \Theta_m, D_n),$

$m \geq 1$}, where Θ_1, Θ_2,... are the final values the distributed variable Θ. These random trees are integrated to estimate the overall regression

$$r_n(X, D_n) = E_\Theta[r|n(X, \Theta_m, D_n)]$$

where E_Θ designates expectation corresponding to the random parameter, provisionally on X and the dataset D_n.

The number of trees in the random forest function is taken as 100. The Gini impurity (*gini*) is considered as the function to measure the quality of split.

4.4.4   K-Nearest Neighbor Classifier

The KNN algorithm is a simple robust and versatile ML algorithm that classifies an input by using its k nearest neighbors. Even though it is simple, it can still perform better than various other classifiers. Assuming for a x feature and y target, the ultimate goal is to train a function $h: X \rightarrow Y$ so that for a new entry in x, $h(x)$ can predict the accurate output y. Basically, for a similarity metric d and an unseen observation, the KNN classifier computes d between x and each observation by performing throughout the dataset. It then computes the conditional probability for each class. Mathematically, this can be expressed as follows:

$$P(y = j \vee X = x) = \frac{1}{K} \sum_{i \in A} I(y^{(i)} = j)$$

where $I(x)$ is the indicator function which equals to 1 when x is true and 0 otherwise.

The KNN classifier is implemented using five neighbors where *uniform* weight is considered so that all points in the neighborhood are equally weighed during prediction.

4.4.5   Decision Tree Classifier

Decision Tree is another supervised learning method which has a flowchart-like structure. Here, each node describes a feature, each branch describes a decision, and output is described by each leaf. The concept is always to produce a similar tree for the entire dataset and produce a single output at every leaf. Out of many, we have discussed two algorithms and its respective metrics which are used to build a decision tree.

1. Classification and Regression Trees (CART)
2. Iterative Dichotomizer (ID3)

CART uses Gini Impurity whereas ID3 adopts Entropy function and Information gain as measurable identities. These three metrics are discussed in detail below.

- Gini Impurity is the metric of impurity in a node. It is an assessment of detecting incorrect labeling of a randomly labeled element chosen randomly from any set. It can be formulated with the below equation:

$$I_G(n) = 1 - \sum_{i=1}^{J} (p_i)^2$$

where p and J are the distribution of the class and the number of classes present in the node, respectively.

- Entropy is also another common approach to split the nodes in a decision tree. It helps in measuring the randomness in a system. Entropy can be described mathematically as the below equation:

$$Entropy = \sum_{i=1}^{c} -p_i * log_2(p_i)$$

where p and C are the distribution of the class and the number of classes present in the node, respectively.

- Information gain $IG(A)$ computes the reduction in uncertainty in the set S after splitting it on feature A. Mathematically, it can be written as follows:

$$IG(A,S) = H(S) - \sum_{t \in T} p(t)H(t)$$

where $H(S)$ and $H(t)$ are the entropy of the set S and the subset t, respectively. T are the subsets formed after splitting the set A. $p(t)$ defines the ratio of the total elements in t to the total elements in the set S.

The decision tree function is used with *gini* criterion for measuring the quality of a split with the *best* splitter strategy to choose the best split at each node.

4.4.6   Logistic Regression Classifier

If a target variable has more than two classes, then multinomial form of logistic regression is used for prediction. Instead of sigmoid function in classical logistic regression, the multinomial logistic regression uses softmax function. All values in a softmax function range between 0 and 1. The below equation shows the mathematical formulation of softmax function.

$$softmax = \frac{e^{x_i}}{\sum_{j=1}^{n} e^{x_j}}$$

Cross entropy is a calculation of how two probability distributions differ from each other. Mathematically, it can be expressed as below:

$$H(p,q) = -\sum_{x} p(x)logq(x)$$

where p and q are discrete. Cross function ranges between 0 and infinity and values to 0 if $p = q$. When $p \ll q$ or $q \ll p$, the function values to be infinity. For a better understanding, let us take an example of a vector $z = Wx + b$, where W is a $C \times M$ matrix and b are the biases of length C. Using one-hot vector, y is defined as 1 for the correct class C and hence 0 everywhere else. For a training set with y as a predicted class and c as true class, the loss can be represented as below:

$$\hat{y} = softmax(z)$$

$$loss = H(y, \hat{y})$$

$$-\sum_i y_i log \hat{y}_i$$

$$-log \hat{y}_c$$

Minimizing the loss over our training examples is therefore equal to increasing the *log* of probability. By using gradient descent on the loss function in relation to these parameters, we can recognize the model parameters W and b. Similar to what we discussed in SVM, there are also two approaches for multi-class classification using logistic regression; one-vs-all and one-vs-one.

Logistic regression classifier is implemented with L2 regularization which specifies the norm used in the penalization. Here, we have considered the inverse of regularization strength as 1 as smaller values specify stronger regularization.

4.4.7 Multilayer Perceptron Classifier

Introduced by Rosenblatt in 1958, a MLP is a structure of basic neurons. A standard result is computed by the perceptron from multiple inputs by creating a linear function with weights, which is then passing the result via an activation function.

Mathematically, this can be represented as

$$y = \varphi\left(\sum_{i=1}^{n} w_i x_i + b\right) = \varphi(w^T x + b)$$

where x is the input, b is the bias, w denotes the weights, and φ is the activation function.

A traditional MLP includes an input and output layer with a group of source nodes and a layer of nodes, respectively. In between input and output, there are single or multiple hidden layers. Layer by layer, the input signal transmits through the neural network. Mathematically, this feedforward network with nonlinear activation, linear output layer, and a single hidden layer can be described as

$$x = f(s) = B\varphi(As + a) + b$$

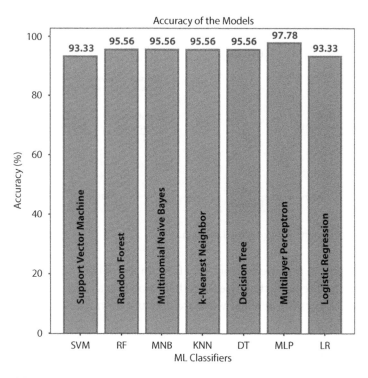

Figure 4.11 List of the implemented algorithms while building the model. MLP provides highest accuracy among the seven classifiers.

where *s* and *x* are vectors of inputs and outputs, respectively. In the first layer, *a* and *A* are the bias vector and matrix of weights, respectively. Similarly, *b* and *B* are the bias vector and the weight matrix of the second layer. Element-wise nonlinearity is denoted by the function φ.

Out of all the algorithms, the highest accuracy provided by MLP was 97.78%. The MLP is implemented with a hidden layer size of 100 which represents the number of neurons in the hidden layer. It was built with a rectified linear unit function (relu) for the hidden layer. The relu activation function can be defined as $f(x) = max(0, x)$. We have used a stochastic gradient optimizer known as adam which performs well on larger datasets. Figure 4.11 lists the accuracy of the seven algorithms used while training the dataset, and the table below compiles their attributes.

4.5 Work Architecture

The training dataset is exposed to all the algorithms discussed above. The algorithm with the highest accuracy is saved in the local to be used for building the end-to-end prediction application. In our case, we have used Pickle to save the model. Since we have a model which can predict a disease, based on given symptoms, we have used Flask to create a Restful API using python.

Then, a web application is designed where the user may input the symptoms, and these information are then fed to the model so that the model can detect and predict the accurate

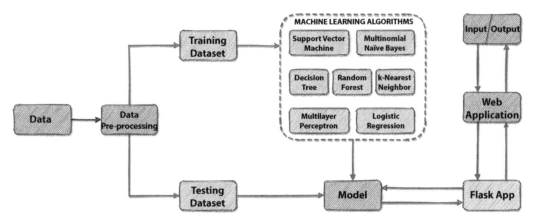

Figure 4.12 Work architecture of the proposed solution.

disease. Accordingly, we prepared a front-end form in React JS to collect the user name and the input symptoms. The predicted disease is then shown as a modal view in the web application. Figure 4.12 shows the detailed work architecture of the built application.

4.6   Conclusion

A detailed analysis of the available ML models is conducted vis-a-vis the data considered, and the best one is applied for training and testing the neural networks developed for the present work to detect and predict a disease based on the symptoms described.

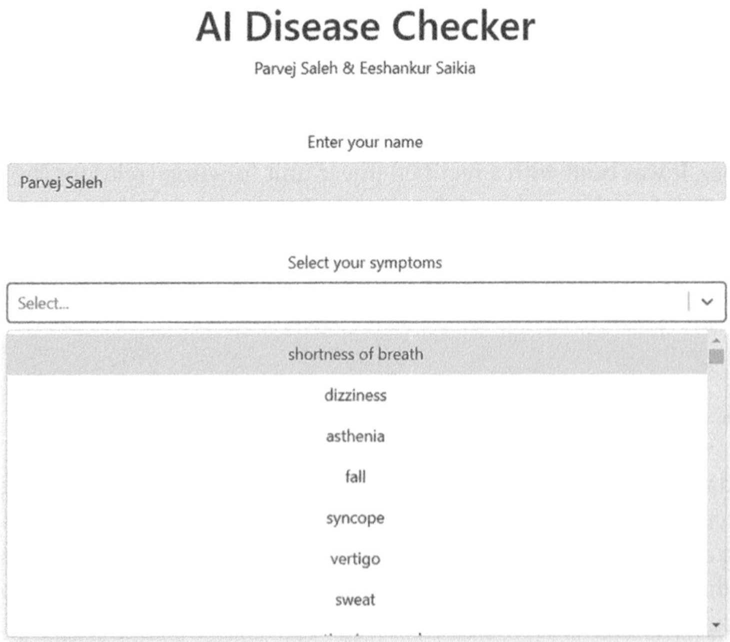

AI Disease Checker

Parvej Saleh & Eeshankur Saikia

Enter your name

Parvej Saleh

Select your symptoms

Select...

shortness of breath

dizziness

asthenia

fall

syncope

vertigo

sweat

Figure 4.13 The web application to predict disease based on symptoms.

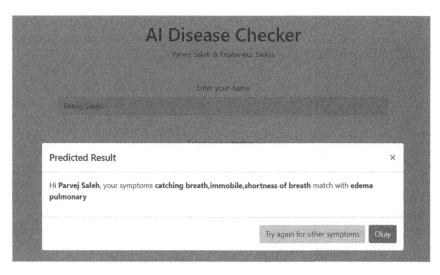

Figure 4.14 The user can input multiple symptoms at a time and get accurate prediction.

As it may be found from the screenshots in Figures 4.13 and 4.14, used here just as a testimony, the AI platform developed in the form of a web application can do its job of disease detection, or prediction, with maximum and minimum statistical accuracies of 97.78 and 93.33, respectively. The user can provide multiple symptoms at a time to predict the disease. However, this initial work needs further validation using different sets of symptoms and diseases from various age, race, and gender groups to take it to the next level.

References

1. Bini, S.A., Artificial Intelligence, Machine Learning, Deep Learning, and Cognitive Computing: What Do These Terms Mean and How Will They Impact Healthcare? *J. Arthroplasty*, 33, 8, 2358–2361, 2018, https://doi.org/10.1016/j.arth.2018.02.067.
2. Buch, V.H., Ahmed, I., Maruthappu, M., Artificial intelligence in medicine: current trends and future possibilities. *Br. J. Gen. Pract.: the journal of the Royal College of General Practitioners*, 68, 668, 143–144, 2018, https://doi.org/10.3399/bjgp18X695213.
3. McClelland, C., *The Difference Between Artificial Intelligence, Machine Learning, and Deep Learning*, 2017, December 4, Retrieved from https://medium.com/iotforall/the-difference-between-artificial-intelligence-machine-learning-and-deep-learning-3aa67bff5991.
4. Chen, M., Hao, Y., Hwang, K., Wang, L., Wang, L.L., Disease Prediction by Machine Learning Over Big Data From Healthcare Communities. *IEEE Access*, 5, 8869–8879, 2017.
5. Darcy, A.M., Louie, A.K., Roberts, L.W., Machine Learning and the Profession of Medicine. *JAMA*, 315, 6, 551–552, 2016, https://doi.org/10.1001/jama.2015.18421.
6. D.P. and Shukla, A. K. S. S. B. P., A Data Mining Technique for Prediction of Coronary Heart Disease Using Neuro-Fuzzy Integrated Approach Two Level. *Int. J. Eng. Comput. Sci.*, 2, 09, 2663–2671, 2013. Retrieved from http://www.ijecs.in/index.php/ijecs/article/view/1855.
7. Hamet, P. and Tremblay, J., Artificial intelligence in medicine. *Metabolism: clinical and experimental*, 69S, S36–S40, 2017, https://doi.org/10.1016/j.metabol.2017.01.011.

8. Danish, I., Introduction to Deep Learning, Deep Learning Series, Chapter 1, Towards AI. Retrieved from https://medium.com/towards-artificial-intelligence/deep-learning-series-chapter-1-introduction-to-deep-learning-d790feb974e2, 2019, June 1.

9. Jiang, M., Chen, Y., Liu, M., Rosenbloom, S.T., Mani, S., Denny, J.C., Xu, H., A study of machine-learning-based approaches to extract clinical entities and their assertions from discharge summaries. *J. Am. Med. Inf. Assoc.: JAMIA*, 18, 5, 601–606, 2011, https://doi.org/10.1136/amiajnl-2011-000163.

10. Johnson, K.W., Torres Soto, J., Glicksberg, B.S., Shameer, K., Miotto, R., Ali, M., Ashley, E., Dudley, J.T., Artificial Intelligence in Cardiology. *J. Am. Coll. Cardiol.*, 71, 23, 2668–2679, 2018, https://doi.org/10.1016/j.jacc.2018.03.521.

11. Kunjir, A., Sawant, H., Shaikh, N.F., Data mining and visualization for prediction of multiple diseases in healthcare. *2017 International Conference on Big Data Analytics and Computational Intelligence (ICBDAC)*, pp. 329–334, 2017.

12. Lison, P., *An introduction to machine learning*, HiOA, University of Oslo, 2015, Retrieved from https://www.nr.no/~plison/pdfs/talks/machinelearning.pdf.

13. Qian, B., Wang, X., Cao, N., Li, H., Jiang, Y., A relative similarity based method for interactive patient risk prediction. *Data Min. Knowl. Discovery*, 29, 1070–1093, 2014.

14. Sharmila, L., Dharuman, C., Venkatesan, P., Disease Classification Using Machine Learning Algorithms-A Comparative Study. *Int. J. Pure Appl. Math.*, 114, 1–10, 2017.

15. Shirsath, S.S. and Patil, S., Disease Prediction Using Machine Learning Over Big Data. *Int. J. Innov. Res. Sci.*, 7, 6, 6752–6757, 2018, http://doi.org/10.15680/IJIRSET.2018.0706059.

16. Sunny, A.D., Kulshreshtha, S., Singh, S., Srinabh, Mr., Ba, M., Sarojadevi, D., Disease Diagnosis System By Exploring Machine Learning Algorithms, *International Journal of Innovations in Engineering and Technology (IJIET)*, 10, 2, 2018. https://dx.doi.org/10.21172/ijiet.102.03

17. Wang, X., Chused, A., Elhadad, N., Friedman, C., Markatou, M., Automated knowledge acquisition from clinical narrative reports. *AMIA .. Annu. Symp. Proc. AMIA Symp.*, 2008, 783–787, 2008.

18. Zhang, Y. and Liu, B., Semantic text classification of disease reporting, in: *Proceedings of the 30th annual international ACM SIGIR conference on Research and development in information retrieval*, Association for Computing Machinery, New York, NY, USA, pp. 747–748, 2007, https://doi.org/10.1145/1277741.1277889.

5

Classification of Heart Sound Signals Using Time-Frequency Image Texture Features

Sujata Vyas[1], Mukesh D. Patil[1] and Gajanan K. Birajdar[2]

[1]*Department of Electronics and Telecommunication Engineering, Ramrao Adik Institute of Technology, Nerul, Navi Mumbai, Maharashtra, India*
[2]*Department of Electronics Engineering, Ramrao Adik Institute of Technology, Nerul, Navi Mumbai, Maharashtra, India*

Abstract

This book chapter presents an approach for heart sound classification based on time-frequency image texture feature and support vector machine classifier. Firstly, the spectrogram image is generated to create a time-frequency representation of small frames from an input speech sample. The spectrogram visual representation provides finest details over resolutions which can be tuned to capture heart sound detailed information. We then acquire a local binary pattern (LBP), and its derivatives like complete local binary pattern (CLBP), dense local binary pattern (dense CLBP), local directional texture pattern (LDTP), and Weber local descriptor (WLD), which is better suited to extract features from heart sound signal spectrogram images. To select prominent features and to discard redundant features, a chaotic moth flame optimization algorithm is employed. Experimental results yield a 5.2% improvement on the PhysioNet 2016 Database compared to the short-time Fourier transform method with LBP. Fusing Mel-spectrogram and IIR constant-Q transform method in pre-processing, a classification accuracy of 99% is achieved.

Keywords: Heart sound classification, PCG signal, time-frequency image, spectrogram image, texture features

5.1 Introduction

As per research by the American College of Cardiology in 2015, around 33% of the world's deaths are because of the cardiovascular infections, and more than 400 million individuals all over the world were diagnosed to have the cardiovascular diseases [26]. Furthermore, according to World Health Organization (WHO), 17.7 million individuals passed on because of cardiovascular diseases in 2015 [22]. Thus, in the current situation, heart disorders are

---

Corresponding author: gajanan.birajdar@rait.ac.in

Om Prakash Jena, Alok Ranjan Tripathy, Ahmed A. Elngar and Zdzislaw Polkowski (eds.) Computational Intelligence and Healthcare Informatics, (81–102) © 2021 Scrivener Publishing LLC

high-mortality killing reason around the world, and therefore, diagnosis and immediate treatment of heart diseases is very important.

The work of computerized diagnosis in the clinical field has improved significantly in recent decades particularly because of signal processing, machine learning techniques, and image processing. While collecting the heart sound signals, samples can easily interfered by the noise of the equipment as well as of the external environment which can affect the processing and interfere the results, and therefore, it is necessary to denoise the heart sound signals first [27]. Samples can also be taken by auscultation. It is very useful and cost effective heart sound listening method with a stethoscope. But doctor's experience, careful analysis, and ear sensitivity are key points to make correct diagnosis [39].

Heart valves opening and closing generates the heart sound and it can be heard by utilizing stethoscopes and can be fed to a computer forfurther processing [3]. During each cardiovascular cycle because of this process, vibration of heart muscle blood flow audible heart sounds is produced. According to previous research, clinical students or interns and newly joined doctors have made about multiple times more mistakes in detecting heart sounds from master specialists; therefore, machine learning–based calculations which make auscultation process both reliable and automatic have been begun to be created.

The normal heart sound consist of two parts S1 and S2 [24]. These are known as fundamental heart sound (FHS). These two sections heard as lub and dub, respectively, through stethoscope and they heard in same sequence, i.e., *lub-dub*. The time interval between the completion of S1 and starting of S2 is named as systolic interval while interval between S2 and S1 is known as diastolic interval. Cardiovascular irregularities occur due to the interruption of this order. Systolic interval is in range of 0.1–0.16 s and diastolic is 0.08–0.12 s. In abnormal condition, some normal beat can be skipped or else sometimes noisy sounds can also occur in the normal cycle. Every abnormality refers to some different problem in the heart. Therefore, heart sound analysis has been very vast and active research area for a long time. Scientists focus primarily on classification or localization and classification at the same time.

5.1.1 Motivation

There are almost 3.6 million people in a world identified with heart failure [22]. This record is according to European Society of Cardiology (ESC), and approximately, 26 million grownups are suffering from Heart failure [26]. Heart diseases can be managed and cured if they are detected at early stage and then it is possible to avoid its adverse effects. Its early detection can control this disease progression and also it can decreases the expenses of medical treatments. In this modern era, machine learning systems help a lot in medical conditions. Medical science has progressed on various patho-physiology–related heart failures. However, detection of heart diseases by using the database of different types of patients is a big challenge nowadays. For early examination of heart failure, machine learning is a broad domain so it is requisite step to detect the condition early and predicting its adverse effects by managing all heart condition so that clinical expenses related with treatment will also be lessen. When cardiovascular abnormality occurs, it affects this concatenation, and normal sequence of "lub-dub" changes which defines the specific abnormality according to heart sound. Therefore, heart sound analysis is active research area in this field.

Here, in this proposed work, processing of heart sound signal is done without segmentation by generating spectrograms in pre-processing section in three different types. Feature extraction and classification methods has also immense effect on the accuracy. Different types of feature extraction tools for the analysis and classify appropriately by mentioned classification method is performed. With this feature extraction, we are also evaluating feature selection in this proposed work which is rarely done in previous work. Feature selection helps to ease this work by saving classification time. Then, classification method is applied to classify the heart signals in normal and abnormal section. The experimental results show that the proposed algorithm performs better than the previous methods on the dataset PhysioNet 2016.

The remainder of the chapter is organized as follows. In this chapter, we have included literature survey in Section 5.2, for major previous work done in this field. Section 5.3 presents theoretical background explaining related theory of all techniques used in the proposed work. Methodology of the work is explained in Section 5.4 with algorithm, and Section 5.5 includes the dataset description and evaluation metrics with its experimental results and discussions. Finally, Section 5.6 concludes the work.

5.2   Related Work

There are various types of research done on the phonocardiogram (PCG) signals, but from past few years, technologies like electrocardiograph were growing with limitation, and therefore, research in this era is growing with improvements in signal processing techniques. Past studies have focused on the localization, identification, and classification of heart sound signals by using extracted features. Techniques used to extract features are statistical features, wavelet transform based features, and FFT. Detailed description from past studies is mentioned here which is as follows.

In 2014, Shivnarayan *et al.* classified a heart sound signal using constrained tunable-Q wavelet transform (TQWT). Proposed method proves its accuracy as well as it reduces complexity as compared to other methods [38]. Heechang *et al.* proposed a technique in which they have used convolutional neural network (CNN) to extract features and construct a classification system. CNN is based on back propagation algorithm. Before feature extraction signal is filtered and segmented finally by collecting probability values of all segmented signals, one can determine normal or abnormal signal as illustrated in [37]. Runnan *et al.* proposed an algorithm to classify normal and abnormal heart sound by using power spectrum analysis. In this, input signal is decomposed by wavelet decomposition method, and then, it is reconstructed bands with various different frequencies [36]. Aortic valve closure (A2) of second fundamental heart sound is extracted using power spectrum analysis of auto regressive model in [36].

In 2016, Michael presented heart sound classification using deep structural features. In this feature, representation is done by wavelet-based deep CNN and used SVM for classification of heart sounds [35]. Shi-Wen Deng *et al.* proposed a framework in which, instead of segmentation, autocorrelation features are extracted from subband envelopes which are calculated by subband coefficients with discrete wavelet transform. Fusion of autocorrelation features is considered to be input to SVM classifier. Results show comparatively better results than the baselines approach [34].

Mohan *et al.* used a supervised classification method to classify normal and abnormal sound in which they have first extracted Mel-frequency cepstral coefficients (MFCCs). The proposed framework resulted in accuracy of 97.30% [33]. Mohammad *et al.* proposed a framework in 2017 which works on random forest algorithm and for that distinctive frequency and time features are extracted from heart sound signal [32]. In [31], a PCG signal is segmented based on a logistic regression hidden semi-Markov model, and then, MFCCs are extracted. Shanti R. Thiyagaraja *et al.* created special mobile health service platform for detecting and classifying heart sounds. They have used MFCC and hidden Markov model (HMM) to detect normal and abnormal heart sound [30].

In 2018, Anjali Yadav *et al.* proposed a framework for classifying heart sound with support vector machine (SVM) classifier [29]. Cepstrum analysis is used for feature extraction and this method achieved the accuracy of 95%. In 2018, Maryam Hamidi *et al.* classified normal and abnormal heart sounds using k-nearest neighbor (KNN). Authors used two feature extraction techniques: first is by curve fitting and second MFCC features fused with the fractal features by stacking [23]. In 2019, M. Mustafa *et al.* presented an algorithm for automatic heartbeat detection and abnormality discrimination [24]. In the presented method, authors used artificial neural network using a multilayer perceptron (MLP) for classification. A novel method to detect abnormal heart sound is developed using the temporal quasi-period features extracted from spectrogram [7]. M. Sheraz Ahmad *et al.* proposed a framework by using SVM and KNN. In this approach, using all systolic and diastolic interval, features are extracted and fed to the classifier, resulting in classification accuracy of 92.6% [22].

The classification algorithm based on the evaluation of the envelope curve of the PCG is presented in [25]. This framework is tested with two different methods for envelope extraction, one with Hilbert transform and short-time Fourier transform. In 2020, Palani *et al.* proposed a classification algorithm without the requirement of feature engineering and segmentation ofheart sound signals. Authors used one-dimensional CNN (1D-CNN) and feed-forward neural network for classification. A.I. Humayun *et al.* used a branched CNN architecture with learnable filter-banks to detect the abnormal heart sound detection [26]. The illustrated work used two different layers in it with eight and four filters, respectively.

A wavelet threshold denoising approach to produce the heart sound signal noise free and then signal envelope is extracted by normalized average Shannon energy method and double threshold method, which is presented in [27]. In 2020, Suyi Li *et al.* explained that every heart sound detection technique most probably contains steps like denoising, segmentation, feature extraction, and classification [28]. They have also explained different techniques which have been used for each step in past few years.

5.3   Theoretical Background

In this section, theoretical background of all the methods used in the proposed work is presented.

5.3.1   Pre-Processing Techniques

Heart sound signals contain real environmental conditions including the sounds of traffic and birds chirping [20]. So, it is requisite to perform pre-processing of any heart sound signal before further processing. In the pre-processing, three main steps are employed as following:

- Filtering: It is used to remove the noise present at low frequency or at very high frequency. The Butterworth sixth-order band-pass filter which has lower cutoff of 25 Hz and higher cutoff of 900 Hz is utilized in this work. Figure 5.1 shows the PCG signal in time-frequency representation format before and after filtered signal.
- Framing: The heart sound signals before processing are converted into the samples of the small frames of 5 s each, and then, these small frames are used for processing.

5.3.2 Spectrogram Generation

Proposed work is based on time-frequency image texture processing techniques so we have used different types of spectrogram generation in this work. In this work, three different types of spectrograms, *viz.*, standard conventional spectrogram, logarithmic Mel-scale spectrogram, and infinite impulse response constant-Q transform spectrogram (IIR-CQT), are utilized [10, 19]. All of these are briefly explained in present section.

(a) Standard Spectrogram Generation

Spectrograms are also shown in time-frequency representation format in which x-axis shows time dimension and y-axis shows frequency dimension while intensity factor is depicted by amplitude [1]. It contains spectral as well as temporal features of sound signal. Sometimes, it can contain noisy data, so it is very crucial to remove it to improve its classification accuracy [2]. It gives variation in energy distribution with respect to frequency so visual representation of spectrograms is important [3].

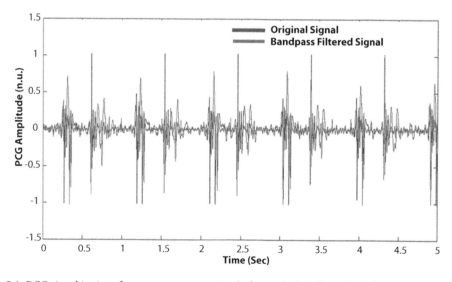

Figure 5.1 PCG signal in time-frequency representation before and after filtered signal.

Steps for spectrogram generation are as follows:

For spectrogram generation, the signal is sampled into window of fixed size of length N.
$\{x(n) : 0 \leq n \leq N-1\}$

Then, Fourier transform is applied to each sample

$$X_t(k) = \sum_{n=0}^{N-1} x(n)\omega(n)e^{\frac{-2\pi tk_n}{N}} \tag{5.1}$$

For k = 0, 1, ..., –N 1 where $\omega(n)$ is the Hamming window function *(k) k.fs/N*, where *fs* is the sampling frequency in Hertz [4]. Figure 5.2a shows the standard spectrogram for normal sample and Figure 5.2b shows the standard spectrogram of abnormal sample, if one carefully observes both figures, it shows the difference in periodical manner. The spectrogram image of normal sample has fixed type of pattern in sequential manner which indicated sequential S1 and S2 of heart sound which is not clear in the spectrogram image of abnormal sample.

(b) Mel-Spectrogram Generation

The Mel-frequency spectrogram is the time-frequency representations inspired by auditory perception of normal human being. It is the initial basic result of psychoacoustics which is result of some nonlinear transformations from the frequency scale. When we convert frequencies into Mel-scale, it generates Mel-spectrogram which attempts to show frequency bands as per the human cognizance [5].

Mel-spectrogram is related to Hertz by

$$m = 2595\,log10\left(1 + \frac{f}{700}\right) \tag{5.2}$$

where m represents in Mel's and f represents in Hertz. By using overlapping triangular filters, it scales the frequency axis to the Mel-scale. The Mel-scale values are approximate values to the non-linear scaling of frequencies in the cochlea. This is followed by variable range compression using the log operator. Figure 5.3a shows Mel-spectrogram image for the normal sample while Figure 5.3b shows Mel-spectrogram image for abnormal sample.

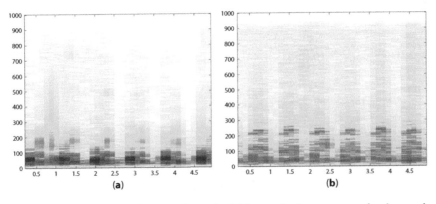

(a)   (b)

Figure 5.2 (a) Standard spectrogram for normal sample. (b) for standard spectrogram for abnormal sample.

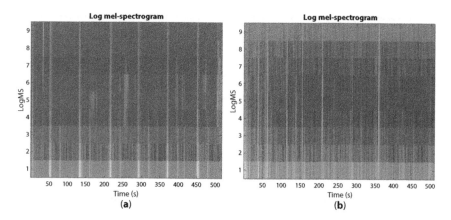

Figure 5.3 (a) Mel-spectrogram for normal sample. (b) Mel-spectrogram for abnormal sample.

When we carefully observe x-axis of both the images, we came to know that normal one is showing yellow vertical string at 60, 140, 220, 300 s, ..., which means this fixed sequence is repeating after each 80 s and that part is absent in abnormal image.

(c) IIR Constant-Q Transform Spectrogram

The IIR-CQT is logarithmically separated frequency bands with respect to time which gives better resolutions at lower frequencies. CQT increases time resolution to higher frequencies, and therefore, it is additionally best to depict environmental sound. By observing CQT time-frequency representation, one can average out various power spectrum patterns across all time and frequencypoints. Its texture pattern changes when its frequency goes on increasing. To improve its time-frequency representation while saving the structures time-frequency of sound scene, it is set to 512 by 512 by using bicubic interpolationwhich will benefit to the less blurring in the image [6].

The IIR-CQT spectrogram is determined by fast Fourier change and CQT of the k-thcomponent is given as follows:

$$X^{cq}[k] = \frac{1}{N[k]} \sum_{n=0}^{N[k]-1} w[n,k]x[n]e^{-j2\pi Qn/N[k]}. \tag{5.3}$$

where n is time index, k represents frequency domain index, $w(n,k)$ gives analysis window, length of window is given by $N(k)$, and Q is quality factor [7].

CQT gives similar resolution in the human acoustic-system as compared with fast Fourier transform which shows uniform spectral resolution, and therefore, CQT is the best option. As short-time Fourier transform has very low computational cost, and therefore, it is used in the evaluation of CQT. At high frequencies, normal spectrogram shows blur images but IIR-CQT shows superior results because of its improved time resolution. These discriminating features motivate to use IIR CQT spectrogram image representation as follows.

Figure 5.4a shows the IIRCQT spectrogram image of normal sample while Figure 5.4b shows for the abnormal sample. It is evident from the figure that there is substantial difference in texture present in normal and abnormal spectrogram image.

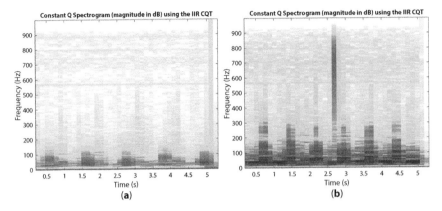

Figure 5.4 (a) IIR-CQT spectrogram for normal sample. (b) IIR-CQT spectrogram for abnormal sample compared to conventional spectrograms [7].

5.3.2   Feature Extraction

Spectrograms generated contain various types of detailspresent in it so textural feature extraction is an important task. This study explores five different types of feature extraction tools to show the comparison with each technique and compare its accuracy. All feature extraction techniques are elaborated in this section.

(a) Local Binary Pattern
Local binary pattern (LBP) is used to find textural clues from the image. The LBP can be explained by considering one pixel as a central pixel C and set of neighbors p are equally spaced at same distance R and intensity difference with textures C and neighbors P is calculated and histogram is drawn by this calculation [8]. Sometimes, this difference calculation can be obtained by interpolation. There are two typesof LBP codes, consistent and inconsistent. If the number of transitions is two or less than two, then it is known as consistent codes otherwise inconsistentcodes [8].

Mathematically LBP values can be calculated as follows:

$$LBP_{P,R}(x_C, y_C) = \sum_{P=0}^{P-1} s(g_P - g_C)2^P \tag{5.4}$$

(b) Complete Local Binary Pattern
Complete local binary pattern (CLBP) is an improved version of LBP, as LBP does not consider the magnitude difference information between central and neighboring pixels [9]. So, LBP most probably generates inconsistent codes, and it may fail to create accurate binary code which inspires us to use CLBP as feature extraction technique. CLBP is an extension of LBP operator which assigns 2P bit code to central pixel based on gray valued of local neighbors. This method uses two bits for each neighbor to represent the sign and magnitude information of the difference between central and neighboring pixels [9].

(c) Local Directional Pattern
Local directional pattern (LDP) operator is based on the information of intensity difference with respect to pixels [11]. It can encode the smallest information regarding edges as well as some other local features. In presence of noise, most probably, most significant responses do not show changes, but magnitude position in some directions can change, and there is lot of chances in lesser significant bits to change because of noise. LDP can create most stable pattern even if noise present in it. But just because of same small noise, LBP code can change from uniform to non-uniform format which shows performance difference of LDP than LBP operator in presence of noise as proved in [11].

LDP finds edge responses in all eight directions and use those to encode the texture features of image. In this, 8-bit binary code is allotted to every pixel of input image. Then, comparing the edge responses in every direction pattern is computed. As Kirsch edge detector detects directional responses more accurately as it calculates it in all eight directions as shown in Figure 5.5. Edge responses in all eight directions are computed in LDP but all are not equally important in all direction. In this, top bit responses are assigned to 1 and all others assigned as 0. Finally, LDP codes are represented as follows:

$$LDP_k = \sum_{i=0}^{7} b_i(m_i - m_k) \times 2^i, b_i(a) = \begin{cases} 1, & a \geq 0, \\ 0, & a < 0, \end{cases} \tag{5.5}$$

where m_k is the highest significant response in specific direction [12].

(d) Local Directional Texture Pattern
Local directional texture pattern (LDTP) is more accurate operator as compared to LBP andCLBP operators as it extracts the textures features from principle axis in every neighborhood pixel [13]. It encodes the intensity difference between two principle directions as well as principle directions into a single number. Because of this method, it can encode very useful information of neighboring pixels divulged by its principle directions. In every

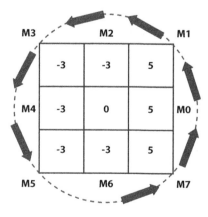

Figure 5.5 Kirschmask in eight different directions [12].

principle direction, the gray value difference in neighboring pixels is encoded as [13] follows:

$$D_f(d_n) = \begin{cases} 0, & -\varepsilon \leq d_n \leq \varepsilon \\ 1, & d_n < -\varepsilon \\ 2, & d_n > \varepsilon, \end{cases} \qquad (5.6)$$

where d_n is gray value difference, ε is the threshold specified by user, and (dn) is encoded difference value. For each pixel, the code of LDTP can be calculated by concatenating the binary form of its first principal directional number $P1$dir. Then, for every pixel, final LDTP code can be computed by sequencing the binary form of its principle direction number $P1$dir, its first and second directional encoded difference $Df(d1)$ and $Df(d2)$ [14].

(e) Weber Local Descriptor

Weber local descriptor (WLD) is recently developed technique for local feature extraction. It is very simple and robust local feature extractor which is motivated by Weber's law which states that ratio of change in threshold to the intensity is constant [15]. To compute WLD features, for each input pixel of image, we have to find two components differential excitation (ξ) and gradient orientation (θ). Differential excitation is the ratio of intensity of current pixel to the relative intensity difference in current and neighboring pixels. Local salient patterns can be extracted by using this component. Current pixel's gradient orientation is also computed with this to find the WLD features [15].

5.3.4 Feature Selection

When we use feature extraction techniques, it extracts large number of features but only some of them are useful. Feature selection helps to select only useful features so it gives better accuracy in lesser time. It is necessary to remove the redundant irrelevant and noisy features and increase its classification generalization.

In this proposed study, chaotic moth flame optimization (CMFO) technique as a feature selection technique. CMFO is one of the most recent techniques invented from the movements of moths at night [16]. Moths generally move in straight line and that too very long distance by maintaining certain angle with the moon light. Dynamic deterministic processes are described by chaotic maps which are mathematical systems and it has better sensitivity to initial conditions. Outcome of this process are not predictable. Chaotic maps have shown their accuracy by enhancing the performance of metaheuristic algorithms when they combined with them for solving specific optimization issue. Chaotic maps are mostly used to provide better convergence capacity, to solve the local minima issues by reaching toward the optimal solution [17].

In present approach, a feature set (total number of features) is coded in a string of certain length (depending on the sample size). During the feature selection process, solution moves and collaborates to find the optimal features set. In this, first we have initialized the parameters and determined the maximum allowed iterations. Then, each moth is randomly assigned to one feature and which should meet all the features and build solution. The algorithm repeats this process for new group generated in previous iteration and determines its accuracy until the stopping criteria is satisfied. Here, classifier error is used as an evaluation measure. At each iteration, feature set is prepared. Then, fitness value is calculated and by operating crossover and mutation next generation is generated. This process repeats until number of generations=gmax. At last, evaluation starts for the selected set of features.

5.3.5 Support Vector Machine

SVM classifies the complex data with a good accuracy and is based on linear separation hyper plane. Sometimes, if data is difficult to linearly separate, then SVM converts it to higher dimensionby using mapping method then obtains separating hyper plane [18]. It is an effective differentiating tool for classification and can be used for pattern classification, regression, problem detection, as well as classification. There are different types available in this group depending on the Kernel function used. They include Linear SVM, Quadratic SVM, Cubic SVM, Fine Gaussian SVM, Medium Gaussian SVM, and Coarse Gaussian SVM.

5.4 Proposed Algorithm

The proposed work consists of four main stages, *viz.*, pre-processing, feature extraction, feature selection, and classification, which are explained in details in previous sections as shown in Figure 5.6.

In pre-processing stage, as explained in above section, filtering and framing of the signal are performed. Framing is done to divide the signal in number of small samples for better accuracy and ease of algorithm. This work used three different types of spectrogram as every method affects the accuracy of the result. Each frame of 5 s is converted to the each type of spectrogram which is used further for feature extraction. After converting RGB spectrogram into grayscale image, feature extraction techniques are applied to spectrogram images. There are five feature extraction techniques used in this proposed work: LBP, CLBP, LDP, LDTP, and WLD. Every feature extraction technique has its own advantages as well as disadvantages.

LBP pours complete information into the code regardless of its necessity and that too is based upon fixed threshold value. So, sometimes, it cannot able to give accurate results in

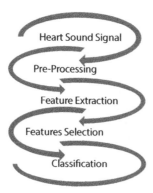

Figure 5.6 Algorithm for the proposed heart sound classification system.

feature extraction. CLBP is an extended version of LBP which also works on neighboring pixels but it encodes the sign as well as magnitude difference from the neighboring pixels. In LDP, encoding process considers only principle directions; any noise present in signal does not affect the accuracy but its intensity variations are difficult to detect and it changes with rotation effect. These limitations are overcome in LDTP; therefore, it contains both directional as well as intensity information.

All the features which are generated using above encoding techniques are not all useful, and to reduce dimensionally CMFO features, selection technique is employed. The CMFO feature selection approach has several advantages as compared to other techniques which inspired us to select for the currentstudy. Some of them are as follows:

1. The CMFO search engine depends on a spiral position that can change the places of moths in a way that accomplishes a promising compromise between the exploration and exploitation and adaptively reachto the correct solution.
2. CMFO had been utilized to take care of numerous issues with obscure and compelled search spaces
3. CMFO algorithm has adaptive parameters which increases the exploration phase in the initial stage of process and increases the exploitation phase in last stage of optimization process.

Experimental evaluation is performed using the PhysioNet database which is binary database. Hence, a binary SVM is utilized for the classification task.

5.5   Experimental Results

Various parameters explaining the efficiency of the system will be discussed in this section with comparison with previous techniques.

5.5.1   Database

This study employs PhysioNet 2016 challenge database which is freely accessible on the internet. These PCG recordings have been collected by considering different locations of the body. The challenge sets consist of total six different classes, from class A to class F. Each class consist of normal and abnormal both the types of samples. The length of each different signal is different, which varies from minimum 5 s to maximum 120 s. Sample rate of recorded heart sound signal is 2,000 Hz. Since the dataset samples are labeled as normal and abnormal, our task is to differentiate it in normal and abnormal classes; therefore, this type of classification is known as binary classification. Database statistics are illustrated in Table 5.1. PhysioNet 2016 challenge dataset contains 3,240 samples in total, out of which 2,575 are normal and 665 are abnormal.

In this work, we have used SVM classifier with its various types depending on the kernel function used. The types we used, *viz.*, Linear SVM, Quadratic SVM, Cubic SVM, Fine Gaussian SVM, Medium Gaussian SVM, and Coarse Gaussian SVM.

These recordings are taken from real world environmental conditions so some of them may contains stethoscope motion, breathing voice which makes it unclean and noisy [20].

Table 5.1 Dataset description collected from PhysioNet 2016 challenge.

| Total dataset | | | Trained (50%) | | | Tested (50%) | | |
Total	Normal	Abnormal	Trained (50%)	Normal	Abnormal	Tested (50%)	Normal	Abnormal
3240	2575	665	1620	1272	348	1620	1303	317
409	117	292	205	58	147	204	59	145
490	386	104	245	189	56	245	197	48
31	7	24	16	3	13	15	4	11
55	27	28	28	15	13	27	12	15
2141	1958	183	1071	970	101	1070	988	82
114	80	34	57	39	18	57	41	16

5.5.2   Evaluation Metrics

The proposed PCG sound classification performance is evaluated using three different parameters, which are specificity (SPE), sensitivity (SEN), and overall accuracy (OAA). Mathematically all terms are defined as follows:

SPE = (No. of correctly identified normal cycles/Total no. of normal cycles from test)*100

SEN = (No. of correctly identified abnormal cycles/Total no. of abnormal cycles from test)*100

OAA = (No. of correctly identified cycles/Total no.of cycles from test)*100

5.5.3   Confusion Matrix

A confusion matrix is used in the performance evaluation. There are different components of confusion matrix like True positive (TP), False positive (FP), True negative (TN), and False negative (FN) and are used to find parameters like OAA, SPE, and SEN [21].

5.5.4   Results and Discussions

As mentioned above, this dataset contains a total of 3,240 samples with 14,951 features. In order to differentiate the performance of feature extraction techniques, the heart sound signals were classified on the basis of LBP, CLBP, dense CLBP, LDTP, and WLD—these five feature extraction techniques. In all these classification processes, we have used the cross validation method to optimize the SVM parameters.

With this work, in order to compare the performance of various spectrograms, we have also used various types of spectrogram generation methods in the pre-processing. In this work, we have used six different types of SVM classifier and calculated results for all types. The classification SPE, SEN, and OAA for standard spectrogram generation as a pre-processing method is shown in Table 5.2. All the mentioned accuracies in Table 5.2 are all highest accuracy obtained from all SVM types. But this type is not fixed for every feature extraction type; it varies according to technique. As shown, highest accuracy of 88.2% is obtained by the WLD feature extraction type. It is because that the derivation of differential excitation and orientation makes the WLD noise redundant. WLD reduces the noises

Table 5.2 Accuracies for conventional spectrogram generation based on various feature extraction methods.

	Specificity (%)	Sensitivity (%)	Accuracy (%)
LBP	95	53.38	85.6
CLBP	94.9	51.8	85
Dense CLBP	90.14	63.6	84.11
LDTP	94.4	61.72	86.7
WLD	94.7	66.01	88.2

present in the sample. So, the WLD can have better classification performance. If we compare SPE and SEN of all techniques, we can observe that specificity is much higher than that of sensitivity. We have calculated these SPE and SEN by the formulas defined in the previous subsection. All the values for this calculation are obtained from the confusion matrix of respective model. Figure 5.7 shows the confusion matrix of dense CLBP for example.

The heart sound signals were also classified based on the pre-processing techniques with different spectrogram generation techniques and for each feature extraction type. As stated above because of robustness to noise, change in scale, illumination these special characteristics, WLD performs obviously better than all other methods.

Table 5.3 shows the variation in accuracy based on different spectrogram generation techniques when we calculated it for the type WLD. Table 5.3 shows that, when we have used standard conventional spectrogram, we got the least accuracy of all three types as it was initial method with some drawbacks which are improved by the time. When we have used logarithmic Mel-spectrogram as pre-processing techniques, it gave the highest accuracy of all. As this method has nonlinear scale instead of linear scale on y-axis i.e., frequency axis. It is better to detect the differences in lower frequencies than the higher

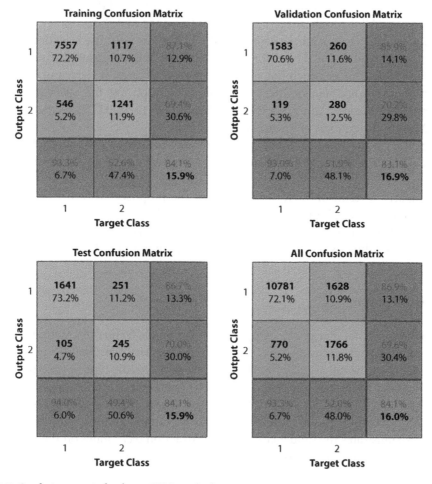

Figure 5.7 Confusion matrix for dense CLBP method.

Table 5.3 Accuracies for various spectrogram generation techniques for WLD feature extraction method.

	Specificity (%)	Sensitivity (%)	Accuracy (%)
Conventional Spectrogram	94.7	66.01	88.2
IIRCQT Spectrogram	98.4	90.1	96.6
Logarithmic Mel-Spectrogram	99.78	94.3	98.5

frequencies. This highest accuracy is 98.5% which is one of the best accuracy from previously done works and algorithms from the literature survey.

As mentioned above, we have used total six types of SVM. Table 5.4 shows all the accuracies of SVM types with different feature extraction types. In this, we have used Mel-spectrogram as pre-processing technique as it gives the better results as compare to both other types. Table 5.4 shows when we used LBP, dense CLBP, and WLD fine Gaussian SVM gives the highest accuracy while when we used CLBP and LDTP cubic SVM type gives highest accuracy. All the highest accuracies are in the range of 95% to 100%.

In this proposed work, we have also used the CMFO as a feature selection technique. Feature selection reduces the dimensions of the features, and as a result, it also reduces the training time of the model which increases the speed of process. If the feature dimensions are very high or low, it does not affect much on recognition rate but affect training time. The best recognition rate of this process is 99.87% when we used LDTP as feature extraction tool and Mel-spectrogram as pre-processing technique.

This accuracy is got by cubic SVM type in training time of 892.65s. But when we have used CMFO features, training time of election algorithm after feature extraction is reduced to 556.24 s.

The comparison result of Table 5.5 shows that the proposed work in this chapter has highest classification rate, indicating that it can better differentiate between various types of heart sound signals while, the model training time is directly related to the feature dimension. If the feature dimensions are high, the model training time will be longer.

5.6 Conclusion

This work presents an empirical comparison of various feature extractions based on time-frequency spectrogram images. Different performance evaluation measures are obtained including overall accuracy to illustrate how the specific type of spectrogram generation affects the algorithm performance of heart sound classification. We found that as compared to conventional and IIR-CQT spectrogram, Mel-spectrogram results significantly better performance as it more precisely shows human auditory system processing. The work also illustrates the influence of feature extraction techniques on the classification accuracy. Feature reduction is also addressed in this work that affects the model training time.

Table 5.4 Accuracies for different types of feature extraction method by Mel-spectrogram technique.

	Linear SVM	Quadratic SVM	Cubic SVM	Fine Gaussian SVM	Medium Gaussian SVM	Coarse Gaussian SVM
LBP	80.5	88.6	92.8	95.7	83.5	77.5
CLBP	80.7	88.4	97.4	95.2	83.5	77.3
Dense CLBP	83.7	93.7	98.8	99.1	90.3	82
LDTP	99.7	99.7	99.8	99.4	99.7	99.7
WLD	77.3	84.7	94.1	98.5	86.7	77.7

Table 5.5 Comparison of proposed work with the related work.

Authors	Year	Pre-processing technique	Feature extraction	Feature selection	Classifier	Accuracy
Wenjie Zheng et al. [7]	2017	Standard Spectrogram generation	Short-time Fourier transform	No	SVM	81%
M. Sheraz Ahmad et al. [22]	2019	Segmentation	MFCC algorithm	No	SVM KNN	92.6% 90%
M. Hamidi et al. [23]	2018	Sampling, Filtering	Curve fitting MFCC algorithm	No	KNN	92% 98%
M. Mustafa et al. [24]	2019	Windowing, Filtering	MFCC	PCA	MLP	94%
Angelika et al. [25]	2020	Synchronization	Envelope curve extraction by Hilbert transform	No		95%
Palani et al. [26]	2020	Sampling, Filtering	-----	No	1D CNN F-NN	75% 86%
Peng chen et al. [27]	2020	Denoising, Normalization	Time-frequency feature extraction	S-transform method	SVM	93%
Proposed method		Mel-Spectrogram generation	Weber Local Descriptor	Chaotic moth flame optimization	SVM	99%

References

1. Abidin, S., Xia, X., Togneri, R., Sohel, F., Local binary pattern with random forest for acoustic scene classification, in: *2018 IEEE International Conference on Multimedia and Expo (ICME)*, 2018, July, IEEE, pp. 1–6.

2. Agera, N., Chapaneri, S., Jayaswal, D., Exploring textural features for automatic music genre classification, in: *2015 International Conference on Computing Communication Control and Automation*, 2015, February, IEEE, pp. 822–826.

3. Agrawal, D.G. and Jangale, P.M., Dynamic texture feature extraction using weber local descriptor. *Int. J. Eng. Res. Appl. (IJERA)*, 4, 3, 502–506, 2014.

4. Ahmad, M.S., Mir, J., Ullah, M.O., Shahid, M.L.U.R., Syed, M.A., An efficient heart murmur recognition and cardiovascular disorders classification system. *Australas. Phys. Eng. Sci. Med.*, 42, 3, 733–743, 2019.

5. Astuti, W., Support vector machine and principal component analysis for microarray data classification, in: *Journal of Physics Conference Series*, 2018, March, vol. 971, No. 1, p. 012003.

6. Ayami, Y.M. and Shabat, A., An Acceleration Scheme to The Local Directional Pattern. *arXiv preprint arXiv:1810.11518*, 2018.

7. Battaglino, D., Lepauloux, L., Pilati, L., Evans, N., Acoustic context recognition using local binary pattern codebooks, in: *2015 IEEE Workshop on Applications of Signal Processing to Audio and Acoustics (WASPAA)*, 2015, October, IEEE, pp. 1–5.

8. Chen, P. and Zhang, Q., Classification of heart sounds using discrete time-frequency energy feature based on S transform and the wavelet threshold denoising. *Biomed. Signal Process. Control*, 57, 101684, 2020.

9. Costa, Y., Oliveira, L., Koerich, A., Gouyon, F., Music genre recognition based on visual features with dynamic ensemble of classifiers selection, in: *2013 20th International Conference on Systems, Signals and Image Processing (IWSSIP)*, 2013, July, IEEE, pp. 55–58.

10. Costa, Y.M., Oliveira, L.S., Koerich, A.L., Gouyon, F., Comparing textural features for music genre classification, in: *The 2012 International Joint Conference on Neural Networks (IJCNN)*, 2012, June, IEEE, pp. 1–6.

11. Demir, F., Şengür, A., Bajaj, V., Polat, K., Towards the classification of heart sounds based on convolutional deep neural network. *Health Inf. Sci. Syst.*, 7, 1, 16, 2019.

12. Deng, S.W. and Han, J.Q., Towards heart sound classification without segmentation via autocorrelation feature and diffusion maps. *Future Gener. Comput. Syst.*, 60, 13–21, 2016.

13. Ghosal, A., Chakraborty, R., Dhara, B.C., Saha, S.K., Song/instrumental classification using spectrogram based contextual features, in: *Proceedings of the CUBE International Information Technology Conference*, 2012, September, pp. 21–25.

14. Hamidi, M., Ghassemian, H., Imani, M., Classification of heart sound signal using curve fitting and fractal dimension. *Biomed. Signal Process. Control*, 39, 351–359, 2018.

15. He, R., Zhang, H., Wang, K., Li, Q., Sheng, Z., Zhao, N., Classification of heart sound signals based on AR model, in: *2016 Computing in Cardiology Conference (CinC)*, 2016, September, IEEE, pp. 605–608.

16. Kabir, M.H., Jabid, T., Chae, O., Local directional pattern variance (ldpv): a robust feature descriptor for facial expression recognition. *Int. Arab J. Inf. Technol.*, 9, 4, 382–391, 2012.

17. Khurma, R.A., Aljarah, I., Sharieh, A., An Efficient Moth Flame Optimization Algorithm using Chaotic Maps for Feature Selection in the Medical Applications, in: *ICPRAM*, pp. 175–182, 2020.

18. Kobayashi, T. and Ye, J., Acoustic feature extraction by statistics based local binary pattern for environmental sound classification, in: *2014 IEEE International Conference on Acoustics, Speech and Signal Processing (ICASSP)*, 2014, May, IEEE, pp. 3052–3056.

19. Krishnan, P.T., Balasubramanian, P., Umapathy, S., Automated heart sound classification system from unsegmented phonocardiogram (PCG) using deep neural network. *Phys. Eng. Sci. Med.*, 43, 505–515, 2020.

20. Li, S., Li, F., Tang, S., Xiong, W., A Review of Computer-Aided Heart Sound Detection Techniques. *BioMed. Res. Int.*, *2020*, 1–10, 2020.

21. Mishra, M., Singh, A., Dutta, M.K., Burget, R., Masek, J., Classification of normal and abnormal heart sounds for automatic diagnosis, in: *2017 40th International Conference on Telecommunications and Signal Processing (TSP)*, 2017, July, IEEE, pp. 753–757.

22. Mustafa, M., Abdalla, G.M.T., Manimurugan, S., Alharbi, A.R., Detection of heartbeat sounds arrhythmia using automatic spectral methods and cardiac auscultatory. *J. Supercomput.*, 76, 8, 1–24, 2019.

23. Nassralla, M., El Zein, Z., Hajj, H., Classification of normal and abnormal heart sounds, in: *2017 Fourth International Conference on Advances in Biomedical Engineering (ICABME)*, 2017, October, IEEE, pp. 1–4.

24. Nogueira, D.M., Ferreira, C.A., Jorge, A.M., Classifying heart sounds using images of MFCC and temporal features, in: *EPIA Conference on Artificial Intelligence*, 2017, September, Springer, Cham, pp. 186–203.

25. Patidar, S. and Pachori, R.B., Classification of cardiac sound signals using constrained tunable-Q wavelet transform. *Expert Syst. Appl.*, 41, 16, 7161–7170, 2014.

26. Rivera, A.R., Castillo, J.R., Chae, O., Local directional texture pattern image descriptor. *Pattern Recognit. Lett.*, *51*, 94–100, 2015.

27. Ryu, H., Park, J., Shin, H., Classification of heart sound recordings using convolution neural network, in: *2016 Computing in Cardiology Conference (CinC)*, 2016, September, IEEE, pp. 1153–1156.

28. Singh, S.A. and Majumder, S., Classification of unsegmented heart sound recording using KNN classifier. *J. Mech. Med. Biol.*, *19*, 04, 1950025, 2019.

29. Thalmayer, A., Zeising, S., Fischer, G., Kirchner, J., A Robust and Real-Time Capable Envelope-Based Algorithm for Heart Sound Classification: Validation under Different Physiological Conditions. *Sensors*, *20*, 4, 972, 2020.

30. Thiyagaraja, S.R., Dantu, R., Shrestha, P.L., Chitnis, A., Thompson, M.A., Anumandla, P.T., Dantu, S., A novel heart-mobile interface for detection and classification of heart sounds. *Biomed. Signal Process. Control*, *45*, 313–324, 2018.

31. Torrisi, A., Farinella, G.M., Puglisi, G., Battiato, S., Selecting discriminative CLBP patterns for age estimation, in: *2015 IEEE International Conference on Multimedia & Expo Workshops (ICMEW)*, 2015, June, IEEE, pp. 1–6.

32. Tschannen, M., Kramer, T., Marti, G., Heinzmann, M., Wiatowski, T., Heart sound classification using deep structured features, in: *2016 Computing in Cardiology Conference (CinC)*, 2016, September, IEEE, pp. 565–568.

33. Umar, A.A., Saaid, I.M., Sulaimon, A.A., An SVM-Based Classification and Stability Analysis of Synthetic Emulsions Co-Stabilized by a Nonionic Surfactant and Laponite Clay, in: *Science and Technology Behind Nanoemulsions*, 2018.

34. Wang, X., Jin, C., Liu, W., Hu, M., Xu, L., Ren, F., Feature fusion of HOG and WLD for facial expression recognition, in: *Proceedings of the 2013 IEEE/SICE International Symposium on System Integration*, 2013, December, IEEE, pp. 227–232.

35. Wu, M.J., Chen, Z.S., Jang, J.S.R., Ren, J.M., Li, Y.H., Lu, C.H., Combining visual and acoustic features for music genre classification, in: *2011 10th International Conference on Machine Learning and Applications and Workshops*, 2011, December, vol. 2, IEEE, pp. 124–129.

36. Xu, Y., Chen, H., Heidari, A.A., Luo, J., Zhang, Q., Zhao, X., Li, C., An efficient chaotic mutative moth-flame-inspired optimizer for global optimization tasks. *Expert Syst. Appl.*, *129*, 135–155, 2019.

37. Yadav, A., Dutta, M.K., Travieso, C.M., Alonso, J.B., Automatic Classification of Normal and Abnormal PCG Recording Heart Sound Recording Using Fourier Transform, in: *2018 IEEE International Work Conference on Bioinspired Intelligence (IWOBI)*, 2018, July, IEEE, pp. 1–9.

38. Zhang, W. and Han, J., Towards heart sound classification without segmentation using convolutional neural network, in: *2017 Computing in Cardiology (CinC)*, 2017, September, IEEE, pp. 1–4.

39. Zeng, H., Zhang, R., Huang, M., Wang, X., Compact local directional texture pattern for local image description. *Adv. Multimedia, 2015*, 2015.

6

Improving Multi-Label Classification in Prototype Selection Scenario

Himanshu Suyal* and Avtar Singh

Department of Computer Science and Engineering, Dr B R Ambedkar National Institute of Technology, Jalandhar, India

Abstract

ML-KNN is the one of the most common multi-label classifications, which is a modified version of the KNN. It is very simple yet powerful algorithm which always gives the promising results. Although it is very simple, the main hindrance of the classifier is the higher time complexity as well as sensitivity toward noise in the data set. To overcome this problem, prototype selection can be performed carefully. Prototype is the process to reduce the training data sets by selecting the most profitable prototype of the training data sets although prototype selections always compromise the accuracy of the algorithms. In this paper, a novel approach has been proposed to select the prototype without dropout the accuracy of the multi-label classification algorithm. To obtain the above objective, the well-known clustering algorithms are used to select the prototype by removing non-prominent data from the training data sets. The results show the improvement on ML-KNN.

Keywords: ML-KNN, prototype, multi-label classification, clustering

6.1 Introduction

Classification has widely played very important roles in many application fields and now became the hot research topic in the last decade. Classification is the process of assigning the incoming data into the predefine classes or labels. Principally, classification process contains the two foremost stages: one is erection, the asymptotic model by using some training mechanisms, training the model, and adopting some relation between input and output (label) using training data by providing inputs (text instances) as well as outputs (labels), so that the model is capable of classifying the unknown incoming text; in the second stage, classifying the unknown text or data by using the train asymptotic model. According to the belongings or labels, classification can be categorized into two classes: one is single-label and the other is multi-label. Single-label classification is assigning the data to single class

---

*Corresponding author: himanshus.cs.19@nitj.ac.in

Om Prakash Jena, Alok Ranjan Tripathy, Ahmed A. Elngar and Zdzislaw Polkowski (eds.) Computational Intelligence and Healthcare Informatics, (103–120) © 2021 Scrivener Publishing LLC

or label simultaneously; although, single-label classification is strong enough to deal with the real-time problems, but for some problems which does not contain single-label rule, for example, a document can be belong to the certain category like financial and economical, simultaneously [1, 2]. In Twitter, a tweet can belong to the deal and event category simultaneously. In image classification, any image can be belong to the certain category like beach, water, and sand [3]. Single-label classification algorithm is not capable to deal that kind of problems, so multi-label classification algorithm came into the picture.

Multi-label classification is the process to classify the data which belongs to the more than one class or labels simultaneously. Comparing the multi class problems, multi-label is more complex because it deals with the multi class problems where each instance will belong to exactly one category or label, but in case of multi-label classification, every instance is supposed to belong to one or more than one category simultaneously. In the past decade, multi-label learning methodology is very healthy in the different domain like machine learning, text classification, information retrieval, pattern recognition, image retrieval, and data mining.

In multi-label classification, a certain document can belong to more than one category at the same time. Multi-label classification problem can be defined as follows: $D = \{d_1, d_2, d_3, d_4, ..., d_I\}$ is the multi-label data set containing I instances, $L = \{l_1, l_2, l_3, ..., l_n\}$ is the set of labels which contain the n labels, and $T = \{(d_1; L (d_1), (d_2; L (d_2), ..., (d_m; L (dim)\}$ is the training data set which is taken by independently and unknown distribution of the multi-label data set D, where $L (d) \in L$, $L (d_1), L (d_2), ..., L (d_m)$ is the label associated with instance $d_1, d_2, ..., d_m$, respectively. In multi-label classification, the value of $L (d_1), L (d_2), ..., L (d_m)$ can be maximum n. The aim of the multi-label classification is to find out the classifier h: $D \rightarrow L$ which map the incoming data into the labels.

In the previous research, several methods are developed by the researcher: one approach to solve the multi-label problems is by treating the multi-label problems as a single label, where each instance belongs to the only single disjoint label simultaneously by decomposing the multi-label problem into a single-label and then using some traditional method used for classification. However, this method is capable to classify the multi-label document, somehow, but contains the weak accuracy due to less Co relations between the labels [1, 4, 5]. So later on, some researcher extends the traditional learning methods with some restriction and add-ons to improve the accuracy of the previous algorithms. Several approaches were designed to solve the multi-label problems like multi-label text categorization algorithms [1, 6, 15, 22], multi-label decision trees [7, 8, 24, 25], multi-label kernel [10], and multi-label neural networks [9, 11, 26, 27]. Another way to solve the problems is by extending the well-known lazy approach k-NN (k-nearest neighbors) [12] to ML-KNN [13], IBLR [14], BSVM [1], and BP-MLL [16].

Prototype selection (PS) methods [17] are the process to select the prototype based on some criteria's without compromising the accuracy of the classifier. Main aim of the PS is to reduce the training data set by selecting the more relevant data for training. Depending on the methods used, it selects the subset from the training set which is less noisy, less redundant, or both. The PS method can be widely classified into mainly three categories: edition, condensation, and hybrid methods. Edition methods remove the noisy and faulty data to increase the accuracy of the classifier, condensation methods remove the irrelevant data which does not take any part of the classification, and finally, the goal of hybrid method is to remove the noisy data as well as irrelevant data.

The structure of the paper can briefly describe as follows: Section 6.2 contains the related work, Section 6.3 contains the ML-KNN, Section 6.4 contains the methodology, Section 6.5 contains the performance evaluation, Section 6.6 contains the experiment and analysis, and Section 6.7 contains the conclusion and future works.

6.2   Related Work

This section briefly explains the previous works. Researchers are mainly motivated toward multi-label classification due to the ambiguity problem in text classification where one document may be belong to several classes simultaneously. Let $X = \{x_1, x_2, x_3, x_4, ..., x_i\}$ be a domain of instances, and then, multi-label data $D = \{(x_1, y_1), (x_2, y_2), (x_3, y_3), ..., (x_i, y_i)\}$ and $Y = \{1, 2, 3, ..., Q\}$ is set of label. In single-label classification $\forall x \in X$, there should be only single value of y, but in multi-label classification $\forall x \in X$, there can be 2^Y value. To resolve the multi-label problem, one of the best and intuitive approaches is to convert multi-label data set into single-label data set. Mainly, there are three types of strategy that can be used: first is make q replica of each instances with their class label, then select those replica with their label which are related to the particular instance, and rest will be ignored. Another approach is used to extend the capabilities of the prevailing single-label classification algorithms so that it can classify the multi-label data set. One of the most intuitive approaches is ML-KNN [13] which extends the most widely used KNN [12] algorithm. ML-KNN used the k nearest instance and maximum posteriori principal for classification. ML-KNN used the most common Binary Relevance (BR) [17] strategy, which distributes the each instances with all labels, and if for instance it belongs to the label, then it is marked as positive, otherwise negative. Although ML-KNN is very simple, it has many drawbacks [18]. Mainly, it has two weaknesses that impact on the greatness of the ML-KNN. First one is the high CPU cost and high space requirement due to the need of training data which led to higher complexity of the algorithm. Second one is the sensitivity toward the noisy data.

Several approaches and studies have been suggested to overcome the above problem, and PS method can be very healthy. PS method is a process to select those prototypes or instances which are relevant to the label and reduce the size of training data as well as reduce the sensitivity toward the noisy data. A formal definition of the PS method is that we have to select the subset S (S from the training data TD where subset S is selected by applying the PS algorithm. There are wide ranges of methods available which can be classified into three categories: editing, condensing, and hybrid. Editing method is used to remove those prototypes which may lead toward the misclassification or eliminating those prototypes which are lying in the boundary with several label so might be confuse the classifier. Condensing method is used to select those prototypes which are nearest to the labels and discard those prototypes which are far away from the labels. Hybrid method compromises both the above method to improve the accuracy.

Although the aim of the PS method is to reduce the training data set without reducing the semantic information of the original training data set, many researchers focus to improve the PS methods through some data reduction [16]. Some researchers extend the algorithms to improve the accuracy by incorporating the PS methods or by using the hybrid feature selection methods with PS using evolutionary algorithms (EA).

ML-KNN

There are several approaches that have been adopted for multi-label from well-known KNN algorithm [18–20]. ML-KNN is one of the multi-label learning approaches, which is basically adopted from the KNN and based on the maximum a posterior principal (MAP) [21]. ML-KNN is basically used the approach in which any instance of the data can belong to the label L based on the information of the neighbor. For given instance, x can belong to certain label L(x) where L(x) ⊆ L, ML-KNN is used firstly find out the k neighbors from the training data set, and it counts the identical neighbors and cluster the neighbors based on the labels. Then, maximum posterior principal is used to find out the label for the given text instance. Posterior probability can be described as follows:

$$P(L_i \in L(x) | v) = \frac{p(v | L_i \in L(x)).p(v | L_i \in L(x))}{p(v)}$$

where v $(0 \le v \le k)$ belongs to the number of neighbors of each class. For each label L_i, a classifier H(x) can be defined as follows:

$$H(x) = \begin{cases} 1, p(L_i \in L(x) | v > p(L_i \notin L(x) | v \\ 0, \text{otherwise} \end{cases}$$

where V is in between 0 and k, if the value of $H_i(x)$ is equal to 1, it indicates that label L_i belongs to the x real label set; otherwise, for the 0, it does not.

KNN has mainly two disadvantages: One is the high time complexity, and whenever number of training data is increase, the CPU time cost is also increase, and another disadvantage of the K-neighbor classifier is that it is very sensitive for the noisy data. To overcome above two problems in this paper, PS methods are used. PS methods reduce the training data as well as remove the noisy data.

6.3   Methodology

Problem Statement

Multi-label classification problem is supposed to be defined as follows: D = {$d_1, d_2, d_3, d_4, \ldots, d_i$} is the multi-label data set containing i instances, and L= {$l_1, l_2, l_3, \ldots, l_n$} is the set of labels which contain the n labels, and T = {$(d_1; L(d_1), (d_2; L(d_2), \ldots, (d_m; L(d_m))$} is the training data set which is taken by independently and unknown distribution of the multi-label data set D, where L(d) ∈ L, $L(d_1), L(d_2), \ldots, L(d_m)$ is the label associated with instance $d_1, d_2, \ldots \ldots d_m$, respectively. In multi-label classification, the value of $L(d_1), L(d_2), \ldots, L(d_m)$ can be maximum n. The aim of the multi-label classification is to get the classifier h: D → L which map the incoming data into the labels.

PS method is used to reduce the training data. PS method takes in training data T as input data and reduces data R as an output where R ⊂ T, R denotes the reduce data and T denotes the training data; as a results of this reduction, the accuracy of the algorithm will be affected. This work proposes a strategy to reduce the training data, thus reducing the data that causes the reduction of the complexity without too much compromising the accuracy. This can be achieved by selecting the prominent data for training. Our work can be concise to the four main phases given as below:

1. PS method given is used to reduce the whole training data.
2. Insist to give the whole training data reduces data given as an input of the classification algorithm to create the hypothesis.
3. Hypothesis generated by the step 2 is used for the classification of the data.

The whole process can be summarized using Figure 6.1.

Algorithm 6.1 *Prototype selection based on the DBSCAN clustering algorithm.*
Input: Training data $T = \{(d_1; L(d_1), (d_2; L(d_2), ..., (d_m; L(d_m)\}$
Output: Reduce Training data R where $R \subset T$

1. Let R be initially set to T
2. Repeat
3. for all $x \in T$ do
4. Apply DBSCAN clustering algorithm
5. If x is misclassified then
6. $R = R-\{x\}$
7. end if
8. end for

Algorithm 6.2 *Prototype selection based on the SUBCLU clustering algorithm.*
Input: Training data $T = \{(d_1; L(d_1), (d_2; L(d_2), ..., (d_m; L(d_m)\}$
Output: Reduce Training data R where $R \subset T$

1. Let R be initially set to T
2. Repeat
for all $x \in T$ do
3. Apply SUBCLU clustering algorithm
4. If x is misclassified then
5. $R = R-\{x\}$
6. end if
7. end for

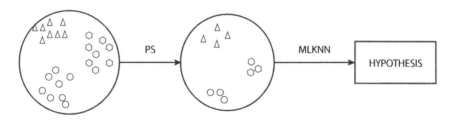

Figure 6.1 Process of proposed model.

6.3.1   Experiments and Evaluation

Experimental Setup
We used well-known clustering algorithms to select the prominent data for classification as PS methods, and these are described below:

> **DBSCAN Using Center (DBS_C) [23]:** Obtain the subset S by selecting the training data T such that DBSCAN method is used to clustering and selecting each center point that forms each cluster.
> **DBSCAN Using Boundary (DBS_B) [23]:** Obtain the subset S by selecting the training data T such that DBSCAN method is used to clustering and selecting each boundary point that forms each cluster.
> **DBSCAN Using Absolute Boundary (DBS_A) [23]:** Obtain the subset S by selecting the training data T such that DBSCAN method is used to clustering and selecting each absolute boundary point that forms each cluster.

> **SUBCLU Using Center (SABS_C) [15]:** Obtain the subset S by selecting the training data T such that SUBCLU method is used to clustering and selecting each center point that forms each cluster.
> **SUBCLU Using Boundary (SABS_B) [15]:** Obtain the subset S by selecting the training data T such that SUBCLU method is used to clustering and selecting each boundary point that forms each cluster.
> **SUBCLU Using Absolute Boundary (SABS_A) [15]:** Obtain the subset S by selecting the training data T such that SUBCLU method is used to clustering and selecting each absolute boundary point that forms each cluster.

6.4   Performance Evaluation

Performance evaluation of the multi-label classification seems to be different from single-label where we can find the accuracy by seeing the test instance that is correctly classified or not, and there exist some sets of standard evaluation metrics like precision and recall [25]. For measuring the performance of our algorithm, we are using three measurement methods. The first one is One-Error, which is used to measure classification error for multi-label classification. Other two is based on the information retrieval and widely used to find the performance of classification algorithm which is based on the label ranking.

The output of the multi-label learning system can be viewed as a function $f: X \times Y \to \mathbb{R}$, in which the rank of the label is according to $f(x, .)$ in such a way that label L_1 is considerably higher rank to the label L_2 if and only if $f(x, L_1) > f(x, L_2)$.

For the sake of the simplicity, this paper refers to the rank of the label L for the any given instance x under the function f that is denoted by the function $rank_f(x, L)$.

One-Error: This measures the error in which how many times the top ranked labels were not belong to the set of possible task. This paper denoted the One-Error of h hypothesis H by the function One-Error (H) for the given test set of TS = $\{(x_1, y_1), (x_2, y_2), ..., (x_n, y_n)\}$

$(x_i \in X, y_i \in Y)$ having the n number of instance and let $Y = \{1, 2, 3, 4, \ldots, L\}$ where L is the no of labels. One-Error (H) can be defined as follows:

$$\text{One-Error}_{TS}(H) = \frac{1}{n} \sum_{i=1}^{n} [H(x_i) \notin y_i] \tag{6.1}$$

where hypothesis H can be defined for the classifier H: $X \rightarrow Y$ which assign the any single-label x by setting $H(x) = arg\ max_{L \in y}\ f(x_1, y)$.

Hamming Loss: Hamming Loss is used to predict how accurately the classifier classifies the data by evaluating how many times instance-label pair misclassified. Hamming Loss denoted as a function H_Loss_{TS} (H) can be defined as follows:

$$H\_Loss_{TS}(H) = \frac{1}{n} \sum_{i=1}^{n} \frac{1}{L} |H(x_i) \boxed{\Delta} y_i|$$

where $\boxed{\Delta}$ denoted the symmetric difference of the two sets.

Average Precision: Average Precision is used to evaluate the document ranking for Information Retrieval (IR) system. Average Precision of a hypothesis can be defined as Avg_Prec (H).

$$\text{Avg\_Prec}(H) = \frac{1}{n} \sum_{i=1}^{n} \frac{1}{|y_i|} \sum_{L \in y_i} \left| \frac{y' | rank_f(x_i, L') \le rank_f(x_i, L)|}{rank_f(x_i, L)} \right|$$

6.5   Experiment Data Set

This paper used a total of four most popular multi-label data sets used from the multiple domain, and the description of the data sets revealed on the Table 6.1. Given a multi-label data $D = (x_1, L_i)$ where $1 <= I <= n$, we use $|D|$ that represents the number of instances, f_D represents the number of features, and L_D represents the total number of labels.

Table 6.1 Experimental data sets description.

Data set	$|D|$	f_D	L_D	Domain
Yeast	2417	103	14	Biology
Scene	2407	294	6	Multimedia
Enron	1702	1001	53	Text
Medical	978	1449	45	Medical
Emotion	593	72	6	Multimedia

6.6   Experiment Results

This section shows the results obtain by using the approach which is represented on Section 6.3.

Experimental results are on the following tables, and for each evaluation criteria, ↓ means the lowest the value having the better performance and ↑ means the highest the value having the better performance. Table 6.2 shows the Hamming Loss of the different data sets, as the percentage reduction increases and eventually loss increases. Percentage reduction means we are reducing the data set, for example, percentage reduction is 0.2, it means that we reduce the data set by 20%.

Table 6.2 shows the comparative study of the hamming loss with the proposed algorithms, and results show the improvement of the ML-KNN as well as we reduce the data set by 20%. SABS_A gives the most promising results in terms of Hamming Loss.

Table 6.3 shows the comparative study of the proposed PS method with the ML-KNN, and results show the promising results. DBS_A gives the best results in terms of One-Error although SABS_C and SABS_A also give the good results.

Table 6.4 shows the comparative study of the proposed PS method with the ML-KNN, and results show the promising results. DBS_A gives the best results in terms of average precision although SABS_A and DBS_C also give the good results.

Table 6.2 Comparative study of Hamming Loss of proposed (at 20% reduction) with ML-KNN ↓.

Data set			Algorithm			
	ML-KNN	DBS_C	DBS_B	DBS_A	SABS_C	SABS_B	SABS_A
Yeast	0.195(4)	0.1907(1)	0.1945(3)	0.1907(1)	0.1924	0.1940(2)	0.1907(1)
Scene	0.169(7)	0.1010(4)	0.1135(6)	0.0970(2)	0.0994(3)	0.1101(5)	0.0933(1)
Enron	0.093(6)	0.0532(2)	0.0566(5)	0.0511(1)	0.0534(4)	0.0556(3)	0.0511(1)
Emotion	0.194(3)	0.2030(6)	0.2030(6)	0.1948(4)	0.1896(2)	0.1881(1)	0.1978(5)
Medical	0.0169(2)	0.0176(3)	0.0204(6)	0.0168(1)	0.0183(4)	0.0190(5)	0.0168(1)
Average	0.1335(5)	0.1131(4)	0.1543(7)	0.1100(2)	0.1106(3)	0.1136(6)	0.1099(1)

Table 6.3 Comparative study of One-Error of proposed (20% reduction) with ML-KNN ↓.

Data set	Algorithm					
	ML-KNN	DBS_C	DBS_B	DBS_A	SABS_C	SABS_B	SABS_A
Yeast	0.2280(5)	0.2209(1)	0.2298(6)	0.2233(3)	0.2218(2)	0.2246(4)	0.2233(3)
Scene	0.3000(7)	0.2591(3)	0.2947(6)	0.2511(1)	0.2650(4)	0.2697(5)	0.2515(2)
Enron	0.3130(4)	0.2632(1)	0.2633(2)	0.2690(3)	0.2632(1)	0.3275(5)	0.2690(3)
Emotion	0.2630(6)	0.2030(5)	0.2030(5)	0.1948(3)	0.1896(2)	0.1881(1)	0.1978(4)
Medical	0.2520(6)	0.0176(2)	0.0204(5)	0.0168(1)	0.0183(3)	0.0190(4)	0.0168(1)
Average	0.2712(7)	0.1929(4)	0.2022(5)	0.1910(1)	0.1915(2)	0.2057(6)	0.1916(3)

Table 6.4 Comparative study of average precision of proposed (20% reduction) with ML-KNN ↑.

Data set				Algorithm			
	ML-KNN	DBS_C	DBS_B	DBS_A	SABS_C	SABS_B	SABS_A
Yeast	0.7660(3)	0.7649(4)	0.7642(5)	0.7684(2)	0.7699(1)	0.7584(6)	0.7684(2)
Scene	0.8030(7)	0.8507(3)	0.8271(5)	0.8574(1)	0.8486(4)	0.8209(6)	0.8561(2)
Enron	0.6260(6)	0.6516(2)	0.6276(5)	0.6568(1)	0.6502(4)	0.6093(7)	0.6508(3)
Emotion	0.7990(3)	0.7959(4)	0.7888(5)	0.8026(1)	0.7831(6)	0.7991(2)	0.8026(1)
Medical	0.8060(1)	0.7949(3)	0.6748(6)	0.7927(4)	0.7989(2)	0.7015(5)	0.7927(4)
Average	.7600(5)	0.7716(3)	0.7365(7)	0.7758(1)	0.7701(4)	0.7379(6)	0.7741(2)

Table 6.5 shows the Hamming Loss of the ML-KNN algorithm by applying the PS algorithms and the results clearly show that the DBSCAN using absolute boundary (DBS_A) and SUBCLU using absolute boundary (SABS_A) give the most promising results. As the percentage reduction increases, Hamming Loss also increases; in the results, we reduce the data set from 20% to 70% which is about 50% reduction of the data that just increase the Hamming Loss of the Yeast data to 1.94%, the Scene data to 1.13%, the Enron data set to 0.02%, the Emotion data set to 3.93%, and the Medical data set to 11%.

Table 6.6 shows the One-Error of the different data set by applying the proposed PS algorithm; the less the One-Error, the more the performance, and it results clearly show that DBSCAN absolute boundary and SUBCLU absolute boundary give the promising results. As the percentage reduction is increasing, the One-Error is also increasing. After reducing data set to about 50%, the One-Error increases about 4.11% for the Yeast data set, 4.06% for the Scene data set, 16% for the Enron data set, 23.32% for the Emotions data set, and 18.74% for the Medical data set.

Table 6.7 shows the average precision of the different data set by applying the proposed algorithms; the more the average precision, the better the performance. The results show that DBSCAN and SUBCLU with absolute boundary give with the most promising results. After reducing the data to about 50%, the average precision of the Yeast data set reduces to 0.6%, 1.1% for the Scene data set, 1.5% for the Enron data set, 4.8% for the Emotion data set, and 4.6% for the Medical data set.

Figure 6.2 shows the performance of the ML-KNN by applying proposed PS algorithm on the Yeast data set. For the yeast data, DBSCAN at absolute boundary gives the most promising results, and SUBCLU at absolute boundary also gives the good results.

Figure 6.3 shows the performance of the ML-KNN by applying the proposed PS algorithm on the Scene data set. For the scene data set, DBSCAN at absolute boundary gives the most promising results.

Figure 6.4 shows the performance of the ML-KNN by applying proposed PS algorithm on the Emotion data set. As shown in the figure, SUBCLU at absolute boundary gives the most prominent results although DBSCAN at absolute boundary also giving the good results.

Figure 6.5 shows the performance of the ML-KNN by applying the proposed PS algorithm on the Enron data set. For the Enron data set, SUBCLU at absolute boundary gives the better results compared to the other proposed algorithms.

Table 6.5 Experimental result 1: Hamming Loss ↓.

Data set	Per_Red	DBS_C	DBS_B	DBS_A	SABS_C	SABS_B	SABS_A
Yeast	.2	0.1907	0.1945	0.1907	0.1924	0.1940	0.1907
	.3	0.1931	0.1946	0.1909	0.1929	0.1938	0.1909
	.4	0.1941	0.1963	0.1916	0.1944	0.1956	0.1916
	.5	0.1979	0.2002	0.1921	0.1995	0.1958	0.1913
	.6	0.1981	0.2001	0.1923	0.2013	0.1961	0.1923
	.7	0.1983	0.2007	0.1944	0.2014	0.2000	0.1944
Scene	.2	0.1010	0.1135	0.0970	0.0994	0.1101	0.0933
	.3	0.1020	0.1146	0.090	0.1054	0.1149	0.0970
	.4	0.1020	0.1138	0.0994	0.1058	0.1184	0.0990
	.5	0.1106	0.1151	0.1010	0.1059	0.1175	0.1010
	.6	0.1177	0.1154	0.1043	0.1077	0.1185	0.1043
	.7	0.1179	0.1156	0.1144	0.1091	0.1188	0.1046
Enron	.2	0.0532	0.0566	0.0511	0.0534	0.0556	0.0511
	.3	0.0527	0.0556	0.0506	0.0529	0.0545	0.0506
	.4	0.0551	0.0554	0.0514	0.0554	0.0536	0.0514
	.5	0.0551	0.0566	0.0518	0.0568	0.0556	0.0518
	.6	0.0547	0.0553	0.0512	0.0580	0.0544	0.0512
	.7	0.0536	0.0556	0.0502	0.0543	0.0538	0.0502
Emotion	.2	0.2030	0.2030	0.1948	0.1896	0.1881	0.1978
	.3	0.2052	0.2126	0.1978	0.2096	0.1956	0.1978
	.4	0.2111	0.2129	0.1978	0.2074	0.2044	0.1988
	.5	0.2244	0.2141	0.2096	0.2119	0.2035	0.2096
	.6	0.2519	0.2259	0.2119	0.2556	0.2089	0.2119
	.7	0.2521	0.2407	0.2281	0.2556	0.2274	0.2281
Medical	.2	0.0176	0.0204	0.0168	0.0183	0.0190	0.0168
	.3	0.0174	0.0209	0.0167	0.0181	0.0192	0.0165
	.4	0.0188	0.0210	0.0168	0.0182	0.0195	0.0168
	.5	0.0190	0.0211	0.0168	0.0183	0.0194	0.0168
	.6	0.0213	0.0215	0.0175	0.0193	0.0219	0.0175
	.7	0.0217	0.0225	0.0188	0.0211	0.0229	0.0188

Table 6.6 Experimental result 2: One-Error ↓.

Data set	Per_Red	DB_C	DB_B	DB_A	SAB_C	SAB_B	SAB_A
Yeast	.2	0.2209	0.2298	0.2233	0.2218	0.2246	0.2233
	.3	0.2298	0.2295	0.2244	0.2298	0.2240	0.2244
	.4	0.2331	0.2294	0.2244	0.2320	0.2375	0.2244
	.5	0.2353	0.2332	0.2288	0.2365	0.2309	0.2288
	.6	0.2440	0.2347	0.2278	0.2462	0.2407	0.2268
	.7	0.2449	0.2348	0.2300	0.2505	0.2497	0.2300
Scene	.2	0.2591	0.2947	0.2511	0.2650	0.2697	0.2515
	.3	0.2625	0.2930	0.2540	0.2684	0.2879	0.2540
	.4	0.2693	0.2972	0.2622	0.2752	0.2913	0.2623
	.5	0.2743	0.2997	0.2666	0.2820	0.2951	0.2666
	.6	0.2820	0.3057	0.2688	0.2859	0.2921	0.2680
	.7	0.2947	0.3058	0.2613	0.2821	0.2937	0.2769
Enron	.2	0.2632	0.2633	0.2690	0.2632	0.3275	0.2690
	.3	0.2924	0.3099	0.2807	0.2865	0.3275	0.2807
	.4	0.3033	0.2924	0.2865	0.3099	0.3567	0.2865
	.5	0.3099	0.3009	0.2849	0.3009	0.3492	0.2849
	.6	0.3275	0.3216	0.2865	0.3216	0.3509	0.2865
	.7	0.3275	0.3241	0.2924	0.3299	0.3524	0.2924
Emotion	.2	0.2844	0.3333	0.2667	0.2756	0.2622	0.2667
	.3	0.3111	0.2889	0.2667	0.2978	0.2933	0.2667
	.4	0.3289	0.2978	0.2800	0.3156	0.2889	0.2800
	.5	0.3689	0.3022	0.2889	0.3467	0.3156	0.2889
	.6	0.3600	0.3467	0.3156	0.3733	0.3289	0.3156
	.7	0.4311	0.3911	0.3289	0.3333	0.3511	0.3289
Medical	.2	0.2668	0.4097	0.2588	0.2507	0.4016	0.2588
	.3	0.2722	0.3423	0.2938	0.2749	0.3720	0.2938
	.4	0.3154	0.4070	0.2642	0.3181	0.3854	0.2642
	.5	0.3127	0.3558	0.2668	0.3235	0.3342	0.2668
	.6	0.3639	0.3558	0.2911	0.3558	0.4124	0.2911
	.7	0.4394	0.4340	0.3073	0.4286	0.4259	0.3073

Table 6.7 Experimental result 3: Average Precision ↑.

Data set	Per_Red	DB_C	DB_B	DB_A	SAB_C	SAB_B	SAB_A
Yeast	.2	0.7649	0.7642	0.7684	0.7699	0.7584	0.7684
	.3	0.7632	0.7642	0.7683	0.7609	0.7585	0.7676
	.4	0.7635	0.7632	0.7676	0.7595	0.7581	0.7683
	.5	0.7641	0.7629	0.7658	0.7592	0.7604	0.7658
	.6	0.7639	0.7635	0.7680	0.7474	0.7538	0.7655
	.7	0.7618	0.7627	0.7660	0.7457	0.7486	0.7650
Scene	.2	0.8507	0.8271	0.8574	0.8486	0.8209	0.8561
	.3	0.8452	0.8280	0.8579	0.8440	0.8355	0.8543
	.4	0.8437	0.8267	0.8501	0.8380	0.8308	0.8479
	.5	0.8363	0.8188	0.8487	0.8336	0.8334	0.8471
	.6	0.8300	0.8144	0.8489	0.8303	0.8268	0.8474
	.7	0.8220	0.8140	0.8479	0.8211	0.8277	0.8470
Enron	.2	0.6516	0.6276	0.6568	0.6502	0.6093	0.6508
	.3	0.6406	0.6206	0.6512	0.6431	0.6191	0.6512
	.4	0.6232	0.6140	0.6451	0.6361	0.6151	0.6451
	.5	0.6251	0.6114	0.6493	0.6141	0.6178	0.6493
	.6	0.6182	0.6144	0.6468	0.6059	0.6145	0.6468
	.7	0.6119	0.6074	0.6469	0.6027	0.6125	0.6469
Emotion	.2	0.7959	0.7888	0.8026	0.7831	0.7991	0.8026
	.3	0.7740	0.7739	0.8026	0.7755	0.7761	0.8031
	.4	0.7656	0.7731	0.7926	0.7704	0.7830	0.7956
	.5	0.7388	0.7762	0.7823	0.7655	0.7669	0.7823
	.6	0.7241	0.7455	0.7762	0.7390	0.7536	0.7762
	.7	0.7194	0.7281	0.7634	0.7161	0.7444	0.7634
Medical	.2	0.7949	0.6748	0.7927	0.7989	0.7015	0.7927
	.3	0.7837	0.7282	0.7770	0.7869	0.6905	0.7770
	.4	0.7602	0.6735	0.7890	0.7581	0.6817	0.7890
	.5	0.7619	0.7195	0.7826	0.7461	0.6529	0.7826
	.6	0.7121	0.6719	0.7681	0.7156	0.6570	0.7681
	.7	0.6536	0.6575	0.7557	0.6481	0.6638	0.7557

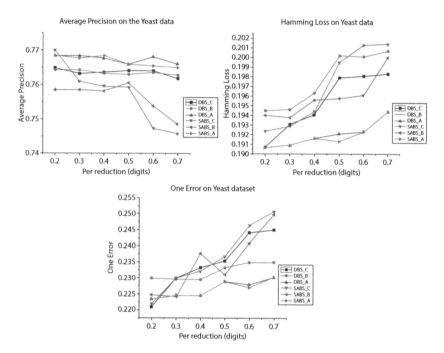

Figure 6.2 Performance on the Yeast data set.

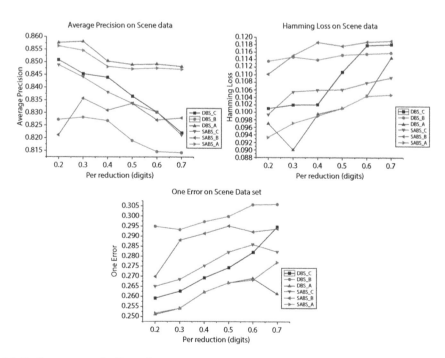

Figure 6.3 Performance on the Scene data set.

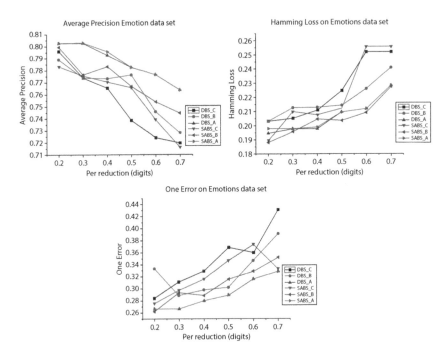

Figure 6.4 Performance of the Emotion data set.

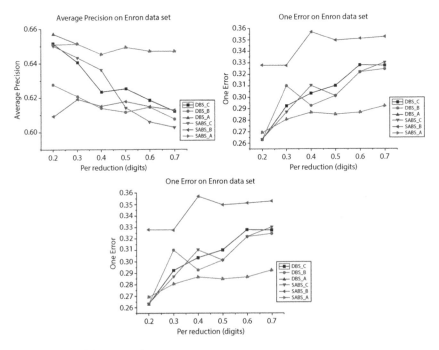

Figure 6.5 Performance if the Enron data set.

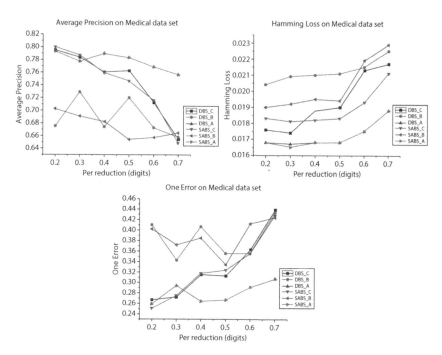

Figure 6.6 Performance if the Medical data set.

Figure 6.6 shows the performance of the ML-KNN by applying the proposed PS algorithm on the Medical data set. As shown in the figure, SUBCLU at absolute boundary gives the most promising results.

6.7 Conclusion

ML-KNN is most simple algorithm for multi-label data set and always gives the most promising results. In this context, PS can be very healthy to improve the accuracy of the ML-KNN as well by reducing the data set by reducing the noisy data. Although, the PS method always lead to reduce the accuracy. In the end of this paper, we proposed novel approach of PS in which we reduce the data by using well-known clustering algorithms and use the reduce data as input for the ML-KNN.

Experimental results show the improvement in the performance of the ML-KNN by approximate 3% as well as reduce the data by 20%. At the end, we reduce the data up to 70% and our experimental results showing that it is not affecting to much the performance of the ML-KNN. In addition, it came into notice that PS method which uses data at absolute boundary giving the remarkable profitable results.

References

1. Boutell, M.R., Luo, J., Shen, X., Brown, C.M., Learning multi-label scene classification. *Pattern Recognit.*, 37, 9, 1757–1771, 2004.

2. Brinker, K. and Hüllermeier, E., Case-Based Multilabel Ranking, in: *IJCAI*, 2007, January, pp. 702–707.

3. Buckland, M. and Gey, F., The relationship between recall and precision. *J. Am. Soc. Inf. Sci.*, 45, 1, 12–19, 1994.

4. Cevikalp, H., Benligiray, B., Gerek, O.N., Semi-supervised robust deep neural networks for multi-label image classification. *Pattern Recognit.*, 100, 107164, 2020.

5. Chen, G., Ye, D., Xing, Z., Chen, J., Cambria, E., Ensemble application of convolutional and recurrent neural networks for multi-label text categorization, in: *2017 International Joint Conference on Neural Networks (IJCNN)*, 2017, May, IEEE, pp. 2377–2383.

6. Cheng, W. and Hüllermeier, E., Combining instance-based learning and logistic regression for multilabel classification. *Mach. Learn.*, 76, 2–3, 211–225, 2009.

7. Clare, A. and King, R.D., Knowledge discovery in multi-label phenotype data, in: *European conference on principles of data mining and knowledge discovery*, 2001, September, Springer, Berlin, Heidelberg, pp. 42–53.

8. Dasarathy, B.V., Data mining tasks and methods: Classification: Nearest-neighbor approaches, in: *Handbook of data mining and knowledge discovery*, pp. 288–298, 2002.

9. De Comité, F., Gilleron, R., Tommasi, M., Learning multi-label alternating decision trees from texts and data, in: *International workshop on machine learning and data mining in pattern recognition*, 2003, July, Springer, Berlin, Heidelberg, pp. 35–49.

10. Elisseeff, A. and Weston, J., A kernel method for multi-labelled classification, in: *NIPS*, 2001, December, vol. 14, pp. 681–687.

11. Cevikalp, H., Benligiray, B., Gerek, O.N., Semi-supervised robust deep neural networks for multi-label image classification. *Pattern Recognit.*, 100, 107164, 2020.

12. Gao, S., Wu, W., Lee, C.H., Chua, T.S., A MFoM learning approach to robust multiclass multi-label text categorization, in: *Proceedings of the twenty-first international conference on Machine learning*, 2004, July, p. 42.

13. García, S., Luengo, J., Herrera, F., *Data pre-processing in data mining*, vol. 72, Springer International Publishing, Cham, Switzerland, 2015.

14. Hinneburg, A. and Gabriel, H.H., Denclue 2.0: Fast clustering based on kernel density estimation, in: *International symposium on intelligent data analysis*, 2007, September, Springer, Berlin, Heidelberg, pp. 70–80.

15. Kailing, K., Kriegel, H.P., Kröger, P., Density-connected subspace clustering for high-dimensional data, in: *Proceedings of the 2004 SIAM international conference on data mining*, 2004, April, Society for Industrial and Applied Mathematics, pp. 246–256.

16. Kazawa, H., Izumitani, T., Taira, H., Maeda, E., Maximal margin labeling for multi-topic text categorization, in: *Proceedings of the 17th International Conference on Neural Information Processing Systems*, 2004, December, pp. 649–656.

17. Khandagale, S., Xiao, H., Babbar, R., Bonsai: diverse and shallow trees for extreme multi-label classification. *Mach. Learn.*, 109, 11, 2099–2119, 2020.

18. Kohavi, R., Sommerfield, D., Dougherty, J., Data mining using a machine learning library in C++. *Int. J. Artif. Intell. Tools*, 6, 04, 537–566, 1997.

19. Lee, J., Yu, I., Park, J., Kim, D.W., Memetic feature selection for multilabel text categorization using label frequency difference. *Inf. Sci.*, 485, 263–280, 2019.

20. McCallum, A.K., Multi-label text classification with a mixture model trained by EM, in: *AAAI 99 workshop on text learning*, 1999.

21. Nanni, L. and Lumini, A., Prototype reduction techniques: A comparison among different approaches. *Expert Syst. Appl.*, 38, 9, 11820–11828, 2011.

22. Schapire, R.E. and Singer, Y., BoosTexter: A boosting-based system for text categorization. *Mach. Learn.*, 39, 2, 135–168, 2000.

23. Schubert, E., Sander, J., Ester, M., Kriegel, H.P., Xu, X., DBSCAN revisited, revisited: why and how you should (still) use DBSCAN. *ACM Trans. Database Syst. (TODS)*, 42, 3, 1–21, 2017.

24. Majzoubi, M., & Choromanska, A. Ldsm: Logarithm-depth streaming multi-label decision trees. In *International Conference on Artificial Intelligence and Statistics*, pp. 4247–4257, PMLR, 2020, June.

25. Wang, D. and Zhang, S., Unsupervised person re-identification via multi-label classification, in: *Proceedings of the IEEE/CVF Conference on Computer Vision and Pattern Recognition*, pp. 10981–10990, 2020.

26. Chen, G., Ye, D., Xing, Z., Chen, J., Cambria, E., Ensemble application of convolutional and recurrent neural networks for multi-label text categorization, in: *2017 International Joint Conference on Neural Networks (IJCNN)*, 2017, May, IEEE, pp. 2377–2383.

27. Kundalia, K., Patel, Y., Shah, M., Multi-label movie genre detection from a movie poster using knowledge transfer learning. *Augment. Hum. Res.*, 5, 1, 1–9, 2020.

7

A Machine Learning–Based Intelligent Computational Framework for the Prediction of Diabetes Disease

Maqsood Hayat*, Yar Muhammad and Muhammad Tahir

Department of Computer Science, Abdul Wali Khan University Mardan, KP, Pakistan

Abstract

In the healthcare system, machine learning performs a vital role because of its high capabilities in the identification and diagnosing of disease. Machine learning hypotheses have been effectively applied in numerous areas of healthcare especially in the diagnosis and prediction of chronic diseases such as Alzheimer's, heart, stroke, blood pressure, and diabetes, which have no permanent cure. Among these diseases, diabetes is a perilous and rapidly growing disease that increases the death ratio particularly in women across the world. The main causes of diabetes disease are immoral lifestyles, unhealthy food, and less awareness about health impacting factors. In order to avoid diabetes disease, there needs a system that can truly identify and diagnose diabetic patients on time and protect them from more damage. In this study, an intelligent computational predictive system is introduced for the identification and diagnosis of diabetes disease. Here, eight machine learning classification hypotheses are examined for the identification and diagnosis of diabetes disease. Numerous performance measuring metrics such as accuracy, sensitivity, specificity, AUC, F1-score, MCC, and ROC curve are applied to inspect the effectiveness and stability of the proposed model. The proposed model obtained quite promising results in terms of all metrics compared to the present models in the literature. It is expected that the recommended system will be valuable and supportive for the physician to identify diabetes disease correctly and successfully. Python is used for the implementation of classification hypotheses and experimental work.

Keywords: Diabetes disease, machine learning, classification hypotheses, disease prediction, computational framework

7.1 Introduction

Diabetes is a fatal and common type of chronic disease. Chronic diseases like Alzheimer's, heart, stroke, blood pressure, and diabetes are long-term diseases and having no permanent cure. Among these chronic diseases, diabetes is a perilous and rapidly growing chronic disease that increases the death ratio especially in women across the world. Diabetes Mellitus

Corresponding author: m.hayat@awkum.edu.pk; maqsood.hayat@gmail.com

Om Prakash Jena, Alok Ranjan Tripathy, Ahmed A. Elngar and Zdzislaw Polkowski (eds.) Computational Intelligence and Healthcare Informatics, (121–138) © 2021 Scrivener Publishing LLC

(DM) is a class of metabolic disorders primarily produced by irregular insulin emission and/or action [1]. In this disease, the blood sugar level of humans increases which causes different malfunctions of the human body. Diabetes is a long-lasting and tenacious disease that occurs because of the inefficient use of insulin generated by the human body. When diabetes disease happens, it increases the chances that various organs of the human body start function abnormally, i.e., it also increases the risk of malfunction of various organs particularly the blood vessels, nerves, kidneys, eyes, and heart [2]. World Health Organization (WHO) accomplished a survey on various diseases that causes death, i.e., deadliest diseases. According to their report, it will be considered the seventh most death-causing disease by 2030 [3]. According to another survey, around 642 million adults (1/10 adults) are likely to have diabetes disease in 2040 [4]. In 2012, 2.2 million people were expired owing to high blood glucose levels and approximately 1.6 million due to diabetes disease [5]. DM does not depend on the age of a human being it can happen to anyone, of any age and any time.

Three main types of diabetes are reported in the literature [5]: a) Type-1 diabetes also called childhood or juvenile diabetes, b) Type-2 diabetes also known as adult diabetes, and c) Type-3 diabetes also called gestational diabetes. Usually, Type-1 diabetes occurs owing to the less production of insulin and is mostly reported in small age human beings [5]. Type-2 is a widely known type of diabetes and is founded in a large number of people, mostly found in young age people [6]. It typically causes excessive weight and physical disorders of the human body. Type-3 diabetes is hyperglycemia that comes during pregnancy due to hormone alteration. Type-1 and type-2 diabetes are the last longings. However, a simple lifestyle and early detection can inhibit it from causing any sort of danger. The ratio of diabetes disease affected people increases day by day across the globe. China is the most affected country by diabetes disease where diabetic patients are founded in a very large number. According to a survey accomplished in 2019, an average of 116.4 million people was diabetic infected in china. According to this survey, India was on the second number with 77 million and the United States was on the third number with 31 million diabetic patients. Bangladesh is a poor country which is the most affected country by diabetes disease based on its financial state, and it is projected that the number of diabetes patients will be more than 16.0 million in 2022 [7].

Conventional techniques implemented for the diagnosis of diabetes disease were based on the medical history of a patient, test results, and inquiry of related symptoms by the doctor [8]. Several limitations, namely, high cost and various side effects, were reported in these methods. Conventional methods often lead to imprecise diagnosis and take more time due to human mistakes. Also, it is a very expensive and computational intensive approach for the diagnosis of disease and takes time in the assessment. Further, medical healthcare is a field in which a huge amount of biomedical data is generating continuously. So, classifying a large amount of data correctly and successfully is the main issue of these models.

Researchers have started to incorporate the concept of intelligence in developing different medical decision support systems to overcome the limitations of conventional methods, etc. [9]. These machine learning–based predictive models helped inaccurate diagnosis of disease, reducing cost and the reduction of death ratio caused by diabetes disease. As discussed in [10] the prediction and accuracy of the machine learning–based classification methods are way better than other data classification techniques. Various researchers conducted their research on diabetes from a different perspective but most of them work on the classification methodologies for the prediction and accuracy of diabetes disease by using various techniques [11]. Diabetes is a fatal disease and increasing death ratio day by day. Therefore, it needs to be diagnosed as early as possible to protect the patient from more damage. The main theme of this attempt is to reduce the cost of disease diagnosing and to obtain more efficient results in Medical Health Services (MHS). Another purpose of this work is to apply various machine learning classification hypotheses to determine whether a person has diabetes disease or not. Eight classification hypotheses such as K-nearest neighbor (KNN), Decision Tree (DT), Random Forest (RF), Logistic Regression (LR), Support Vector Machine (SVM), AdaBoost (AB), Gradient Boosting (GB), and Extra-Tree (ET) are applied for the identification of diabetes. In literature, the Pima Indian Diabetes Dataset (PIDD) has been extensively utilized by the researchers [12–14].

Quan Zou *et al.* [15] have used three classification hypotheses, i.e., DT, RF, and ANN, for the prediction of diabetes disease and yielded an accuracy of 72.75%, 76.04%, and 76.76%, respectively. Likewise, Nagarajan *et al.* [16] have used two classifiers such as Naïve Bayes (NB) and KNN and attained the classification accuracies of 73.87% and 75.96%, respectively. In the sequel, Hasan *et al.* [14] have used six classification hypotheses for diagnosing diabetes disease and attained the best accuracy of 74.0% through the NB classifier. Similarly, Sivanesan *et al.* [14] have investigated the J48 DT classifier for the identification of diabetes disease as a result obtained 76.58% of accuracy.

The contribution of the developed work is to introduce machine learning–based an intelligent medical decision support system for the diagnosis of diabetes disease. Different nature of learning classification hypotheses is analyzed. K-fold cross-validation is applied in this work for validating the results of utilized classification hypotheses. In K-fold cross-validation, the investigation was accomplished on different values of K (5, 7, and 10). The performance of learning hypotheses was evaluated by various performance evaluation matrices like accuracy, sensitivity, specificity, recall, f1-score, AUC-score, Matthews correlation coefficient (MCC), and ROC curve. Python has been used as a tool for implementing all the classifiers.

7.2 Materials and Methods

The subsection given below considers the research resources used and the approaches followed in this paper.

7.2.1 Dataset

The problem-related and well-organized dataset has a great effect on the performance of a computational model. Looking at the prominent role of the dataset, PIDD was utilized which is available online on the University of California Irvine (UCI) machine learning repository. PIDD is provided by the national institute of Kidney, Digestive, and Diabetes diseases [18]. It consists of 768 instances; each instance has eight distinct features. All the patients in the dataset are female and the minimum age of a patient in the dataset is 21 years. The true cases are 268, i.e., 268 females have diabetes disease and the numbers of false cases are 500, i.e., 500 females do not have diabetes disease. The ratio of true and false cases is 35.0% and 65.0%, respectively. To remove missing values from the dataset pre-processing techniques are applied. The target class consists of two subclasses, i.e., presence or absence of diabetes disease. Table 7.1 represents the complete description and information of the dataset [19].

Table 7.1 Information regarding Pima Indian diabetes dataset.

Feature no.	Feature name	Feature description
F1	Pregnancies	Pregnancy records
F2	Glucose	Plasma glucose concentration (2 hours in OGTT)
F3	BP	Blood Pressure in (mm Hg)
F4	Skin Thickness	Triceps with skin fold thickness (mm)
F5	Insulin	2-hour level of serum insulin record of patient
F6	BMI	Body Mass Index of patient
F7	DPF	Diabetes pedigree function
F8	Age	Age in years

7.2.2 Proposed Framework for Diabetes System

The core objective of the developed system is to diagnose diabetes disease in human beings. The framework of the developed system is accomplished in four stages that include dataset pre-processing, cross-validation technique, classification hypotheses, and performance evaluation of classifiers, which is depicted in Figure 7.1.

7.2.3 Pre-Processing of Data

The technique that transforms raw data into meaningful format and patterns is called data pre-processing. It is considered essential for a decent representation of data along with proper training and testing of learning hypotheses. Two pre-processing techniques, i.e., standard scalar and Min-Max scalar are used in this study and are applied to the dataset to use it efficiently.

7.3 Machine Learning Classification Hypotheses

Various machine learning hypotheses are used for the identification of diabetes disease. The importance of each classification hypothesis varies from application to application. Here, eight machine learning classification hypotheses are explored, to choose the preeminent and generalize prediction model. The classification hypotheses used in this study are discussed briefly below.

7.3.1 K-Nearest Neighbor

KNN is supervised learning applied for both classification and regression problems. Supervised learning is one in which the data is labeled, i.e., output is known while unsupervised learning is one in which data is unlabeled. In the KNN model, K values represent K

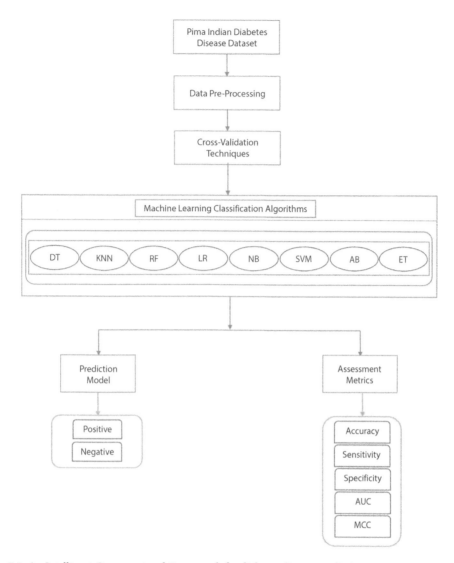

Figure 7.1 An Intelligent Computational Framework for diabetes disease prediction.

neighbor elements near to a point and then find the Euclidean distance between the point and K number of nearest neighbors, then it decides on the bases of average if it is near to more instances of a class then that point belongs to that class.

7.3.2   Decision Tree

DT is supervised learning, breaks a dataset into several small subsets, then at last combines these subsets and take a decision [20]. DT adopts a very simple and easily comprehendible approach for making a decision. DT has two types of nodes: internal and external. The internal nodes are responsible for making a decision. The leaf node has no child nodes and is associated with a label, i.e., one single output value.

7.3.3 Random Forest

RF creates several DTs and then combines the results of these DTs and takes a decision based on the result of these DTs. The predicted results obtained from this is more accurate and efficient. RF uses the bagging method which is an ensemble method and is more efficient as compared to a single DT because this approach optimizes overfitting by taking the average of results [21].

7.3.4 Logistic Regression

LR is a statistical technique based on probability and is applied extensively in classification. LR is reported very effective for binary classification problems. LR uses cost function which is more complex compared to the linear one. The cost function which the LR uses is called either sigmoid function or logistic function. The LR hypothesis tends to limit the cost function between 0 and 1. Therefore, linear functions fail to represent it as it can have a value greater than 1 or less than 0 which is not possible as per the hypothesis of LR.

7.3.5 Naïve Bayes

NB is another popular supervised learning model utilized for classification problems. NB classifier follows the concept of Bayes theorem which assumes that attributes are statistically independent. Further, Bayes's theorem itself follows the concept of conditional probability. It operates on datasets and finds the conditional probability of a class [22]. Here, in this case, there are two classes "1" for the presence of diabetes disease and "0" for the absence of diabetes disease. In addition, NB is an efficient classifier that results in good prediction results and has proven itself to be good.

7.3.6 Support Vector Machine

SVM is a broadly applicable supervised learning model, mostly applied for classification related problems. SVM has a lot of applications in many fields, but it plays a vital role in healthcare where it classifies a huge amount of data accurately and effectively. SVM can solve both linear and non-linear problems. Two researchers Vapnik and Chervonekis [23, 24] introduced SVM for the linear classification of the dataset into two classes by passing a linear hyper plan between two classes. SVM has four kernel types such as linear, RBF, poly, and sigmoid. These kernel types are used according to the nature of the problem.

7.3.7 Adaptive Boosting

Adaptive Boosting (AB) is a powerful machine learning classification technique. It was proposed by two scientists Yoav Freund and Robert Schapire in 1996. It is an iterative ensemble method that combines multiple weak classifiers and builds a strong classifier which is good in terms of accuracy and other performance evaluation metrics. AB is very useful and sensitive to data that contains noise, i.e., noisy data and outliers, which degrades the performance. AB with DT as a weak learner is often considered the best classification model and is more preferred as the best out-of-the-box classifier.

7.3.8 Extra-Tree Classifier

ET is an ensemble learning technique that is used mostly for classification problems. It takes the aggregate of the outcomes of multiple de-correlated DTs combined in a forest to output its classification results. The idea of RF and ET is almost the same, but the method of creation of DTs in the forest is different. In ET, each DT is created from the original training instance. Further, a random sample of "k" attributes from the attributes sub-space is provided to every tree at each test node, from which each DT must select the best features to divide the data based on some mathematical criteria, i.e., mostly the Gini Index. This random sample of features results in the generation of various de-correlated DTs. Gini Index is used to rank the feature according to their importance and select the best features from the feature space, this rank given is called the Gini importance of the feature. Besides, to perform the feature selection, features are listed in descending order according to their score. After doing this, it is up to the user how many features he/she wants to select. ET produces good results and has proven itself to be the best classification hypothesis.

7.4 Classifier Validation Method

Validation of the results of the prediction model is an important and necessary step of Machine learning processes. In this study, the K-fold cross-validation method is adopted for validating the results of the above-stated classification models.

7.4.1 K-Fold Cross-Validation Technique

In K-fold cross-validation, the whole dataset is distributed into k equal parts. The (k − 1) parts are utilized for training and the rest is provided for testing the model at each iteration. This process continues for k-iterations. Various researchers have used different values of k for cross-validation. Here, in our case, we perform multiple experiments for values of K (5, 7, and 10), i.e., we have applied 5-, 7-, and 10-fold cross-validation techniques for our experimental work.

7.5 Performance Evaluation Metrics

Various evaluation metrics have been applied in this study for measuring the performance of classification hypotheses such as accuracy, specificity, sensitivity, f1-score, recall, AUC, Mathew correlation coefficient (MCC), and ROC curve. A confusion matrix is used for the production of these measures as presented in Table 7.2.

Table 7.2 Confusion matrix.

	Predicted (normal)	Predicted (disease)
Actual (Normal)	TN	FP
Actual (Disease)	FN	TP

In the confusion matrix, True Negative (TN) demonstrates that the actual and prediction are the same which represents that the person does not have the disease a healthy person is correctly classified by the model.

True Positive (TP) represents that, in actual, the person has the disease and the model also predicts that the person has diabetes disease, i.e., an unhealthy person is correctly classified by the model.

False Positive (FP) shows that the model predicted contradictory means a healthy person is wrongly classified by the model. This is also called a type-1 error.

False Negative (FN) notifies that the model predicted that the outcome opposing means a person having diabetes disease is incorrectly classified by the model. This is also called a type-2 error.

Accuracy: Accuracy of classifier demonstrates how accurately the instances are classified by the classification model and can be calculated with the help of the following formula:

$$\text{Accuracy}: \frac{TP+TN}{TP+TN+FP+FN} * 100$$

Sensitivity: Sensitivity is the percentage of correctly identified diabetic patients. It means the model has predicted that the patient has diabetes disease. Sensitivity can be calculated by the following formula:

$$\text{Sensitivity}: \frac{TP}{TP+FN} * 100$$

Specificity: Specificity is the ratio of the correctly identified healthy people. It means the model has predicted that the person is healthy. Specificity can be calculated by the following formula:

$$\text{Specificity}: \frac{TN}{TN+FP} * 100$$

Precision: Precision demonstrates the percentage of positive classes predicted by my model. It can be formulated as follows:

$$\text{Precision}: \frac{TP}{TP+FP} * 100$$

F1-Score: F1-score is the weighted measure of both recall and precision. Its value ranges between 0 and 1. If the value is 0, it means the worst performance, and if the value is 1, it means the good performance of the classification model. F1-score can calculate as follows:

$$\text{F1-Score}: \frac{2 * (\text{Precision}* \text{Recall})}{\text{Precision}+ \text{Recall}}$$

MCC: MCC is a correlation coefficient between the predicted and actual results. MCC gives resulting values between −1 and +1, where −1 represents completely wrong prediction, 0 means that the classifier produces random prediction, and +1 represents the ideal prediction of the classification models. MCC is computed as follows:

$$MCC: \frac{TP}{\sqrt{(TP+FP)(TP+FN)(TN+FP)(TN+FN)}}$$

Finally, the prediction competency of the machine learning classification hypotheses is analyzed with the help of the receiver optimistic curve (ROC) which shows a graphical representation of the performance of the classification hypothesis. The area under the curve (AUC) describes the ROC of a classifier and the performance of the classification hypotheses is directly linked with AUC, i.e., larger the value of AUC greater will be the performance of the classification hypothesis.

7.6   Results and Discussion

The experimental results of various learning hypotheses are represented in this section. We instigate the performance of eight classification hypotheses, namely, KNN, DT, RF, LR, NB, SVM, AB, and ET, on the Pima Indian Diabetes Disease Dataset (PIDD). To normalize the dataset and remove the missing values, various pre-processing techniques are applied to the dataset before used by the classification hypotheses. The CV technique, i.e., k-fold, is used to assess the results of each classification model. Multiple experiments for different values of K (5, 7, and 10) were performed. For measuring the performance of classification models various performance evaluation metrics are used. For experimental work and implementation, Python is used as a tool.

7.6.1   Performance of All Classifiers Using 5-Fold CV Method

In this experiment, the performance of all eight classification hypotheses was investigated on PIDD using the 5-fold CV method. The success rates of all eight classification models are demonstrated in Table 7.3.

Table 7.3 shows that SVM with kernel='rbf' performs excellently in terms of all evaluating metrics among used classification models by achieving the classification accuracy of 80.40%, sensitivity of 54.64%, specificity of 93.12%, precision of 80.0%, AUC of 90.04%, F1-score of 0.80, and MCC of 0.55. Sensitivity demonstrates that the diagnostic result was positive and the person has diabetes disease. On the other hand, specificity notifies that the diagnostic result was negative and the person is healthy. Again, SVM with kernel='linear' performs very well and attained classification accuracy of 79.65 and stood second in terms of all performance evaluation metrics as shown in Table 7.3. KNN stood last in this regard as compared to other classification hypotheses by attaining accuracy of 75.02%. We accomplished multiple trials for the KNN classifier by taking numerous values for "K" (3, 5, 7, 9, 11, 13, and 15). KNN attained good results at k = 9 as shown in Table 7.3.

Table 7.3 Outcomes of all eight classification hypotheses on PIDD using 5-fold CV.

Classification model	Accuracy	Specificity	Sensitivity	Precision	AUC	F1-score	MCC
DT	77.22	83.72	62.04	77.0	86.0	0.77	0.48
KNN (K = 9)	75.02	86.18	54.46	74.0	82.24	0.74	0.40
RF	78.68	86.22	58.32	78.0	86.0	0.78	0.46
LR	79.30	89.52	59.56	78.0	89.10	0.78	0.52
NB	78.70	86.80	63.25	77.0	88.64	0.77	0.51
SVM (Linear)	79.65	91.12	56.68	79.0	88.98	0.79	0.53
SVM (rbf)	80.40	93.12	54.64	80.0	90.04	0.80	0.55
AB	77.80	90.72	53.10	77.0	87.76	0.77	0.48
ET	78.44	85.48	60.65	78.0	85.83	0.78	0.49

The performance (accuracy, sensitivity, and specificity) of all eight classification hypotheses is demonstrated in Figure 7.2.

Figure 7.3 shows the F1-score and MCC results of all eight classifiers using 5-fold CV techniques.

Precision and AUC-score of all eight classification hypotheses on PIDD using the 5-fold CV method are shown in Figure 7.4.

Figure 7.5 represents the ROC curve of all eight classifiers on PIDD using 5-fold CV techniques.

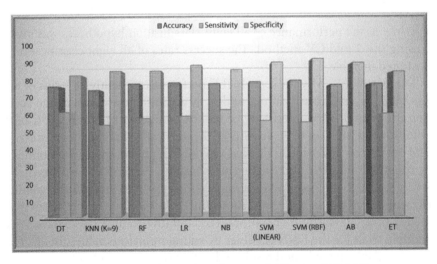

Figure 7.2 Performance of all eight classification hypotheses on PIDD using 5-fold CV.

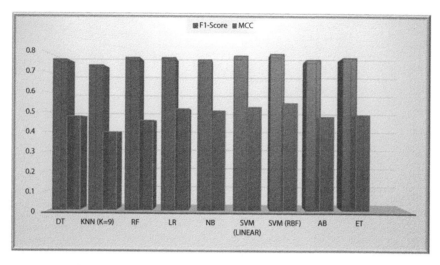

Figure 7.3 F1-score and MCC of all eight classification hypotheses on PIDD applying 5-fold CV.

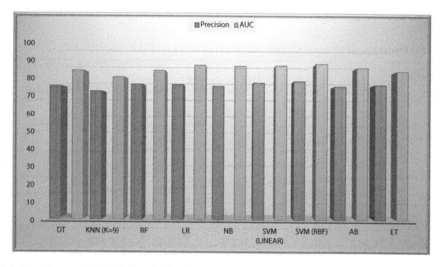

Figure 7.4 Precision and AUC of all eight classification hypotheses on PIDD using 5-fold CV.

7.6.2   Performance of All Classifiers Using the 7-Fold Cross-Validation Method

The success rates of all used classifiers on PIDD applying 7-fold CV techniques are reported in Table 7.4.

Table 7.4 demonstrates that SVM with kernel='rbf' performs very well as compared to the rest of the models, by attaining the classification accuracy of 80.45%, 55.64% of sensitivity, and specificity of 93.14%. KNN showed poor performance and stood last in this regard by achieving an accuracy of 75.02%. Multiple experiments were performed for the KNN classifier by taking numerous values for "K" (3, 5, 7, 9, 11, 13, and 15). KNN showed good performance at k = 9 as noted in Table 7.4.

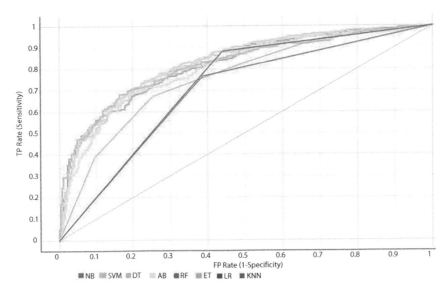

Figure 7.5 ROC curves of all used classification hypotheses applying 5-fold CV.

Table 7.4 Performance of all eight classification hypotheses on PIDD using 7-fold CV.

Classification model	Accuracy	Specificity	Sensitivity	Precision	AUC	F1-score	MCC
DT	77.22	83.72	62.04	77.00	86.0	0.77	0.48
KNN (K = 9)	75.02	86.18	54.46	74.00	82.24	0.74	0.40
RF	78.68	86.22	58.32	78.00	86.00	0.78	0.46
LR	79.30	89.52	59.56	78.00	89.10	0.78	0.52
NB	78.72	86.80	63.28	77.00	88.68	0.77	0.51
SVM (Linear)	79.68	91.16	56.70	79.00	89.10	0.79	0.53
SVM (rbf)	80.45	93.14	55.64	80.00	90.12	0.80	0.55
AB	77.81	90.74	53.10	77.00	87.78	0.77	0.48
ET	78.42	85.46	60.68	78.00	85.85	0.78	0.49

The performance (accuracy, sensitivity, and specificity) of all eight classifiers on PIDD using 7-fold CV is represented in Figure 7.6.

The F1-score and MCC results of all eight classifiers using 5-fold CV are shown in Figure 7.7.

Figure 7.8 illustrates the precision and AUC-score of all eight classification hypotheses on PIDD using the 7-fold CV method.

Figure 7.9 demonstrates the ROC curve of all eight classification hypotheses on PIDD using 7-fold CV techniques.

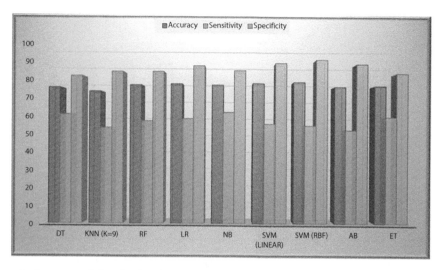

Figure 7.6 Performance of all eight classification hypotheses on PIDD using 7-fold CV.

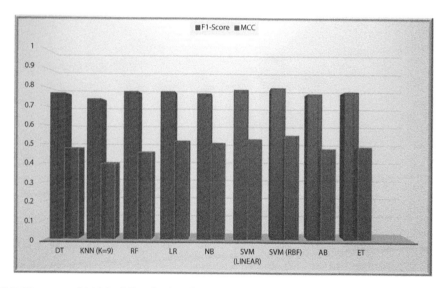

Figure 7.7 F1-score and MCC of all eight classification hypotheses on PIDD using 7-fold CV.

7.6.3   Performance of All Classifiers Using 10-Fold CV Method

This section represents the performance of all classification models and their experimental results attained using the 10-fold cross-validation method on PIDD. The performance of all classifiers is represented in Table 7.5.

Table 7.5 shows that SVM with kernel='rbf' performs excellently in terms of all evaluating metrics compared to other classification models. SVM achieved classification accuracy of 80.51%, 54.43% of sensitivity, specificity of 94.07%, precision of 80.0%, AUC of 90.74%, F1-score of 0.80, and MCC of 0.55. Again, SVM with kernel='linear' performs very well and attained classification accuracy of 79.65% and stood second in terms of all performance

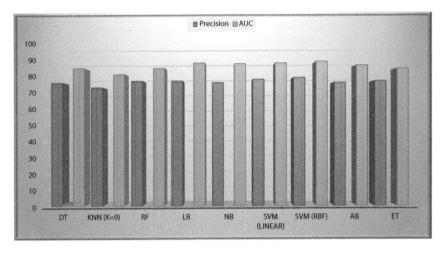

Figure 7.8 Precision and AUC of all eight classification hypotheses on PIDD using 7-fold CV.

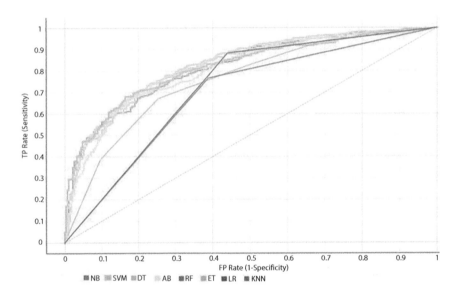

Figure 7.9 ROC curves of all used classification hypotheses using 7-fold CV.

evaluation metrics as shown in Table 7.5. KNN stood last in this regard as compared to other classifiers. We accomplished multiple trials for the KNN classifier by taking numerous values for "K" (3, 5, 7, 9, 11, 13, and 15). KNN showed good performance at k = 9 as shown in Table 7.5.

The performance (accuracy, sensitivity, and specificity) of all eight classification hypotheses is shown in Figure 7.10.

Figure 7.11 shows the F1-score and MCC results of all eight classifiers using 10-fold CV techniques.

Table 7.5 Performance of all eight classification hypotheses on PIDD using 10-fold CV.

Classification model	Accuracy	Specificity	Sensitivity	Precision	AUC	F1-score	MCC
DT	77.60	84.86	62.03	77.0	87.0	0.77	0.48
KNN (K = 9)	75.01	86.21	54.43	74.0	82.23	0.74	0.40
RF	78.64	86.18	58.22	78.0	86.0	0.78	0.46
LR	79.22	89.47	59.49	78.0	89.04	0.77	0.52
NB	78.78	86.84	63.29	78.0	88.67	0.78	0.51
SVM (Linear)	79.65	92.10	55.69	79.0	89.41	0.79	0.53
SVM (rbf)	80.51	94.07	54.43	80.0	90.74	0.80	0.55
AB	77.92	90.78	53.16	77.0	87.95	0.76	0.48
ET	78.64	85.52	60.75	78.0	86.13	0.78	0.49

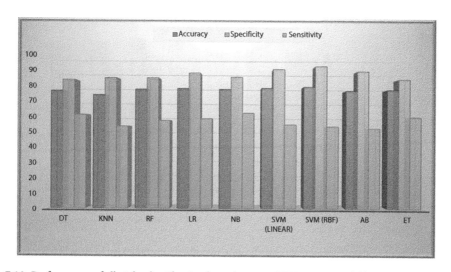

Figure 7.10 Performance of all eight classification hypotheses on PIDD using 10-fold CV.

Precision and AUC-score of all eight classification hypotheses on PIDD using the 10-fold class validation method are shown in Figure 7.12.

Figure 7.13 represents the ROC curve of all eight classifiers on PIDD using the 10-fold CV technique.

Multiple experiments for various values of "K" (5, 7, and 10) of the K-fold CV technique are applied. The empirical outcomes demonstrated that all the classification hypotheses achieved good results in terms of all performance measures on a 10-fold CV.

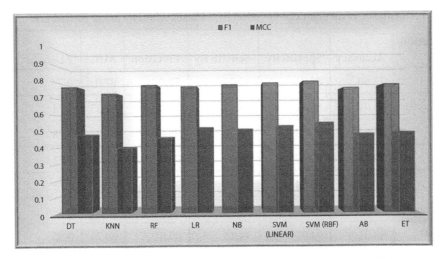

Figure 7.11 F1-score and MCC of all eight classification hypotheses on PIDD using 10-fold CV.

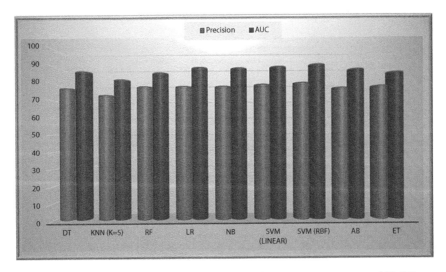

Figure 7.12 Precision and AUC of all eight classification hypotheses on PIDD using 10-fold CV.

Up to now, we have discussed research guidelines and the scope of machine learning in healthcare service (HCS). Nowadays, machine learning classification hypotheses play a vital role in medical fields by predicting and diagnosing various diseases accurately and effectively. The identification and diagnosing process of different diseases such as chronic diseases is considerably improved by applying machine learning classification models. Here, in our study, we have discussed and implemented various popular machine learning classification hypotheses and proposed a hybrid integrated framework for the identification and prediction of diabetes disease. The proposed system is expected to be helpful for the physician in effectively diagnosing diabetes disease.

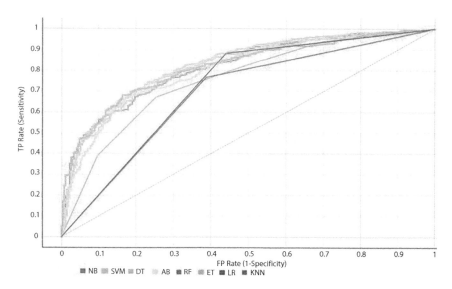

Figure 7.13 ROC curves of all eight classification hypotheses on PIDD using 10-fold CV.

7.7 Conclusion

Diabetes is a fatal and one of the most perilous diseases which grows rapidly all over the world. Early-stage and on time curing can reduce the death ratio caused by diabetes disease. Here, a machine learning–based intelligent predictive system for diagnosing diabetes disease is introduced. PIDD was carried out for testing the proposed system. Eight popular machine learning hypotheses were utilized to investigate the success rates of the proposed system. To normalize the dataset and remove the missing values dataset, various preprocessing techniques are applied to the dataset before implementing classification hypotheses. The CV technique, i.e., k-fold, is applied to investigate the results of each classification model. To measure the true outcomes of each classification hypothesis. Experimental work shows that SVM outperforms all other classification models in terms of performance metrics. Python is used for implementation and experimental work. The proposed system is expected to be helpful for the physician in diagnosing diabetic patients.

References

1. Association, A.D., Diagnosis and classification of diabetes mellitus. *Diabetes Care*, 37, 1, S81–S90, 2013.
2. Association, A.D., Diagnosis and classification of diabetes disease. *Diabetes Care*, 48, 2, S101–S110, 2014.
3. Mathers, C.D. and Loncar, D., Projections of global mortality and burden of disease from 2002 to 2030. *PloS Med.*, 3, 11, e442, 2006.
4. Dhatariya, K., Levy, N., Kilvert, A., Watson, B., Cousins, D., Flanagan, D., Lipp, A., NHS Diabetes guideline for the perioperative management of the adult patient with diabetes. *Diabet. Med.*, 29, 4, 420–433, 2012.
5. Diabetes, 2017. http://www.who.int/newsroom/factsheets/detail/diabetes.Accessed:2018-06-08.

6. Samant, P. and Agarwal, R., Machine learning techniques for medical diagnosis of diabetes using iris images. *Comput. Methods Programs Biomed.*, 157, 121–128, 2018.

7. Islam, S.M.S., Lechner, A., Ferrari, U., Froeschl, G., Niessen, L.W., Seissler, J., Alam, D.S., Social and economic impact of diabetics in Bangladesh: protocol for a case–control study. *BMC Public Health*, 13, 1, 1217, 2013.

8. Samuel, O.W., Asogbon, G.M., Sangaiah, A.K. *et al.*, An integrated decision support system based on ANN and Fuzzy_AHP for heart failure risk prediction. *Expert Syst. Appl.*, 68, 163–172, 2017.

9. Edmonds, B., Using localised 'Gossip' to structure distributed learning, in: *Proceedings of AISB Symposium on Socially Inspired Computing*, 1–12, Hatfield, UK, 2008.

10. Dwivedi, A.K., Analysis of computational intelligence techniques for diabetes mellitus prediction. *Neural. Comput. Appl.*, 30, 12, 3837–3845, 2018.

11. Heydari, M., Teimouri, M., Heshmati, Z., Alavinia, S.M., Comparison of various classification algorithms in the diagnosis of type 2 diabetes in Iran. *Int. J. Diabetes Dev. Ctries.*, 36, 2, 167–173, 2016.

12. Zehra, A., Asmawaty, T., Aznan, M., A Comparative Study on the Pre-Processing and Mining of Pima Indian Diabetes Dataset. In: *3rd International Conference on Software Engineering & Computer Systems (ICSECS - 2013)*, Universiti Malaysia Pahang, pp. 1-10, 20-22 August 2013.

13. Choubey, D.K., Paul, S., Kumar, S., Kumar, S., Classification of Pima indian diabetes dataset using naive bayes with genetic algorithm as an attribute selection. *Paper presented at the Communication and Computing Systems: Proceedings of the International Conference on Communication and Computing System (ICCCS 2016)*, 2017.

14. Sivanesan, R. and Dhivya, K.D.R., A Review on diabetes mellitus diagnoses using classification on Pima Indian diabetes data set. *Int. J. Adv. Res. Comput. Sci. Manage. Stud.*, 5, 1, 12–17, 2017.

15. Zou, Q., Qu, K., Luo, Y. *et al.*, Predicting diabetes mellitus with machine learning techniques. *Front. Genet.*, 9, 515, 2018.

16. Thirumal, P. and Nagarajan, N., Utilization of data mining techniques for diagnosis of diabetes mellitus-a case study. *ARPN J. Eng. Appl. Sci.*, 10, 1, 8–13, 2016.

17. Mahmud, S.H., Hossin, M.A., Ahmed, M.R. *et al.*, *Machine Learning Based Unified Framework for Diabetes Prediction*, BDET 2018: *Proceedings of the 2018 International Conference on Big Data Engineering and Technology*, pp. 46–50, 2018

18. *Research Summary*, National Institute of Diabetes and Digestive and Kidney Diseases (NIDDK), [Online]. Available: https://www.niddk.nih.gov/aboutniddk/staffdirectory/intramural/lesliebaier/Pages/researchsummary.aspx. [Accessed: 25-march-2020].

19. Smith, J.W., Everhart, J.E., Dickson, W.C., Knowler, W.C., Johannes, R.S., Using the ADAP learning algorithm to forecast the onset of diabetes mellitus. *Proc. Annu. Symp. Comput. Appl. Med. Care*, 261–265, 2005.

20. Safavian, S.R. and Landgrebe, D., A survey of decision tree classifier methodology. *IEEE Trans. Syst. Man. Cyb.*, 21, 3, 660–674, 1991.

21. Masci, C., Johnes, G., Agasisti, T., Student and school performance across countries: A machine learning approach. *Eur. J. Oper. Res.*, 269, 3, 1072–1085, 2018.

22. Leung, K.M., *Naive bayesian classifier*, Polytechnic University Department of Computer Science/Finance and Risk Engineering, pp. 123–156, 2007

23. Vapnik, V., Guyon, I., T., H.-M., Learn, and undefined 1995, Support vector machines. statweb.stanford.edu. 3, 7, 2011.

24. Chervonenkis, A.Y., *Early history of support vector machines Empirical Inference*, Springer, pp. 13–20, 2013.

8

Hyperparameter Tuning of Ensemble Classifiers Using Grid Search and Random Search for Prediction of Heart Disease

Dhilsath Fathima M.[1*] and S. Justin Samuel[2]

[1]Sathyabama Institute of Science and Technology, Chennai, Tamil Nadu, India
[2]Department of Computer Science and Engineering, PSN Engineering College, Tirunelveli, Tamil Nadu, India

Abstract

Tuning the model hyperparameters is an essential step in developing a high-performance machine learning model. Grid search algorithms and random search algorithms are used in machine learning to tune the hyperparameters of ML algorithms. Ensemble learners are a category of a machine learning algorithm. Ensemble classifiers are divided into two types: bagging, which is a parallel ensemble model, and boosting, which is a sequential ensemble model. The proposed work uses two boosting classifiers, the Adaboost Algorithm and Gradient boosting algorithm, and one bagging classifier, the Random forest algorithm. A model for early heart disease prediction has developed using the Adaboost classifier, random forest, and gradient boosting classifier. The Cleveland heart disease dataset is used to train and validate the ensemble classifiers in this heart disease prediction model. When comparing the performance of these ensemble learners, gradient boosting algorithms outperform AdaBoost and random forest classifiers. This paper evaluated the efficiency of the grid search algorithm and random search algorithm via tuning the hyperparameters of the Gradient boosting algorithm, Adaboost algorithm, and Random forest algorithm. We conclude from the performance analysis, tuning the ensemble classifier hyperparameters using the grid search method and the random search method can increase an ensemble learner's efficiency.

Keywords: Hyperparameter tuning, ensemble learners, grid search, random search, heart disease prediction

Corresponding author: dilsathveltech123@gmail.com

Om Prakash Jena, Alok Ranjan Tripathy, Ahmed A. Elngar and Zdzislaw Polkowski (eds.) Computational Intelligence and Healthcare Informatics, (139–158) © 2021 Scrivener Publishing LLC

8.1   Introduction

In developing nations like India, including poorer states and rural areas, cardiovascular disease (CVD) has become one of the leading causes of mortality. The increase in the prevalence of CVD and CVD risk factors in India is primarily due to an epidemiological change [1, 2]. The estimated prevalence of CVD in India became reported at 54.5 million in 2016. One in four fatalities in India is now due to CVD with stroke and ischemic heart disease affecting Indians, a minimum 10 years earlier as well as in their more active mid-life times prior to people of European descent. For instance, around 23% of CVD deaths occur before the age of 70 years in western countries; this statistic is 52% in India.

Abnormal functionality of a heart and blood vessels is known as CVD due to some reason. A various type of CVD exists. The most common kind of CVD is coronary artery disease (CAD) [3]. CAD, such decreased myocardial perfusion, induces angina, acute myocardial infarction (AMI), and heart failure. AMI, commonly referred as a heart attack, often is accompanied by diminished and blocked blood flow to a chamber of the heart, resulting in necrosis of the heart muscle [4]. Congestive heart failure and mortality are common complications for AMI. Clinical studies and medical research have identified the risk factors of AMI and these risk factors are divided into two key groups, like demographic risk factors and medical risk factors. The demographic risk factors which cannot be changed are gender, age, and family history. A healthy lifestyle and treatment can modify clinical complications blood pressure, high cholesterol, smoking, obesity, and diabetes.

Different approaches are used by medical professionals to predict or diagnose AMI. Angiography is the most frequently used diagnostic procedure for the diagnosis of AMI and is known to be the most reliable method of identification of CAD or AMI. Even so, the major limitations in the manner of diagnosis of CAD or AMI are higher medical costs and significant side effects of angiography. In general, the diagnosis of CAD involves some conventional methods for detailed examination of various factors such as blood test, electrocardiogram (ECG), physical examination, and evaluating patient's medical history, which can make the cardiologist job complicated. These challenges motivate the development of a non-invasive framework for heart failure detection. The conventional methods used to predict AMI are often time consuming and, due to human errors, may give inaccurate prediction performance [5]. To avoid these limitations, it is therefore vital to strengthen an automated diagnostic model to predict CAD and AMI accurately and efficiently.

8.2   Related Work

From the literature review, it has been surveyed that within the past, different automated frameworks have been recommended utilizing diverse ML techniques for identifying the existence of CAD and acute myocardial infarction. Support vector machine (SVM), logistic regression (LR), K-nearest neighbor (KNN), artificial neural network (ANN), decision tree (DT), random Forest (RF) are typical ML algorithms which are useful for building a predictive model intended aimed at the automated heart disease diagnosis. The classification performance of different ML algorithms upon this Cleveland heart disease dataset was stated by various researchers. In the machine learning (ML) library of the University of California Irvine (UCI), the Cleveland heart disease dataset is publicly available [6–8]. This is the dataset used by different researchers to evaluate different classification challenges associated with heart diseases using various ML classification algorithms.

Amin Ul Haq et al. [6] suggested a hybrid intelligent architecture using different ML techniques for prediction of heart disease, like logistic regression, K-nearest neighbor (KNN) algorithm, linear SVM, ANN, radial Basis Function SVM (RBF-SVM), RF, and DT. In order to select the significant risk factors for heart disease, this study used three feature selection methods, namely, minimal-redundancy-maximal-relevance method, relief feature selection algorithm, and least absolute shrinkage and selection operator technique. The accuracy of logistic regression algorithm and RBF-SVM is 84% and 86%, respectively, before selection of features. A high classification accuracy of 89% with the logistic regression algorithm and 88% with RBF-SVM was obtained after feature selection. Thus, the classification efficiency of the ML classifier depends on the feature selection algorithms.

Srabanti Maji et al. [9] proposed the hybridization ML model (hybrid-DT) in which a DT algorithm and ANN are combined aimed at enhancing accuracy of automated heart disease diagnosis model. This is done by using WEKA tool. Ten-fold validation is used to validate the efficiency of the suggested classifier. An output of the individual classifiers (ANN and DT) and hybridized model (hybrid-DT) are analyzed using classifier estimation measures like specificity, sensitivity, and accuracy. An author further states that hybridized model achieves highest accuracy of 78.14% than ANN model with accuracy of 77.40% and DT with 76.66% of accuracy. It is assessed that with respect to the individual algorithms, hybrid ML models work out the best for the given dataset.

Latha, C. Beulah Christalin et al. [10] analyze a process called ensemble classification, which can be used to enhance the efficiency of weak classifiers by joining multiple ML models. Experiments were conducted using UCI heart disease dataset. Boosting, bagging, and stacking are three forms of ensemble classification used in this analysis. An ensemble with the algorithms of C4.5, Bayes Net, Naïve Bayes (NB), RF, PART algorithm, and multilayer perceptron is done by the Bagging algorithm. The AdaBoost M1 algorithm is used as a boosting algorithm and the NB classifier is being used in the stacking model as default classifier. The ensemble classifier's performance was further improved with the support of brute force feature selection method, and the result of this analysis showed a significant improvement in prediction accuracy.

VirenViraj Shankar et al. [11] suggested a prediction model that uses the convolutional neural network (CNN), a subset of neural networks for training and building heart disease diagnosis model. The prediction model is implemented on real-life patient data obtained from hospital. The findings of the CNN model equate with the KNN classifiers and NB. An accuracy of the heart disease diagnosis model is found to be 85% highest for CNN, and afterward, 80% for the NB algorithm and 74% for KNN.

An automated framework was suggested by G. Thippa Reddy *et al.* [12] for predicting heart disease using ML method called the OFBAT-RBFL algorithm. This experimentation is carried out using publicly accessible dataset from the University of California, Irvine (UCI) datasets, such as Hungary, Switzerland, and Cleveland. Thus, the significant features were first selected from the UCI dataset using the locality preservation projection (LPP) algorithm to help the proposed methodology for constructing a classification model using the rule-based fuzzy classifier (RBFL). Then after, from the sample data, the rules are generated for the RBFL framework. The significant rules are extracted from the entire fuzzy rules using the oppositional firefly with BAT(OFBAT) algorithm. The outcome of the experiment indicates that the RBFL algorithm outperforms the existing method by achieving 78% accuracy. This proposed model used MATLAB tool to implement the OFBAT-RBFL technique.

It is evident from the literature analysis that numerous researchers have taken advantage of feature selection methods to boost the predictive ability of ML models. Encouraged by this knowledge, we are trying to further enhance the precision of CAD disease diagnosis by tuning hyperparameters of ensemble learners in this paper.

8.3   Proposed Method

This framework has been developed for AMI detection using ensemble learning models. Ensemble learners help to enhance ML model outcomes by integrating multiple weak ML classifiers [13]. These ensemble learners enable good prediction output to be achieved compared with a single ML algorithm. Main objective of using ensemble learners is to reduce the variance and bias of ML model or to boost the performance of ML model. Ensemble learning refers to a method used to train different learning ML algorithms and integrate their performances, treating them as a decision-making "group". The idea is of ensemble learner is that the group's decision, properly combined with individual predictions, should, on average, have greater overall accuracy than any independent member of the group [14]. Many conceptual and empirical studies have shown that ensemble classifiers achieve greater accuracy than single ML classifiers, very frequently. The proposed method has been designed to identify individuals with the goal of classifying individuals with acute myocardial infarction and healthy individuals. Cleveland heart disease has been utilized by many researchers which is used in our proposed work. The ensemble ML classifiers such as AdaBoost classifier, gradient boosting classifier, and RF classifier are used in this proposed system. The efficiency of this proposed model is further improved using hyperparameter optimization or hyperparameter tuning methods. This suggested model uses two hyperparameter tuning methods, namely, a grid search method and the random search method. To test the efficiency of this ensemble classifier, classifier assessment metrics like F1-score, ensemble learner accuracy, misclassification rate, sensitivity, Matthews correlation coefficient, specificity, and receiver optimistic curve are used to compare the performance of this model. The components of the heart disease prediction model based on ensemble learners are shown in Figure 8.1. The train-test split technique for evaluating an ensemble learning algorithm's output is applied. The proposed framework is composed of four steps, namely, (1) dataset collection, (2) ensemble classification modeling, (3) hyperparameter tuning of ensemble classifiers, and (4) performance assessment methods of proposed model.

8.3.1   Dataset Description

As input for ensemble learners training and validation, the proposed model uses Cleveland heart disease dataset [15]. From the UCI ML library, this heart disease dataset was gathered. The objective of this method paper is to decide whether an individual has heart disease depending on risk factors for heart disease. This dataset consists of 303 samples and 13 input features of individuals with a binary target class for identifying whether or not an individual has heart disease. In the target class, there are two class labels, as target class = 1 means that the person suffers from heart disease and target class = 0 indicates that the person does not suffer. In this dataset, there are 165 positive cases tested in this dataset, and 138 negative samples tested. This dataset is being used to evaluate whether or not a patient has heart disease. The 14-input attribute of this dataset are listed below:

- Individual's age (Age)
- Shows the person's gender (Sex)
- Chest-pain type suffered by the person is displayed (cp)
- Individual's resting blood pressure level in mmHgg (unit) (Trestbps)
- Shows serum cholesterol in mg/dl (unit) (Chol)
- Fasting blood sugar value; Compare an individual's fasting blood glucose value to 120mg/dl. If the blood glucose concentration is > 120 mg/dl, then: 1 (true); Otherwise: 0 (false) (Fbs)
- Shows resting electrocardiographic observations Restecg (Restecg)
- The maximal heart rate experienced by a person is shown (Thalach)

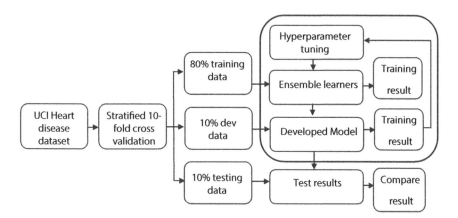

Figure 8.1 General schematic diagram of the proposed method for predicting heart disease.

- Shows exercise induced angina (Exang)
- Exercise-induced ST depression compared to rest (Oldpeak)
- Shows Segment of ST peak exercise (Slope)
- Number of major flourosopy-colored vessels (Ca)
- Shows Thalassemia (Thal)
- Shows whether or not the patient suffers from heart disease (Target)

Statistical analysis is a methodology to evaluating the features of the heart disease dataset. This provides an insight into every attribute's missing data and types of data values. Through the statistical analysis, we analyzed the attributes of the target dataset and we observed no missing values exist in the target dataset.

8.3.2   Ensemble Learners for Classification Modeling

Input dataset (target dataset) is used for build a classifier using ensemble learners. Two stages are involved in classification modeling which are model training stage and model validation stage. During training phase, model is built using ensemble classifiers. In this training phase, ensemble learners develop a model by learning parameter of base learners and input dataset to construct a model to minimize loss function; Second phase of classification modeling is validation phase; during this phase, outcomes of training stage are evaluated using validation dataset for tuning the hyperparameters of ensemble classifier using random search and grid search algorithms for boosting the overall accuracy of classification model. Ensemble learners [16] are used to achieve better predictive performance than could be obtained from any of the simple ML learning algorithms alone, and many weak learning algorithms are combined with ensemble techniques. Experimentally and theoretically, the combination of

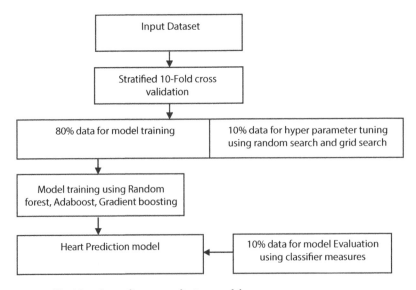

Figure 8.2 Process of building heart disease prediction model.

various learning models has shown to achieve considerably excellent performance than the individual base learners. The classification modeling process is shown in Figure 8.2.

Ensemble learners include the methods used to train different weak learners and integrate their performances, treating them as a decision-making "committee". The idea is that the committee's decision, correctly paired with individual estimates, should have higher overall accuracy on average than any individual member of the committee. There are many methods to combine the decisions of an individual classifier such as voting method, averaging method, and probabilistic method [17]. In ML, there are two categories of ensemble technique such as boosting and bagging. The functionality of this proposed work is shown in Figure 8.3.

8.3.2.1 Bagging Ensemble Learners

Bagging ensemble learner is called as bootstrap aggregation method which is a type of ensemble learner. This method combines bootstrapping and aggregation to build an ensemble learner. Several bootstrapped subsets are obtained from a data set. On each of the bootstrapped subsets, a DT is constructed. After the DT subsample has been created, a voting algorithm is being used to aggregate the most effective predictor over the DTs. The bagging method works based on Algorithm 8.1. This bagging method used to reduce the variance and helps to avoid overfitting when it is implemented with the weak base learner.

Algorithm 8.1 Bagging ensemble learner.

Inputs

- Input dataset D with N training samples $D = \left((x_1, y_1), (x_2, y_2), ..., (x_N, y_N) \right)$ and $x_i \epsilon X$, $y_i \epsilon Y$ is a class labels of associated input features x_i. Value of $y \epsilon \{1, 0\}$
- Weak learner L
- Number of iterations or learning rounds R

Ouput

- Ensemble learner E_L

Training Process

    for k = 1 to R
    B_k = *Generate bootstrap subset from D*
    L_k = Training a weak learner from the bootstrap samples B_k
    end for k

$$E_L = arg\ max_{y \in Y} \sum_{k=1}^{R} 1(y = L_k(x))$$

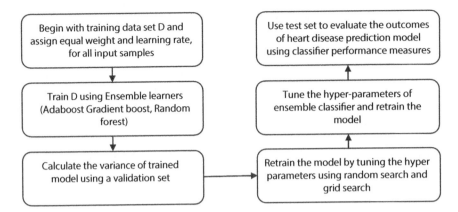

Figure 8.3 Proposed classifier workflow.

Random Forest Classifier

It is a classifier [18] which follows bagging principle. It is an efficient classification algorithm for ensemble ML which yields accurate results among several classification models due to its robust nature. It is an enhanced DT algorithm method of ensemble bagging to build a minimal variance model. Through reducing the variance as well as minimizing the overfitting problem, the RF algorithm (RFA) enhances the classifier's performance by developing several DTs upon this training subset samples and packing a performance of all DTs by implementing the task of majority voting. Even if there is a missing value in an input samples, the random forest model shows better accuracy. This classifier, which generates a DT from the bootstrap subsampling process, is a form of statistical sampling, involves a random selection of input samples with substitution, and is utilized to assessing problem of uncertainty also minimize model overfitting. Figure 8.4 shows the RF classifier workflow.

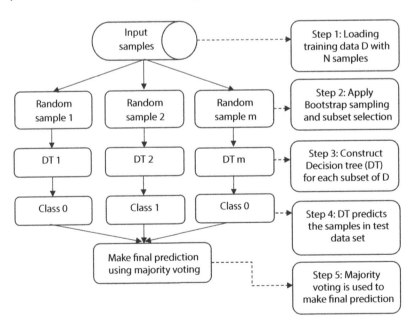

Figure 8.4 Random forest classifier workflow.

Major Steps of Random Forest Classifier

Step 1: Apply bootstrap sampling with replacement method on D to select m subsets of D where $m < D$.

Step 2: For each m, create a DT which utilizes the Gini index as an attribute or feature selection method to efficiently divide the input features for the generating DT. For each feature A of m, the Gini index [10] is determined and the input feature with the minimum Gini index is nominated as a best splitting feature to divide the m to form a DT. Equation (8.1) describes the Gini index's mathematical derivation.

$$\Delta Gini(A) = Gini(m) - Gini_A(m) \cdots \tag{8.1}$$

where $Gini(A)$ is the Gini index value of input feature A of m subset, $Gini(m)$ is the Gini index of m, and Gini index of subset m is expanded in Equation (8.2) as

$$Gini(m) = 1 - \sum_{j=1}^{y} p_k^2 \tag{8.2}$$

where p_k is the relative probability of class k in subset m, this can be calculated as $p_k = \dfrac{|c_k, M|}{|M|}$ where $|M|$ implies the total number of samples in m and $|c_k, M|$ is the number of class labels in m. If m is split into two subsets on attribute A like m_1 and m_2, $Gini_A(m)$ is defined in Equation (8.3) as

$$Gini_A(m) = \frac{|m_1|}{|m|} Gini(m_1) + \frac{|m_2|}{|m|} Gini(m_2) \tag{8.3}$$

n_estimator is the RF algorithm parameter for evaluating the volume of DT developed for each m. Without pruning, each DT is full-grown to the full extent possible.

Step 3: The sample in the test data set is uniquely predicted by an independent DT.

Step 4: To make a final hypothesis on the test data set, apply the majority voting function.

8.3.2.2   Boosting Ensemble Learner

Boosting ensemble learner is a type of ensemble learning technique used to improve the robustness of weak classifier via combining multiple learners toward a more accurate estimate and reducing the model bias error [19]. Boosting is accomplished by creating a weak model from the training samples, and making a second model that tries to fix the first model's mistake. Final model is implemented until perfectly predict the class label of the training samples or an adequate range of models are implemented. It is a type of sequential practice, in which each subsequent model tries to correct the previous model's errors. The successor models depend on the preceding model.

Major Steps of Boosting Ensemble Learner

Step 1: Select a random subset of training samples to train a weak learner *Classifier*$_{c1}$ without substitution from the training set *D*, generate an initial *model*$_1$.

Step 2: This *model*$_1$ is being used to make a prediction about the entire dataset. Using the actual values and expected values, errors are estimated.

Step 3: Higher weights are assigned to the wrongly predicted observations. Another model *model*$_2$ is developed and make predictions based on the dataset. *model*$_2$ aims to correct the previous model's errors to improve the accuracy.

Step 4: Similarly, several models are developed, each fixing the prior model's errors. The final model is a strong model or learner which is a weighted mean of all models (weak learners). So as to make a final strong learner, majority voting is applied to associates the prediction of weak learner.

This proposed model uses two common methods of boosting learners, Ada boosting algorithm (ABA) and gradient boosting algorithm (GBA).

AdaBoost Algorithm

AdaBoost is an adaptive boosting algorithm which solves binary classification problems [20, 21]. It is used as a weighted sum of weak learners to define an ensemble model. It uses iterative ensembled technique for converting a weak classifier into a strong learner. Two conditions should be satisfied in AdaBoost such as different weighted training examples must be iteratively trained by the weak classifier, and for each iteration, this model aims to gives a correct prediction for the training samples by reducing training errors.

Major Steps of AdaBoost algorithm

Step 1: AdaBoost model uses any weak classifier like DT to develop a weak learner using input training data *D* using weighted samples. Here, *D* is an input training set with N training samples $D = ((x_1, y_1), (x_2, y_2), ..., (x_N, y_N))$, and $x_i \in X, y_i \in Y$ is a class labels of associated input features x_i. Value of y$\in$\{1,0\}.

Step 2: For a number of iterations *R*, the ABA iteratively calls the base learner called weak learner. Each input feature vector x_i in the *D* is weighted in each iteration, denoting the likelihood of the samples being selected for an input training set. As in the Equation (8.4), the initial weight is assigned to x_i is w_1 (i) = 1/N for all x_i, i = 1,2, ...N.

Step 3: Before starting training process, the same weight w_i will be applied to all samples of training set, the w_i of the miclassified samples will be increased and changed during the training process of weak learner to get the high probability correct prediction from all training samples of *D*. This process is useful to a get a high probability prediction.

Step 4: This procedure continues till the entire training data make predictions without any error or when the maximum estimator iteration specified is reached.

Step 5: Ada boosting makes final prediction by linearly integrates outcomes of weak learners by carry out a voting classifier to minimize the weighted error. This classifier calculates the weighted error of a model using an Equation (8.4).

$$e_w = \frac{sum(w_x(i) * terror_x(i))}{sum(w_x)} \tag{8.4}$$

where e_w is the weighted sum of error, w is the weight of training samples x_i and $terror_x$ is the prediction error that is 1 for the misclassified samples and 0 if correctly classified samples for training instance x_i.

The ABA works on Algorithm 8.2.

Algorithm 8.2 AdaBoost learner.

Input

- Input dataset D with N training samples $D = ((x_1, y_1), (x_2, y_2), ..., (x_N, y_N))$ and $x_i \in X$, $y_i \in Y$ is a class labels of associated input features x_i. Value of y $\in \{1, 0\}$

Parameters

- *base_learner*: Select any weak learner used to train the AdaBoost learner
- *est_ad*: The max limit of estimators over which the boost stops.
- $w_x(i)$: Setting weight of the classifier.

Output

- hyp_{op} is a final hypothesis with less error rate.

Training Process

- Load $D = ((x_1, y_1), (x_2, y_2), ..., (x_N, y_N))$
- Set initial weight of training samples: $w_i = \dfrac{1}{N}$ for all x_i, $i = 1, 2, ..., N$
- For $t = 1$ to *est_ad*:do
  a. D_i = samples from D according to distribution
  b. L_i = Train a classifier using D_i via *base_learner* with weight w_i
  c. $h_t = L_i(D, D_i)$
  d. Compute error of a h_t as e_t

$$e_t = \frac{sum(w_i I(h_t(x_i) \neq y_i))}{sum(w_i)}$$

  e. Set w_i as $w_i = w_i . \exp[\alpha_t . I(h_t(\alpha_t) \neq y_i)]$
  f. Output $hyp_{op} = sign \sum_{t=1}^{est\_ad} \alpha_t h_t(x)$

Gradient Boosting Algorithm

GBA is s type of ensemble learner for developing predictive models [22]. It is an appropriate algorithm to change the weak hypotheses into strong hypotheses [23]. A poor learner is described as the one with at least moderately better performance than a random chance. GBA is an ensemble of weak learner designed in a forward stagewise fashion to optimise certain distinct loss function. GBA uses gradient descent technique to minimise the cost function whenever a weak learner is added one at a time in the stagewise method. Cost function is a function for any given data which calculates the accuracy of a model. The Cost Function attempts to measure the loss and represents it in the form of a single real number among the calculated value and actual value. Estimating a cost function after building a hypothesis with initial parameters and adjust the model parameters using the Gradient descent function over the given data with the objective of reducing the cost function. The aim of GBA is to minimizing cost function by iteratively performs the following steps as:

Step 1: At a certain point, calculate the slope (gradient), the function's first-order derivative.

Step 2: Make a step in the opposing direction of gradient, increase the opposing slope direction from the current point by alpha (learning rate) times the gradient at that point.
   The GBA works on Algorithm 8.3.

Algorithm 8.3 Gradient boosting learner.

Input

- Input dataset D with N training samples $D = ((x_1, y_1), (x_2, y_2), ..., (x_N, y_N))$ and $x_i \in X, y_i \in Y$ is a class labels of associated input features x_i. Value of $y \in \{1, 0\}$

Parameters

- **base_learner:** Select any weak learner used to train the AdaBoost learner
- **T:** The max number of learning iteration
- $f_0(x)$: Loss function to minimize $f_0(x) = arg\ min_\gamma \sum_{i=1}^{N} L(y_i, \gamma)$
- **γ:** Step size

Training Process

- Load $D = ((x_1, y_1), (x_2, y_2), ..., (x_N, y_N))$
- for $t = 1$ to T:do
   a.   For $i = 1, 2, ..., N$ compute the pseudo residuals

$$r_{it} = -\left[\frac{\partial L(y_i, F(x_i))}{\partial F(x_i)} \right]$$

   b.   Fit a weak model **base_learner** to $h_t(x)$ to pseudo residuals, i.e., training it using $D\ \{(x_i, r_{it})\}$ for $i = 1, 2, ..., N$
   c.   Compute multiplier r_t by solving the following optimization problem as

$$\gamma_t = arg\ min \sum_{i=1}^{N} L(y_i, F_{t-1}(x_i) + \gamma\ h_t(x_i))$$

d.   Update the model

$$F_t(x) = F_{t-1}(x) + \gamma_t h_t(x_i))$$

- Output model $F_T(x)$

8.3.3   Hyperparameter Tuning of Ensemble Learners

This proposed methodology uses the two optimization techniques, which are used to adjust the ensemble learner hyperparameters for improving the prediction precision of a heart disease diagnosis system and for enhancing the classification modeling efficiency by optimizing the loss function by adjusting or tuning the default values of the hyperparameters using random search method and grid search method. ML classifier's hyperparameter tuning helps to improve the classifier prediction [24]. Hyperparameters are parameters used by ML classifiers to regulate and control the classifier's learning method, modeling, and estimation. The method of choosing the right hyperparameter for ML classifiers is hyperparameter tuning, which is called model selection and optimization of hyperparameters. As a problem statement, the basic hyperparameter tuning of ML classifiers is described below:

Define y with the N hyperparameters (H) as classifier. The nth hyperparameter domain is defined as H_n and the configuration space of all ML classifier hyperparameters is denoted as $H = H_1 \times H_2 \times ....\times H_N$. The y hyperparameter vector space is denoted as $V \in H$ and y is assigned to V with its hyperparameter by y_v. The hyperparameter domain space is integer-valued (e.g., minimum number of samples needed and maximum tree depth), real-value or floating value (e.g., early stop tree growth threshold value and learning rate), categorical (e.g., loss function selection and type of attribute selection metric), and bool values (e.g., whether or not to use bootstrap sampling) [25].

The validation set is applied to evaluate the performance of the trained model as it is independent of a training data set. Tuning model hyperparameter is important to improve the efficiency of the ML model. For tuning a hyperparameter of heart disease prediction model and to minimise the loss function of the ensemble classifier, this proposed model is applied to the validation dataset (x). In this proposed model, the optimization algorithms are used for minimizing the loss function of model as D ($argmin_x: f(x)$) or for maximizing the accuracy of training and validation set as D ($argmax_x: f(x)$) by identifying the hyperparameter specification which works best for this model. Grid search method and random search method are used as a tuning algorithm in this proposed model. An outcome of our proposed model is improved using grid search technique and random search technique through the tuning hyperparameters of RF, AdaBoost and gradient boosting classifier.

8.3.3.1   Grid Search Algorithm

Grid search is an optimization algorithm that aims to find the appropriate set of hyperparameters for the suggested model. Hyperparameters are not the model's parameters and the best parameter cannot be determined from the training set. When minimizing a loss function, model parameters become learned through training a proposed model. The optimization algorithm used to create a model for each combination of different hyperparameters and validate each model. The model that provides the greatest accuracy is selected as an optimal hyperparameter of given classifier. Grid search is an approach of optimizing hyperparameters. Since the ML algorithm parameter space may include spaces with real or infinite values for certain parameters, it is likely that essential to define a boundary for applying grid search, which simply allows a complete search over a specified hyperparameters search space [26]. Grid search technique applies exhaustive search for selecting the optimal hyperparameters of proposed model. For implementing grid searching, create a grid of hyperparameter values and train a model and evaluate the trained model on the validation data on each combination. Every combination of hyperparameter values is attempted in this grid search, which can be very inefficient. To overcome the limitation of grid search, random search method is used for model's hyperparameter tuning.

8.3.3.2 Random Search Algorithm

Random search is a procedure in which the best solution for the constructed model is determined using random combinations of hyperparameters [27]. By choosing hyperparameter randomly, random search eliminates the exhaustive evaluation of all combinations of different hyperparameter. To train and validate the proposed model, random search creates a grid of hyperparameter search values and identifies the random combination of hyperparameter. This helps to directly regulate the combination of parameters that are performed. The hyperparameter of ensemble learners using grid search technique is shown in Table 8.1 and tuning of ensemble learner with random search is given in Table 8.2.

Table 8.1 Grid search hyperparameter tuning of ensemble classifier with hyperparameter search space and optimized hyperparameters and optimized parameter value.

Ensemble classifier	Hyperparameter name	Hyperparameter search space	Optimized hyperparameter value of ensemble classifier
Random Forest Algorithm	n_est	[10, 50, 100, 500]	500
	selection_criterion	['gini'.'entropy']	Entropy
	max_depth	[50,100]	100
	bootstrap	[True, False]	False
AdaBoost Algorithm	base_est	[Gaussian NB (), Random ForestClassifier ()]	RandomForestClassifier
	n_est	[10, 50, 100, 500]	500
	lr_rate	[0.0001, 0.001, 0.01, 0.1, 1.0]	1.0
	random_state	[50, 30, 40]	40
Gradient Boosting Algorithm	n_est	[10, 50, 100, 500]	500
	lr_rate	[0.0001, 0.001, 0.01, 0.1, 1.0]	0.01

Table 8.2 Random search hyperparameter tuning of ensemble classifier with hyperparameter search space and optimized hyperparameters and optimized parameter value.

Ensemble classifier	Hyperparameter name	Hyperparameter search space	Optimized hyperparameter value of ensemble classifier
Random Forest algorithm	*n_est*	[10, 50, 100, 500]	50
	selection_criterion	['gini', 'entropy']	Entropy
	max_depth	[50,100]	100
	bootstrap	[True, False]	False
	min_sample_split	[2,5]	5
AdaBoost Algorithm	*base_est*	[Gaussian NB (), Random ForestClassifier ()]	Gaussian NB ()
	n_est	[10, 50, 100, 500]	10
	lr_rate	[0.0001, 0.001, 0.01, 0.1, 1.0]	0.001
	random_state	[50,30,40]	30
Gradient boosting Algorithm	*n_est*	[10, 50, 100, 500]	100
	lr_rate	[0.0001, 0.001, 0.01, 0.1, 1.0]	0.01

The outcomes of the proposed model are improved by tuning the hyperparameters of the RF classifier, AdaBoost, and GBAs using a grid search method and random search technique which is defined in Equation (8.5).

$$\textit{Ensemble classifier Perf} = \textit{argmax}_x \, f\,(\textit{Ensemble classifier}, H, x) \qquad (8.5)$$

where **Ensemble classifier Perf** provides a set of optimized hyperparameters which are helpful to maximize an efficiency of this proposed model; **Ensemble classifier** denotes RF, AdaBoost, and GBA; **H** denotes hyperparameter search space; **x** denotes the validation dataset. Ensemble learners provide good training score and validation score after tuning its parameter using optimization algorithms such as grid search method and random search method. Using different key metrics, the outcome of the suggested model is evaluated and results are tabulated in Table 8.4.

8.4 Experimental Outcomes and Analyses

8.4.1 Characteristics of UCI Heart Disease Dataset

The proposed ensemble classifier utilized UCI heart disease dataset. The detailed description of UCI heart disease dataset's input attributes is explained in Section 8.3.1. The characteristics of this dataset are given below in Table 8.3.

Table 8.3 UCI heart disease dataset properties.

Dataset	Count of attributes	Count of output classes	Count of samples	Missing values
UCI heart disease dataset	13	2	303	No

8.4.2 Experimental Result of Ensemble Learners and Performance Comparison

Thirteen heart disease risk factors called predictor attributes and one target attribute with two classes are being used as an input for the proposed ensemble classifier. Ten-fold repeated stratified cross-validation is utilized to build a generalized classifier and to prevent overfitting problems. Criteria such as assuming where each folding has almost the same proportions of samples with a specified outcome value may regulate the separation of data into folds; this is referred to as stratified cross-validation. The chosen features of the input samples are given to the ensemble classifier along with the target attribute. Three-way split [28] is used for developing heart prediction model on UCI heart disease dataset; this approach divides the input dataset into three subsets such as 70% of the inputs used for the proposed model training. For validating and tuning the hyperparameters of ensemble classifiers using grid search and random search algorithms, 15% of inputs is used, and for the evaluation of this model, 15% of the input called test data set is used. Using different classifier performance metrics, the outcomes of the final heart disease prediction model are examined. Table 8.4 represents the description of classifier performance metrics which are used for evaluating the proposed model [29, 30].

Table 8.5 for the RF classifier, Table 8.6 for the AdaBoost classifier, and Table 8.7 for the gradient boosting classifier indicate the performance of the model proposed.

Figure 8.5 shows the accuracy of three ensemble learners such as RFA, AdaBoost classifier, and gradient boosting classifier before and after applying hyper tuning optimization algorithms such as grid search and random search algorithm. To illustrate the efficiency of grid search and random search algorithms that are used to enhance the efficiency of the proposed model, Tables 8.3 to 8.5 and Figure 8.5 are used.

8.4.3 Analysis of Experimental Result

The proposed ensemble learner is evaluated using 10% test dataset of UCI heart disease dataset. Six classifier performance metrics are classifier accuracy, Matthews correlation coefficient, receiver operating characteristics curve, sensitivity, specificity, and precision. For the output analysis of this proposed classifier with grid search and random search, comparative study tables and graphs are given in Section 8.4.2. From Tables 8.3 to 8.5, we observed that grid search and random search are used to boost the classifier's performance. Figure 8.5 is used to interpret the efficiency of random search technique over grid search technique as it uses random combination of hyperparameter search space to identify the best hyperparameter for the proposed model. GBA provides 84% accuracy before tuning its hyperparameters and gives 91% and 93% improved accuracy after optimizing its hyperparameter using grid

Table 8.4 Performance evaluation measure of the proposed model.

Metrics	Definition	Formula
Classifier Accuracy	This is a ratio of the total number of accurate estimates to the total set of input observations given.	$Acc = \dfrac{Number\ of\ accurate\ estimates}{Total\ input\ observation}$
Sensitivity (Sen)	The ratio of the number of true positives (TP) to the total number of true positives and false negative (FN).	$Sen = \dfrac{TP}{TP+FN}$
Specificity (Spe)	The ratio between number of true negatives and the samples of true negatives and samples of false positives.	$Spe = \dfrac{TN}{TN+FP}$
Precision (Pre)	It is ration between true positives and the overall true positives and total false positives.	$Pre = \dfrac{TP}{TP+FP}$
Receiver operating characteristics curve (ROC)	This is a curve plotted with the true positive rate (TPR) against the false positive rate (FPR).	$TPR = \dfrac{Total\ True\ Positives}{Total\ positive\ samples}$ $FPR = \dfrac{Total\ False\ Positives}{Total\ negative\ samples}$
Matthews correlation coefficient (MCC)	Using the formula given, this measure rates the effectiveness of the model.	$MCC = \dfrac{TP \star TN - FP \star FN}{\sqrt{(TP+FN)(TP+FP)(TN+FP)(TN+FN)}}$

FP, False positive samples; FN, False negative samples; TP, True positive samples; TN, True negative samples.

Table 8.5 The outcomes of random forest (RF) before and after applying grid search and random search techniques.

Ensemble learner	Accuracy	MCC	ROC	Sen	Spe	Pre
RF without optimization	0.89	0.77	0.88	0.91	0.86	0.88
RF with grid search optimization	0.89	0.77	0.88	0.89	0.88	0.89
RF with random search optimization	0.91	0.82	0.91	0.89	0.93	0.93

Table 8.6 The performance of AdaBoost (AB) classifier before and after applying grid search and random search techniques.

Ensemble learner	Accuracy	MCC	ROC	Sen	Spe	Pre
AB without optimization	0.84	0.69	0.84	0.89	0.79	0.82
AB with grid search optimization	0.93	0.86	0.93	0.91	0.95	0.95
AB with random search optimization	0.91	0.82	0.91	0.89	0.93	0.93

Table 8.7 The performance of gradient boosting (GB) classifier before and after applying grid search and random search techniques.

Ensemble learner	Accuracy	MCC	ROC	Sen	Spe	Pre
GB without optimization	0.84	0.69	0.84	0.81	0.88	0.88
GB with grid search optimization	0.91	0.82	0.91	0.93	0.88	0.9
GB with random search optimization	0.93	0.86	0.93	0.95	0.90	0.92

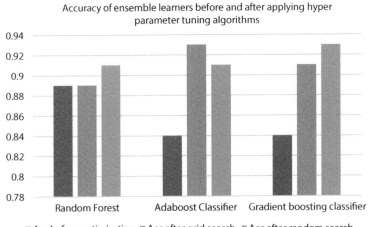

Figure 8.5 Comparison of three ensemble classifier accuracy before and after grid search and random search algorithm.

search method and random search method, respectively. ABA gives 84% accuracy before hyperparameter tuning, showing 93% higher efficiency after tuning its hyperparameter with grid search algorithm and 91% after optimizing its hyperparameters with the random search algorithm. The accuracy of the RFA before hyperparameter tuning is 89%, but after tuning, its hyperparameter using the grid search algorithm, the accuracy of RFA is not enhanced. Random search tuning algorithm which increases RFA accuracy from 89% to 91% after fine tuning of RFA hyperparameters such as the criterion for DT splitting, the number of trees generated in the RF. We conclude that the proposed classifier (ensembled classifier) gives good output when optimizing the hyperparameters of RF, AdaBoost, using model optimization techniques called grid search and random search; gradient boosting is well suited for classifying unseen samples of heart disease. We state that the optimization methods are finely tuned and boost model efficiency of this proposed classifier, and this suggested model can be used to predict the risk of heart disease in a patient well.

8.5   Conclusion

This proposed model is an effective automated disease diagnosis system for the diagnosis of the heart disease. This automated heart diagnosis system uses the UCI heart disease dataset. This proposed model uses grid search and random search techniques for improving outcomes of ensemble learners. The outcomes of this suggested model illustrate that the grid search and random search are used for tuning the hyperparameter of ensemble learners. This proposed model can be extended to apply with cardiac MRI and heart sounds for prediction of myocardial infarction. Automated regularization method can be used to further enhance the efficiency of the proposed classifier.

References

1. Abdul-Aziz, A.A., Desikan, P., Prabhakaran, D., Schroeder, L.F., Tackling the burden of cardiovascular diseases in India: The essential diagnostics list. *Circ. Cardiovasc. Qual. Outcomes*, 12, 4, e005195, 2019.
2. Prabhakaran, D., Jeemon, P., Roy, A., Cardiovascular diseases in India: current epidemiology and future directions. *Circulation*, 133, 16, 1605–1620, 2016.
3. Olvera Lopez, E., Ballard, B.D., Jan, A., Cardiovascular Disease, in: *StatPearls [Internet]*, StatPearls Publishing, Treasure Island (FL), Aug 10 2020, 2021 Jan–. PMID: 30571040, 2020.
4. Moussa, S. and Ambrose, J.A., *Understanding myocardial infarction*, NCBI, https://www.ncbi.nlm.nih.gov/pmc/articles/PMC6124376/ 2018, F1000Research, 7.
5. Kopec, D., Kabir, M.H., Reinharth, D., Rothschild, O., Castiglione, J.A., Human errors in medical practice: systematic classification and reduction with automated information systems. *J. Med. Syst.*, 27, 4, 297–313, 2003.
6. Haq, A.U., Li, J.P., Memon, M.H., Nazir, S., Sun, R., A hybrid intelligent system framework for the prediction of heart disease using machine learning algorithms. *Mob. Inf. Syst.*, 2018, 3, 2018.
7. Javeed, A., Zhou, S., Yongjian, L., Qasim, I., Noor, A., Nour, R., An intelligent learning system based on random search algorithm and optimized random forest model for improved heart disease detection. *IEEE Access*, 7, 180235–180243, 2019.
8. Garate-Escamilla, A.K., EL Hassani, A.H., Andres, E., Classification models for heart disease prediction using feature selection and PCA. *Inform. Med. Unlocked*, 19, 2, 2020, 100330.

9. Maji, S. and Arora, S., Decision tree algorithms for prediction of heart disease, in: *Information and communication technology for competitive strategies*, pp. 447–454, Springer, Singapore, 2019.

10. Latha, C.B.C. and Jeeva, S.C., Improving the accuracy of prediction of heart disease risk based on ensemble classification techniques. *Inform. Med. Unlocked*, 16, 100203, 2019.

11. Shankar, V., Kumar, V., Devagade, U., Karanth, V., Rohitaksha, K., Heart disease prediction using CNN algorithm. *SN Comput. Sci.*, 1, 1–8, 2020.

12. Reddy, G.T. and Khare, N., An efficient system for heart disease prediction using hybrid OFBAT with rule-based fuzzy logic model. *J. Circuits, Syst. Comput.*, 26, 04, 1750061, 2017.

13. Rokach, L., Ensemble methods for classifiers, in: *Data mining and knowledge discovery handbook*, pp. 957–980, Springer, Boston, MA, 2005.

14. Brown, G., Ensemble Learning, in: *Encyclopedia of machine learning*, vol. 312, pp. 15–19, 2010.

15. Janosi, A., Steinbrunn, W., Pfisterer, M., Detrano, R., *Heart Disease Data Set*, UCI machine learning repository, https://www.kaggle.com/ronitf/heart-disease-uci. Available online: https://archive.ics.uci.edu/ml/datasets/Heart+Disease (Accessed on 25 September 2020), 2018.

16. Pintelas, P. and Livieris, I.E., *Special issue on ensemble learning and applications*, MDPI, https://www.mdpi.com/1999-4893/13/6/140, 2020.

17. Brown, G., Ensemble Learning, in: *Encyclopedia of machine learning*, vol. 312, pp. 15–19, 2010.

18. Breiman, L., Random forests. *Mach. Learn.*, 45, 1, 5–32, 2001.

19. Kearns, M., Valiant, L., Cryptographic limitations on learning Boolean formulae and finite automata. *J. ACM (JACM)*, 41, 1, 67–95, 1994.

20. Freund, Y. and Schapire, R.E., A decision-theoretic generalization of on-line learning and an application to boosting. *J. Comput. Syst. Sci.*, 55, 1, 119–139, 1997.

21. Freund, Y. and Schapire, R.E., Experiments with a new boosting algorithm, in: *icml*, vol. 96, pp. 148–156, 1996.

22. Friedman, J.H., Greedy function approximation: a gradient boosting machine. *Ann. Statist.*, 29, 5, 1189–1232, 2001.

23. Kearns, M., *Thoughts on hypothesis boosting*, vol. 45, p. 105, Machine Learning class project https://www.cis.upenn.edu/~mkearns/papers/boostnote.pdf, 1988, Unpublished manuscript.

24. Khan, F., Kanwal, S., Alamri, S., Mumtaz, B., Hyper-Parameter Optimization of Classifiers, Using an Artificial Immune Network and Its Application to Software Bug Prediction. *IEEE Access*, 8, 20954–20964, 2020.

25. Feurer, M. and Hutter, F., Hyperparameter optimization, in: *Automated Machine Learning*, pp. 3–33, Springer, Cham, 2019.

26. Liashchynskyi, P. and Liashchynskyi, P., *Grid search, random search, genetic algorithm: A big comparison for nas*, arXiv preprint arXiv:1912.06059, 2019.

27. Bergstra, J. and Bengio, Y., Random search for hyper-parameter optimization. *J. Mach. Learn. Res.*, 13, 2, 282–287, 2012.

28. Reitermanová, Z., Data Splitting. *WDS'10 Proceedings of Contributed Papers, Part I*, pp. 31–36, 2010. Copyright MATFYZPRESS. https://www.mff.cuni.cz/veda/konference/wds/proc/pdf10/WDS10_105_i1_Reitermanova.pdf

29. Hossin, M. and Sulaiman, M.N., A review on evaluation metrics for data classification evaluations. *Int. J. Data Min. Knowl. Manage. Process.*, 5, 2, 1, 2015.

30. Chicco, D. and Jurman, G., The advantages of the Matthews correlation coefficient (MCC) over F1 score and accuracy in binary classification evaluation. *BMC Genom.*, 21, 1, 1–13, 2020.

Computational Intelligence and Healthcare Informatics Part III— Recent Development and Advanced Methodologies

Sankar Pariserum Perumal[1]*, Ganapathy Sannasi[2], Santhosh Kumar S.V.N.[3] and Kannan Arputharaj[4]

[1]*Department of Information Science and Technology, College of Engineering Guindy, Anna University, Chennai, Tamil Nadu, India*
[2] *School of Computer Science and Engineering, Vellore Institute of Technology, Chennai Campus, Tamil Nadu, India*
[3]*School of Information Technology & Engineering, Vellore Institute of Technology, Vellore, Tamil Nadu, India*
[4]*School of Computer Science and Engineering, Vellore Institute of Technology, Vellore, Tamil Nadu, India*

Abstract

There are different types of healthcare simulations currently available varying from simulation of patient records in hospital emergency wards, specific disease level simulation of patient history to human resource management in clinical environments. Role of Machine Learning (ML)/Deep Learning (DL) models in such simulations is very significant and it produces hybrid results by imbibing advantages of ML and simulation modeling techniques. These models bring out the interdependent relationship between the biomedical and computational factors in complex healthcare simulations leveraged by different practitioners and management authorities. Healthcare simulations can be of two types—Agent-Based Methods (ABM) and Discrete Event Simulations (DES). Such simulations involve study of enormous data generated from various biomedical applications, diagnostic arrays and medical devices which are put into standard analytical procedures to extract logical patterns used for further medical analysis. Various ML algorithms like Random Forest, XG Boosting, and Support Vector Machine used for modeling such simulations and aimed at improved prediction scores are studied. Biomedical feature selection and quality training set labeling processes play important role in stabilizing such ML algorithms. As an advanced level, DL models are deployed by making use of different types of Artificial Neural Networks (ANNs) like Recurrent Neural Networks (RNN) and Convolutional Neural Networks (CNN) to improve the simulation vs. real-time output synchronization. Different DL models leveraged for different biomedical simulations are illustrated. There is an important need to strike a trade-off between handling high dimensional data

Corresponding author: tell.sankar@gmail.com; ORCID 0000-0002-6004-3534

Om Prakash Jena, Alok Ranjan Tripathy, Ahmed A. Elngar and Zdzislaw Polkowski (eds.) Computational Intelligence and Healthcare Informatics, (159–178) © 2021 Scrivener Publishing LLC

and improved prediction accuracies. ML/DL models developed for such healthcare simulations will clearly focus on writing suitable healthcare policies for high quality medical care.

Keywords: Healthcare simulation, machine learning, random forest, support vector machine, stochastic gradient descent, logistic regression, ROC, AUC, deep learning, RNN, bi-LSTM

9.1   Introduction: Simulation in Healthcare

Simulation process is necessary to get a good grip of the functional processes and workflows used in the healthcare domain and their reactive properties when the system under use undergoes several changes over time [25]. Visual representations and data analytical models from such simulation platforms open avenues for improving the efficiency and quality of healthcare services extended by specific simulation systems. Various types of healthcare offerings starting from patient flow in different hospital departments [30] to scheduling the operating equipment and personnel for emergency room services [7] to usage of healthcare services by patients with specific medical cases [14] are capable of being upheld in simulation environments.

Before simulating a real-time healthcare scenario, it is primarily important to draw the process map as to identify the exact problem area in the whole picture to be focused on, which needs to be resolved using the simulator tools or environments, to obtain clarify on the objective of the simulation process. In certain cases, a prototype of the whole simulation process is developed to gain confidence from the domain experts on the direction of the main process in achieving the proposed results. This would help in mutual agreement on the righteousness of the process map. Based on the feedback on the prototype results, the process map may or may not be revisited to realign with the initial simulation objectives. This would also probe the need to enhance the main simulation strategy to coincide with the real-time results. Once the final simulated metrics are derived and compared against the desired data points, domain experts provide their solution alternatives in different stages of the simulation process map. After several rounds of such process betterment steps, the approved simulation process is documented and sometimes extended for further study with continuous real-time data.

9.2   Need for a Healthcare Simulation Process

Since the simulation process as a whole is based out of its evidences, it immensely helped in the decision making step for complex healthcare scenarios. The great advantage of simulating a healthcare scenario is that it gives the courage to conduct the otherwise riskier tasks that are not advisable in real-time cases. It also boosted the idea of knowledgeable discussion among domain experts on various avenues of inconsistencies to look at a medical emergency situation which is not patiently possible in a live operation. It helps in tapping metrics and results faster than a real-time incident where data science or Machine Learning (ML) comes to rescue on the automatic predictive analytics of decisions in complex healthcare instances.

Simulation helps to envisage the health condition of the patient under study ahead of his/her time, i.e., based on the current medical condition and several observations of the bodily reactions to the surgical processes, the potential medical monitoring at a future instant could be achieved in no time. Visual representation of the metric performances as well as the bodily reactions communicate the situation to the healthcare professionals in a way beyond than the plain textual reports could do. The broader problem statement like hospital staff management issues [50] or inventory maintenance issues [15, 27] is circled down to the precise questions with respect to particular resource utilizations, bed coverages or surgical steps. Since each and every step and its requirement in a healthcare simulation process is open to the table, the participant enjoys the ability to vary the input parameters, augment, or cut down the intermediate steps which might be necessary in executing different use cases of highly organized medical proposals. This clearly enables the subsequent task of revisiting the initial numbers of certain input variables and the corresponding hypotheses made on them before kicking off the main simulation process, thereby double confirming on the stability of the output model.

9.3   Types of Healthcare Simulations

There are different types of simulation processes evolved over the period of time, among which the most commonly used three types are as follows:

- Discrete Event Simulation (DES),
- Agent-Based Models (ABM), and
- System Dynamics (SD).

In healthcare context, DES [52] refers to the respective medical system functionality defined at discrete intervals rather than their continuous availability. This method conduces the iterative identification of reactive system changes as and when it happens and reduces the necessity to gauge these changes separately. The requirements and their objectives in a DES type are quantifiable and tend to enable the hypothetical analyses before the actual implementation of their outcomes. The performance shift in the discrete intervals gives a fair chance to fasten or decelerate the simulation process for better dissection of the healthcare applications.

ABM method [24] gives importance to the behavior of every agent used in the concerned healthcare management system. The reference of such an agent can vary from a specific tool used in the medical process or a set of processes aimed at a particular simulation output. These agents play vital role in impacting the overall simulation efficiency. As and when the correspondence among different healthcare application agents vary in direction and contents, their time and execution dependencies also vary [13], for example, in a hospital operational management, emergency department, operational personnel, health policymakers, and health economists.

SD model [51] gives more importance to the system flow than the discrete elements and their behaviors. The overall system performance is gauged based on the skeleton of the functional flow. Unlike DES and ABM methods, SD is not a stochastic model where the output is derived in a single instance. Naturally, SD models spend more time on the conceptual design of the model than the complexity of the model. The model is designed in such a way to reduce the delay between the flow metrics and the follow up action items on the top of it. For example, overall functional structure of an emergency surgical unit is given more weightage in its SD model than the individual discrete elements like its tools or equipment and trusted agents employed for intact surgical performance.

Nowadays, there are hybrid healthcare simulation processes used for better system performance and improved operational clarity. This can either be a combination of DES and SD models or a combination of ABM and SD models. DES and SD models [9] together provide the advantage of discrete units' performance within a healthcare department and at the same time, its functional dependencies with other departments in the same healthcare ecosystem. Brailsford *et al.* [5] provide a simulation platform where DES and SD methods are combined to model a STI clinic as a discrete event system and the local infections are designed as susceptible, infected, and recovered (SIR) SD model. Also, though there are operational differences between DES and ABS systems, their combination is preferred by certain simulation processes where several iterations need to be run to model their discrete random distribution [46]. Table 9.1 provides a detailed list of literature references, their simulation types, contexts, and tools/softwares used in these healthcare simulations.

Table 9.1 Healthcare simulation instances.

Reference	Simulation type	Context	Year	Tool/software
[48]	ABM	Betterment of Hospital emergency services	2010	FSM
[6]	DES	Emergency Department modeling	2010	SIMUL8
[3]	ABM	distributed memory based emergency response	2006	EpiSimS
[21]	DES	Handling long patient waiting times	2019	FlexSim
[22]	ABM	Resource allocation in emergency response	2015	STORMI
[19]	DES	Demand management of emergency department from closed care centers	2020	FlexSim
[28]	ABM	Control strategy on Influenza pandemic spread	2012	GIS
[8]	SD	Impact of Emergency Department on hospital's surgery activities	2013	iThink 9.1.4
[20]	SD	Theory of Constraints in Healthcare	2019	AnyLogic
[42]	SD	Reducing Childhood Overweight	2019	iThink V10
[31]	SD	Demand & Supply projection of physical therapists	2019	Stella 8.1.1

9.4   AI in Healthcare Simulation

Artificial Intelligence (AI) in healthcare simulation [2, 10, 32, 43] extends a needy hand to mitigate the practical issues in all complex aspects of healthcare management services, starting from service speed, issue diagnosis to the genomics prediction, as well as disease classification based on medical history and biological symptoms and possible treatment suggestions. AI is used in both pre-clinical and clinical trials to provide meaningful insight on medical datasets and thereby yield predictive analytics on the specific healthcare problem statements. Under the broad category of AI, both ML and deep learning (DL) are used to develop and rerun data science models for business application predictions.

9.4.1   Machine Learning Models in Healthcare Simulation

ML is the heuristic process to produce suitable algorithms on top of domain specific datasets and come up with stable models for analytic predictions or patterns that best suit the past data. In healthcare simulation, ML models can be developed for various analytical case studies like computational biology where drug patterns are rationally designed based on earlier molecular or atomic cell information and healthcare recommendation models where user level suggestions are populated based on their medical history and widely followed current treatment methods. There are variety of recommendation systems [39–41] deployed in different domains including healthcare domain by leveraging collaborative filtering, content based recommendations and hybrid models. Also, there are several ML algorithms that could be applied based on the business requirement, healthcare context, nature of the available dataset and the required prediction output type. In this section, a novel healthcare simulation problem statement and application of ML model for its resolution are discussed in detail.

9.4.1.1   Machine Learning Model for Post-Surgical Risk Prediction

This case study deals with the invasive surgical procedural dataset that constitutes various types of data including patients' demographic details, EHR medical history, and surgery descriptive records. There is always a high degree of postoperative complicate risks in invasive surgical procedures where the patients are succumbed to mild to major health complications. Hence, this necessitates the requirement on the development of a ML model that can predict such postoperative risks, thereby supporting clinical system workflows and interoperability. This system also presents alarming signals to the surgeons and supportive clinical resources with the risky profiles that need careful patient re-evaluations before proceeding with their surgical procedures as well as enhanced pre-operative care focused on continuous monitoring of patients health metrics for high surgical quality.

Though there are various pre-operative health risk assessors like National Surgical Quality Improvement Program (NSQIP) [4] representing cross-continental participations, these are not locally reliable since the curated metrics get averaged out across different populations and races. Cologne *et al.* [11] pointed out that such differences arose because of pressing factors like duration of the in-house patients' accommodation, malignant tumor types, and different health complications [12] with respect to the particular hospital's geographical location. Leveraging health risk assessors like NSQIP need not necessarily result in the betterment of post-surgical medical history and they do not guarantee in lowering down the patients' financial burden after their surgeries [16, 34]. So, this calls out for a locally customized ML model to predict such post-operative health complications based on the locally available datasets.

A total of 4,582 patients' pre-surgical as well as post-surgical data were collected from three surgical critical care centers in Chennai, India spanning across the timeline of 3 months (January to March 2020). These data were sourced from simulated EHR system supported by the surgical centers as well as the task-wise clinical data facilitated and simulated by the surgical instruments used by these centers. Post-surgical complications are not directly available in this dataset and hence a detailed analysis was carried out to group them into nine major categories and a final category to host all other unclassified complications, to predominantly align with the wide range of ICD-10-CM codes (International Classification of Diseases) as shown in Figure 9.1. Though the number of deaths in both genders is very less, it is equally important to note that the post-operative complications in terms of infections, inpatient procedures, and neurological disorders are notably high.

9.4.1.1.1   High-Level Machine Learning Model Architecture

Figure 9.2 provides the high-level system flow of a ML model aimed at post-operative risk prediction process. This consists of four major sections—Data Processing, Factor Selection, ML Algorithm, and Parameter Optimization. At the end of several training iterations, the ML model is stabilized with refined parameter values upon which health complication scores are predicted.

Since the post-surgical dataset is sourced from three different surgical critical care centers that are specialized in hematological malignancy treatments, a data hub for collecting and curating these data is needed. The factors used in the individual data repositories vary from one center to another and do not share common metadata format. Firstly, these data are fed into a Big Data Pipeline which automatically cleanses the data sourced from different repositories and standardizes it based on the data mapping rules for standard health records. Data harmonization and normalization also happens in this stage so that the input data frame is on par with industry standards before being fed for training a ML model.

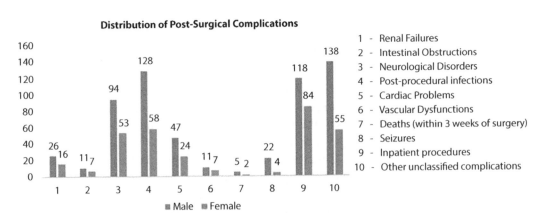

Figure 9.1 Distribution of post-surgical complications in the selected dataset.

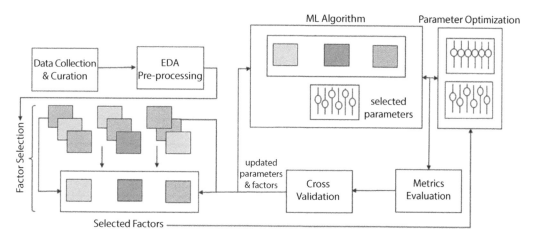

Figure 9.2 High-level ML model architecture.

Exploratory Data Analysis (EDA) on the normalized dataset is then carried out where inter-correlations among various factors/attributes used in this hematological malignancy focussed surgical dataset are evaluated. Both univariate and multivariate analyses are performed to find the relationships among different attributes and aggregate them into specific factor sets to ease the continuous training process of the subsequent ML model. At the end of this stage, the curated dataset is well segregated into different sets of patients' medical and surgical attributes invariably contributing to hematological malignancies.

Table 9.2 presents the list of clinical characteristics of the patients who had undergone invasive surgical procedures for hematological malignant tumors. The different tumor attributes that are taken into consideration in this dataset are Chronic Myelogenous Leukemia (CML), Chronic Lymphocytic Leukemia (CLL), Acute Myeloid Leukemia (AML), Acute Lymphoblastic Leukemia (ALL), MyeloDysplastic Syndrome with Severe Aplastic Anaemia (MDS/SAA), and Lymphoma and Myeloma. The percentages of such tumor treatments vary among surgical centers as well as different genders as shown in Table 9.2.

The binary classification of different factors like hypothyroidism, diabetes mellitus, rheumatoid arthritis, and COPD (Chronic Obstructive Pulmonary Disease) that includes chronic bronchitis, emphysema, and other lung diseases impacting the normal breathing process are carried out to conduce the model training stage where these factors are trained with different weightage metrics. It is evident from Table 9.2 that, though there are higher or lower percentages for certain attributes on females compared to males, most of these factors share general pattern among both genders. Other factors that also contribute to the model training stage are, whether the surgical patients have drug abuse history in the recent past and they are HIV infected or not.

The second section deals with the dimensionality reduction where the objective is to reduce the number of factors to be fed into the training process from 724 elements to a sizeable number fit for the ML model. Based on the univariate and multivariate analyses done in the previous step among the existing factors and the non-negative matrix factorization (NMF) method resulting in the selected factors list. The chosen non-negative matrix factorization method considers the entire input matrix with 4,582 patients' records × 724 factors. It results in two reduced matrices—one 4,582 × 15 matrix with the selected factors and the next 15 × 724 matrix with trained weights.

Table 9.2 Clinical characteristics of surgical patients treated for hematological malignancies.

Attributes	Invasive surgical procedures for hematological malignancies (Jan 2020–Mar 2020)	
	Male (%)	Female (%)
Patients	2861 (62.44)	1721 (37.56)
Age		
> 60 years	912 (31.88)	395 (22.95)
<= 60 years	1949 (68.12)	1326 (77.05)
Surgical Procedure Classes	73	62
Hypothyroidism		
Yes	722 (25.24)	682 (39.63)
No	2139 (74.76)	1039 (60.37)
Diabetes Mellitus		
Yes	1039 (36.32)	327 (19)
No	1822 (63.68)	1394 (81)
Rheumatoid Arthritis		
Yes	301 (10.52)	129 (7.5)
No	2560 (89.48)	1592 (92.5)
COPD		
Yes	758 (26.49)	377 (21.91)
No	2103 (73.51)	1344 (78.09)
Drug Addicts		
Yes	488 (17.06)	163 (9.47)
No	2373 (82.94)	1558 (90.53)
HIV Infected		
Yes	126 (4.4)	151 (8.77)
No	2735 (95.6)	1570 (91.23)
Tumor Types		
CML	121 (4.23)	74 (4.3)
CLL	335 (11.71)	222 (12.9)
AML	776 (27.12)	546 (31.73)

(Continued)

Table 9.2 Clinical characteristics of surgical patients treated for hematological malignancies. (*Continued*)

Attributes	Invasive surgical procedures for hematological malignancies (Jan 2020–Mar 2020)	
	Male (%)	Female (%)
ALL	792 (27.68)	443 (25.74)
MDS/SAA	211 (7.38)	148 (8.6)
Lymphoma	546 (19.08)	267 (15.51)
Myeloma	80 (2.8)	21 (1.22)

9.4.1.1.2   ML Methods, Evaluation, and Optimization

The ML models considered in this case study of predicting the post-surgical health complications are Random Forest (RF) [29], Support Vector Machine (SVM) [17], and Stochastic Gradient Descent (SGD) [18] algorithms trained on 4582 surgical patients' records over 15 selected factors from the previous step. Each algorithm is trained individually with different factors set and their derived combinations to achieve maximum possible accuracy on the complication outcomes. Python library class used for RF algorithm was scikit learn library's sklearn.ensemble.RandomForestClassifier() class [35] which tries to fit as many decision trees as possible on different bootstrapped subsets of the input dataset. To improve the prediction accuracy of the model, RF algorithm either averages out the accuracies or picks the mode of all predictions resulting from individual subsets. Though it is computationally intensive considering all decision trees it internally handles, it performs better in identifying the highly related important factors from the selected factor set for complication prediction.

Though there are many SVM algorithms supported in Python library Scikit-learn, the suitable one for predicting the specific post-surgical complication class is sklearn.svm. NuSVC() class [36] which is similar to SVC class [37] but it has an extra regularization argument "nu" to control the number (between 0 and 1) of support vectors being used in the classification process. This class, by default, returns "OVR" (One-Vs-Rest) decision function among the list of complication outcomes to be predicted and this can be explicitly overwritten with "OVO" (One-Vs-One) function. Nu-SVC algorithms find a hyperplane between data classes, which can maximize the margin between those classes, though many such planes can potentially separate these classes. This SVM algorithm efficiently handled the post-operative complication dataset of high input dimensionality.

To implement SGD-based classification, Python library class used is sklearn.linear_model.SGDClassifier() class [38]. This is nothing but a linear classifier with SGD training, i.e., each sample's gradient loss is estimated every time when the model gets trained and updated with a decaying learning rate. The regularizer used in this algorithm is based on the penalty added to the loss function, defined as squared Euclidean variation L2 or absolute difference L1 or an Elastic Net, a weighted combination of both. Among these three ML algorithms, SGD classifier is selected since its accuracy metrics compared to other two ML models was higher. Also, the optimization parameters used in each of these ML models improve the performance and stability of respective algorithms with local convergence. In the case of SGD Classifier, the "coef_init" and "intercept_init" parameters were initialized to 0.21 and 0.06, respectively, to kick start the optimized learning process. Also, SVM algorithm's fit() function makes use of "sample_weight" argument that provides per-sample weights by rescaling the regularizer component per sample. RF classifier makes use of "ccp_alpha" parameter for minimal cost complexity pruning, i.e., among the list of split trees chosen to make up the decision path, only those with cost complexity less than the optimized "ccp_alpha" value are chosen.

As shown in Figures 9.3, 9.4 and 9.5, "area_*" parameters in the AUC curve graphs represent the area covered by each of 10 post-operative complication outcomes predicted out of the selected factors set. Based on Area under the Curve (AUC) performance of Receiver Operating Characteristics (ROC) of all 10 post-operative complication outcomes for each of 3 ML algorithms, SGD classifier is chosen to have the higher AUC value for most of the complication outcomes and the model training for each algorithm type is cross validated 10-fold to extract the optimized hyper-parameters for each of these outcomes.

Model inference gives surplus metadata including final factor set weights and the bias coefficients which provide promising interpretations for improved risk control methods by the surgeons and pre-clinical resources on the patients with hematological malignancies. Post-surgical complication outcomes that are more than 10% of the total population in such tumor surgeries are presented along with an alarm signal so that the clinicians could take a serious look in such cases and plan for extended care and evaluation of the respective patients with higher risk. Similar to this simulation case study, there are quite a few ML algorithms that are deployed today aimed at improved accuracy and performance on the simulation objective. The key factor is the efficient and relative factor set selection and rigorous model training that make the due ML algorithm advantageous over the rest.

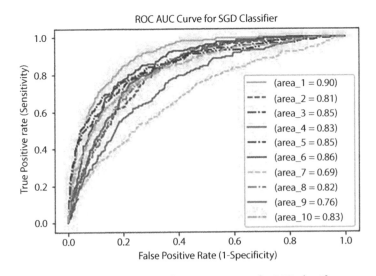

Figure 9.3 ROC-AUC curve of post-surgical complication outcomes for SGD classifier.

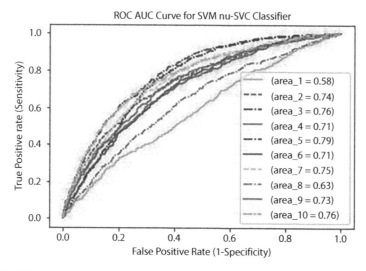

Figure 9.4 ROC-AUC curve of post-surgical complication outcomes for SVM nu-SVC classifier.

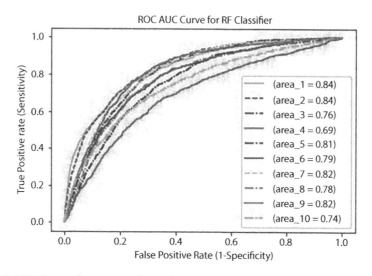

Figure 9.5 ROC-AUC Curve of post-surgical complication outcomes for RF classifier.

9.4.2   Deep Learning Models in Healthcare Simulation

DL algorithms create Artificial Neural Networks (ANNs) that can learn from the input features and produce their own intelligent results. Though both ML and DL come under the umbrella of AI, DL executes every single step by means of human-like AI. In this section, a healthcare simulation case study that leverages one of the most widely used DL algorithm and proves its performance over ML algorithms is presented.

9.4.2.1   Bi-LSTM–Based Surgical Participant Prediction Model

This case study deals with filtering out surgical and clinical attributes from the locally collected dataset of medical professionals who take part in neurosurgical procedures and their surgical measure values. The surgical and clinical attributes are extracted from VR (Virtual Reality) surgical simulator—NeuroTouch [44] developed by National Research Council of Canada and are trained in a DL model to predict specific set of medical experts' characteristics. These professionals are further classified into four classes—neurointensivists, neurosurgeons, neurosurgical residents, and final year medical college students. A special case of RNN (Recurrent Neural Network)–LSTM (Long Short-Term Memory) is used in this study. The dataset was locally collected from 90 medical professionals working in the neurosurgery section of three different surgical critical care centres in Chennai, India and 10 computer simulated records are also added for class balancing. LSTM model is deployed in Keras neural network API in TensorFlow 2.0 library for DL.

9.4.2.1.1   Basic LSTM Unit

These medical professionals, whose data are exported from NeuroTouch VR simulator as CSV files in the timeframe of January 2020 to March 2020, have participated in several simulated hematological tumor resections. The performance measures of this bi-LSTM–based prediction model are then compared against those of two ML algorithms—LR (Logistic Regression) and RF (Random Forest). LSTM is the specific version of RNN as proposed by Hochreiter and Schmidhuber [23] who introduced two new parts to a RNN—Memory C and gate structure. As shown in Figure 9.6, there are four gates in a LSTM cell—input gate I, output gate o, forget gate f, and control gate c.

The input gate i_t is the gatekeeper that inspects which weighted vector could get into the LSTM cell. The forget gate f_t is in charge of getting rid of unwanted weighted vectors from the last memory. The control gate updates the LSTM cell state from C_{t-1} to C_t based on $\hat{C}_t$. The output gate o_t keeps a tab on the hidden vector h_{t-1} and controls what goes in as input to the next LSTM cell. "tanh" function is used to flatten out the output vector within −1 to

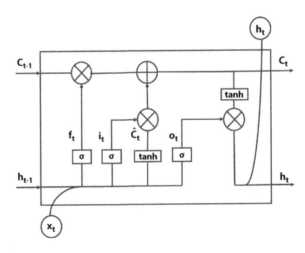

Figure 9.6 Basic LSTM unit.

1 and σ refers to the sigmoid activation function applied between two gates. These LSTM gates fit in between the input layer and the hidden layers in a RNN architecture.

9.4.2.1.2   Bidirectional LSTM Model Network Architecture

Bidirectional LSTM, introduced by Schuster and Paliwal [45], necessitates the need to split the LSTM outputs into forward and backward directions. Both positive and negative feedback is propagated in this LSTM network, thereby maintaining the consistency of LSTM cell state to the maximum expectation. Figure 9.7 explains how bi-LSTM unit gets and gives directional weighted vectors from and to input and hidden layers.

This surgical participant prediction model is built on Python Keras library on TensorFlow model which is more user-friendly on high-level APIs. For this case study, 1 bidirectional LSTM layer with 4 units, 2 hidden layers with 8 units, 2 fully connected layers with 8 and 64 units, and output layer with 8 units are used to output the different participant classes among the neurosurgical teams using VR simulator NeuroTouch. Among 552 different features in this simulator dataset, Singular Value Decomposition (SVD) is followed based on Eigen values to reduce them into 10 prominent features. LSTM mainly overcomes sequential persistence feature of RNNs where RNN needs to retain the past information closer to the current data for sequential connect, though it is not very important as a whole for a sequential network. Since LSTM makes use of long term dependencies [33, 49], it can get rid of such irrelevant information in its forget gate. Ten-fold cross-validation is again used to overcome overfitting and epoch number is chosen based on performance results from 500–2,500 iterations. The same set of features selected for this model training are fed into RF and LR algorithm and the evaluation metrics are then plotted.

Misclassification among these 100 records are evaluated using confusion matrix determined for each of these algorithms. The comparison results are shown in Tables 9.3 to 9.5, where bi-LSTM model outruns two ML algorithms in prediction accuracy. Overall, misclassification of "Neurointensivists" and "Neurosurgeons" are less compared to other two surgical participants' prediction in all three algorithms. Also, it is important to note that LSTM model achieved prediction accuracy of 81% with only 10 surgical attributes compared to 68 attributes present in the surgical simulation CSV file provided by VR simulator.

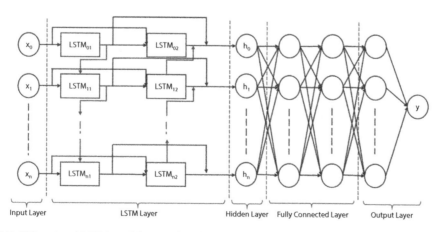

Figure 9.7 Bidirectional LSTM model network architecture.

Table 9.3 Misclassification—Confusion matrix for bi-LSTM model.

bi-LSTM model		Predicted			
		Neurointensivists	Neurosurgeons	Residents	Final year students
Actual	Neurointensivists	12 (86%)	1 (7%)	1 (7%)	0 (0%)
	Neurosurgeons	1 (4%)	19 (83%)	1 (4%)	2 (9%)
	Residents	0 (0%)	3 (19%)	13 (81%)	0 (0%)
	Final Year Students	1 (2%)	3 (6%)	6 (13%)	37 (79%)

Table 9.4 Misclassification—Confusion matrix for LR model.

LR model		Predicted			
		Neurointensivists	Neurosurgeons	Residents	Final year students
Actual	Neurointensivists	11 (79%)	1 (7%)	0 (0%)	2 (14%)
	Neurosurgeons	1 (4%)	18 (78%)	1 (4%)	3 (13%)
	Residents	0 (0%)	2 (13%)	12 (75%)	2 (13%)
	Final Year Students	3 (6%)	3 (6%)	6 (13%)	35 (74%)

Table 9.5 Misclassification—Confusion matrix for RF model.

RF model		Predicted			
		Neurointensivists	Neurosurgeons	Residents	Final year students
Actual	Neurointensivists	10 (71%)	2 (14%)	1 (7%)	1 (7%)
	Neurosurgeons	1 (4%)	16 (70%)	2 (9%)	4 (17%)
	Residents	0 (0%)	1 (6%)	11 (69%)	4 (25%)
	Final Year Students	0 (0%)	7 (15%)	10 (21%)	30 (64%)

This study has taken the reduced feature set, i.e., surgical and clinical attributes, into account, like decrease in blood loss, convergence in instrument tips, bleeding speed, and total blood emitted. This can be extended to variety of other features [53] in this NeuroTouch VR simulator dataset like so that correlation between predominant features and these additional features could also be examined.

In all the above three, Tables 9.3 to 9.5, percentages indicate the proportion among the rows (actuals).

Precision measure is also calculated as shown in Equation (9.1) whose metrics again prove that bis-LSTM model outperforms RF and LR models. It is represented in Figure 9.8.

$$Precision = \frac{Number\ of\ Correctly\ Predicted\ Outcomes}{Number\ of\ Total\ Outcomes\ Predicted} \tag{9.1}$$

Bi-LSTM model's two-way feedback helped achieving better performance for this surgical core team professionals' dataset and their classification. Also, there should be a flag check for striking right balance between reduction of misclassification error rates and improvement of overall prediction accuracy. Since we cannot just rely upon certified credentials for neurosurgeons and educational qualification for residents and final year students to estimate their surgical performance, this classification prediction task will be useful for practical evaluation of their skillsets.

There are quite a few other DL algorithms being commonly used for practical advantages like Convolutional Neural Network (CNN) in the field of Computer Vision—for patients' CT (Computer Tomography) Scan image analysis [26, 47]. RNNs are favored in some use cases where sequential learning of sentiment text analytics [1, 54] is required. Here, overall sentiment of the given text/comment is given more importance than the sequential yet inconsistent domain words.

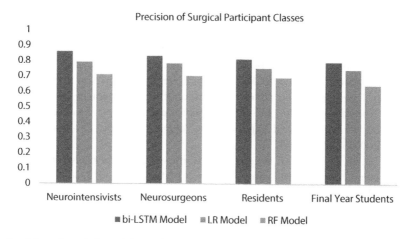

Figure 9.8 Precision of surgical participant classes.

9.5   Conclusion

A detailed analysis on the different types of healthcare simulations is done in this chapter—starting from DES to ABM to SD. Literature study of these simulation types and their contexts are elucidated. Role of AI in healthcare simulation is then discussed where two types of AI—ML and DL models trained and stabilized for various research problems in healthcare simulation are analyzed in this chapter. A detailed case study to classify and predict the post-surgical complication outcomes using ML algorithms is carried out where ROC-AUC performance measure is compared among these algorithms in detail. Then, another case study to identify different surgical and clinical attributes from the given neurosurgical simulation export file and thereby classify them into various classes of neurosurgical professionals using bidirectional LSTM DL model is presented. Performance metrics of this specific version of RNN trained on hyper parameters are compared against those of ML algorithms and tabulated.

References

1. Abdi, A., Shamsuddin, S.M., Hasan, S., Piran, J., Deep learning-based sentiment classification of evaluative text based on Multi-feature fusion. *Inf. Process. Manag*, 56, 4, 1245–1259, 2019, https://doi.org/10.1016/j.ipm.2019.02.018.
2. Ahuja, A.S., The impact of artificial intelligence in medicine on the future role of the physician. *PeerJ*, 7, e7702, 2019. https://doi.org/10.7717/peerj.7702.
3. Alotaibi, M.F. and Ibrahim, D.M., Agent-Based Simulation for Coordination Emergency Response: A Review Study, in: *1st International Conference on Computer Applications & Information Security (ICCAIS)*, Riyadh, pp. 1–5, 2018, https://doi.org/10.1109/CAIS.2018.8441949.
4. Bilimoria, K.Y., Liu, Y., Paruch, J.L., Zhou, L., Kmiecik, T.E., Ko, C.Y., Cohen, M.E., Development and evaluation of the universal ACS NSQIP surgical risk calculator: a decision aid and informed consent tool for patients and surgeons. *J. Am. Coll. Surg.*, 217, 5, 833–842, 2013, https://doi.org/10.2016/j.jamcollsurg.2013.07.385.
5. Brailsford, S., Desai, S., Viana, J., Towards the holy grail: Combining system dynamics and discrete-event simulation in healthcare, in: *Proceedings of the 2010 Winter Simulation Conference*, Baltimore, MD, USA, pp. 2293–2303, 2010, https://doi.org/10.1109/WSC.2010.5678927.
6. Brenner, S., Zeng, Z., Liu, Y., Wang, J., Li, J., Howard, P.K., Modeling and Analysis of Emergency Department at University of Kentucky Chandler Hospital Using Simulations. *J. Emerg. Nurs.*, 36, 4, 303–310, 2010, https://doi.org/10.1016/j.jen.2009.07.018.
7. Brown, E.G., Howard, P.K., Moore, D., Simulating Emergency Department Boarding Using a Difference Equation. *medRxiv*, 1–14, 2020, https://doi.org/10.1101/2020.03.19.20039040.
8. Cassettari, L., Mosca, R., Orfeo, A., Revetria, R., Rolando, F., Morrison, J., A System Dynamics Study of an Emergency Department Impact on the Management of Hospital's Surgery Activities. *Proceedings of the 3rd International Conference on Simulation and Modeling Methodologies, Technologies and Applications – Volume 1: HA*, pp. 597–604, 2013, https://doi.org/10.5220/0004617205970604.
9. Chahal, K., Eldabi, T., Young, T., A conceptual framework for hybrid system dynamics and discrete event simulation for healthcare. *J. Enterp. Inf. Manage.*, 26, 1/2, 50–74, 2013, https://doi.org/10.1108/17410391311289541.
10. Christo, V.R.E., Nehemiah, K.H., Nahato, K.B., Brighty, J., Kannan, A., Computer assisted medical decision-making system using genetic algorithm and extreme learning machine for diagnosing allergic rhinitis. *Int. J. Bio-Inspir. Com.*, 16, 3, https://doi.org/10.1504/IJBIC.2020.111279, 2020.

11. Cologne, K.G., Keller, D.S., Liwanag, L., Devaraj, B., Senagore, A.J., Use of the American College of Surgeons NSQIP Surgical Risk Calculator for Laparoscopic Colectomy: how good is it and how can we improve it? *J. Am. Coll. Surg.*, 220, 3, 281–286, 2015, https://doi.org/10.1016/j.jamcollsurg.2014.12.007.

12. Corey, K.M., Kashyap, S., Lorenzi, E., Lagoo-Deenadayalan, S.A., Heller, K., Whalen, K., Balu, S., Heflin, M.T., McDonald, S.R., Swaminathan, M., Sendak, M., Development and Validation of Machine Learning Models to identify high-risk surgical patients using automatically curated Electronic Health Record data (Pythia): A retrospective, single-site study. *PloS Med.*, 15, 11, e1002701, 2018.

13. Daknou, A., Hammadi, S., Zgaya, H., Hubert, H., Agent based optimization and management of healthcare processes at the emergency department. *Int. J. Math. Comput. Simul.*, 2, 3, 285–294, 2008.

14. Dobson, T.H.W. and Gopalakrishnan, V., Preclinical Models of Pediatric Brain Tumors—Forging Ahead. *Bioeng. (Basel)*, 5, 4, 1–13, 2018, https://doi.org/10.3390/bioengineering5040081.

15. Efe, K., Raghavan, V., Choubey, S., Simulation modeling movable hospital assets managed with RFID sensors, in: *Proceedings of the 2009 Winter Simulation Conference (WSC)*, Austin, TX, USA, 2009, pp. 2054–2064, 2009, https://doi.org/10.1109/WSC.2009.5429662.

16. Etzioni, D.A., Wasif, N., Dueck, A.C., Cima, R.R., Hohmann, S.F., Naessens, J.M., Mathur, A.K., Habermann, E.B., Association of hospital participation in a surgical outcomes monitoring program with inpatient complications and mortality. *J. Assoc. Am. Med. Coll. JAMA*, 313, 5, 505–511, 2015, https://doi.org/10.1001/jama.2015.90.

17. Evgeniou, T. and Pontil, M., Support Vector Machines: Theory and Applications, in: *Machine Learning and Its Applications. ACAI 1999. Lecture Notes in Computer Science*, vol. 2049, G. Paliouras, V. Karkaletsis, C.D. Spyropoulos (Eds.), Springer, Berlin, Heidelberg, 2001, https://doi.org/10.1007/3-540-44673-7_12.

18. Friedman, J.H., Stochastic gradient boosting. *Comput. Stat. Data Anal.*, 38, 4, 367–378, 2002, https:doi.org/10.1016/S0167-9473(01)00065-2.

19. Gabriel, G.T., Campos, A.T., Magacho, A.L., Segismondi, L.C., Vilela, F.F., Queiroz, J.A.D., Montevechi, J.A.B., Lean thinking by integrating with discrete event simulation and design of experiments: an emergency department expansion. *Peer J Comput. Sci.*, 6, e284, 2020, https://doi.org/10.7717/peerj-cs.284.

20. Grida, M. and Zeid, M., A System Dynamics-based Model to implement the Theory of Constraints in a Healthcare System. *Simul-T. Soc Mod. Sim.*, 95, 7, 593–605, 2019, https://doi.org/10.1177/0037549718788953.

21. Hajrizi, E. and Berisha, D., Application of Discrete Events Simulation for the Department of Emergency at Peja Regional Hospital Case Study Kosovo. *IFAC-PapersOnLine.*, 52, 25, 376–381, 2019, https://doi.org/10.1016/j.ifacol.2019.12.556.

22. Hawe, G.I., Coates, G., Wilson, D.T., Crouch, R.S., Agent-based simulation of emergency response to plan the allocation of resources for a hypothetical two-site major incident. *Eng. Appl. Artif. Intell.*, 46, 2, 336–345, 2015, https://doi.org/10.1016/j.engappai.2015.06.023.

23. Hochreiter, S. and Schmidhuber, J., Long Short-Term Memory. *Neural Comput., ACM.*, 9, 8, 1735–1780, 1997, https://doi.org/10.1162/neco.1997.9.8.1735.

24. Huang, J., Jennings, N., Fox, J., Agent-based approach to healthcare management. *Appl. Artif. Intell.*, 9, 4, 1–36, 1995, https://doi.org/10.1080/08839519508945482.

25. Jain, S. and McLean, C., A framework for modeling and simulation for emergency response, in: *Proceedings of the 2003 Winter Simulation Conference*, New Orleans, LA, USA, Vol. 1, pp. 1068–1076, 2003, https://doi.org/10.1109/WSC.2003.1261532.

26. Karabulut, E.M. and Ibrikci, T., Emphysema discrimination from raw HRCT images by Convolutional Neural Networks, *9th International Conference on Electrical and Electronics Engineering*, 705–708, 2015, https://doi.org/10.1109/ELECO.2015.7394441.

27. Khaleghi, T., Murat, A., Neemuchwala, H., Use of simulation in managing reusable medical equipment inventory in surgical services. *Proceedings of the Summer Computer Simulation Conference*, 39, 1–7, 2016, https://dl.acm.org/doi/10.5555/3015574.3015613.

28. Khalil, K.M., Abdel-Aziz, M., Nazmy, T.T., Salem, A.B.M., An Agent-Based Modeling for Pandemic Influenza in Egypt, in: *Handbook on Decision Making*, vol. *Intelligent Systems Reference Library*. Vol.33, J. Lu, L.C. Jain, G. Zhang (Eds.), Springer, Berlin, Heidelberg, 2012, https://doi.org/10.1007/978-3-642-25755-1_11.

29. Liaw, A. and Wiener, M., Classification and Regression by randomForest. *R News, Newslett. R Project.*, 2, 3, 18–22, 2002.

30. McLean, C., Jain, S., Lee, Y., Hutchings, C., *Technical Guidance for the Specification and Development of Homeland Security Simulation Applications*, pp. 1–110, National Institute of Standards and Technology, USA, 2012, http://dx.doi.org/10.6028/NIST.TN.1742.

31. Morii, Y., Ishikawa, T., Suzuki, T., Tsuji, S., Yamanaka, M., Ogasawara, K., Yamashina, H., Projecting future supply and demand for physical therapists in Japan using system dynamics. *Health Policy Technol.*, 8, 2, 118–127, 2019, https://doi.org/10.1016/j.hlpt.2019.05.003.

32. Nahato, K.B., Nehemiah, K.H., Kannan, A., Hybrid approach using fuzzy sets and extreme learning machine for classifying clinical datasets. *Inform. Med. Unlocked.*, 2, 1–11, 2016, https://doi.org/10.1016/j.imu.2016.01.001.

33. Nas, S. and Koyuncu, M., Emergency Department Capacity Planning: A Recurrent Neural Network and Simulation Approach. *Comput. Math Methods Med.*, 4359719, 1–13, 2019, https://doi.org/10.1155/2019/4359719.

34. Osborne, N.H., Nicholas, L.H., Ryan, A.M., Thumma, J.R., Dimick, J.B., Association of hospital participation in a quality reporting program with surgical outcomes and expenditures for Medicare beneficiaries. *J. Am. Med. Assoc.*, 313, 5, 496–504, 2015, https://doi.org/10.1001/jama.2015.25.

35. Pedregosa, F., Varoquaux, G., Gramfort, A., Michel, V., Thirion, B., Grisel, O., Blondel, M., Prettenhofer, P., Weiss, R., Dubourg, V., Vanderplas, J., Passos, A., Cournapeau, D., Brucher, M., Perrot, M., Duchesnay, E., Scikit-learn: Machine Learning in Python. *J. Mach. Learn. Res.*, 12, 2825–2830, 2011. sklearn.ensemble.RandomForestClassifier(), https://scikit-learn.org/stable/modules/generated/sklearn.ensemble.RandomForestClassifier.html.

36. Pedregosa, F., Varoquaux, G., Gramfort, A., Michel, V., Thirion, B., Grisel, O., Blondel, M., Prettenhofer, P., Weiss, R., Dubourg, V., Vanderplas, J., Passos, A., Cournapeau, D., Brucher, M., Perrot, M., Duchesnay, E., Scikit-learn: Machine Learning in Python. *J. Mach. Learn. Res.*, 12, 2825–2830, 2011. sklearn.svm.NuSVC(), https://scikit-learn.org/stable/modules/generated/sklearn.svm.NuSVC.html#sklearn.svm.NuSVC.

37. Pedregosa, F., Varoquaux, G., Gramfort, A., Michel, V., Thirion, B., Grisel, O., Blondel, M., Prettenhofer, P., Weiss, R., Dubourg, V., Vanderplas, J., Passos, A., Cournapeau, D., Brucher, M., Perrot, M., Duchesnay, E., Scikit-learn: Machine Learning in Python. *J. Mach. Learn. Res.*, 12, 2825–2830, 2011. sklearn.svm.NuSVC(), https://scikit-learn.org/stable/modules/generated/sklearn.svm.SVC.html#sklearn.svm.SVC.

38. Pedregosa, F., Varoquaux, G., Gramfort, A., Michel, V., Thirion, B., Grisel, O., Blondel, M., Prettenhofer, P., Weiss, R., Dubourg, V., Vanderplas, J., Passos, A., Cournapeau, D., Brucher, M., Perrot, M., Duchesnay, E., Scikit-learn: Machine Learning in Python. *J. Mach. Learn. Res.*, 12, 2825–2830, 2011. sklearn.linear_model.SGDClassifier(), https://scikit-learn.org/stable/modules/generated/sklearn.linear_model.SGDClassifier.html.

39. Perumal, S., Sannasi, G., Arputharaj, K., An intelligent fuzzy rule-based e-learning recommendation system for dynamic user interests. *J. Supercomput.*, 75, 5145–5160, 2019, https://doi.org/10.1007/s11227-019-02791-z.

40. Perumal, S., Sannasi, G., Arputharaj, K., REFERS: refined and effective fuzzy e-commerce recommendation system. *Int. J. Bus. Intell. Data Min.*, 17, 1, 117–137, 2020, https://doi.org/10.1504/IJBIDM.2020.108031.

41. Perumal, S., Sannasi, G., Arputharaj, K., FIRMACA-Fuzzy Intelligent Recommendation Model using Ant Clustering Algorithm for Social Networking. *SN Appl. Sci.*, 2, 1704, 2020, https://doi.org/10.1007/s42452-020-03486-4.

42. Roberts, N., Li, V., Atkinson, J.-A., Heffernan, M., McDonnell, G., Prodan, A., Freebairn, L., Lloyd, B., Nieuwenhuizen, S., Mitchell, J., Can the Target Set for Reducing Childhood Overweight and Obesity Be Met? A System Dynamics Modelling Study in New South Wales, Australia. *Syst. Res. Behav. Sci.*, 36, 36–52, 2019, https://doi.org/10.1002/sres.2555.

43. Rong, G., Mendez, A., Assi, E.B., Zhao, B., Sawan, M., Artificial Intelligence in Healthcare: Review and Prediction Case Studies. *Engineering*, 6, 3, 291–301, 2020, https://doi.org/10.1016/j.eng.2019.08.015.

44. Rosseau, G., Bailes, J., Maestro, R.D., Cabral, A., Choudhury, N., Comas, O., Debergue, P., Luca, G.D., Hovdebo, J., Jiang, D., Laroche, D., Neubauer, A., Pazos, V., Thibault, F., Diraddo, R., The Development of a Virtual Simulator for training neurosurgeons to perform and perfect Endoscopic Endonasal Transsphenoidal Surgery. *Neurosurgery*, 73, 1, 85–93, 2013, https://doi.org/10.1227/NEU.0000000000000112.

45. Schuster, M. and Paliwal, K.K., Bidirectional Recurrent Neural Networks. *IEEE Trans. Signal Process.*, 45, 11, 2673–2681, 1997.

46. Siebers, P., Macal, C., Garnett, J., Buxton, D., Pidd, M., Discrete-event simulation is dead, long live agent-based simulation! *J. Simul.*, 4, 3, 204–210, 2010, https://doi.org/10.1057/jos.2010.14.

47. Srivastava, V. and Purwar, R.K., Classification of CT Scan Images of Lungs Using Deep Convolutional Neural Network with External Shape-Based Features. *J. Digit. Imaging*, 33, 252–261, 2020, https://doi.org/10.1007/s10278-019-00245-9.

48. Stainsby, H., Taboada, M., Luque, E., Agent-based Simulation to Support Decision Making in Healthcare Management Planning, in: *Proceedings of 3rd International Conference on Health Informatics*, Valencia, Spain, pp. 436–441, 2010.

49. Sun, Q., Jankovic, M.V., Bally, L., Mougiakakou, S.G., Predicting Blood Glucose with an LSTM and Bi-LSTM Based Deep Neural Network, in: *Symposium on Neural Networks and Applications (NEUREL)*, Belgrade, Serbia, pp. 1–5, 2018, https://doi.org/10.1109/NEUREL.2018.8586990.

50. Tanaka, K., Sato, J., Guo, J., Takada, A., Yoshihara, H., A Simulation Model of Hospital Management Based on Cost Accounting Analysis According to Disease. *J. Med. Syst.*, 28, 689–710, 2004, https://doi.org/10.1023/B:JOMS.0000044970.82170.ae.

51. Vazquez-Seraano, J.I. and Peimbert-Garcia, R.E., System Dynamics Applications in Healthcare: A Literature Review, in: *Proceedings of the International Conference on Industrial Engineering and Operations Management*, Dubai, UAE, pp. 92–103, 2020.

52. Virtue, A., Kelly, J., Chaussalet, T., Using simplified discrete-event simulation models for healthcare applications, in: *Proceedings of the 2011 Winter Simulation Conference (WSC)*, pp. 1154–1165, 2011, https://doi.org/10.1109/WSC.2011.6147838.

53. Winkler-Schwartz, A., Yilmaz, R., Mirchi, N., Bissonnette, V., Ledwos, N., Siyar, S., Azarnoush, H., Karlik, B., Maestro, R.D., Machine Learning Identification of Surgical and Operative Factors Associated With Surgical Expertise in Virtual Reality Simulation. *J. Am. Med. Assoc., JAMA Netw. Open*, 2, 8, e198363, 2019, https://doi.org/10.1001/jamanetworkopen.2019.8363.

54. Zhang, L., Wang, S., Liu, B., Deep learning for Sentiment Analysis: A survey. *Wiley Interdiscip. Rev. Data Min. Knowl. Discovery*, 8, 4, 1–34, 2018, https://doi.org/10.1002/widm.1253.

10

Wolfram's Cellular Automata Model in Health Informatics

Sutapa Sarkar[1]* and Mousumi Saha[2]

[1]ECE, Seacom Engineering College, Howrah, India
[2]CSE, NIT, Durgapur, India

Abstract

Von Neumann was the first person who introduced cellular automata (CA) as a powerful computational tool to model complex physical systems. But the study of Wolfram on one-dimensional three-neighborhood linear and additive CA puts the conventional study one step forward. Quite a large number of researchers concentrated to investigate the best features of the following CA and for exploiting its adaptability, scalability, and reversibility. CA are found convenient to model complex and discrete dynamical systems for its simple, modular, and repetitive cellular structure. CA cells are evolved with discrete time and space depending on the present states of self and neighboring cells and a combinational logic. Therefore, it can provide global behavior through local interactions and vice versa by using appropriate CA rules. CA tools can extensively be applied in medical image processing for follicle image recognition, to detect heart defects, medical image edge detection, grayscale images, etc. This work targets to discuss recent CA applications for medical image processing, heart diseases, and mammograms. CA are discussed in the context of health informatics.

Keywords: Health informatics, cellular automata, machine learning, E-healthcare modelling with CA, HL-DL-CA

10.1 Introduction

The theoretical concept of cellular automata (CA) was introduced by J. Von Neumann and Stan Ulam in 1950s. Introduced CA had found to be a universal modeling tool that can perform any computing operations. CA is analogous in operation to finite state machine (FSM). Each cell was having 29 states and complex neighborhood structure that had reflected a very complex behavioral pattern [1]. Further, CA behavior can be analyzed or synthesized to produce local to global structure or vice versa. The complexity of introduced CA pattern makes it impracticable for physical system implementation. Von Neumann's CA rules were never found application in modern computers also. It had also become very complex for computer-based simulation. This research though enriched by a strong potentiality in computing shows dichotomy in theoretical and practical aspects. So, the research

---

Corresponding author: sutapa321@gmail.com

Om Prakash Jena, Alok Ranjan Tripathy, Ahmed A. Elngar and Zdzislaw Polkowski (eds.) *Computational Intelligence and Healthcare Informatics*, (179–192) © 2021 Scrivener Publishing LLC

hunt continued to eliminate the dichotomy in CA research. On the other hand, a simple CA structure was required to design for formulation of any arbitrary physical system functionality. On the other hand, CA need to be simulated by digital systems.

The dichotomy had been started to be eliminated by Wolfram's and Conway's research from the year 1970. Conway's research in computing proposed CA theory of *game of life had escalated* computing based on CA [13]. It had attracted interest toward representation of CA model for a well-understood model of complete cycle of life. Stephen Wolfram's *two-state* model puts a simpler CA structure that suits in modern computing from early eighties. He had shown that this special class of one-dimensional three-neighborhood CA can be emulated through simple computing systems easily and does not need to handle the complexity like previous CA structure of Von Neumann. It had drawn attention of the researchers for its simple modular repetitive structure in its one-dimensional three-neighborhood CA model with the exploration of 256 CA rules. It has a regular cellular structure that is preferable in modeling of discrete dynamical systems. It can find its use in various application domains of physical and biological systems including digital image processing, pattern recognition, VLSI circuits and systems, cryptography, networks, cache applications [4], and also in health sciences. As it had proven a very powerful tool for its versatility, it has started to be used in health sciences [2] as well as medical imaging [3, 5].

CA structures are found in various neighborhood constructions like Null boundary or periodic boundary, linear or nonlinear, and uniform or non-uniform [1]. Different types of CA tools can extensively be applied in medical image processing for follicle image recognition, to detect heart defects, medical image edge detection, grayscale images, binary images, noise filtering, spot detection, mammograms, etc. [3, 10]. Machine learning (ML) as well as deep learning (DL) is a derived branch of Artificial Intelligence that has tremendous impact in medical applications nowadays. This upcoming field has extensively applied to medical informatics, bioinformatics and medical imaging for heart diseases, human behavior, gene prediction, skin cancer, diabetes, etc. In this chapter, recent CA applications with different CA rules and neighborhood pattern are discussed for medical image processing, heart diseases, and mammograms [5, 10]. For pattern recognition, a *two-dimensional* image is mapped into two-dimensional CA with 256 states. Cell pattern is used to frame CA model with different neighborhood pattern as used in Greenberg-Hastings proposal as Moore neighborhood, hexagonal grid, extended Moore, Brickwall, etc. Then, those 2-D CA model is verified with simulation using software like MATLAB [6].

Here, proposed CA-based algorithms are discussed for pectorial muscle detection and mass segmentation from images of mammograms. The chapter also throws light on the ML and DL algorithms those are used in medical image processing [7]. Artificial neural network (ANN) is the backbone of ML- and DL-based systems used in health informatics. ANN algorithms are constructed with layers of connected nodes. The inputs to the system have radiomic features extracted from imaging files (CT, MRI, SPECT) or images in convolution neural network (CNN). Application of ML and DL in medical imaging lowers the error rate, provides better detection and classification of lesions, gives precise data analysis and radiomic feature extraction, etc. Three-dimensional imaging for oncological treatment has also become possible with AI. DL medical applications when augmented to nonlinear CA tools can provide greater advantages in terms of better security and rapid storage with greater efficiency in computation of big data processing. Design of health informatics-DL-CA (HL-DL-CA) is discussed in the context of medical imaging and health informatics. Problem formulation, algorithms, and sensitivity parameters are discussed in detail [11]. The chapter is organized into six sections with the effort of analyzing CA applications into health sciences. CA rules and its characterization in time and space are given in Section 10.2. Local and global behavior of CAs with Wolfram's modeling is tried to describe for health science in Section 10.3. Various other application domains of CA including health informatics are given in Section 10.4. Section 10.5 is used to mention CA applications augmented with DL used in health informatics. Section 10.6 details health informatics with added concluding notes.

10.2 Cellular Automata

CA structures can be distinguished by various boundary structures as well as neighborhood pattern. CA rules can also be used for its characterization to make its application simpler and domain specific. Von Neumann's complex CA structure has 29 states, whereas Codd utilizes eight states per CA cells. It is reduced to four states followed by the research of banks and that is further reduced to two-state CA which is the interest of health informatics. CA states can also be assumed by the elements of Galois field GF(q) where q gives the number of states. Paul introduced two-state CA concepts of the pattern $GF(2^p)$. Here, p gives the number of memory elements. The most cultured neighborhood patterns are Von Neumann's (five) and Moore neighborhoods (nine). The neighborhood patterns vary from three or five or nine, etc., which can also be generalized by the R-radial and R-axial neighborhoods, respectively. One-dimensional three-neighborhood CA can be classified as linear and additive CA. Additive CA can be implemented by xor or xnor logics only. Nonlinear CA can be implemented by other basic gates. Each CA cells can be applied with identical or different rule and termed as uniform and non-uniform or hybrid CA. According to boundary conditions, there are variations of CA structure like periodic boundary, null boundary, adiabatic boundary, and intermediate boundary. For null boundary CA, left terminal of left most cell is kept to zero state, whereas right of right most cell is also kept to zero state. For periodic boundary CA (PBCA), right terminal of right most cell is connected to left terminal of left-most cell and vice-versa as shown in Figure 10.1.

Characterization of CA behavior is very much required which puts insight into the power of modelling of a CA. Wolfram's CA is having 256 rules within ECA set and few of them are given in Table 10.1.

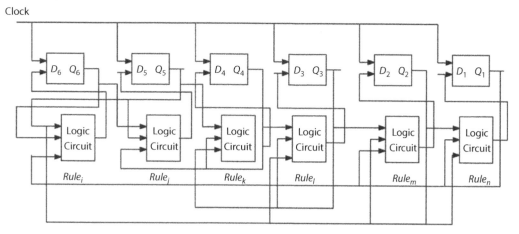

Figure 10.1 Block diagram of n-cell periodic boundary cellular automata with hybrid rule.

Table 10.1 Truth table.

PS	111	110	101	100	011	010	001	000	Rule	Logic function
RMT	(7)	(6)	(5)	(4)	(3)	(2)	(1)	(0)		f_i
NS	1	1	1	1	1	1	1	1	30	$S_i^{t+1} = \overline{S_{i+1}^t} \cdot S_{i-1}^t + \overline{S_{i+1}^t} \cdot S_i^t$
NS	1	1	1	0	1	0	0	0	232	$S_i^{t+1} = S_i^t \cdot S_{i-1}^t + S_{i+1}^t \cdot S_{i-1}^t + S_{i+1}^t \cdot S_i^t$
NS	1	0	1	1	1	0	0	0	184	$S_i^{t+1} = \overline{S_i^t} \cdot S_{i-1}^t + S_{i+1}^t \cdot S_i^t$
NS	1	1	1	0	0	0	1	0	226	$S_i^{t+1} = \overline{S_i^t} \cdot S_{i-1}^t + S_{i+1}^t \cdot S_i^t$
NS	1	1	1	1	1	1	1	1	255	$S_i^{t+1} = 1$

They can be categorized under different classes as per their dynamics like (1) Class 1: CA cells evolve to a homogeneous state; (ii) Class 2: showing periodic structures; (iii) Class 3: CAs show chaotic/pseudo-random behavior; and (iv) Class 4: Complex patterns within localized structures distinguishes global structure for modern computation.

10.3   Application of Cellular Automata in Health Science

Wolfram's CA are found to be applied in various application domain. The reason behind its versatility is depicted in his book "*A New Kind of Science*" where he found few generalized rules that can evolve to represent complex abstract and natural systems. CA modeling has been found in different machine designing like *parallel multiplier, sorting machines,* and *prime number sieves*. It has also found applications in gaming like *firing squad, firing mob, queen bee, iterated prisoners, and dilemma*. Taffoli and others named CA-based machines (CAMs) those have the capacity of computation at a larger scale of parallelism. The cost of computation is reduced but not at the cost of limited capacity. It functions at autonomous mode and that suitable for complex system modeling with localized interactions among CA cells. CA has also found application in VLSI systems, memory testing (Built in self-testing), fault-tolerant systems, cache systems of CMPs, etc. [1]. PBCA-based wear leveling [12] and NBCA-based fault-tolerant designs are found in cache systems [4]. CA models are found applications in pattern recognition, cryptography, and VLSI designing and testing [4].

Wolfram's CA structure has become a powerful tool for addressing problems of biological sciences starting from the granularity of small cells, cluster of cells, and up to the level of organs. Celada, Seidan, De Boer *et al.* have developed CA-based models for immune systems [13]. HIV drug therapy, detection of cancerous cell, tumor development, detection of genetic disorders, etc., are found to be devised with CA. CA applications are also found in genetic algorithms (GAs) and DNA sequencing. CA rules are used to find the patterns of DNA using GA. 2D and 3D CA modeling is used to provide the patterns of gene regulatory networks [8]. CA are extensively used in medical image processing for heart diseases, cancerous cell detection, abnormal growth of tumor detection, etc. Modeling is very much essential in health sciences because real-life experimentation is not always possible or rather painful in few cases. CA modeling is also helpful for computer simulation that can extensively support detailed clinical diagnosis. CA models can be mathematically represented in terms of time, space, and state. Four types of neighborhood configurations are used (as described by Greenberg-Hastings as Moore, extended Moore, Brickwall, and hexagonal) to detect the electrical activities of cardiac cells and finally abnormal heart pumping behavior is observed [6].

CA can be thought of a natural tool in medical image processing to analyze mammogram images in gray and binary scale. CA algorithms are used in edge and spot detection, noise filtering, and pectorial muscle detection for breast cancer diagnosis [5]. CA algorithms, when they are based on two-dimensional CA and Von Neumann type of neighborhood, can make use of the rules taken from rule set = {0,1, 2,..., 255}. Specialized hardware is developed like CLIP for image processing but it was generalized afterward to the use of available computers. The work is further extended to develop cellular neural networks (CNNs) for continuous and discrete time image processing [3]. Noise filtering targets to detect irregularity in the patterns from MRI, etc. Medical image processing takes input

Table 10.2 Application of cellular automata in health sciences.

Sl. no.	Domain	Input data	Application
1.	Medical image processing [3, 5, 10, 15]	Clinically detected images like medio-lateral oblique views of mammogram	Ultra sonography, image edge detection, spot detection, malignancy identification, pectoral muscle detection, mass segmentation from mammograms, etc.
2.	Medical informatics [6, 7]	Report or health record	Heart diseases, skin cancer, diabetes
3.	Bioinformatics [2]	Genomic record	Gene prediction, promoter prediction
4.	Genetic algorithms [8]	-	DNA sequencing, Gene regulatory networks
5.	Others [6, 13, 14]	CT scan, magnetic resonance image (MRI), 3D ultrasound computer tomography, single-photon emission computed tomography (SPECT)	HIV drug therapy, brain function through eye movement, cardiac modeling, immune systems

from report of health records. Various images are taken for medical diagnosis of different diseases and few of them are given in Table 10.2. In mammogram images along with the use of medio-lateral oblique (MLO) views, malignant diseases can be detected. Various CA algorithms are used for binary and grayscale images in spot detection and pectoral muscle. Here also, Wolfram's three-neighborhood two-dimensional CA with Moore's neighborhood is used [5].

G. Moe *et al.* and Barbosa suggested few cardiac models like *fibrillation (asymmetric rhythm of heart)* and others that are realized by CA models. These models are realized by the various structure or neighborhood patterns of Moore, extended Moore, Brickwall, hexagonal, etc. These CA models are two-dimensional and excitable in nature having CA rules and excitable function [7]. MATLAB is used in this study to simulate and analyze those four neighborhood models. It has been found that innovative visual modeling and computer-based learning (CBL) produces detailed analysis of abnormal heart beats and diagnosis of heart diseases. This bio-computational CA-based analysis and use of MATLAB tool is described in [7]. Different CA models are utilized in various health science applications are exemplified in Table 10.3.

10.4 Cellular Automata in Health Informatics

Clinical reports written by doctors are in the form of textual data. These reports are very much useful for different purposes like (a) Reports carry information about the pathological records of a patient, (b) personal medical history of the patient and his background,

Table 10.3 Cellular automata modeling in health sciences.

Sl. no.	Domain	Methodology	Tool	Application
1.	Epidemic spread [14]	Susceptible, infected, and recovered (SIR) epidemic model is modeled through CA	Two-dimensional CA	Real-time data is captured to get the real-time informatics of epidemic
2.	Immunity systems in tumor [13]	Tumor-immunity system cellular automaton model (TISCAM) organized with CA structure as {Cells, space, Neighborhood conditions, CA Rule}	Two-dimensional stochastic and discrete CA	Detection of malignant cells from cell space with Moore and extended Moore's neighborhood conditions
3.	Brain cancer detection [16, 17]	Cellular automata (CA)–based segmentation method like MR Images. CA algorithm is used for selection of thresholds for expectation maximization and Otsu's method.	Monte Carlo and gray level co-occurrence matrix (GLCM) Cellular Automata	This scheme works on a CA-based feature extraction methods applicable for cancer detection
4.	Heart disease [19]	Streeter's model of fiber orientation in a transmural block of left ventricular (LV) tissue is considered for detailed analysis and simulation.	A three-dimensional cubical grid CA structure	A cellular automata model engine is developed to analyze activation pattern of tissues of left and right ventricles of heart
5.	Breast Cancer [20]	This work uses per KEGG pathway enriching survey for findings of correlation network with the use of priority checking.	2D ECA with null boundary condition and using rule "30"	It is a method of predicting pathways to cancer detection using gene regulatory networks (silencing). Putting a bio-markers and cross domain mapping of oncology into CA is done

(c) important findings during interactions with patients and preliminary procedures. But extraction of data for clinical diagnosis and future use becomes difficult. Mostly, the data is not in structured format so that it can be used for the following purposes:

i.   Medical research data
ii.   Epidemiological disease study
iii. Decision or detection purposes
iv.   Statistical analysis for medical diagnosis (mainly infectious disease)
v.   Data mining
vi.   To diagnose new patients using previous information

So, difficulty is faced during storage of data and access the data easily. Health informatics mainly deals with the structuring of a system to get easy data access from a large volume of data. The purpose of data extraction and medical diagnosis can be achieved through non-linear CA. Flow diagram of the system starting from clinical reports and upto the decision stages of medical decision and diagnosis is given by the Figure 10.2. Though, the detailed description with the use of CA in different stages is given in Figure 10.3.

A typical E-healthcare information generation system is composed of three stages: collection of health data or records, processing those data, and analyzing those data for results/findings. Healthcare data/records are collected over different networks and storage of data in healthcare data base is made available for clinical diagnosis. Starting from pre-processing stage, extraction of data and analysis of data with various clustering algorithms such as big bang-big crunch (BB-BC), memory enriched big bang big crunch algorithm (MEBB-BC), artificial bee colony (ABC), hybrid version artificial bee colony algorithm (CABC), ACO, GA, GWO, particle swarm optimization (PSO), charged system search (CSS), and K-means algorithms are used. CA-based approach is taken to implement BB-BC algorithm to get improved convergent speed and optimal solution. Few other clustering algorithms are also implemented through CA like MEBB-BC. To implement through CA-based BB-BC approach, dimension, number of instances, and each cell are associated with a transition function (heat) is used in clustering the data set [9]. CA-based approach can provide optimal findings in data analysis in E-healthcare informatics. This healthcare model is simulated through MATLAB 2016a that has detailed visual aids to support diagnosis.

CA-based E-healthcare model can be used to find clinical data patterns for clinical diagnosis. But few CA models are developed with neural networks augmented with the process or methodology. Training of CA for medical image processing with *sequential floating forward search method* enhances the feature extraction of data records (noise filtering).

Medical data or health records are in the form of unstructured format written by doctors. In another CA-based approach, medical data or health records can be processed to get the important information from those data that can be used in decision support, diagnosis of new patient, research works in epidemics, etc. [14]. In Figure 10.3, a CA-based system architecture is shown with the details of health informatics. The features are extracted in the form of entity and feature extraction parameter. The information processing is done though CA-based Boolean inference engine that provides storage optimization and response time of feature extraction about the entities and their features. The feature

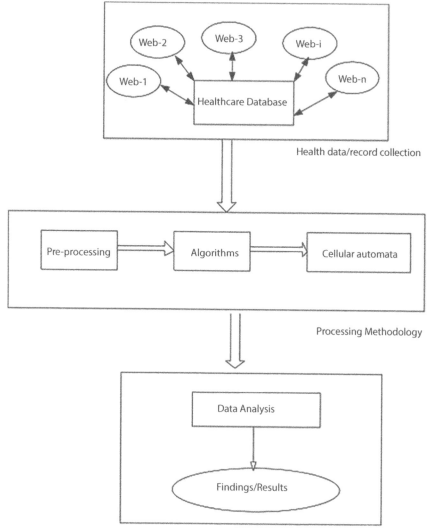

Figure 10.2 E-healthcare steps toward medical diagnosis or disease detection.

extraction is performed in two phases. In first phase, methods of processing unstructured textual format are derived to extract medical history and pathological information about the patients to be stored in a healthcare data base. (2) Second phase is related to named entities like name of the patients, symptoms, detected diseases, and drugs used derived from those data base.

Named entity extraction (NEE) can take two approaches: (1) rules of pattern matching and (2) ML. First one is tedious but gives a good result using dictionaries and linguistic rules. ML approach is a promising one in health informatics but consumes appreciable time in training. NEE can be applicable for extracting information of patient details as well as pathological information and data extraction of radiology and mammogram. A typical

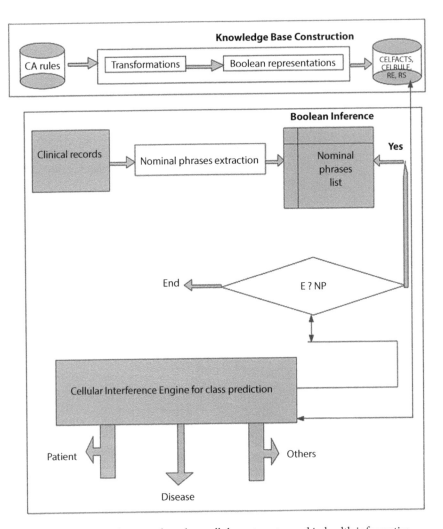

Figure 10.3 A typical system architecture based on cellular automata used in health informatics.

NEE system works on two steps. The first one is used for acquiring Boolean knowledge base using Cellular Automata for Symbolic Induction (CSAI) model shown in Figure 10.4. In next steps, Boolean entities are classified with Cellular Inference Engine (CIE) as shown in Figure 10.3. The steps of NEE are as follows:

- Entities are extracted on the basis of few previously constructed rules named as entities classification rules and set manually;
- Boolean modeling is prepared of those constructed rules;
- Clinical reports are extracted through linguistic analysis by checking their nominal phrases using morphosyntactic and semantic properties;
- Boolean inference files used or classification of nominal phrases into different classes or entities (nominal phrases) like person's name, date of diagnosis, suffering symptoms, and detected disease;
- By using CA rules and neighborhood pattern, NPs are identified.

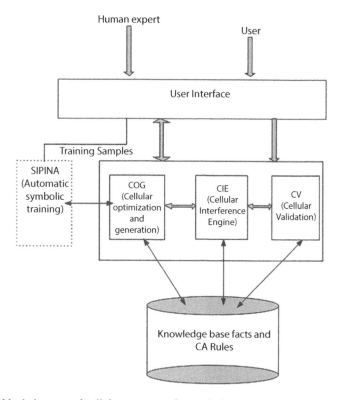

Figure 10.4 Basic block diagram of Cellular Automata for Symbolic Induction (CASI) model [2].

Table 10.4 Deep learning applications in health informatics.

Area	Application	Input	Method
Bioinformatics	Medicine/drug design	Molecule compounds	Deep neural network
	Compound-protein interaction	DNA/RNA protein structure	Deep belief networks
	Cancer diagnosis	Gene expression	Deep autoencoders
Medical image processing	Brain reconstruction	Magnetic resonance image	Deep autoencoders
	Tissue categorization	Magnetic resonance image/computerized tomography images	Convolution deep belief networks
	Alzheimer symptoms diagnosis	Positron emission tomography scan	Deep near networks
Pervasive sensing	Anomaly symptoms detection	Electroencephalogram (EEG)	Deep belief networks

Few other NLP-based systems are also proposed by the researchers like MeDLEE, SymTEX, MetaMap, and NegEx [2] for NEE. A work on discharge summaries is used to identify smoker, nonsmoker, not known, etc. On the basis of training data, a hybrid system is developed which is integrated heuristic rule-based modules with ML-based named entity recognition process [2].

ML techniques are started to be used in different domain including detection of disease in health informatics. In [18], an innovative effort is made to detect heart disease and given in Figure 10.4.

Few applications of DL are given in Table 10.4 for various domains like bio-informatics and medical imaging.

10.5   Health Informatics–Deep Learning–Cellular Automata

Health informatics deals with a large volume of data. Therefore, ML and DL had started to be used in processing and analysing the big data [18]. It can provide a) required parallelism, (b) rapid storage of data, (c) high security with proper confidentiality (using advanced encryption system), authorization (against DdoS like other attacks), and integrity (with the use of repeated hashing techniques), (d) powerful computational capacity, etc. DL when augmented to CA can give much benefit in handling large volume of complex health records or medical images. In medical informatics, large data is available to training a CA which can give solution of real-time complicated problems. In Figure 10.5, a neural network is shown

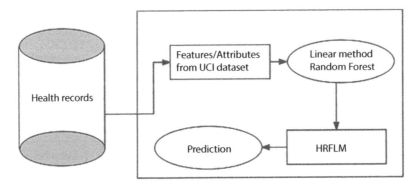

Figure 10.5 Detection of heart disease with hybrid random forest with linear model [18].

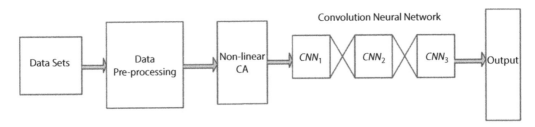

Figure 10.6 Basic block diagram of HL-DL-CA used in health informatics.

with convolution operation and trained with nonlinear CA as an input to CNN. Health data records are taken from Uniform Hospital Discharge Data Set (UHDDS) and the typical processing of the same through HL-DL-CA networks [11] are shown in Figure 10.6.

Different CA rules are used in its non-linear architecture taken from the rule sets like 108, 162, 252, and 255 and with transition function. CA rules are allowed to iterate for state transitions upto the point of reaching an attractor state. The above architecture can effectively be applied in medical informatics, bioinformatics, and health informatics for named entity classification.

10.6 Conclusion

CA are powerful tool for modeling different discrete physical real-time systems. Its versatility attracted researchers toward big data analysis as required in health informatics. But it can provide a great advantage of big data analytics when augmented to ML and DL. This chapter focuses on application of CA on different domain of health informatics, medical informatics, and bioinformatics. It also reports the analysis of medical imaging, mammogram, heart diseases, tumor detection, and others using CA. Its augmented structure with ML to provide higher accuracy, precision, security, speed, etc., is discussed. CA-based system architecture is detailed for NEE and UHDSS analysis with its current state of application.

References

1. Ganguly, N., Sikdar, B.K., Deutsch, A., Canright, G., Chaudhuri, P., *A Survey on Cellular Automata*, 2003, http://www.cs.unibo.it/.
2. Barigou, F., Atmani, B., Beldjilali, B., Using a Cellular Automaton to Extract Medical Information from Clinical Reports. *J. Inf. Process. Syst.*, 8, 1, 67–84, 2012, https://doi.org/10.3745/JIPS.2012.8.1.067.
3. Rosin, P.L., Training cellular automata for image processing. *IEEE Trans. Image Process.*, 15, 7, 2076–2087, 2006, https://doi.org/10.1109/tip.
4. Sarkar, S., Saha, M., Sikdar, B.K., Multi-bit fault tolerant design for resistive memories through dynamic partitioning, in: *2017 IEEE East-West Design & Test Symposium (EWDTS)*, Novi Sad, 2017, pp. 1–6, https://doi.org/10.1109/EWDTS.2017.8110053.
5. Wongthanavasu, S., Tangvoraphonkchai, V., Cellular Automata-Based Algorithm and its Application in Medical Image Processing, in: *2007 IEEE International Conference on Image Processing*, 2007.
6. Akdur, G., The use of biological cellular automaton models in medical, health and biological studies. *Proc. Soc Behav. Sci.*, 28, 825–831, 2011.
7. Currie, G., Hawk, K.E., Rohren, E., Vial, A., Klein, R., Machine Learning and Deep Learning in Medical Imaging: Intelligent Imaging. *J. Med. Imaging. Radiat. Sci.*, 50, 4, 477–487, 2019, https://doi.org/10.1016/j.jmir.
8. Chavoya, A., Duthen, Y., Using a genetic algorithm to evolve cellular automata for 2D/3D computational development, in: *Proceedings of the 8th Annual Conference on Genetic and Evolutionary Computation - GECCO '06*, 2006, https://doi.org/10.1145/1143997.
9. Singh, H., Kumar, Y., Cellular Automata Based Model for E-Healthcare Data Analysis. *Int. J. Inf. Syst. Model. Des.*, 10, 3, 1–18, 2019, https://doi.org/10.4018/ijismd.

10. Ghosh, P., Antani, S.K., Long, L.R., Thoma, G.R., Unsupervised Grow-Cut: Cellular Automata-Based Medical Image Segmentation, in: *2011 IEEE First International Conference on Healthcare Informatics, Imaging and Systems Biology*, San Jose, CA, 2011, pp. 40–47.

11. Arslan, F., Deep Learning for Health Informatics: A Secure Cellular Automata. *Int. J. Adv. Res.*, 8, Jun, 879–888, 2020, https:// doi.org /10.21474/IJAR01/11167.

12. Sarkar, S., Ghosh M. Biplab, K.S., Saha, M., Periodic Boundary Cellular Automata Based Wear Leveling for Resistive Memory. *IAENG Int. J. Comput. Sci.*, 47, 2, 310–321, Jun 2020.

13. Hu, R. and Ruan, X., A simple cellular automaton model for tumor-immunity system, in: *IEEE International Conference on Robotics, Intelligent Systems and Signal Processing, 2003. Proceedings. 2003*, Changsha, Hunan, China, 2003, vol. pp2, pp. 1031–1035.

14. Zhang, Q. and Xu, L., Simulation of the Spread of Epidemics with Individuals Contact Using Cellular Automata Modeling, in: *2012 Fifth International Conference on Information and Computing Science*, Liverpool, pp. 60–62, 2012.

15. Ranaee, I., Nia, M.M., Jahantigh, R., Gharib, A., Introducing a new algorithm for medical image encryption based on chaotic feature of cellular automata, in: *8th International Conference for Internet Technology and Secured Transactions (ICITST-2013)*, London, pp. 582–587, 2013.

16. Darshini Velusamy, P. and Karandharaj, P., Medical image processing schemes for cancer detection: A survey, in: *2014 International Conference on Green Computing Communication and Electrical Engineering (ICGCCEE)*, Coimbatore, pp. 1–6, 2014.

17. Sompong, C. and Wongthanavasu, S., MRI brain tumor segmentation using GLCM cellular automata-based texture feature, in: *2014 International Computer Science and Engineering Conference (ICSEC)*, Khon Kaen, pp. 192–197, 2014.

18. Mohan, S., Thirumalai, C., Srivastava, G., Effective Heart Disease Prediction Using Hybrid Machine Learning Techniques, in: *IEEE Access*, vol. 7, pp. 81542–81554, 2019.

19. Bollacker, K.D. *et al.*, A Cellular Automata Three-dimensional Model Of Ventricular Cardiac Activation, in: *Proceedings of the Annual International Conference of the IEEE Engineering in Medicine and Biology Society*, Orlando, FL, USA, 1991, vol. 13, pp. 627–628, 1991.

20. Mahata, K. and Sarkar, A., Cancer gene silencing network analysis using cellular automata, in: *Proceedings of the 2015 Third International Conference on Computer, Communication, Control and Information Technology (C3IT)*, Hooghly, pp. 1–5, 2015.

Part III

MACHINE LEARNING AND COVID PROSPECTIVE

11

COVID-19: Classification of Countries for Analysis and Prediction of Global Novel Corona Virus Infections Disease Using Data Mining Techniques

Sachin Kamley[1]*, Shailesh Jaloree[2], R.S. Thakur[3] and Kapil Saxena[4]

[1]Department of Computer Applications, S.AT.I., Vidisha, India
[2]Department of Applied Math's and Science, S.AT.I., Vidisha, India
[3]Department of Computer Applications, M.A.N.I.T., Bhopal, India
[4]Department of Computer Science and Applications, Career College, Bhopal, India

Abstract

For the couple of days, Novel Corona Virus Infection Disease (COVID-19) pandemic has become a major challenge as well as threat to the society. Presently, more than 170 countries are infected from this virus including India. However, no medicines and antidote have been made at present to cure this disease. Preventing these infections to large community level immediate actions are required. In this way, data mining has capability to handle data quickly and effectively tracking and controlling the spread of virus infections. In this study, global dataset of 204 countries for the period of 31 January to 19 May from Worldometer website are considered for study purpose and data from 20 May to 8 June is considered to predict the evaluation of the outbreak, i.e., 3 weeks ahead. Three most prominent data mining techniques like Linear Regression (LR), Association Rule Mining (ARM), and Back Propagation Neural Network (BPNN) are utilized to predict and analyze the COVID-19 dataset. Finally, BPNN and ARM methods have outperformed LR, and results obtained in this study are permitted to classify the countries based on the low, medium, and high risk in future, respectively.

Keywords: COVID-19, Corona Virus, data mining, prediction, ARM, regression, Statistica 13.2

11.1   Introduction

These days, Novel Corona Virus Infection Disease (COVID-19) outbreak has spread all over the world and created a problem for human civilization. The first case of COVID-19 was identified in Wuhan, China, as on 31 December 2019. Later, on 23 January 2020, Wuhan was locked down on the basis of the reports that it is spreading due to the communication transmission in the cities [20, 28]. Due to the widely spread of COVID-19, presently more than 170 countries around the world have been suffered from this pandemic. Till now on 20 May 2020, no specific drugs or vaccines against the disease have been caused [7, 22].

---

*Corresponding author: sachinkamley.mca@satiengg.in

Om Prakash Jena, Alok Ranjan Tripathy, Ahmed A. Elngar and Zdzislaw Polkowski (eds.) Computational Intelligence and Healthcare Informatics, (195–214) © 2021 Scrivener Publishing LLC

On May 20, 2020, the World Health Organization (WHO) reported that a total of 4,897,492 confirmed cases and 323,285 deaths around the world. Therefore, the fertility rate for COVID-19 has been recorded is 4.5% but for old age people especially (65–79) has been recorded up to 8%, while for above 80, it has been recorded up to 14.8%. Thus, the people specially age greater than 50 to be considered at the highest risk having underlying diseases like diabetes, Cardiovascular Disease (CVD), and Parkinson's disease [8].

In order to prevent this deadly virus globally, government will have to take harsh policies, i.e., lock-down strategy, improve medical facilities like testing kits, masks, ventilators, and sanitizers, for protection of millions of people. However, it has been entered in the body through common symptoms like fever, cough, droplets, and breath shortness (pneumonia), and these symptoms take 2–14 days to appear for patients [19]. In order to fight against the virus, patients' clinical conditions as well as highly supportive care are very important concern.

The key part of managing this pandemic is to reduce the epidemic peak, i.e., flattening the effect of the virus. In this direction, data mining (DM) techniques are very helpful to fight against COVID-19 in order to help governments and healthcare management to figure out the best preparation and response to such pandemics [29]. Moreover, DM techniques have ability to handle and analyze large data quickly as well as effectively tracking and controlling the spread of COVID-19 [12]. In this study, we have used three most prominent DM techniques like Linear Regression (LR), Association Rule Mining (ARM), and Neural Network (NN) to monitor the COVID-19 infections around the world.

Now, the world has entered in to week 20 in COVID-19 cases. The main focus of this study is to predict the trend related to death, recovery, total tests, serious cases (SC), and case fertility rate (CFR) expected 3 weeks ahead (COVID-19) in the world.

After background discussions, some significant research works are described in brief by Section 11.2. Data pre-processing process and proposed methodology of the study are described by Sections 11.3 and 11.4, respectively. Experimental result analysis and conclusion and future scopes of the study are described in Sections 11.5 and 11.6, respectively.

11.2   Literature Review

This section briefly highlights some significant research works in healthcare field.

Alimadadi *et al.* [3] have suggested the role of Artificial Intelligence (AI) and machine learning techniques to fight over COVID-19.

Anastassopoulou *et al.* [5] have considered epidemiological data for Hubei, China, for the period of 1 month, i.e., 11 January to 10 February 2020. However, they have adopted Susceptible-Infectious-Recovered-Dead (SIDR) model for data analysis task. Finally, they have made predictions 3 weeks ahead till 29 February based on the output parameters like recovery rate (RR), per day infection mortality, and basic reproduction number in order to forecast the evaluation of the pandemic. Finally, based on the experimental results, they have recorded the high epidemic peak of the confirmed number of infected cases, confirmed number of recovered cases, and the case fertility ratio is found around 0.15% of the total population.

Song *et al.* [25] have designed a multi-class classification model by using a modified version of pre-trained ResNet-50 network called as DRE-Net. They have classified based on the

COVID patients, non-COVID patients, and bacterial phenomena with C-T images. Finally, the proposed model has recorded the 86% classification accuracy.

Wang and Wong [27] have implemented COVID-Net Deep Neural Network (DNN) model for COVID cases detection. However, they have recorded 92.4% accuracy in classifying normal, non-COVID pneumonia, and COVID-19 classes.

Jiaweili MS *et al.* [17] have presented content analysis method for the Chinese social media platform, i.e., Weibo with LR technique during the early COVID-19 outbreak. In order to predict the early stages of COVID-19, they have used infoveillance approaches with social media platform to characterize attributes behavioral, disease distribution, and public knowledge. At last, they have found that positive correlation between number of reported cases from Wuhan, China, and the number of Weibo posts.

Ozturk *et al.* [23] have presented deep learning neural network model with raw chest X-ray images as an input for automatic detection of COVID-19 cases. In order to provide accurate diagnostics, they have classified the model based on binary classification (COVID vs. No-Findings) and multi-class classification (COVID vs. No-Findings vs. Pneumonia). At last, proposed model had recorded the 98.08% classification accuracy for binary classes and 87.02% for multi-class cases, respectively.

Ghosal *et al.* [14] have applied LR and multiple regression approaches to predict the number of deaths, fifth to sixth week in India. Their experimental results had stated that projected death rate (DR) at the end of fifth and sixth weeks would be 211 and 417 with a 95% CI: 1.31–2.60, respectively.

Khaitan *et al.* [18] have performed the statistical analysis of COVID-19 dataset based on the demographic factors like age, sex, travel history, and symptoms for the infected country China. However, they have used clustering technique for categorizing the symptoms based on the age group ranging from 1 to 87 years.

At last, based on the literature survey, this study is augmented by using DM techniques like LR, ARM, and NN, as well as presents a risk classification of COVID-19 countries based on various parameters.

11.3 Data Pre-Processing

The real worldwide data of Corona Virus (COVID-19) for the period of 22nd January 2020 to 19 May 2020 is obtained from the Worldometer website [21]. In the beginning, dataset is too much noisy and containing redundant information. In this way, data pre-possessing methods are used to remove noise, missing or inaccurate information, or tuple from dataset [15, 21]. Therefore, dataset employed 204 samples and consisting of 17 important parameters like country, actual cases, total cases, total deaths, total recovery, CFR, diabetes, median age, old age, population density, male smokers, female smokers, hand washing facility, and hospital beds facility per 100k. Table 11.1 shows COVID-19 dataset attributes in an abbreviated form.

In order to make COVID-19 dataset feasible for computation dataset, it is represented in symbolic form. However, all numeric variables are used for this purpose. However, classifications of data values are done based on the low, medium, and high category. Thus, a value comes below average classified under low category and value comes under above average classified under high category. Samples of range-wise classifications of attributes are shown by Table 11.2.

Table 11.1 COVID-19 dataset attributes in an abbreviated form [15, 21].

S. no.	Attributes	Abbreviation
1	Country	Country
2	Total Cases	TC
3	Total Deaths	TD
4	Total Recovered	TREV
5	Active Cases	AC
6	Serious Cases	SC
7	Death Rate	DR
8	Case Fertility Rate	CFR
9	Recovery Rate	RR
10	Diabetes Patients	DP
11	Median Age	MAGE
12	Old Age	OAGE
13	Population Density	PD
14	Male Smokers	MS
15	Female Smokers	FS
16	Hand Washing Facility	HWF
17	Hospital Beds Facility per 100k	HBF

11.4   Proposed Methodologies

In this section, different DM techniques are discussed in order to predict COVID-19 parameters.

11.4.1   Simple Linear Regression

Regression analysis is one of the well-known and powerful concept provides a way to iden-tify the relation between two or more variables, i.e., dependent and independent variable about which knowledge is available [6]. In this direction, Simple LR (SLR) method has capability to make predictions based on two variables. Equation (11.1) shows the simplest form of LR with a single dependent variable (response) and single independent variable (predictor) [6, 13].

Table 11.2 Sample of range-wise classification of attributes [15, 21].

Classification	TC	AC	TD	TREV	PD
	Range {51, 1631457}	Range {0, 1149398}	Range {0, 96989}	Range {18, 385070}	Range {0, 26337}
Low	51	0	0	18	0
Medium	71875.64	50181.5	6024.2	29122.6	475
High	1631457	1149398	96989	385070	26337
Classification	CFR	DP	MAGE	OAGE	MS
	Range {0, 19.557}	Range {0, 22.02}	Range {7.15, 48.2}	Range {1.14, 27.04}	Range {7.7, 85.84]
Low	0	0	7.15	1.14	7.7
Medium	4.55	7.87	34.15	10.94	33.55
High	19.557	22.02	48.2	27.04	85.74

Equation (11.1) denotes the basic regression equation with single predictable variable and one response variable.

$$Y = \alpha_0 + \alpha_1 X \tag{11.1}$$

where α_0 and α_1 denote regression coefficients as well as specifying the intercept and slope of the line, respectively.

In order to minimize the error between actual and predicted variable, least square method is used to solve Equation (11.1). In this study, different predictor and response variables are used for better prediction performance. However, correlation formula is used to find the association between the variables which is shown by Equation (11.2) [11].

$$\text{Correlation } (r) = \frac{\sum (X-\overline{X})(Y-\overline{Y})}{\sqrt{[\sum (X-\overline{X})^2 (Y-\overline{Y})^2]}} \tag{11.2}$$

Here, Table 11.3 shows classification of correlation values.

Correlation between variables (predictor vs. response) is shown by Table 11.4.

Based on Table 11.4, CFR, TD, SC, RR, TTPMP, DP, DR, OAGE, and TREV are selected as variables for regression model. Now, Equations (11.3) and (11.4) are used to solve the regression coefficients, i.e., α_0 and α_1, respectively.

$$\alpha_1 = \sum_{i=1}^{N} \frac{(X_i-\overline{X})(Y_i-\overline{Y})}{(X_i-\overline{X})^2} \tag{11.3}$$

$$\alpha_0 = \overline{Y} - \alpha_1 \overline{X} \tag{11.4}$$

where　$\overline{Y}$ = average of response variable,
　　　　$\overline{X}$ = average of predictor variable,
　　　　N = total number of samples.

Table 11.3 Classification of correlation values [11].

S. no.	Symbolic convention	Meaning
1	$0.7 < |r| \leq 1$	Strong
2	$0.4 < |r| < 0.7$	Moderate
3	$0.2 < |r| < 0.4$	Weak
4	$0 \leq |r| < 0.2$	No Correlation

Table 11.4 Correlation between variables (predictor vs. response).

Variables/associations	Correlation (r)	Interpretation
TD and TTPMP	0.93	Strong
SC and TD	0.86	Strong
TREV and CFR	0.81	Strong
PD and CFR	−0.15	Negative
RR and AC	0.86	Strong
CFR and DR	0.85	Strong
DP and DR	0.78	Strong
MAGE and DR	−0.07	Negative
OAGE and DR	0.84	Strong
MS and RR	−0.005	Negative
HWF and CFR	0.34	Weak
HBF and RR	−0.14	Negative
DP and RR	0.23	Weak

In this study, DR, RR, CFR, SC, and TTPMP are selected as response variables and OAGE, TD, TREV, AC, and DP are considered as predictor variables. However, LR coefficients are solved by Equations (11.3) and (11.4). Table 11.5 shows straight line trend with regression coefficients.

Table 11.5 Straight line trend with regression coefficients.

S. no.	Attributes	Regression equation	Coefficients value
1	OAGE and DR	Y = 422.45-5.75X	$\alpha_0 = 422.45$, $\alpha_1 = -5.75$
2	TD and SC	Y = −783.98 + 0.19X	$\alpha_0 = -783.98$, $\alpha_1 = 0.19$
3	TREV and CFR	Y = 1868.06 + 0.083X	$\alpha_0 = 1868.06$, $\alpha_1 = 1.083$
4	AC and RR	Y = 17254.07 + 0.341X	$\alpha_0 = 17254.07$, $\alpha_1 = 0.341$
5	TD and TTPMP	Y = 325.774 + 0.061X	$\alpha_0 = 325.774$, $\alpha_1 = 0.061$
6	DP and DR	Y = 6.36 + 0.65X	$\alpha_0 = 6.36$, $\alpha_1 = 0.65$

11.4.2   Association Rule Mining

In order to find the unrelated frequent items in databases, one of the prominent and well-known techniques is known as ARM. However, ARM has capability to define relationships between the items as well as finding frequent rules with minimum support and confidence constraint [15, 16]. Basically, it is a two-step process.

1. Generating all frequent items based on satisfying the minimum support and minimum confidence constraint criteria.
2. Generating frequent rules using step 1.

In symbolic form, association rules are often shown as R → S meaning that whenever R occurs, then S also tends to be occurs, where R and S may be single item or sets of items. Generally, support confidence and lift measures are used to evaluate the ARM process. Hence, frequency of the pattern is denoted by support. In order to find some interesting business rules, minimum support constraint is necessary. Lift measure is used to denote how much more often antecedent and consequent occur together than expected, if they were statistically independent. The formula numbers (11.5), (11.6), and (11.7) denote the support, confidence, and lift measures [1, 16].

$$\text{Support (R)} = \frac{\text{Frequency of the Itemset R in Transations}}{\text{Total No. of Transactions (D)}} \tag{11.5}$$

Strength of the association between items R and S is shown by confidence.

$$\text{Confidence}\,(R \to S) = \frac{\text{Support (RUS)}}{\text{Support(R)}} \tag{11.6}$$

$$\text{Lift}\,(R \to S) = \frac{\text{Confidence}\,(R \to S)}{\text{Support(S)}} \tag{11.7}$$

A lift value between 0 and 1 shows a negative correlation between the items, the lift value 1 shows that no association between the items, and a lift value above than 1 shows stronger relationships between the items.

In order to find the association rule on a COVID-19 dataset, one of the most prominent ARM algorithm named as apriori is used in this study developed by Agrawal and Shrikant in 1994 [24]. Therefore, algorithm is popularly known as to use downward closure property or level by search where n-items are used to explore n+ 1 item. If no more n frequent item set found in the last, then algorithm terminates. Algorithm 11.1 shows the step-by-step procedure of apriori method.

Algorithm 11.1 Apriori method [26].

Input: COVD-19 Dataset, Min_support, Min_confidence, Min_lift
Output: Rules Generated
Step 1) Start
Step 2) Loop until the following:
    2.1) Get frequent-1 itemset.
    2.2) Searches and find for K-frequent itemset on D.
    2.3) Calculate support value using formula no. (11.5).
    2.4) Based on generated frequent itemset-I generate rules. For each rule (A→BϵD).
    2.5) Calculate confidence and lift value (A→B) on D using the formula nos. (11.6)
        & (11.7).
Step 3) Eliminating rules based on Min_support, Min_confidence and Min_lift constraint.
Step 4) If rules generated are frequent
    4.1) Use that rules for decision-making purpose.
        Otherwise
    4.2) Go to Step 2 and repeat the same procedure.
Step 5) Stop.

11.4.3 Back Propagation Neural Network

In order to train Multi-Layer Perceptron (MLP) networks, one of the most popular supervised learning algorithms is named as Back Propagation Neural Network (BPNN) [2]. Therefore, in MLP architecture, errors are always computed at an output layer and propagating in the "backwards" direction at hidden layers, where some activation functions like Sigmoid or Tangent is used so it is called as back propagation [10]. In this study, most popular back propagation techniques like Levenberg Marquardt (LM) are used to train the MLP networks. However, LM technique is well suited for solving small and medium size training problems and provides faster and stable convergence speed. Algorithm 11.2 shows step-by-step LM procedure.

Algorithm 11.2 Levenberg Marquardt (LM) [4, 9].

Input: AC, TD, TR, MAGE, OAGE, HWF, HBF, PD, MS, FS
Output: CFR, DR, RR, TTPMP, SC
Set constraint as: Min_error (α) < 10, Max_epoch (β)=1000
1) Start
2) Initialize the network training parameters, i.e., weights (W) and biases (b).
3) Start network training and calculate error value for proposed output.
4) Calculate Jacobian Matrix JM (W).
5) Update weight ΔW by using following formula.

$$\Delta W = (JM^T(W)J(W) + \mu I)^{-1} JM^T(W)e(W) \qquad (11.8)$$

6) Compute new error value w.r.t. eq. no. (11.8):
$\overline{W}=W+\Delta W$
7) If Errors < Min_error (α)
    7.1) Stop the network training and calculate output performance.
        Otherwise
    7.2) Check if Epoch ≥ Max_epoch (β) if yes stop network training.
        Otherwise
        Go to step 5 (update weights)
8) Epoch++
9) Go to step 2 and continue the same procedure.
10) Stop

11.5 Experimental Results

In this study, real dataset of different countries from Worldometer websites from the 31 December 2019 (week 1) to 19 May 2020 (20th week, 204 samples) are considered for study purpose. However, SC, Total Test per Million Population (TTPMP), RR, DR, and CFR of week 21, 22, and 23 are used as output parameters to predict the COVID-19 dataset. The SLR model based on two variables, ARM model and MLP model 17*8*1, is considered. Thus, 17 denotes number of input variables, 8 denotes number of hidden neurons, and 1 denotes output layer or neuron. In order to train the model, dataset is divided into three parts: training (70%), validation (15%), and testing (15%). Moreover, training parts contain 142 samples, validation parts contain 31 samples and testing part contains 31 samples. Finally, Statistica 13.2 machine learning tool is used to evaluate and analysis the results. Table 11.6 states the sample of frequency count of variables.

Table 11.6 Sample of frequency count of variables.

ID	Count	Item
1	31	TREV_Low
2	41	TREV_High
3	23	TD_Medium
4	41	DR_Low
5	35	DP_High
6	52	DP_Low
7	47	HBF_Poor
8	33	HBF_Medium
9	39	CFR_Low
10	51	CFR_High

In this study, 48 items and 204 records are considered for rule generation purpose. However, different constraint on support, confidence, and lift values are used in order to generate more frequent association rules. Table 11.7 shows maximum number of rule generation based on support 20%, 30%, 40%, and confidence value is greater than 90%.

Table 11.7 clearly states that when we increasing support %, then number of rules {1-length, 2-length, 3-length, 4-length, and 5-length} decreases. However, we got the frequent rule on 40% support value and confidence greater than 90%. In this study, we have considered only top 14 interesting rules based on constraints. Table 11.8 shows some interesting rules for COVID-19 dataset.

Table 11.7 Maximum number of rule generation based on support values 20%, 30%, 40%, and 50%.

Confidence (% ≥90)	1-Length	2-Length	3-Length	4-Length	5-Length
Support 20%	32	47	35	15	3
Support 30%	14	17	6	1	-
Support 40%	8	5	1	-	-
Support 50%	12	23	20	9	3

Table 11.8 Some interesting rules for COVID-19 dataset.

ID	Rules	Confidence (%)	Lift
1	TD=Low & PD=Low⇒AC=Low	100	1.1
2	TREV=Low TD=Low AC=Low PD=Low⇒TC=Low	100	1.26
3	CFR=Low PD=Low⇒DR=Low	92	1.21
4	CFR=High TREV=Low⇒TD=High	97	1.25
5	TREV=Low TC=High PD=Medium⇒TD=Low	98	1.14
6	TD=Low FS=Low⇒AC=Low	97	1.07
7	MS=High HBF=Poor⇒AC=Medium TREV=Low	94	1.15
8	OAGE =High CFR=Medium⇒DR=Medium TREV=Low	95	1.26
9	TD=High AC =Low TREV=Low⇒TC=Low	99	1.31
10	DP=Low⇒TD=Low AC=Low	92	1.12
11	MAGE=High DP=Medium⇒CFR=Low TD=High	97	1.27
12	HWF=Poor HBF=Medium CFR=Medium⇒DP=Low MAGE=Medium	100	1.24
13	TREV=Low⇒AC=High TC=Low TD=High	99	1.29
14	PD=High OAGE=Medium DP=High⇒DR=High HWF=Poor	100	1.34

Based on the Table 11.8 results, i.e., extracted rules can be described in the following manner. According to ID-1, when total deaths and population density are low, then actual case is also low (100% confidence). When CFR and population density are low, then DR is also low (according to ID-3, 92% confidence). Similarly, when total recovery is low, total cases are high and population density is medium and then total deaths are also low (ID-5, 98% confidence). According to ID-8, when old age people are high and CFR is medium, then DR is medium and total recovery is also low (95% confidence). When median age people are high and diabetes patient are medium, then CFR rate is low and total deaths are high (ID-11, 97% confidence). Similarly, when population density is high, old age people are medium and diabetes patient are high, then death rate is high and hand washing facility is poor (ID-14, 100% confidence). Figure 11.1 states the performance graph of the LM algorithm against Mean Square Error (MSE) and epochs.

It is clearly stated by Figure 11.1 that best validation performance is achieved at epoch 36, i.e., 1,511.4905. Table 11.9 states the various performance indicators in order to assess the proposed model performance.

Performance of proposed model is shown by Table 11.10.

Table 11.10 clearly states that LM and ARM method has outperformed well than SLR method. Country-wise performance comparison of actual and predicted output based on DR, RR, and CFR is shown by Table 11.11. Table 11.12 shows country-wise performance comparison of actual and predicted output based on SC and TTMP. Based on the Tables 11.11 and 11.12 results, we have classified the country based on some risk measurement.

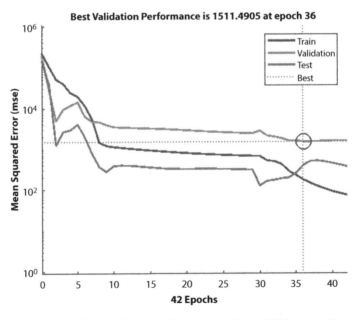

Figure 11.1 Performance graph of LMBP algorithm Mean Square Error (MSE) vs. epochs.

Table 11.9 Performance assessment of the proposed model.

S. no.	Performance assessment indicators	Description	Formula
1	Mean Absolute Error (MAE)	Measuring the performance w.r.t. Mean of squared errors	$\sum \dfrac{(\alpha_i - \beta_i)^2}{N}$
2	Root Mean Squared Error (RMSE)	Square Root of Mean Squared Error	$\sqrt{\sum \dfrac{(\alpha_i - \beta_i)^2}{N}}$
3	Mean Absolute Percentage Error (MAPE)	Simple average of absolute percentage errors	$\dfrac{\sum \dfrac{\lvert \alpha_i - \beta_i \rvert}{\alpha_i} \ast 100}{N}$

Here, α_1 = Actual Data, β_i = Predicted Data, N = Number of Sample.

Table 11.10 Performance of the proposed model.

Techniques	Performance measures		
Simple Linear Regression (SLR)	MAE	RMSE	MAPE
	833.43	47.63	546.31
Levenberg Marquardt (LM)	256.32	21.51	11.56
Association Rule Mining (ARM)	Best Rule Generated based on Support = 40%, Confidence >= 90%		

Table 11.13 shows risk classification of output parameters.

Based on Table 11.13 values, all the countries are classified into three levels, i.e., low, medium, and high, respectively. In this study, 204 countries are considered for study purpose. Here, representations of all countries data are not possible. However, we have recognized some well-known countries based on risk categorization. Table 11.14 shows sample of risk-wise categorization of countries based on output parameters.

Table 11.14 clearly classifies the countries based on DR, RR, CFR, SC, and TTPMP. We have classified the countries form lowest risk to highest risk based on color combination. The country France, Belgium, Italy, and UK have identified as highest risk in DR category and countries like Pakistan, Belgium, USA, and UK have lowest RR. In the case of fertility rate category, France, Belgium, Italy, and UK have identified as highest risk country. Moreover, the countries like USA, India, Russia, Peru, and Iran have highest serious patients of COVID-19. Similarly, the countries Ghana, Philippines, India, Algeria, Pakistan,

Table 11.11 Country-wise performance comparison of actual and predicted output based on DR, RR, and CFR.

Country	Actual value (death rate)	Predicted value (death rate)	Actual value (recovery rate)	Predicted value (recovery rate)	Actual value (case fertility rate)	Predicted value (case fertility rate)
Australia	1.4	1.95	92.46	89.81	1.4	1.43
Peru	2.79	3.61	44.85	46.87	2.78	3.36
Ukraine	2.9	3.39	44.41	52.11	2.91	2.93
Portugal	4.26	4.61	60.64	79.8	4.28	4.37
Philippines	4.5	5.65	20.63	47.61	4.58	4.59
France	18.94	19.44	46.09	46.51	18.93	16.08
Belgium	16.19	16.48	27.49	30.03	16.2	16.2
UK	14.13	14.26	28.42	33.12	14.16	14.24
Italy	14.44	17.01	70.08	65.79	14.42	14.39
Iran	4.8	4.87	78.44	84.65	4.82	4.84
Germany	4.72	5.34	91.08	104.39	4.71	4.74
Russia	1.25	1.45	48.04	45	1.25	1.08
Austria	3.96	4.84	93.35	82.71	3.98	3.97
USA	5.58	5.37	38.17	38.28	5.69	5.69
India	2.8	1.10	48.47	40.61	2.78	2.87
Algeria	6.97	6.91	66.23	49.08	6.96	6.01
Indonesia	5.88	6.07	34.04	48.58	5.93	6

Table 11.12 Country-wise performance comparison of actual and predicted output based on serious cases (SC) and total test per million population (TTMP).

Country	Actual value (SC)	Predicted value (SC)	Actual value (TTMP)	Predicted value (TTMP)
Australia	3	8	64,723	57,559
Peru	1,065	1,000	36,548	37,832
Ukraine	306	365	9,854	13,824
Portugal	70	84	85,700	83,593
Philippines	82	58.83	4,032	3,912
France	933	930	21,216	26,754
Belgium	104	94	81,963	79,896
UK	516	400	84,456	104,824
Italy	249	440	70,064	64,801
Iran	2,639	2,137	13,193	25,432
Germany	492	731	51,916	36,978
Russia	2,300	2,942	89,193	84,578
Austria	17	23	54,953	57,578
USA	16,838	13,453	65,657	65,161

Table 11.13 Risk classification of output parameters.

Parameters	Interpretation		
DR	Low	Medium	High
	0–4.99	5–9.99	10–20
RR	10–39	40–69	70–100
CFR	0–3.99	4–6.99	7–20
SC	0–299	300–999	≥1,000
TTPMP	0–10,000	11,000–49,000	≥50,000

Indonesia, and China have very low total tests of COVID-19. Figure 11.2 indicates the rise-wise classification of other popular countries.

In Figure 11.2, countries are classified, i.e., lower risk to higher risk level based on CFR and TTPMP. However, we have recognized some new countries like Netherland, Mexico, Afghanistan, Canada, Sweden, Uganda, Kenya, Taiwan, Poland, Ireland, Greece, Finland,

Table 11.14 Sample of risk-wise categorization of countries based on output parameters.

DR	RR	CFR	SC	TTPMP
France	Pakistan	France	USA	Ghana
Italy	Belgium	Belgium	India	Philippines
Belgium	USA	Italy	Iran	India
UK	UK	UK	Russia	Pakistan
Indonesia	France	Algeria	Peru	Indonesia
Philippines	Russia	Indonesia	France	China
Algeria	India	USA	Ukraine	Algeria
Germany	Peru	Germany	UK	Ukraine
USA	Ghana	China	Germany	Iran
China	Philippines	Iran	Italy	Australia
Peru	Algeria	Philippines	Pakistan	Austria
Iran	Indonesia	Portugal	Belgium	Germany
Austria	Ukraine	Austria	Portugal	Russia
Portugal	Italy	Ukraine	Philippines	Portugal
Ukraine	Iran	India	Israel	UK
Israel	China	Australia	Algeria	USA
Australia	Israel	Pakistan	Austria	Israel
Ghana	Austria	Russia	Ghana	Italy
India	Portugal	Ghana	Australia	Portugal
Russia	Australia	Israel	Indonesia	Belgium
Pakistan	Germany	Peru	China	UK

*Red Color = High Risk.
*Dark Blue = Medium Risk.
*Green Color = Low Risk.

Denmark, Romania, Egypt, Norway, Bangladesh, Nepal, S. Africa, S. Korea, Qatar, and Chile, which come under highest to lowest risk levels, respectively. The countries shown in low- and medium-risk category which might be come in high-risk category in future, if proper strategy is not followed by the government. Thus, government should implement the proper lock-down strategy, maintaining social distancing among people, and compulsorily

Figure 11.2 Rise-wise classification of countries.

allow wearing surgical masks and keeping sanitizer for hand wash, weekly two days shutdown in order to spread COVID-19 outbreak.

11.6   Conclusion and Future Scopes

In this study, three most popular DM techniques like SLR, ARM, and BPNN are implemented. The performance of proposed techniques like SLR and BPNN are assessed based on Root Mean Square Error (RMSE), Mean Absolute Percentage Error (MAPE), and Mean Absolute Error (MAE), as well as performance of ARM technique is assed based on constraints like support, confidence, and lift measures. The BPNN method has recorded the lowest error 256.32 (MAE), 11.56 (MAPE), and 21.51 (RMSE), respectively.

The main focus of this study is to recognize the countries based on risk level, i.e., low to high. However, DR, RR, CFR, SC, and TTPMP are considered as output parameters and we have found that countries like France, Italy, Belgium, UK, Pakistan, USA, India, Iran, Russia, Peru, Ghana, Philippines, Indonesia, Algeria, China, Germany, Ukraine, Portugal, Spain, Canada, Sweden, Brazil, Switzerland, and Kenya are recognized as in high-risk category. In low-risk category level, we have recognized the countries like Austria, Israel, Australia, Nepal, Chile, Qatar, Egypt, and Bangladesh. In future, countries might be changed their level from higher to lower or vice versa due to the carelessness of the government. The government adopt the proper strategy or planning to fight against the COVID-19 and should take some preventive actions.

The government should take some preventive actions like implementing lock-down rule, use inferred camera to maintain social distance, compulsorily allow wearing surgical masks, and manage automatic sanitizer machine in government offices, schools, colleges, and public places in order to save the life of the millions of people.

This study will be helpful for government, medical professionals, business persons, and police staff to know the global status of COVID-19 countries. Additionally, it would be helpful for government to manage the hospital beds, surgical masks, sanitizers' machines, medical staff, enhancing COVID test center so that proper strategy could be implemented on right time to fight against this serious outbreak.

In future, some other well-known machine learning classification techniques like support vector machine (SVM) and neuro-fuzzy would be adopted for better analysis and decision-making purpose.

References

1. Agrawal, R. and Srikant, R., Fast Algorithms for Mining Association Rules in Large Databases, in: *Proc. of the 20th International Conference on VLDB*, pp. 478–499, 1994.
2. Akhtar, M., Kraemer, M., Gardner, L., A Dynamic Neural Network Model for Predicting Risk of Zika in Real Time. *BMC Med.*, 17, 171, 1–16, 2019, https://doi.org/10.1186/s12916{019-1389-3.
3. Alimadadi, A., Aryal, S., Manandhar, I., Munroe, P.B., Joe, B., Cheng, Xi, Artificial Intelligence and Machine Learning to Fight COVID-19. *Physiol. Genom.*, 52, 200–202, 2020.
4. Alpaydin, E., *Introduction to Machine Learning*, 2nd Edition, The MIT Press, Cambridge, M.A. U.S.A., 2010.
5. Anastassopoulou, C., Russo, L., Tsakris, A., Siettos, C., Data based Analysis, Modeling and Forecasting of the COVID-19 Outbreak. *PloS One*, 15, 3, 1–21, 2020, https://doi.org/10.1371/journal.pone.0230405.
6. Berk, R.A., *Regression Analysis: A Constructive Critique*, 1st Edition, Sage Publications, SAGE Publishing, U.S.A., 2003.
7. Cascella, M., Rajnik, M., Cuomo, A., Dulebohn, S.C., Napoli, R.D., *Features, Evaluation and Treatment Corona Virus (COVID-19)*, StatPearls Publishing-NCBI BookShelf, Treasure Island (FL), 1–17, 2020, [Online] Available on https://www.ncbi.nlm.nih.gov/books/NBK554776/. Accessed on 26th March 2020.
8. Centers for Disease Control and Prevention, *Corona Virus Disease 2019 (COVID-19)*, Published 2020, [Online] Available: https://www.cdc.gov/coronavirus/2019-ncov/summary.html#background. Accessed on 5th May, 2020.
9. Chen, J.H. and Asch, S.M., Machine Learning and Prediction in Medicine-beyond the Peak of Inflated Expectations. *N. Engl. J. Med.*, 376, 26, 2507–2509, 2017.
10. Cheng, B. and Titterington, D.M., Neural Networks: A Review from a Statistical Perspective. *Stat. Sci.*, 9, 1, 2–54, 1994.
11. Chicco, D. and Jurman, G., The Advantages of the Matthews Correlation Coefficient (MCC) over F1 Score and Accuracy in Binary Classification Evaluation. *BMC Genom.*, 21, 1, 1–13, 2020.
12. Connolly, T. and Begg, C., *Database Systems: A Practical Approach to Design, Implementation and Management*, 6th Edition, Pearson Education LTD, Harlow, 2015.
13. Cryer, J.D. and Miller, R.B., *Statistics for Business: Data Analysis and Modeling*, 2nd Edition, Brooks/Cole, South-Western College Publishing, U.S.A., 2004.
14. Ghosal, S., Sengupta, S., Majumder, M., Sinha, B., Linear Regression Analysis to Predict the Number of Deaths in India due to SARS-COV-2 at 6 Weeks from Day 0 (100 Cases- March 14th 2020). *Diabetes. Metab. Syndr. Clin. Res. Rev.*, 14, 4, 311–315, 2020.

15. Han, J. and Kamber, M., *Data Mining: Concepts and Techniques*, 2nd Edition, Morgan Kaufmann, San Francisco, U.S.A, 2006.

16. Hong, S.J. and Weiss, S.M., Advances in Predictive Models for Data Mining. *Pattern Recognit. Lett.*, 22, 55–61, 2001.

17. Jiawei, L., MS, Qing, X., MAS, Raphael, C., MPH, Purushothaman, V., Mackey, T., Data Mining and Content Analysis of the Chinese Social Media Platform Weibo During the Early COVID-19 Outbreak: Retrospective Observational Infoveillance Study. *JMIR Public Health Surveill.*, 6, 2, 1–10, 2020. e18700.

18. Khaitan, S., Mitra, A., Shukla, P., Chakraborty, S., Statistical Investigation of Novel Corona Virus COVID-19, *Int. J. Control Autom.*, 13, 2s, 1–6, 2020.

19. Long, J.B. and Ehrenfeld, J.M., The Role of Augmented Intelligence (AI) in Detecting and Preventing the Spread of Novel Corona Virus. *J. Med. Syst.*, 44, 3, 59–66, 2020.

20. National Health Commission of the People's Republic of China, Update on Pneumonia of New Corona virus Infection as of 21:00 on January 31 Available Online: http://www.nhc.gov.cnxcs/yqtb/202002/84faf71e096446fdb1ae44939ba5c528.shtm. Accessed on 25 March, 2020.

21. Online Data Source Available on http://www.worldometer.com. Accessed on 20th May 2020.

22. Organization WH. Novel Corona Virus (2019-NCoV), *Situation report 21*, World Health Organization, Geneva, Switzerland, 2020, 2020; Available from: https://www.who.int/docs/default-source/coronaviruse/situation-reports/20200210-sitrep-21-ncov.pdf?sfvrsn=947679ef_2. Accessed on May 24, 2020.

23. Ozturk, T., Talo, M., Yildirim, E.A., Baloglu, U.B., Yildirim, O., Acharya, U.R., Automated Detection of COVID-19 Cases Using Deep Neural Networks with X-ray Images. *Comput. Biol. Med.*, 121, 1–11, 2020.

24. Perng, C., Wang, H., Ma, S., Hellerstein, J., Discovery in Multi-attribute Data with User-defined Constraints. *ACM SIGKDD Explor. Newslett.*, 4, 1, 56–64, 2002.

25. Song, F., Shi, N., Shan, F., Emerging Corona Virus 2019-NCoV Pneumonia. *Radiology*, 295, 1, 210–217, 2020.

26. Srikant, R. and Agrawal, R., Mining Generalized Association Rules, in: *Proc. of the 21st International Conference on Very Large Databases*, Zurich, Switzerland, September 1995.

27. Wang, L. and Wong, A., *COVID-Net: A Tailored Deep Convolutional Neural Network Design for Detection of COVID-19 Cases from Chest Radiography Images arXiv*, pp. 1–12, 2020, 22 (https://arxiv.org/abs/2003.09871).

28. WHO, *Novel Corona Virus–Thailand (ex-China)*, Jan 14, 2020, http://www.who.int/csr/don/14-january-2020-novel-coronavirusthailand/en/. Accessed on April 19, 2020.

29. Xie, J. and Coggeshall, S., Prediction of Transfers to Tertiary Care and Hospital Mortality: A Gradient Boosting Decision Tree Approach. *Stat. Anal. Data. Min.*, 3, 4, 253–258, 2010, doi: 10.1002/sam.10079.

Sentiment Analysis on Social Media for Emotional Prediction During COVID-19 Pandemic Using Efficient Machine Learning Approach

Sivanantham Kalimuthu

Research and Development Team, Crapersoft, Coimbatore

Abstract

The growth of social websites, electronic media, and blogging services is increased day by day, and they contribute many user messages like customer comments, reviews, and opinions. These mes-sages are used for measuring the quality of various products and services but it is very large. Therefore, sentiment analysis (SA) or opinion mining (OM) was introduced, and it involves in collecting the data from the web by using Natural Language Processing (NLP) techniques and examine the opinions. The opinions are collected by NLP, and then, it is classified as positive, neutral, and negative. This research investigates the SA for COVID-19 data by using various machine learning and swarm intelligence optimization algorithms. In this research, new types of SA models have been studied and performance has been evaluated for COVID-19 data by using MATLAB. The proposed HSVMCSO scheme achieves a high accuracy rate of 92.80%, sensitivity rate of 93.20%, specificity rate of 90.42%, precision rate of 95.38%, recall rate of 90.24%, and F-measure rate of 89.78% when compared with the existing SA schemes like SVM, logistic regression, and neural network. The proposed HSVMCSO attained less processing time of 29.12 s and processing cost compared to existing schemes.

Keywords: COVID-19, sentimental analysis, opinion mining, machine learning algorithms, chicken swarm optimization, support vector machine

12.1 Introduction

Data mining is the uprooting or extraction of informations from large datasets, or it can be defined as a method of detecting knowledge from data, and the other activities performed by data mining are cleaning of data, transformation of data, integration of data, evaluation pattern, and presentation of data

In the web, many text data exist, and it can be organized approximately into two most important classifications: truth and opinion. The truth is the objective state-ments, whereas opinions are the subjective statements. The objective statements are on

Email: sivanantham.kalimuthu@crapersoft.com

Om Prakash Jena, Alok Ranjan Tripathy, Ahmed A. Elngar and Zdzislaw Polkowski (eds.) Computational Intelligence and Healthcare Informatics, (215–234) © 2021 Scrivener Publishing LLC

components for instance. Opinions are individual sentiments, feelings, evaluations, and mindsets associated with the specific object. The major component of the research on text-based data has been focused on mining from truth based data, for instance, web based searching, retrieval of information, text grouping, topicalization, text classification, etc. There are many numbers of clients rising for every year, and it has become more popular in these times and as a result, this has developed into the important source to extract opinions.

There available many number of text that is posted by various users on the web. The number of persons transmitting in the social web is growing more and more. Their feedbacks are eminently precious for governments, institutions, organizations, and also for other users. Twitter is the more familiar website for micro-blogging, and it is more popular for rapid messages called as "Tweets". This restricts the message up to 140 characters. For every day, there are more than three hundred and forty million tweets are posted and subsequently a better source of information. Users are often speaking about the present dealings and generate their feedbacks on the similar through their tweets. Twitter possess many benefits that include, uncomplicated in accessing with the help of API, tweets are very small in length; therefore, it is less unclear, it gathers the information of the various socio-social domain, and it is impartial.

Opinion mining (OM) is a too long process that comprises of many number of actions which includes discovering sources of opinion, identifying, and evaluating statements, and summarizing it. There available many numbers of opinion-based sources and all may further have a massive amount of opinion based data. Customer's statements are commonly engaged in extensive conversation posts and websites for review. It is inconvenient for the customers to outline such sources, discovering right opinion statements, comprehend them, and summarize them into positive and negative opinions.

It is a practice of discovering the opinions, statements, or analyses of users associated to the distinct product, subject, and services. Still, the particular statement can have the composition of both the information of truth based and opinion based. Right now, there available many distinguished search systems that may provide many numbers of attractive applications in various domains from business to academics.

Experimental dataset, such as twitter COVID-19 and people situation sequences of pandemic durations, and the purpose of data mining techniques, is to discover useful information from this biological twitter datasets. The use of Internet possesses a beneficial place for online learning, for interchanging their opinions, views, and ideas for services or items/products due to the availability of excessive bandwidth through wireless. The discussions on the internet play a very critical role in choosing the service or items/products. Intuitive research, a computational study of reviews, statements, sentiments, and opinions that are conveyed in text on their reviews which is found on the internet has become obligatory.

Initially, the issue of extraction from Twitter and Facebook for which an algorithm has been proposed for identifying and extracting the tweets pertaining to the policy passed as a keyword has been discussed. In terms of thoughtful comment extraction and on the social, the process was evaluated by performing a comparative study of different approaches to extracting the data. Then, the basic classification algorithms have been improvised by incorporating the concept of negation handling mechanism. The model presented here in this thesis has been formulated based on probabilities, initially training the data and then proceeding to test the new data with respect to the policies launched by the government of India. These needs have inspired a new line of research on summarizing the opinions. An algorithm has been proposed which combines the concepts of extractive and abstractive versions to generate an abstractive summary. Comparisons with respect to the existing techniques have been done during all the stages of this investigation.

Proposed models are used to calculate risk estimates for development of COVID-19 disease. The models are also be used to estimate the risk after adjusted for potential confounders and possible interactions between risk factors. In reality, enhancing and comparing the user's diverse viewpoints that are readily available in the sites calls for a consideration in determining valuable perception. OM is one of the rising areas in research that reviews the user's product views and services as well as the learning system. This reveals whether the viewpoints are encouraging or discouraging. The main intention of OM is to decide the polarity of feedbacks by deriving the features and constituents of the object that have been mentioned in every document.

The high-speed development of mobile communication and miniature devices offer an inventive and a novel instructive strategy in the learning system. Hence, it is essential to develop the system of machine learning and to recognize the user's viewpoint and assessment about them. This encompasses practicing the self-activating text evaluation to derive the opinions and designating self-activating text evaluation to discover the opinion's sentiment from the viewpoint on which the users are examining or expressing their personal opinions and rating of services. The latest researches on sentiment analysis (SA) experience many numbers of restrictions, very small accuracy in classification, and also document level views are not discovered. This proposed research work tackles all these issues.

In this research, an hybrid SVM with chicken swarm optimization (CSO) algorithm has been proposed for efficient SA. Part-of-Speech (POS) tagged text is used in this algorithm for extracting the potential features. Based on the opinion score, the efficient features have been selected, and the opinion scores and ranks are provided by CSO scheme for every noun. After that, the highest opinions of features are predicted by using max opinion score scheme. The predicted features are transferred to classification phase and the Interactive has been used for classifying the sentiments like positive, neutral, and negative.

In the proposed research, the results of a comprehensive comparative study of data mining, statistical, and machine learning algorithms, including artificial neural networks (ANN), neural network, and hybrid support vector machines (SVMs) with chicken swarm optimization (HSVMCSO), were examined. The main focus of this research was to study the effective classification learning techniques for prediction of COVID-19 survivability. There are two main aspects in prediction of COVID-19 pandemic situation survivability: accuracy and efficiency. Data reduction technique was applied to the dataset and obtained a reduced representation of the COVID-19 twitter dataset that was much smaller in volume, yet closely maintains the originality of the data. The python function was used to reduce a large dataset (the patients in this case) to smaller components of objects related according to their expression patterns with character size.

The significant intention of this research acquires the high precision in the classification of user viewpoints and to strengthen the campaign success and user service of a specific product on the basis of reviews. At this time, the techniques based on machine learning are established for deriving the opinions from the online user viewpoints.

This proposed research comprises of two phases in order to derive the features like identification of features and ranking the phase of prediction. In primary one, the features are derived or decided from the customer reviews. The next is to illustrate the numerical features for derived attributes of products. At last, the viewpoints are systematized into good, bad or neutral depends on the various users' opinions. The essential goal of the anticipated research work is as follows:

1. To obtain the better precision of analysis, the feature extraction is presented.
2. To systematize the reviews, the opinion ratings and mining system is proposed.
3. To upgrade the method, the machine learning categorization schemes are used.

The reminder of paper is organized as follows. Section 12.2 presents SA on social media for emotional prediction and its related work. Section 12.3 discussed to HSVMCSO Algorithm. Section 12.4 presents proposed system and existing systems experimental results comparison. Finally, Section 12.5 provides the concluding remarks and future scope of the proposed COVID-19 sentimental analysis.

12.2 Literature Review

The literature survey gathers the researches exist on OM. This describes the SA and the various tools existed for it. There exist many strategies that include techniques for pattern mining and machine learning with several degrees of automation. In this segment, the surveys about the previously existing study which are evolved by various developers are presented. All the difficulties in the survey were stated clearly.

Padmaja & Sameen Fatima [8] surveyed about the OM and SA. OM is considered as the procedure of deriving the knowledge automatically from the view of others regarding few specific areas. There were exists many applications and development regarding OM and this research concentrates on the OM definitions, examination of linguistic resources needed for OM, usage of machine learning schemes and its significance for investigation, and assessing the classification of sentiments and its numerous applications. It also focused on an extensive range of applications of NLP tools which are generally used for SA.

Vinodhini & Chandrasekaran [16] reviewed about the SA and OM. SA is one of the more focused areas because there is a great volume of views rich web resources that include blogs, review sites, discussion forum, and news corpora. People are deliberated to evolve a system which is to find and categorize the views or statement that is depicted in an electronic text. A perfect method for forecasting sentiments allows us to derive the viewpoints from the internet and estimate online users wish that provide evidence for valuable research of economic or marketing. Until now, there also exist some distinct issues dominating in this research community such as feature-based classification, sentiment classification, and managing negations. This research work describes the approaches and practices in SA and the issues arise in this field.

Bing Liu [6] deals with sentiment analysis and opinion mining. The important intent of this work is to provide the extensive review about OM and provide the complete survey of every significant topic in this field. It also considers the natural language text that is frequently regarded as the unstructured data. This work deals with the structured approach in establishing the issue with the intent of connecting the unstructured world with the structured world, and it promotes the quantitative and qualitative analysis of opinions. But it is more critical for realistic applications. This work distinguishes the problems existed in many previous works. It also discussed the tools that solve these problems and sub-problems. This research work is very much useful for all students and researchers who are very much interested in this field.

Richa Sharma *et al.* [11] estimated the attribute sets and classifiers for SA of financial news. The studies of SA are restricted due to several reasons. It includes insufficient of clearly defined goal, complexity in partitioning the good and bad news from positive and negative sentiments, and the seeming need of, complexity in, depending on domain specific interpretations and perception of knowledge. In this research work, it presents, describes, conducts experiment, and estimates four various attribute classifications, and it contains 26 article attributes for SA. By utilizing five distinct approaches to machine learning, it trains sentiment classifiers of Norwegian financial internet news articles and attains the accuracy of classification of 71%. This is equivalent to the state of the art in current domains, and it is near to the human baseline. This shows that it yields better performance.

Lizhen Liu *et al.* [5] examined about the automated evaluation of the sentiments expressed in online user comments enable both institutions' business strategy growth and separate user's comparison shopping. This technique automatically builds FDSOT (Fuzzy Domain Ontology Tree) that depends on the opinions of products involving the derivation of sentiment words, attributes of products, and the associations in between the attributes. The feature of product denotes the components or attributes of the product. The experiment is conducted with the reviews expressed by the users of the Chinese product which is gathered from the 360buy.com and evaluation shows that the presented method attains high precision and very much better in predicting polarity.

Sumathi *et al.* [13] discussed the disadvantages in the previous research on feature based OM, and it includes choosing an attribute by only considering the grammatical information or considering attributes with similar meanings as dissimilar. Though this causes a huge corpus that later affects the precision of classification. Statistical methods like CFS (Correlation-based Feature Selection) that are used highly for choosing feature in order to minimize the size of the corpus. The decided attributes are sub-optimal because of Non-Polynomial (NP) hard nature of the used strategy. Therefore, in OM, an algorithm of Artificial Bee Colony (ABC) is introduced for optimization of feature subset. For purpose of classification, Naive Bayes, Fuzzy Unordered Rule Induction Algorithm (FURIA), and Ripple down Rule Learner classifiers (RIDOR) are used. This introduced approach is compared with the attributes derived depends on the Inverse Document Frequency (IDF). Therefore, this strategy is more helpful for minimizing the size of feature subset and difficulty in computation that may maximize the accuracy of classification.

Revathi Manju *et al.* [7] addressed the problems of navigation of information and attainment of knowledge as the essential reviews are not correctly arranged because there are a lot of reviews submitted on the web by users. These reviews are varied on multiple features of products. To tackle this issue, product feature ranking is considered to find the attributes or characteristics of essential products automatically from online user viewpoints using semantically oriented sentiment classifier. The algorithm of probabilistic feature ranking is presented with kNN-based sentiment classifier. In this approach, semantic-oriented subjective information is derived initially and ranking is computed depends on the frequency of features. The algorithm is examined by using T-Mobile dataset to exhibit the usefulness of the ranking method. The presented approach scope is to arrange the viewpoints of the user in a suitable way so that the product promotion can be carried out that effectively depends on the user comments.

Mohammad Ehsan Basiri et al. [1] examined the techniques of sentiment prediction that are frequently utilized for allocating numerical scores for reviews submitted by users in online. For properly utilizing the fine-grained structural information, viewpoints should be gathered as a sentence all with their own rank and sentiment orientation. It is found that, in this way, rank aggregation approach is required for integrating the sentence-level rank into complete viewpoint score. But many of the aggregation techniques perform badly from the investigation. Therefore, a new aggregation technique is presented depending on the Dempster-Shafer theory of evidence. In this approach, it initially finds the polarity of views with the help of machine learning method then it records the sentence rank as proof for entire review rating. The experiment is conducted with two public social web datasets and the results show that the technique attains high performance.

Gautami Tripathi & Naganna [14] presented a review based on OM. The access of social media and other applications of the web like e-commerce sites, micro-blogging, and news portal have resulted in huge amount of user-created content in the form of feedbacks, suggestions, comments, views, ratings, rankings, and scores. It presents the survey on these things and the associated methods. This describes the SA and the existed techniques used for it. By investigating, the user comments are greatly helpful for the government, individuals, and business organizations.

Valakunde, N & Patwardhan [15] surveyed about the feature level SA. This explains about the learning algorithms like supervised learning, unsupervised learning, and hybrid methods and the process of steps involved in these techniques. From the analysis, it is shown that the supervised learning attains better performance when compared to the unsupervised learning but supervised learning is more expensive. It is found that SVM has a high accuracy. The data is categorized into two main subclasses with the binary classification, namely, positive and negative. The positive class exhibits the excellent opinion and negative class exhibits the poor decision opinion. One more essential challenge for this method is the polarity of words. These words are interconnected with the sentiment in a specific domain.

Yang et al. [18] introduced an approach called gloss based approach. With this method, it enhances the efficiency of identifying the viewpoint orientation in the domain of SA. This analysis is done with using the reviews collected from the customers.

Chetashri Bhadane et al. [2] measured the opinions in the SA. This describes the numerous approaches that are employed for categorizing the given piece of natural language text based on the views conveyed in it. That categorizes the views whether the common attitude is positive or negative. It also examined about the two-step approaches that includes aspect classification and polarity classification in the experiment for reviewing a product by using machine learning SVM integrated with the domain specific lexicons and the output from the experiments proves that this presented approach attains about 78% of precision, and it is essential for executing its task.

Richa Sharma et al. [12] proposed an OM system to discover the polarity of sentences using the unsupervised procedure. The main intent of this work is to categorize the sentences as positive, negative, or neutral and to decide the polarity of a huge number of user reviews of a product. In this system, negation is also managed. The outlined results produced by the system will be useful for the customers in considering the decision. The effectiveness of the system is seen from the outcome of conducted experiments with the opinions of products. This outcome denotes that the sentiment orientation system performs much better when compared to the AIRC Sentiment Analyzer System. This process is essential as peoples are more rely on the reviews conveyed on the web. This is more useful for any business or institution because it decides the advantages and disadvantages of their manufactured item.

Jeevanandam Jotheeswaran and Kumaraswamy [4] analyzed that feature selection is required for any applications of data mining to get successful as it minimizes the dimensions of data by eliminating the unnecessary attributes. These features are derived from the data for categorizing the sentiment. The process of feature selection has obtained more significance because of its involvement to preserve the cost of classification corresponding to the time and computation load. This work concentrates on the feature selection for OM with the support of Manhattan hierarchical cluster measure for decision tree–based feature selection. This presented approach is estimated by using IMDb (Internet Movie Database) dataset, and it is compared with PCA. LVQ-type learning models comprise of trendy learning algorithms because of its easy learning rule, its instinctive formation of a classifier through prototypical locality in the data space, and its effective appropriateness to any given number of classes. The attributes of movie views derived from the IMDb were derived using frequency of inverse document and the significance of the founded word. PCA was employed for selecting feature that depends on the significance of work corresponding to complete document. The precision of classification that is derived by LVQ was about 75%. It is found that the accuracy of positive opinions was very less. This event was noticed not only on LVQ but also in other classifiers comprising Naive Bayes and CART (Classification and Regression Tree). The proposed feature selection method is considered as the promising one from the experiment conducted.

Christopher Yang *et al.* [17] deal with the SA by using machine learning to understand the review opinions of customers in online. It concentrates on viewpoints that are provided by user's regards on products that many numbers of customers in online employs to maintain the choice of purchase by finding out the products which fit better for the first choice. For now, sentiment classification and investigation of user viewpoints in online have drawn essential research attention. Many of existing procedures depend on the tools of NLP (Natural Language Processing) in order to parse and examine the statements in a review, although it provides incorrect accuracy, as the writing in online leads to be minimal formal compared to writing in news or journal articles. More number of opinion statements that consist of grammatical errors and unidentified terms that are not present in dictionaries. Hence, two supervised learning approaches are found, namely, Naive Bayes Classifier and Class Association rule for categorizing opinion statements into suitable classes of product attributes and generate an overview of user viewpoints. The comparison is made between the two for SA, and it proves that it attains greater than 70% of micro and macro F-measures.

Honglei Guo *et al.* [3] proposed a classification approach of unsupervised product attributes along with the multilevel latent semantic association (LaSA). Once the attributes of products are derived from the semistructured viewpoints, then the model is introduced as LaSA model to cluster the words into a group of perceptions based on its virtual text documents. This provides the latent semantic formation for every product attribute. After that, a second LaSA model is established to sort out the product-attributes based on its latent semantic arrangements and framework snippets in the viewpoints. It is illustrated with the experiments that attain the higher performance and the approach is domain and language independent.

Hong Yu & Vasileios Hatzivassiloglou [20] discussed a sufficient factor for a system of opinion question answering, partitioning opinion from facts in both sentence level and document level. It suggests a Bayesian classifier for perceptive among the documents with the prevalence of opinions like editorials from usual news stories and narrates three unsupervised, statistical methods for the essentially rigid task for identifying opinions at the sentence level. It also provides the initial model for categorizing the opinion sentences as positive or negative. The output obtained from the huge collection of news stories and a human estimation of 400 sentences are investigated that denotes it attains higher performance nearly 97% in the classification of the document and honorable performance in identifying opinions and categorizing them at the sentence level as positive, negative or neutral.

In this chapter, it reveals the existing researches on OM. It also detailed about the SA and the various tools used for it. It describes many numbers of strategies which comprises of techniques for pattern mining and machine learning with several degrees of automation. The problems with the existed methods are also stated properly. The next chapter covers the proposals for SA, and it overcomes the difficulties existed in the previous approaches.

12.3   System Design

SA is a method that groups the body of textual information to decide attitudes, feelings, and emotions in the direction of a specific matter or object. SA of people with COVID-19 endeavors to decide the speaker's attitude or a writer's attitude concerning few topics or the complete contextual polarity of a document. This attitude can be any one's assessment, judgment, responsiveness, or affecting the state of the writer at the time of conveying their statements about a subject on the web. OM attends to finding and categorizing the sentiments that are available in a text.

In these days, there exist a lot of websites that have been inaugurated for collecting user viewpoints of diseases, and it is much needful for peoples and medical perceptions. In the field of emotional dataset of people with COVID-19, viewpoints are helpful for examining the response of various users and at the mean time; it enhances the severity of COVID-19 diseases. As the number of user reviews is raised quickly, it becomes difficult for users to accomplish the entire view of user reviews associated with the diseases of complications by manually. Hence, for evolving an effective and efficient SA, the reviews of users are essential, and it is a significant method for inferring the people reviews automatically. This investigation possesses two essential functions. First is deriving all item attributes in the user viewpoint and the second is finding opinion orientation.

Hence, for evolving an effective and efficient SA, the reviews of users are essential, and it is a significant method for inferring the people reviews automatically. This investigation possesses two essential functions. First is deriving all emotionally expressed attributes of people with COVID-19 diseases in the user viewpoint and the second is finding opinion orientation.

However, several researches existed on COVID-19 SA, and still, there are many issues and they are not resolved efficiently. There also few issues like deriving product attributes that was not finding the right attributes and organizing or classifying the product attribute were not addressed properly and also in the subtask of opinion orientation recognition the complications of the absence of opinion words and changes of context or domain are not approached efficiently. The mission was utilizing the opinion words to determine the kind of people emotional of derived COVID-19 features. All these issues are addressed previously only in a single point and also exists an integrated structure for effective SA.

For that reason, the goal of this research work is to put forward a scheme of SA competent of compacting with all the above mentioned complications. Specifically, this work introduces the algorithm.

Initially, the emotional dataset of people with COVID-19 was collected. The data preprocessing is applied to the dataset by using ICA. Then, the process of feature extraction is accomplished with WMAR. After deriving the features, ranking and scores are provided by using IBA. At last, classification of reviews is carried out by using SVM. The output for COVID-19 dataset is obtained from this SA architecture explained Figure 12.1. The process of SA has been described gradually in given below subsections.

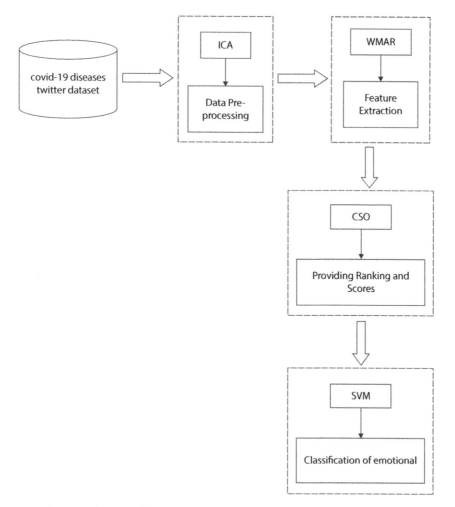

Figure 12.1 Architecture diagram of COVID-19 emotional classification.

Inputs: ICA COVID-19 dataset, number of attributes, missing values or unobserved hidden data z and vector of α, an unknown parameter

Output: Predict the cleaned data

Step 1: Stop words, commas, periods and punctuations should be removed from the dataset. Data which possess the frequency of occurrence greater than one in the dataset is collected.

Step 2: The repeated words treated in datasets by comparing the words that are available in vocabulary and also training datasets.

Step 3: Examine for matching word s-sets or its subgroup that is comprised of items greater than one in the dataset checklist gathered from the training data with that of s-subset that, comprises the items greater than one of the repeated dataset of the new dataset.

Step 4: The equivalent possibility values of matched dataset for every target class are gathered and the probability should be deliberated.

Step 5: Score algorithm is practiced to compute the range in which the attributes must be lying.

Step 6: The probability class should be evaluated by executing the algorithm of expectation maximization.

Step 7: The dataset arranged in the class maintaining maximum probability as cleaned dataset.

Figure 12.2 Pseudocode for Independent Component Analysis pre-processing (Prastyo, Pulung Hendro, *et al.* [9]).

Data pre-processing set is more important and much helpful in eliminating the stop words and stemming words and lessen the dimension of COVID-19 emotional data with the help of Independent Component Analysis. This not only concentrates on the dimension reduction, and it also restricts the data dimensionality. This process fundamental practice is, at first the data is continuously varied with a group of specific independent signal sources. Consequently, these signal sources are different consistent in between their numerical independency evaluated by mutual data. Figure 12.2 pseudocode explains the pre-processing method of independent component analysis to remove noise from the imputed dataset and generate the final dataset.

In the method of ICA, the inappropriate data are revealed as the high dimensionality, and it will take out from the dataset. Assumed, N-dimensional data vectors specified as $[V^{(1)}, V^{(2)}, ..., VX^{(N)}]$, the vectors are self-governing elements, that the data of projections of the data vectors are not dependent of one another. At this point, T is considered as unknown matrix, and it specifies the transformation from the existent reference data to the self-governing element reference data and the arbitrary variables are specified as follows.

12.3.1 Extracting Feature With WMAR

The model of WMAR derives the attributes from customer viewpoints for separate products/items accordingly the values of feature vector are stated as the linear summation of past actions. Assume that, to be the time series review data with features and in which m

Step 1 : Establish p = SMP copies of the present position of Ck and C denotes the cat. If the SPC"s value is right, consider p = (SMP – 1), and one of the cat"s present position is preserved.

Step 2 : For all copy, SRD offered random plus or minus rates and exchanged the former values besides CDC.

Step 3 : The Fitness Values (FV) should be computed for all candidate points.

Step 4 : If every FV are not equal, then for all candidate point the selecting possibility evaluated, otherwise the value of 1 is set for every selecting probability of every candidate point.

Step 5 : Elect the point in random from the candidate points to move, and vary the point of Ck.

In case of, the objective of the FV is to discover the minimum solution, then FVx= FVmax, or else FVx= FVmin

Figure 12.3 Pseudocode for WMAR features extraction (Satu, Md Shahriare, *et al.* [10]).

denotes the order of WMAR model for deriving the potential feature, and yn is the linear summation, and it is given as key distribution for WMAR approach (Figure 12.3).

It is the subsequent mode of algorithm past the seeking mode. In this mode, cats wanted to detect foods and targets. The course of tracing mode is specified below. Figures 12.4 and 12.5 explained features optimization using CSO techniques.

The SVM can decompose problems into many numbers of hierarchical sub-problems that can be quickly understandable and computed subjectively. The subjective estimations are transformed into numerical values and processed in order to rate every alternative on the numerical scale. The process of vector can be given in the following steps.

Step 1: The problem can be fragmented into the sub-problems and makes a hierarchy and this task is considered as the most essential in the part of decision-making, and it is the basic one in relevance vector. In this hierarchy, every element is connected with the every other with the levels at least in an indirect manner. Figure 12.6 shows SA for the structure of support vector machine. The root is objective and the problem is examined. After the root level, the levels of criteria and sub-problems are taken place. Finally, the leaves are alternatives. While comparing the elements in every level, it should be compared from lower level to higher level.

Step 2: Data are gathered from the decision makers with respect to the structure of hierarchy in the pair-wise comparison of alternatives on the qualitative scale. These decision makers or experts give the rate of comparison like equal, marginally strong, strong, very strong, and extremely strong. The format of pair-wise comparisons is given in Figure 12.7.

These comparisons are carried out for all criteria and transformed into quantitative numbers like in Table 12.1.

Step 3: For all criteria, the pair-wise comparisons are made, and it is established as the square matrix. The diagonal elements of the matrix are 1. The value of element (i, j) is greater than one in case of the ith row criterion is more effective compared to the jth row criterion. Else, the jth row criterion is more effective than ith row.

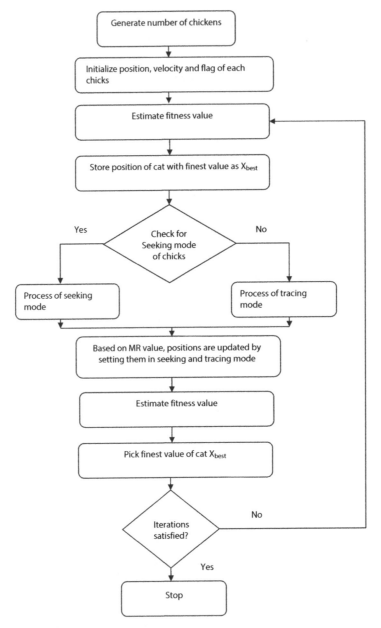

Figure 12.4 Chicken swarm optimization for COVID-19 emotional features optimization flow chart (Kalimuthu, S., F. Naït-Abdesselam, and B. Jaishankar [21]).

Step 4: The comparison matrix's principle Eigen value and the relative normalized right Eigen vector provide the comparable significance of the several criteria being compared. The normalized Eigen vector elements are termed weights corresponding to criteria and the ranks of alternatives.

Step 5: Compute the consistency index of matrix denotes with CI and the value is compared with the arbitrary matrix AI. The ratio of CI/AI is referred as the consistency ratio. It is recommended that the value of consistency ratio should be less than 0.1.

Step 1: as stated For all dimension the velocities are reorganized.

Step 2: the value of velocity is examined for whether it is in the range of maximum velocity or not. In the event if the new velocity is go beyond the range it is set equal to the limit.

$$Vk, = Vk, + r1c1\,(, -Xk,d\,)$$

in which,

Xbest,d: denotes the finest value of fitness of cat position, Xk,d: denotes the position of Ck, C1 : indicates an acceleration coefficient (equal to 2.05) and is employed to expand the velocity of the cat,
r1 : denotes the arbitrary value evenly created in the range of [0,1].

Step 3: as stated in equation (step2) the position of Ck is improved

$$Xk,d = Xk,d + Vk,d$$

Figure 12.5 Pseudocode for chicken swarm optimization (Yang, Liping, Alan M. MacEachren, and Prasenjit Mitra [19]).

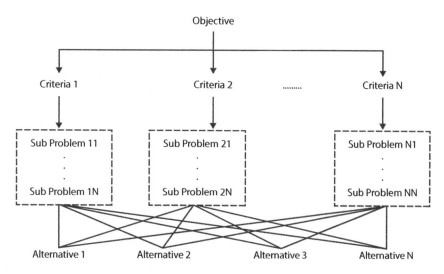

Figure 12.6 Structure of SVM.

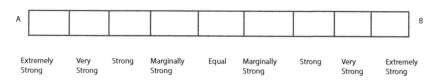

Figure 12.7 Pair-wise comparison format.

Table 12.1 Scale for comparing alternatives.

Choices	COVID-19	Numerical values
Equal	Emotionally balanced	1
Marginally strong	Emotionally marginally strong	3
Strong	Mentally strong	5
Very strong	Emotionally very strong	7
Extremely strong	Emotionally no impact	9
Intermediate values to reflect inputs	In between values are forwarded input	2, 4, 6, 8

Step 6: Every alternative rating is multiplied by the sub-problem weights and accumulated in order to obtain the local ratings concerning every criterion. These local ratings are then multiplied by weights of criteria to obtain the global ratings.

The SVM provides values of weight for all alternatives that depend on the determined significance of one alternative over another concerning a common criterion. It is essential to know better about the pair-wise comparison. Consider that there are two items: Item A and Item B. It is to be found that the item which is more liked by the user by comparing both the items. In order to solve this, a relative scale is made to measure the most likely item on the left when compared to the item on the right.

Figure 12.8 shows the relative scale to compare the two tweets. If the user likes the Item A more than Item B, then it is indicated on left side in between the numbers 1 and 9. Similarly, in the case where Item B is more favorite than Item A, then it is marked in between 1 and 9 on the right side.

If Item B is more favorable compared to Item A, then it is marked like as in Figure 12.9.

It is found that the number of comparisons is a grouping of number of items to be compared. As there are three items A, B, and C, therefore there are three comparisons. Table 12.2 shows the number of comparisons.

The scaling is not compulsory 1 to 9, but for qualitative data like subjective opinions, ranking, and preferences, it is recommended to employ scale 1 to 9. These evaluations are practiced in order to acquire the weights of the importance of the decision criteria and the performance of evaluation quantifies the options concerning all distinct decision criteria. In the case where comparisons are not consistent thoroughly, then it recommends a system for enhancing reliability.

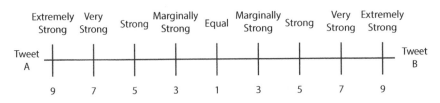

Figure 12.8 Relative scale to compare COVID-19 two tweets.

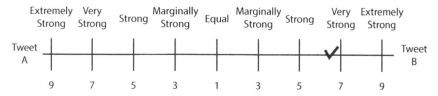

Figure 12.9 Choosing COVID-19 emotional prediction.

Table 12.2 Number of comparisons.

Number of Tweets	1	2	3	4	5	6	7	n
Number of Comparisons	0	1	3	6	10	15	21	$N(n-1)/2$

The proposed approach is more adaptable and potential tool as the scores and also the final ranking are acquired based on the evaluation of pair-wise comparison of both the conditions and the viewpoints given by the user. The evaluations made by the proposed HSVMCSO are always lead by the decision founder experience, and therefore, MATLAB tool possesses the capacity to transform the computations that are made by the decision maker includes both the qualitative and quantitative into the multi-criteria ranking. Furthermore, it is easy tool as there is not requires constructing a compound expert system with the decision maker's perception integrated with it.

12.4   Result and Discussion

To analyze the performance of the proposed model, accuracy, precision and recall were used for evaluating classification results and mean squared error (MSE) and R2 score were used for evaluating regression results. The Improved SVM Algorithm was chosen to solve this problem. Two independent result sets were requested for the same test data using each of these evaluation measures.

The performance of proposed scheme HSVMCSO SA is investigated in this segment with the previous scheme of SA that includes SVM, Logistics Regression, and Neural Network.

The graphical representation for comparison of accuracy, sensitivity, and specificity for the methods of SA HSVMCSO, SVM, NN, and logistic regression is shown in Figure 12.10 and Table 12.3. In the case where there is more products and if the reviews of the product get higher, the performance is also increased. The proposed HSVMCSO attains the high accuracy rate of 90.25%, sensitivity rate of 96.15%, and specificity rate of 90.25% when compared to existing SVM, NN, and LR.

The graphical representation of a comparison of precision, recall, and F-measure for the methods of SA HSVMCSO, SVM, NN, and LR is shown in Figure 12.11. The proposed HSVMCSO obtains the higher rate of precision, recall, and F-measure when compared to existing methods. This shows that the proposed HSVMCSO scheme has a high precision rate of 95.23%, recall rate of 90.20%, and F-measure rate of 89.78% when compared to other existing methods of SVM, NN, and LR.

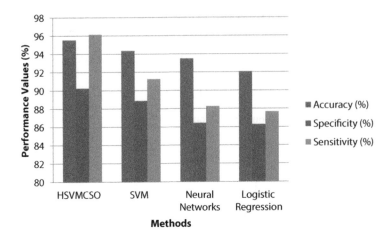

Figure 12.10 Comparisons of accuracy, sensitivity, and specificity for various methods.

Table 12.3 Comparisons of precision, recall, and F-measure for various sentiment analysis schemes.

Measures	Methods			
	HSVMCSO	SVM	Neural networks	Logistic regression
Sensitivity (%)	96.15	91.25	88.25	87.66
Specificity (%)	90.25	88.88	86.44	86.28
Accuracy (%)	95.56	94.35	93.50	92.05

Figure 12.12 represents the graphical representation of processing time of the proposed HSVMCSO and other existing methods such as SVM, NN, and LR. This proves that the proposed HSVMCSO accomplishes more efficiency when compared to other existing methods as it uses only less time for evaluation in order to estimate the review of users. In many numbers of cases, the HSVMCSO is effectively executed, and it is quicker than SVM, NN, and LR.

Table 12.4 Comparisons of precision, recall, and F-measure for various sentiment analysis schemes (Satu, Md Shahriare, *et al.* [10]).

Measures	Methods			
	HSVMCSO	SVM	Neural networks	Logistic regression
Precision (%)	95.23	94.15	92.95	91.85
Recall (%)	90.20	89.35	88.88	86.95
F-measure (%)	89.78	87.42	85.16	76.15

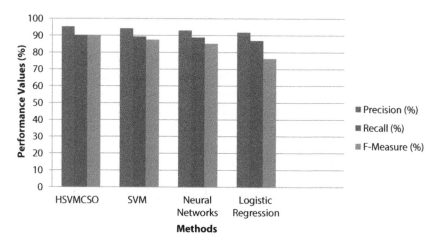

Figure 12.11 Comparisons of precision, recall, and F-measure for various SA methods.

Table 12.5 Time consumption of various sentiment analysis schemes (Satu, Md Shahriare, *et al.* [10]).

	Methods			
Measures	**HSVMCSO**	**SVM**	**Neural networks**	**Logistic regression**
Time (s)	29	33	35	38

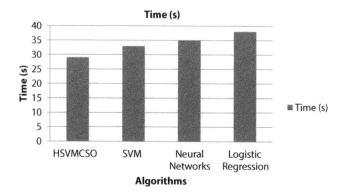

Figure 12.12 Comparison of processing time vs. no of products.

In this research work, the method of SA HSVMCSO is described. This shows clearly about the task of pre-processing by using ICA and efficiency of model WMAR for feature extraction. The performance of HSVMCSO was evaluated with the product reviews. These reviews were examined with the values of precision, recall, accuracy, and F-measure. This shows the effective method of SA and in this chapter; it also demonstrates the results of the comparison of existing methods SVM, NN, and LR with HSVMCSO and shows the precision value of every method.

12.5 Conclusion

The entire research work concentrated on the scheme of COVID-19 SA on the basis of machine learning and swarm intelligence with effectual feature extraction methods. The main intent of this work is to lessen the error based derivation of opinions from people emotions at COVID-19 pandemic situation. The proposed hybrid method aims to enhance the COVID-19 emotion based sentimental analysis accuracy, precision and minimize processing time.

The HSVMCSO algorithm is employed in order to categorize the customer's sentiments in the applications of the COVID-19 tweets. The process of pre-processing is carried out by using ICA, and it removes the inefficient data. After that for the potential extracting feature, WMAR is utilized. Then, the ranking and opinion scores are given for the derived features of all nouns with the help of CSO. Then, HSVMCSO algorithm derives the highly used opinion words, which categorize the review data depending on the opinion. Furthermore, CSO technique is employed to decide on the input weights and hidden biases. This is utilized to decide the output weights analytically and the algorithm called ILM algorithm is practiced for learning the review via HSVMCSO. It is set by evolving a probabilistic Bayesian learning structure that has high ability to develop the models of correct prediction. The experiment is carried out and the performance of SA classifier models based on few evaluation metrics is examined.

The proposed simulation results show that the proposed HSVMCSO has achieved 0.96% of accuracy rate more than existing SVM, NN, and LR. Similarly, sensitivity rate of 4.1%, specificity rate of 1.6%, the precision rate of 1.1%, recall rate of 1.1%, and F-measure rate of 2.36% are more than the existing schemes with better processing time. It accomplishes the effective SA with minimum processing cost.

References

1. Basiri, M.E., Naghsh-Nilchi, A.R., Ghasem-Aghaee, N., Sentiment prediction based on dempster-shafer theory of evidence. *Math. Probl. Eng.*, 2014, 361201, 13, 2014.
2. Bhadane, C., Dalal, H., Doshi, H., Sentiment analysis: Measuring opinions. *Proc. Comput. Sci.*, 45, 808–814, 2015.
3. Guo, H., Zhu, H., Guo, Z., Zhang, X., Su, Z., Product feature categorization with multilevel latent semantic association. *Proceedings of the 18th ACM conference on information and knowledge management*, pp. 1087–1096, November 2009.
4. Jeevanandam Jotheeswaran, D.R. and Kumaraswamy, Y.S., Opinion mining using decision tree based feature selection through manhattan hierarchical cluster measure. *J. Theor. Appl. Inf. Technol.*, 58, 1, 72–80, 2013.
5. Liu, L., Nie, X., Wang, H., Toward a fuzzy domain sentiment ontology tree for sentiment analysis, in: *2012 5th International Congress on Image and Signal Processing*, IEEE, pp. 1620–1624, October 2012.
6. Liu, B., Nie, X., Wang, H., Toward a fuzzy domain sentiment ontology tree for sentiment analysis, in: *2012 5th International Congress on Image and Signal Processing*, IEEE, pp. 1620–1624, October 2012.
7. Manju, S.R., Kalaimani, E.V.R.M., Bhavani, R., Product Aspect Ranking Using Semantic Oriented Sentiment Classifier. *Int. J. Sci. Eng. Res. (IJSER)*, 2, 10, 25–28, 2014.

8. Padmaja, S. and Fatima, S.S., Opinion mining and sentiment analysis-an assessment of peoples' belief: A survey. *Int. J. Ad Hoc Sens. Ubiquitous Comput.*, 4, 1, 21, 2013.

9. Prastyo, P.H., Sumi, A.S., Dian, A.W., Permanasari, A.E. Tweets Responding to the Indonesian Government's Handling of COVID-19: Sentiment Analysis Using SVM with Normalized Poly Kernel. *J. Inform. Syst. Eng. Bussiness Intelligence.*, 6, 2, 112–122, 2020.

10. Satu, Md.S., Khan, I., Mahmud, M., Uddin, S., Summers, M., Quinn, J., Ali Moni, M., TClustVID: a novel machine learning classification model to investigate topics and sentiment in COVID-19 Tweets. Knowledge-Based Systems, 107126–10, 2021.

11. Sharma, R., Nigam, S., & Jain, R. Polarity detection at sentence level. *Int. J. Comput. Appl.*, 86, 11, 29–33, 2014.

12. Sharma, R., Nigam, S., Jain, R. Mining of product reviews at aspect level. *International Journal in Foundations of Computer Science & Technology (IJFCST)*, 4, 3, 87–95, 2014.

13. Sumathi, T., Karthik, S., Marikkannan, M., Artificial bee colony optimization for feature selection in opinion mining. *J. Theor. Appl. Inf. Technol.*, 66, 1, 17–23, 2014.

14. Tripathi, G. and Naganna, S., Opinion mining: A review. *Int. J. Inf. Comput. Technol.*, 4, 16, 1625–1635, 2014

15. Valakunde, N.D. and Patwardhan, M.S., Multi-aspect and multi-class based document sentiment analysis of educational data catering accreditation process, in: *2013 International Conference on Cloud & Ubiquitous Computing & Emerging Technologies IEEE*, pp. 188–192 November 2013.

16. Vinodhini, G. and Chandrasekaran, R.M., Sentiment analysis and opinion mining: a survey. *Int. J.*, 2, 6, 282–292, 2012.

17. Yang, C.C., Tang, X., Wong, Y.C., Wei, C.P., Understanding online consumer review opinions, with sentiment analysis using machine learning. *Pacific Asia J. Assoc. Inf. Syst.*, 2, 3, pp. 73–89, 2010.

18. Yang, C.S., Chen, C.H., Chang, C., Improving the effectiveness of opinion orientation identification in sentiment analysis of consumer reviews: A gloss-based approach, in: Bell the Cat? IT, Channel Conflicts, Transparency and the Theory of Strategic Decommoditization" and the other by Dr. Varghese Jacob on "MIS Research over the Years -Rolling Stone or Leading Edge", and (ii) two panels on issues related to Success, Collaboration, Opportunities, Risks, and Enterprise (SCORE) of Information Systems: one in English (Panelists: Han Zhang (Chair), Ming Fan, Ram Gopal, Ting, Proceedings of The Fifth China Summer Workshop on Information Management (CSWIM 2011), vol. 2011, pp. 7–11, 2011.

19. Yang, L., MacEachren, A.M., Mitra, P., Geographical feature classification from text using (active) convolutional neural networks. In *2020 19th IEEE International Conference on Machine Learning and Applications (ICMLA)*, pp. 1182–1198, IEEE, 2020.

20. Yu, H. and Hatzivassiloglou, V., Towards answering opinion questions: Separating facts from opinions and identifying the polarity of opinion sentences, in: *Proceedings of the 2003 conference on Empirical methods in natural language processing*, pp. 129–136, 2003.

21. Kalimuthu, S., Naït-Abdesselam, F., Jaishankar, B., Multimedia Data Protection Using Hybridized Crystal Payload Algorithm With Chicken Swarm Optimization, in: *Multidisciplinary Approach to Modern Digital Steganography*, IGI Global, pp. 235–257, 2021.

13

Primary Healthcare Model for Remote Area Using Self-Organizing Map Network

Sayan Das* and Jaya Sil

Department of Computer Science and Technology, Indian Institute of Engineering Science and Technology, Shibpur, West Bengal, India

Abstract

Around 66% of total population in India lives in rural areas, where the availability of primary healthcare is a real problem due to the lack of physicians and trained manpower. Health kiosks are deployed in rural villages and health workers are engaged in acquiring specific individual health data such as blood pressure, pulse rate, temperature, BMI, and level of oxygen saturation (SpO_2). However, the sensors used to measure the basic health data are not standardized, resulting in measurement errors in symptom values. Therefore, when people are diagnosed based on the measured health attribute values, there is always risk due to limited domain knowledge and skill of the health workers. A fuzzy-based health assistance framework was suggested in this study that analyzes the specific health characteristics of individuals to decide if a person is in good health or needs medical attention. First, to deal with vagueness in measuring error of symptom values, we use fuzzy variables with proper semantics with reference to the corresponding standard values, available in the literature. States of health of the patients are derived by analyzing their symptoms, and it is obvious that instead of an individual symptom, combination of symptoms is more effective in diagnosing the patients. Based on this observation, *severity_factor* has been designed which evaluates degree of relevance of the combination of symptoms (two and three symptoms at a time irrespective of the order) with respect to health of each patient. Dimension of input feature vector represents *severity_factor* corresponding to the number of unique combinations of the symptoms and applied to the Self-Organizing Map network to group the patients according to their health. Finally, the mapped network categorizes a person into one of five clusters as asymptomatic, mild symptomatic, moderate symptomatic, severe symptomatic, and critical illness. Various methods are used to assess the efficiency of the proposed model with respect to precision, sensitivity, specificity, and accuracy, giving better performance. In the domain of primary healthcare, the proposed approach reduces vagueness in measurement of symptom values and provides a precise, cost-effective solution for the people of remote areas. The model, though, is not replaced by doctors, and patients are referred to expertise in emergencies.

Keywords: Remote healthcare, fuzzy, self-organizing mapping, *severity_factor*

Corresponding author: sayan.das57@gmail.com

Om Prakash Jena, Alok Ranjan Tripathy, Ahmed A. Elngar and Zdzislaw Polkowski (eds.) Computational Intelligence and Healthcare Informatics, (235–254) © 2021 Scrivener Publishing LLC

13.1 Introduction

In India, nearly 66% of populations are rural based [1] and India's rural healthcare sector faces numerous challenges due to shortage of experts, skilled manpower, and poor accessibility of facilities. A three-tier system has been developed for healthcare system of India which consists of (i) Sub-Centers (SCs), (ii) Primary Healthcare Centers (PHCs), and (iii) Community Healthcare Centers (CHCs) [2]. Sub-centers provide the basic healthcare facilities to the primary healthcare system and local community. PHCs provide integrated healthcare services to village communities and emphasis on preventive and promotive aspects. CHCs provide obstetric treatment services and expert consultations maintained by governments and the first referral unit of four PHCs [3]. There are about 26,000 PHCs in India, with 60% each having just one doctor and about 7.5% of PHCs having none. In West Bengal, almost 8% of PHCs run without doctors [4]. The lack of adequate manpower, health infrastructure, and distance, in particular for poor women and children, are the reasons for the poor quality of care in the public health system.

In remote villages, health kiosks are arranged where specific health-related attribute values such as blood pressure, pulse rate, and temperature of people visited in kiosks are recorded using different types of sensors by health assistants. After training some of the trained personnel belonging to rural areas will be selected as health assistants and they will be provided with sensing devices for collection of health data. However, occurrence of the error in measuring the basic symptoms is common due to lack of precise signs and symptoms [5], human bias factor, non-standardization, and lack of precision of the sensors, which invite uncertainty in the health data set. Uncertainty in healthcare receives wide attention and researchers look at it in multiple perspectives as there are different meanings and varieties of uncertainty in healthcare [6].

Uncertainty depends on precision and standardization of the medical equipment, maybe the consequence of a lack of knowledge of the agents who analyze the facts. Probability theory for dealing with uncertainty has been utilized by the researchers since 1960s and recently the advancement of fuzzy sets [7], evidence [8], and possibility theory [9] gaining momentum to manage different types of uncertainty [10]. The acquisition of prior probability distributions with few data sets that are not acquired is the key issue of probability-based approaches. Other approaches draw upon subjective knowledge and human perception to model systems in the presence of limited and vague information. The data set is transformed into fuzzy variables with adequate semantics considering medical data acquired from medical literature as gold standard, given in Table 13.1. The fuzzy sets are considered health attributes and their specific combination represents the severity of the patient was used in the paper to evaluate the condition of the patients. To comprehend the health status of a person, basic health attributes, although heterogeneous in units are assessed. In order to facilitate processing and to deal with measurement error of the data, fuzzy sets are used with proper semantics such as "*Low*", "*Normal*", and "*High*" to simplify processing and to deal with measurement error of the data, depending on the deviation from the standard data obtained from medical journals and medical books [11–13] as shown in Table 13.1. As of example, a patient with blood pressure 160/90 mmHg and pulse rate 85 bpm are represented with reference to gold standard value as "*Stage 2_Hypertensive*" and "*Poor*", respectively. In the chapter, a fuzzy-based method was introduced to combine human reasoning

Table 13.1 Discretized features represented using fuzzy variables.

Features/unit	Range	Fuzzy variable	Features/unit	Range	Fuzzy variable
BMI/(kg/m²)	BMI < 15	Severe_thinness	Pulse (PU)/(bpm)	PU < 60	Slow
	15 ≤ BMI <19	Mild_thinness		60 ≤ PU < 73	Normal
	19 ≤ BMI < 25	Normal		73 ≤ PU < 83	Average
	25 ≤ BMI <30	Overweight		PU ≥ 83	Poor
	BMI ≥ 30	Obese			
SpO_2 (SO)/(percentage)	SO < 85	Severe_hypoxic	Temperature (T)/(degree Fahrenheit)	T < 97	Hypothermia
	85 ≤ SO <90	Hypoxic		97 ≤ T < 99.5	Normal
	90 ≤ SO <95	COPD		99.5 ≤ T< 104	Hyperthermia
	SO ≥95	Healthy		T ≥ 104	Hyperpyrexia

Features/unit	Range	Fuzzy variable
Systolic (BPS)/Diastolic (BPD)/(mmHG)	BPS < 90/BPD < 60	Low
	90 ≤ BPS < 120/60 ≤ BPD < 80	Normal
	120 ≤ BPS < 140/80 ≤ BPD < 100	High
	140 ≤ BPS < 160/100 ≤ BPD < 110	Stage 1_Hypertensive
	160 ≤ BPS < 180/110 ≤ BPD < 120	Stage 2_Hypertensive
	BPS ≥ 180/BPD ≥ 120	Crisis_Hypertensive

power and measurement error tolerance by implementing the *severity_factor* of the patient depending on the variation of health characteristics and demonstrating divergence from the respective standard values. In addition, the Self-Organizing Map (SOM) network [14] clusters the health condition of the patients to asymptomatic, mild symptomatic, moderate symptomatic, severe symptomatic, and critical disease, where the SOM input is the *severity_factor* corresponding to the number of unique health attributes combinations.

The block diagram of various steps of the methodology proposed is shown in Figure 13.1 and the paper's contribution is summarized below:

> (i) Vagueness of health attribute values that occur due to measuring error have been dealt with using fuzzy variables representing proper semantics.
>
> (ii) The parameter *severity_factor* was suggested to measure the health status of patient's on the combination of health characteristics, indicating deviation from the normal values.
>
> (iii) Finally, *severity_factor* corresponding to the number of different combinations of health attributes is applied to the SOM network, grouping the patients according to their health.

The chapter is organized as follows: Section 13.2 describes background details and literature review. Section 13.3 provides methodology applied to manage uncertainty and SOM-based clustering for health assistance systems. Section 13.4 highlights experimental results and discussions and conclusion appears in Section 13.5.

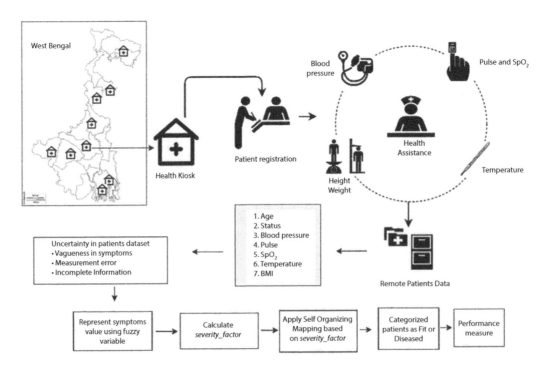

Figure 13.1 Different steps in the block diagram of the proposed methodology.

13.2   Background Details and Literature Review

Knowledge randomness, ambiguity, and incomplete information are associated with uncertainty. However, it is difficult to handle health uncertainty, since each uncertainty may have or involve specific effects, which motivates each case to take various measures. The situation is worse in rural areas, where the shortage of expertise, scarce resources, the lack of patient awareness are the facts, drawing researchers to offer cost-effective approaches to remote populations. Beresford [15] defined three modes of uncertainties: (i) conceptual uncertainty, (ii) technological uncertainty, and (iii) uncertainty in measurement. Instead of Beresford classification, parameters, structural, methodological, and uncertainty of decisions are distinguished in healthcare domain [16, 17].

Researchers have established various approaches and methodologies to cope with the diversified problems related to medical diagnosis. Human experts' reasoning and decision-making can easily deal with the vagueness and incompleteness of evidence that could be integrated into the application of an autonomous health assistance system using observational approaches. To deal with vagueness in detail, researchers have proposed fuzzy expert models and applied in real-life applications. The theoretical aspects of fuzzy set theory and self-organizing mapping will be discussed in the next section.

13.2.1   Fuzzy Set

Fuzzy set theory developed around the seminal work of Zadeh's paper in 1965 [18], which was successfully extended to information sciences, medical systems, control systems, and many areas [19–21]. The value of fuzzy sets [22, 23] lies to model the uncertain or ambiguous details to deal efficiently with vague (ill-defined) data, and the idea of fuzzy sets can therefore be integrated into the neural network.

A fuzzy set G defined as function $G{\to}M$ [0, 1] where M is universe of discourse represented by membership function (MF) that graphically represents the degree of truth for an item. MF expressed as μ_G and expressed as μ_G: $m{\to}$ [0, 1]. The value $\mu_G(m)$ of an element m ϵ M determines the degree of membership in the fuzzy set G. Conversion of input crisp set to fuzzy set using fuzzy linguistic variables, fuzzy linguistic terminology, and MFs is used in fuzzification of fuzzy systems. However, linguistic variables are represented using natural language or sentences. In fuzzy set, defuzzification is used to get crisp values.

13.2.2   Self-Organizing Mapping

Kohonen's Self-organizing Mapping (SOM) is unsupervised clustering artificial neural network mapped from a high dimension to low-dimensional data space and represents the distribution of high-dimensional through a topological representation in low dimension [24]. SOM clusters and graphically demonstrate data vectors that adopt related approaches and are used in applications such as pattern recognition, medical analysis, anomaly identification, knowledge retrieval, and data compression as visualization methods and data pattern classification [25–30].

SOM has two layers: high-dimensional data is obtained by input layer, and output layer (referred to as competition layer) is responsible for analyzing and comparing input modes as shown in Figure 13.2. Kohonen uses dimensional networks in which the neurons in some regular topology are placed on a flat grid either rectangular or hexagonal. The grid's all nodes

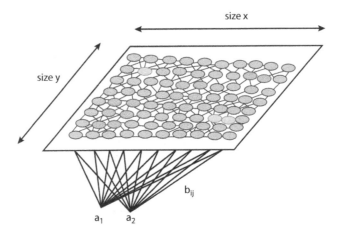

Figure 13.2 Kohonen SOM network model.

are connected to the input vector directly, but not to each other, which means the nodes do not know their neighbor's values and only change the weight of their neighbors to the given inputs. The grid is arranged in accordance with the input of input data for each iteration.

- Every input sample finds its optimal partner neuron in the output layer, called its winning neuron, through "competitive learning." By training, the parameters of the active neuron are constantly changed and at the same time, according to the distance of winning neuron, the points adjacent to the winning neuron are modified accordingly. After training, if the subsamples are close to each other in the original high-dimensional sample space, the gap between the winning neurons mapped on the output layer of the SOM is also near.
- In an unseen data set, these self-organizing networks can learn the general features of related objects and organize them into various classifications or clusters. The network's winning neuron is defined as having the smallest Euclidean distance to the new input data and is determined that classification of the new input is the same as that of winning neuron.
- The main benefit of SOM is the creation of clusters, which allows using a self-organization mechanism to minimize the input space into representative features. The underlying structure is therefore retained, while dimensionality of space is reduced.

In terms of volume, variety, and values, remote healthcare datasets are very complicated and have multiple dimensions. The identification of the associations between the attributes of these datasets will lead significantly to improving not only healthcare facilities but also to the excavation of hidden trends to determine the causes of symptom severity.

13.3   Methodology

There are various attributes in the medical record, of which the specific health-related attributes [blood pressure (BPS/BPD), pulse rate (PU), temperature (T), SpO_2, and BMI] are

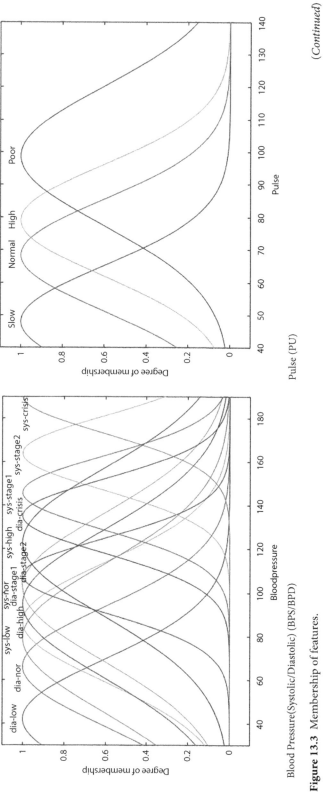

Blood Pressure(Systolic/Diastolic) (BPS/BPD)

Pulse (PU)

(Continued)

Figure 13.3 Membership of features.

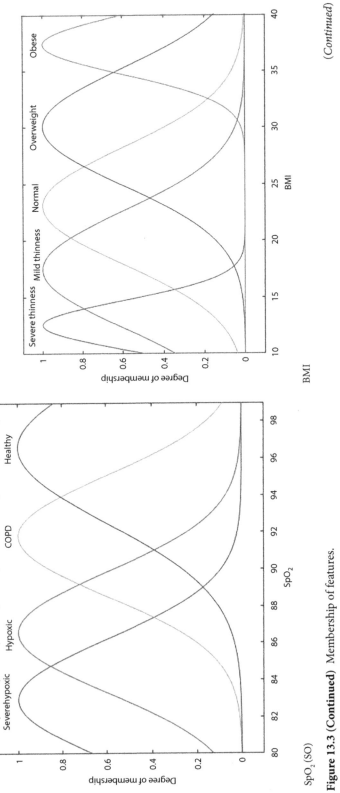

Figure 13.3 (Continued) Membership of features.

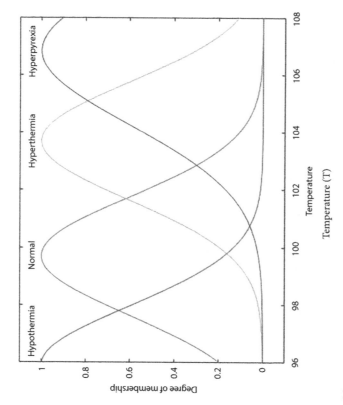

Figure 13.3 (Continued) Membership of features.

applied for patients' primary diagnosis. However, due to measurement error, the raw data is inconsistent and often heterogeneous with respect to measurement units. The collected data is then transformed into fuzzy variables with appropriate semantic, considering medical science as ground truth provided in Table 13.1. Figure 13.3 indicates membership of health-related BPS/BPD, PU, T, SpO$_2$, and BMI attributes. In the chapter, the particular combination of health attributes reflects the patient's severity was used to determine the patient's condition.

13.3.1　*Severity_Factor* of Patient

The primary task of automatically diagnosing the patient relies on the interaction between health attributes and evaluation processes that are likely to reflect the reasoning power of the experts. A *severity_factor* parameter [Equation (13.1)] is proposed in the chapter to determine the patient's severity based on the assessed health parameters. For example, the condition of a patient with "*High*" BPS/BPD and "*Slow*" PU is more severe than that of the patient with "*High*" BPS/BPD and "*Normal*" PU. The combination of health attributes reflecting the severity of the patients is shown in Table 13.2, formulated after consulting with experts.

$$Severity\_factor = \frac{1}{(\max(e, f, g, ..., n))^{l+1}} \qquad (13.1)$$

e, *f*, and *g* are the membership value of health attributes. Here, *max* indicates maximum membership of health attributes and *n* is total number of health attributes.

Variable *l* indicates maximum difference between the levels of two different health attributes as represented by ordered values.

For example, different *l* values are as follows:

BP: "*Low*", 0; "*Normal*", 1; "*High*", 2; "*Stage 1_Hypertensive*", 3; "*Stage 2_Hypertensive*", 4; "*Crisis_Hypertensive*", 5.

PU: "*Slow*", 0; "*Normal*", 1; "*Average*", 2; "*Poor*", 3.

SpO$_2$: "*Healthy*", 0; "*COPD*", 1; "*Hypoxic*", 2; "*Severe_hypoxic*", 3.

T: "*Hypothermia*", 0; "*Normal*", 1; "*Hyperthermia*", 2; "*Hyperyrexia*", 3.

BMI: "*Severe_thinness*", 0; "*Mild_thinness*", 1; "*Normal*", 2; "*Overweight*", 3; "*Obese*", 4.

For example, a patient who has "*Stage 2_Hypertensive*" BPS and "*Poor*" PU the value of *l* is 1. If a patient has "*Low*" BPS, "*Average*" PU, and "*Severe_hypoxic*" SpO$_2$ the value of *l* is (3 − 0) = 3.

Table 13.3 indicates how *severity_factor* is measured as the following cases are considered:

Case 1: A patient has "*Stage 1_Hypertensive*" BPS and "*Low*" PU.

Case 2: A patient has "*Very Very High*" BPS and "*High*" PU.

Since the amount of patient data in the remote area is huge, SOM plays an important role in better classifying patients in the disease cluster. The application of SOM has certain benefits, such that it is unsupervised and does not need a predetermined number of groups; thus, SOM has a more visually appealing topological diagram that is insensitive to the impact of initialization. The component of the input function vector in this chapter reflects the *severity_factor* corresponding to the number of specific health attribute combinations added to the SOM network to classify patients according to their health. Finally, the mapped network classifies an individual as asymptomatic, mild symptomatic, moderate symptomatic, moderate symptomatic, and critical illness in one of five clusters.

Table 13.2 Different severity condition.

BP and SpO₂		BP and PU	
BP	**SpO₂**	**BP**	**PU**
Crisis_Hypertensive	Severe_hypoxic	High	Slow
Crisis_Hypertensive	Hypoxic	Low	Poor
Crisis_Hypertensive	COPD	Crisis_Hypertensive	Slow
Stage 2_Hypertensive	Severe_hypoxic	Stage 2_Hypertensive	Slow
Stage 2_Hypertensive	Hypoxic	Stage 1_Hypertensive	Slow
Stage 2_Hypertensive	COPD	Crisis_Hypertensive	Poor
Low	Severe_hypoxic	Low	Slow

BP and BMI		BP and T	
BP	**BMI**	**BP**	**T**
Crisis_Hypertensive	Severe_thinness	Crisis_Hypertensive	Hyperpyrexia
Stage 1_Hypertensive	Severe_thinness	Stage 2_Hypertensive	Hyperpyrexia
Stage 2_Hypertensive	Severe_thinness	Stage 1_Hypertensive	Hyperpyrexia
Crisis_Hypertensive	Obese	Low	Hyperpyrexia
Low	Severe_thinness	Crisis_Hypertensive	Hypothermia
Stage 2_Hypertensive	Obese	Stage 2_Hypertensive	Hypothermia

(Continued)

Table 13.2 Different severity condition. (Continued)

	Low	Obese	Stage 1_Hypertensive	Hypothermia
SpO_2 and T	**PU and SpO_2**		**PU and T**	
SpO_2	**PU**	**SpO_2**	**PU**	**T**
Severe_hypoxic	Slow	Severe_hypoxic	Slow	Hyperpyrexia
Hypoxic	Slow	Hypoxic	Slow	Hyperpyrexia
COPD	Slow	COPD	Slow	Hyperpyrexia
Severe_hypoxic	Poor	Severe_hypoxic	Poor	Hypothermia
Hypoxic	Poor	Hypoxic	Poor	Hypothermia
COPD	Poor	COPD	Poor	Hypothermia
			SpO_2 and BMI	
			SpO_2	**BMI**
			Severe_hypoxic	Severe_thinness
			Hypoxic	Severe_thinness
			COPD	Severe_thinness
			Severe_hypoxic	Obese
			Hypoxic	Obese
			COPD	Obese

(Continued)

Table 13.2 Different severity condition. (Continued)

PU and BMI

PU	BMI
Slow	Severe_thinness
Slow	Severe_thinness
Poor	Obese
Poor	Obese

T and BMI

BMI	T
Severe_thinness	Hyperpyrexia
Severe_thinness	Hyperpyrexia
Obese	Hypothermia
Obese	Hypothermia

BP, PU, and SpO₂

BP	PU	SpO₂
High	Slow	Severe_hypoxic
Low	Poor	Severe_hypoxic
Crisis_Hypertensive	Slow	Severe_hypoxic
Stage 2_Hypertensive	Slow	Severe_hypoxic
Stage 1_Hypertensive	Slow	Severe_hypoxic
Crisis_Hypertensive	Poor	Severe_hypoxic
Low	Slow	Severe_hypoxic
High	Slow	Hypoxic
Low	Poor	Hypoxic
Crisis_Hypertensive	Slow	Hypoxic
Stage 2_Hypertensive	Slow	Hypoxic
Stage 1_Hypertensive	Slow	Hypoxic
Crisis_Hypertensive	Poor	Hypoxic
Low	Slow	Hypoxic

BP, PU, and T

BP	PU	T
High	Slow	Hyperpyrexia
Low	Poor	Hyperpyrexia
Crisis_Hypertensive	Slow	Hyperpyrexia
Stage 2_Hypertensive	Slow	Hyperpyrexia
Stage 1_Hypertensive	Slow	Hyperpyrexia
Crisis_Hypertensive	Poor	Hyperpyrexia
Low	Slow	Hyperpyrexia
High	Slow	Hypothermia
Low	Poor	Hypothermia
Crisis_Hypertensive	Slow	Hypothermia
Stage 2_Hypertensive	Slow	Hypothermia
Stage 1_Hypertensive	Slow	Hypothermia
Crisis_Hypertensive	Poor	Hypothermia
Low	Slow	Hypothermia

(Continued)

Table 13.2 Different severity condition. (Continued)

BP, PU, and BMI			PU, SpO$_2$, and T		
BP	PU	BMI	PU	SpO$_2$	T
High	Slow	Severe_thinness	Slow	Severe_hypoxic	Hyperpyrexia
Low	Poor	Severe_thinness	Slow	Hypoxic	Hyperpyrexia
Crisis_Hypertensive	Slow	Severe_thinness	Slow	COPD	Hyperpyrexia
Stage 2_Hypertensive	Slow	Severe_thinness	Poor	Severe_hypoxic	Hyperpyrexia
Stage 1_Hypertensive	Slow	Severe_thinness	Poor	Hypoxic	Hyperpyrexia
Crisis_Hypertensive	Poor	Severe_thinness	Poor	COPD	Hyperpyrexia
Low	Slow	Severe_thinness	Slow	Severe_hypoxic	Hypothermia
High	Slow	Obese	Slow	Hypoxic	Hypothermia
Low	Poor	Obese	Slow	COPD	Hypothermia
Crisis_Hypertensive	Slow	Obese	Poor	Severe_hypoxic	Hypothermia
Stage 2_Hypertensive	Slow	Obese	Poor	Hypoxic	Hypothermia
Stage 1_Hypertensive	Slow	Obese	Poor	COPD	Hypothermia
Crisis_Hypertensive	Poor	Obese			
Low	Slow	Obese			

Table 13.3 Calculation of severity factor.

Case	Membership of BPS/BPD and PU	$\dfrac{1}{(\max(e,f,g,...,n))^{l+1}}$	Severity_factor
1.	"Very High" (0.89) and "Slow"(0.31)	1.59	1.59
2.	"Very Very High"(0.95) and "High"(0.78)	1.28	1.28

13.3.2 Clustering by Self-Organizing Mapping

The input layer neurons are fully connected to the output layer neurons in SOM and clustering is implemented using competitive learning algorithm.

The *Euclidean distance* is determined between input pattern $A \subseteq R^d$ and each neuron weight B of the output layer, and the "winning" neuron is the output layer neuron corresponding to the shortest distance, known as best matching unit (BMU). The following is the formula:

$$D(A,C_k) = \min\{\| A - B \|\} \tag{13.2}$$

where C_k is BMU, and B is weight vector of neuron k on the output layer.

The *weight update formula* for winning neuron and its neighbors by considering the winning neuron k is as follows:

$$b_k(nw) = b_k(od) + \alpha(a - b_k) \tag{13.3}$$

Neuron n is the winning neuron neighbor, k, and α is the rate of learning which declines over time.

Algorithm 13.1 Self-Organizing Algorithm.

1.	Randomly initialize each neuron weight
2.	Set $B = [b_1, b_2, ..., b_m]$ and $A = [a_1, a_2,...., a_n]$, where B is weight vector and A is input data, m is number of output layers neuron and n is number of input data.
3.	**for** $i = 1$ to length(A) **do**
4.	**for** $j = 1$ to length(B) **do**
5.	Calculate the Euclidean distance between current input node a_i and output node b_j as $\{\| a_i - b_j \|\}$.
6.	**end for**
7.	$D(a_i, C_j) = min\{\| a_i - B \|\}$
8.	Adjust the weight value of the winning C_j and the neighborhood nodes of C_j so that the weight value is close to the current input of sample data a_i.
9.	**end for**
10.	return $D(A, C)$.

For the winner itself and neuron nearest to the winner, weights are changed according to Equation (13.3). Clearly, weight of neuron that is far away from central neuron does not change. This method is repeated until the weight vectors change by less than a predetermined amount.

SOM network algorithm is given in Algorithm 13.1.

The SOM network model is capable of managing the input health properties of both precise and incorrect types. Exact information is easier to translate into linguistic form; we consider the key linguistic properties *"Low"*, *"High"*, etc., in this chapter and apply the combination of health attributes *severity-factor* as input. In terms of any combination of membership values for these properties, any input feature value can be represented and further classifies a person into one of five clusters as asymptomatic, mild symptomatic, moderate symptomatic, severe symptomatic, and critical disease.

The next section describes result and discussion where the data is collected from the different health kiosks of West Bengal.

13.4   Results and Discussion

The proposed method is demonstrated using the kiosk datasets and compared with other methods followed by performance evaluation measures. The patients' health data and other important parameters are acquired from the health kiosks, situated in remote areas of West Bengal like Sundarban, Purulia, Bankura, Malda, Jalpaiguri, and Darjeeling. Patients' dataset comprises samples with health parameters like age, systolic and diastolic blood pressure, pulse, SpO_2, BMI, and temperature.

Five thousand samples are used as a training set and five hundred test samples are considered to cluster in appropriate disease classes as asymptomatic, mild symptomatic, moderate symptomatic, severe symptomatic, and critical illness. The patient data is composed of both male and female characteristics.

The proposed method is evaluated based on (i) accuracy (AC), (ii) sensitivity (SE), (iii) specificity (SP), and (iv) precision (PR) using 10-fold cross-validation technique [31, 32]. Accuracy is an estimation parameter that measures the number of observations that the model makes correctly. Sensitivity measure shows how well the positive class samples are predicted and specificity shows how well the negative class examples are predicted. As a performance metric, precision is used where value of false positives is high, whereas value of false negatives is low. Table 13.4 shows the performance of each measure which increases (3% to 5%) as the number of patients increases.

Figure 13.4 shows ROC [33] curve which reflects true positive rate with lowest false positive rate.

In the chapter, by using SOMs, we visualize and analyze clusters of disease classes as asymptomatic, mild symptomatic, moderate symptomatic, severe symptomatic, and critical illness in various ways and also find correlations between health attributes. The performance tests were made in a machine with Intel Core i7-4702MQ CPU 2.20 GHz, 12 GBs of RAM, and Windows operating system with MATLAB version R2018a.

Table 13.4 Performance measure with patients samples.

Performance	Number of patients sample				
	500	1,000	2,000	3,000	5,000
AC in percentage	89.4	89.5	91.3	92.5	**94.2**
SE in percentage	86.4	88.2	89.6	90.8	**93.8**
SP in percentage	88.2	88.4	90.6	93.5	**94.5**
PR	0.88	0.9	0.92	0.94	**0.95**

Bold denote better performance.

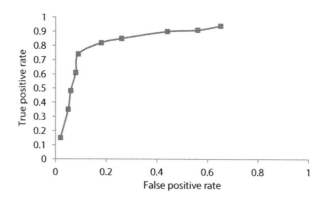

Figure 13.4 ROC curve of proposed methodology.

Figure 13.5a shows the neuron locations in the hexagonal topology in the two dimensions space and the topology is a 30-by-30 grid. In addition, Figure 13.5b shows the weight plane for each element of the input vector, where larger weights are represented by darker colors. The patterns of connection between two inputs are different; therefore, inputs are not associated with each other. The weight positions of SOM are seen in Figure 13.5c and the weight is distributed within the two-dimensional space. The SOM weight distance matrix (U-matrix) [34] is shown in Figure 13.5d where blue hexagons represent neurons and adjacent neurons are connected by red lines. The colors represent distances between neurons in the regions comprising the red lines. Larger distances reflect the darker colors, and smaller distances are represented by the brighter colors. Dark segments thus pass through the SOM network, clustered in five different classes as asymptomatic, mild symptomatic, moderate symptomatic, severe symptomatic, and critical illness.

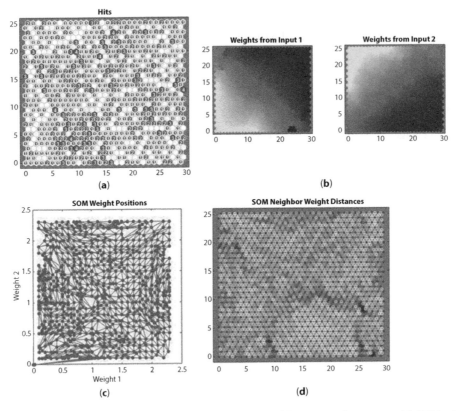

Figure 13.5 (a) SOM Hit map. (b) SOM weight for input vectors. (c) SOM weight position. (d) SOM neighbor weight distance.

13.5 Conclusion

The fuzzy set-based approach has been suggested to manage uncertainty, which significantly reduces uncertainty in remote areas. Firstly, fuzzy sets with proper semantics are used for managing uncertainty measuring symptoms; secondly, severity of patients are measured by using most basic health attributes of patients; and finally, a patient is classified into asymptomatic, mild symptomatic, moderate symptomatic, severe symptomatic, and critical illness by the mapped SOM network. Without any additional information or assumption, the proposed method reduces uncertainty to diagnose the people of rural areas, where experts' involvement is least and also remote health data is easily interpreted and understood by SOM network. An autonomous, cost-effective device has been developed with high precision and accuracy to diagnose patients' diseases in rural areas. Accessibility of genuine patient records is the basic bottleneck to establish the proposed rural healthcare model. Finally, we must rely on the opinions of experts, which is expensive.

References

1. Kumar, A., Nayar, K.R., Koya, S.F., COVID-19: Challenges and its consequences for rural healthcare in India. *Public Health Pract.*, 1, 100009, 2020.

2. Chokshi, M., Patil, B., Khanna, R., Neogi, S.B., Sharma, J., Paul, V.K., Zodpey, S., Health systems in India. *J. Perinatol.*, 36, 3, S9–S12, 2016.

3. Kumar, R. and Pal, R., India achieves WHO recommended doctor population ratio: A call for paradigm shift in public health discourse! *J. Fam. Med. Prim. Care*, 7, 5, 841, 2018.

4. Bhardwaj, S., Garg, V., Kumar, K., Rural Healthcare in India: A paucity between prerequisites and provisions. *J. Adv. Med. Dent. Sci. Res.*, 6, 7, 141–143, 2018.

5. Das, S. and Sil, J., Uncertainity management of health attributes for primary diagnosis, in: *2017 International Conference on Big Data Analytics and Computational Intelligence (ICBDAC)*, IEEE, pp. 360–365, March 2017.

6. Han, P.K., Babrow, A., Hillen, M.A., Gulbrandsen, P., Smets, E.M., Ofstad, E.H., Uncertainty in healthcare: Towards a more systematic program of research. *Patient. Educ. Couns.*, 102, 10, 1756–1766, 2019.

7. Rahimi, S.A., Application of Fuzzy Soft Set in Patients' Prioritization, in: *Theoretical and Practical Advancements for Fuzzy System Integration*, D. Li (eds.), pp. 221–244, IGI Global, Hershey, PA, 2017.

8. Greenhalgh, T., *How to implement evidence-based healthcare; and, How to read a paper: the basics of evidence-based medicine*, fifth edition. Hoboken, Nj, Usa; Chichester, West Sussex, Uk: Wiley Blackwell, 2018.

9. Chiffi, D., *Clinical Reasoning: Knowledge, Uncertainty, and Values in Healthcare*, pp. 79–89, Cham, Springer, 2020.

10. Han, P.K., Klein, W.M., Arora, N.K., Varieties of uncertainty in healthcare: a conceptual taxonomy. *Med. Decis. Making*, 31, 6, 828–838, 2011.

11. Jameson, J.L., Harrison's principles of internal medicine (20th ed.). New York Mcgraw-Hill Education, 2018.

12. Alagappan, R., *Manual of practical medicine*, JP Medical Ltd, 2018.

13. Longmore, M., Wilkinson, I., Baldwin, A., Wallin, E., *Oxford Handbook of Clinical Medicine-Mini Edition*, Oxford OUP Oxford, 2014.

14. Kohonen, T., The self-organizing map. *Proc. IEEE*, 78, 9, 1464–1480, 1990.

15. Beresford, E.B., Uncertainty and the shaping of medical decisions. *Hastings Cent. Rep.*, 21, 4, 6–11, 1991.

16. Pomare, C., Churruca, K., Ellis, L.A., Long, J.C., Braithwaite, J., A revised model of uncertainty in complex healthcare settings: a scoping review. *J. Eval. Clin. Pract.*, 25, 2, 176–182, 2019.

17. Alam, R., Cheraghi-Sohi, S., Panagioti, M., Esmail, A., Campbell, S., Panagopoulou, E., Managing diagnostic uncertainty in primary care: a systematic critical review. *BMC Fam. Pract.*, 18, 1, 79, 2017.

18. Zadeh, L.A., Klir, G.J., Yuan, B., *Fuzzy sets, fuzzy logic, and fuzzy systems: selected papers*, Vol. 6, Singapore; River Edge, N.J., World Scientific, 1996.

19. Zimmermann, H.J., *Fuzzy set theory—and its applications*, Springer Science & Business Media, New York, 2011.

20. Gürsel, G., Healthcare, uncertainty, and fuzzy logic. *Digit. Med.*, 2, 3, 101, 2016.

21. Shihabudheen, K.V. and Pillai, G.N., Recent advances in neuro-fuzzy system: A survey. *Knowl. Based Syst.*, 152, 136–162, 2018.

22. Mendel, J.M., Uncertain rule-based fuzzy systems, in: *Introduction and new directions*, p. 684, Cham Springer International Publishing, 2017.

23. Hamada, M., Odu, N.B., Hassan, M., A fuzzy-based approach for modelling preferences of users in multi-criteria recommender systems, in: *2018 IEEE 12th International Symposium on Embedded Multicore/Many-core Systems-on-Chip (MCSoC)*, IEEE, pp. 87–94, September 2018.

24. Zhang, J., Kohonen Self-Organizing Map–An Artificial Neural Network, in: *Visualization for Information Retrieval*, pp. 107–125, Springer, Berlin, Heidelberg, 2008.

25. Oja, M., Kaski, S., Kohonen, T., Bibliography of self-organizing map (SOM) papers: 1998–2001 addendum. *Neural Comput. Surv.*, 3, 1, 1–156, 2003.

26. Hua, W. and Mo, L., Clustering Ensemble Model Based on Self-Organizing Map Network. *Comput. Intell. Neurosci.*, 2020, 2971565, 11, 2020. https://doi.org/10.1155/2020/2971565.

27. Mayaud, J.R., Anderson, S., Tran, M., Radić, V., Insights from self-organizing maps for predicting accessibility demand for healthcare infrastructure. *Urban Sci.*, 3, 1, 33, 2019.

28. Jena, O.P., Pradhan, S.K., Biswal, P.K., Nayak, S., Recognition of Printed Odia Characters and Digits using Optimized Self-Organizing Map Network, in: *2020 International Conference on Computer Science, Engineering and Applications (ICCSEA)*, IEEE, March 2020.

29. Hoglund, A.J., Hatonen, K., Sorvari, A.S., A computer host-based user anomaly detection system using the self-organizing map, in: *Proceedings of the IEEE-INNS-ENNS International Joint Conference on Neural Networks. IJCNN 2000. Neural Computing: New Challenges and Perspectives for the New Millennium*, Vol. 5, IEEE, pp. 411–416, July 2000.

30. Aggarwal, M. and Tiwari, A.K., Approach for Information Retrieval by Using Self-Organizing Map and Crisp Set, in: *Speech and Language Processing for Human-Machine Communications*, pp. 51–56, Springer, Singapore, 2018.

31. Sackett, D.L., A primer on the precision and accuracy of the clinical examination. *Jama*, 267, 19, 2638–2644, 1992.

32. Bank, H.L. and Schmehl, M.K., Parameters for evaluation of viability assays: accuracy, precision, specificity, sensitivity, and standardization. *Cryobiology*, 26, 3, 203–211, 1989.

33. Narkhede, S., Understanding AUC-ROC Curve. *Towards Data Sci.*, 26, 220–227, 2018.

34. Thrun, M., Pape, F., Ultsch, A., Interactive machine learning tool for clustering in visual analytics, in: *2020 IEEE 7th International Conference on Data Science and Advanced Analytics (DSAA)*, IEEE, pp. 479–487, October 2020.

14

Face Mask Detection in Real-Time Video Stream Using Deep Learning

Alok Negi and Krishan Kumar*

Department of Computer Science and Engineering, National Institute of Technology, Uttarakhand, Srinagar (Garhwal), India

Abstract

On 11 March 2020, World Health Organization (WHO) recorded the Novel Coronavirus Disease (COVID-19) pandemic outbreak and reiterated the call for countries to take decisive action and scale up their response to treat, identify, and minimize transmission in order to save the lives of people. Healthcare organizations have an immediate need for decision-making strategies to deal with this virus and to assist them in having proper real-time suggestions to prevent its spread. With the continuing pandemic, in order to reduce risk, it is much more important to have advanced analytics apps and services in place. Artificial Intelligence (AI) is an emerging technology that is successful in combating the pandemic of COVID-19. AI is used as a weapon to help the fight against the viral pandemic that has been impacting the planet since the start of 2020. This technology helps to screen, monitor, and forecast current and potential patients properly. Mostly with assistance of real-time data processing, AI will provide up-to-date information to help in prevention of this disease. During this crisis, it is being used to monitor possible transmission sites, the proliferation of virus, and need for rooms and medical services. WHO studies indicate that respiratory droplets and physical contact are the two primary transmission routes of the COVID-19 virus. Respiratory tiny particles are formed while an infected person is coughing or sneezing. Particles can indeed fall on surfaces in which virus can remain alive, so the infected person's immediate environment can constitute a source of contact transmission. One of the preventive measures that can restrict the spread of such respiratory viral diseases like COVID-19 is wearing a medical face mask. For public safety and hygiene, the use of face masks and covers to monitor the spread of COVID-19 is recommended by the authorities. In this chapter, we propose an advanced Deep Learning model for face mask detection in real-time video streams. The study analyses a series of video stream/images to recognize individuals who comply with the regulation of wearing medical masks by the government. This could allow the government to take sufficient action against non-compliant persons.

Keywords: Artificial Intelligence (AI), Corona virus, Deep Learning, face mask detection, World Health Organization (WHO)

Corresponding author: kkberwal@nituk.ac.in

Om Prakash Jena, Alok Ranjan Tripathy, Ahmed A. Elngar and Zdzislaw Polkowski (eds.) Computational Intelligence and Healthcare Informatics, (255–268) © 2021 Scrivener Publishing LLC

14.1 Introduction

The persistent spreading of Coronavirus [4] has contributed to a gradual rise in the death rate in several countries around the globe since its inception in Wuhan, China. Globally, there have been 68,845,368 confirmed cases with 1,570,304 deaths, reported to WHO till 11 December 2020. At this time, as there is no vaccine or antidote, the WHO has recommended usage of surgical masks that minimize the outbreak of virus. According to WHO, any use of masks is obligatory in societies, predominantly populated regions, throughout residential care and also in healthcare facilities in regions recognized by COVID-19. Carrying masks before and after the pandemic will be of utmost importance before the vaccine has been invented. Even during COVID-19 epidemic, this measure obtained a number of recommendations from numerous public health organizations and governments.

Coronavirus airborne disease (COVID-19) is indeed an infectious disease. People that are diagnosed with that kind of virus may have moderate to severe respiratory disease and may not survive without the need for special care. Aging people and children that already have health issues such as cardiovascular disease, diabetes, chronic respiratory disorders, and cancer are often more likely to experience serious illnesses. The effective way to avoid or slow down transfer is to get more knowledge of the COVID-19 virus; the epidemic it can induce, or how it is transmitted.

Artificial Intelligence (AI) focused on Machine Learning (ML) and Deep Learning (DL) will benefit to tackle COVID-19 in several ways. ML helps practitioners and researchers to analyze large amounts of data to predict the propagation of COVID-19, to act as an active warning system for future pandemics, and also to identify vulnerable members of society. In addition to best grasp the rate of infection or to monitor and easily diagnose infections, the power of the AI to deal with the COVID-19 disease outbreak is now being optimized. The law persuades citizens to wear face masks in public place in many nations. These policies and regulations have been formulated as an intervention for rapid growth in suspected cases in several locations. However, the task of observing vast numbers of people is now becoming extremely difficult and the risk monitoring includes the identification of someone who does not wear a face mask.

Face detection recently surfaced as quite an important topic in computer vision and image processing. It seems to have a series of applications, from face movement to facial expression recognition that allows the face to be identified with relatively good precision at the end. Nowadays, face detection is more important since it is utilized in not only images, as well as in video implementations such as real-time surveillance [5–8] and then faces detection.

By motivating this, we developed a DL approach for real-time face mask detection [9, 10] using VGG19. Firstly, we trained a face mask detection classifier using VGG19. Then, results are tested through webcam generated video stream. The proposed methodology can be combined with real-time video to prevent dissemination of COVID-19 by enabling the identification of people that wear masks or who are not wearing face masks. By using this data, we can determine if the individual can be admitted to public areas including the market or indeed the hospital. The whole proposal can be used in restaurants, bus terminals, and certain other social occasions whereby monitoring is required.

The rest of the chapter is arranged as follows: Related work is given in Section 14.2 and Section 14.3 describes the proposed work. Section 14.4 describes result and analysis followed by conclusion in Section 14.5 and references.

14.2 Related Work

Jagadeeswari *et al.* [1] highlighted usage of DL models to recognize individuals who do not wear masks. The machine was trained to recognize precisely whether or not an individual was wearing a mask. When a machine detects an individual without a mask, a warning should be triggered to warn people nearby or around the relevant authorities such that the appropriate action must be initiated against these offenders. This paper showed a comparison study of classifiers such as VGG16, RESNET50, MobileNetV2 with ADAGRAD, ADAM, and SGD optimizers. Based on the analysis of the various classifiers, the ADAM optimizing output was quite high and the SGD testing accuracy was roughly equal to ADAM for all three classifiers mentioned above. During research, it was found that only the MobileNetV2 classifier offered the highest performance with greater accuracy.

Chavda *et al.* [2] presented two-stage detection system for face mask. The first step was using a pre-trained RetinaFace method for comprehensive facial detection after compared the accuracy with Dlib and MTCNN. An unbiased independent dataset of covered and uncovered faces has been formed. The stage 2 implicated the training of three distinct lightweight face mask classification methods on a dataset constructed and based on results; the NASNetMobile method was adopted to classify faces as masked or non-masked. In addition, the proposed algorithm was introduced to Centroid Tracking that mostly sought to increase its efficiency on video streams.

Ejaz *et al.* [3] proposed the FaceNet pre-trained system to enhance masked face identification. The researchers have reviewed this approach to two excellently well-known datasets and self-made datasets. The method tested on all these datasets indicates improved recognition rates. So, the FaceNet model was trained on masked and unmasked images gives more accurate results for basic masked recognition of the face. While it also focused on hat-induced masks, goggles, mustache, long blonde hair, beard, and surgical mask. The obscured face detection issue was solved using the Multi-Task Cascaded Conv Nets (MTCNN).

Meenpal *et al.* [11] aimed to develop a binary face classifier that detects every face existing throughout the frame, regardless about its orientation. Authors provided a way for any arbitrary form of the input image to create precise face analytics masks. Starting from RGB images of any dimension, the approach used is VGG's Predefined Training Weights–16 Architecture for Extraction Function. Training is done through Completely Fully convolutional Nets to conceptually classify the face features of an image. When Binomial Cross Entropy is used as a weight matrix, Gradient Descent is used for training. Furthermore, output image from its FCN was manipulated to eliminate unnecessary noise and prevent false predictions, if there are any, and to create a feature vector across the faces. In addition, the proposed system has shown excellent results in the identification of non-frontal faces. In addition, several face masks may also be identified in single frame.

Research on Multi-Parsing Human Dataset was conducted to attain an average pixel precision of 93.884% on differentiated face masks.

Rosebrok [12] used OpenCV, TensorFlow, Keras, PyTorch, and CNN to determine whether or not individuals were wearing the face masks. The models have been examined with images and video streams in real time. The precision of the model is obtained and the enhancement of the system is a continual procedure and authors creating a reasonably precise solution by refining the hyper parameters. This particular model may also consider as a test case for edge analysis. In addition, the proposed novel approach provides state-of-the-art findings on known face mask dataset. By developing face mask detection, they detect if an individual is wearing a face mask and allowing their entry might be of tremendous benefit to society.

14.3   Proposed Work

- The proposed work is designed to face detection and decide whether or not the person is wearing a face mask. Using this technique, we can determine if it is possible to allow the individual concerned within public places such as a hospital or the market.
- The proposed work has two parts. A Python script is used to train the face mask classifier with VGG19 model in the first part. In the second part, the results are tested in a real-time video stream generated through webcam using OpenCV.
- The proposed work utilizes the concept of data augmentation, transfer learning, and dropout, using the VGG19 model. Accuracy curve, loss curve, confusion matrix, precision, recall, F1-score, and specificity-based analysis have been performed for this work.
- This technique can also be used in hospitals, malls, transport hubs, restaurants, and some other community meetings where surveillance is required. This work involves a camera to record the image of users approaching public places and to discern whether or not a person uses their facial features to wear a face mask. The block diagram for the proposed work is shown in Figure 14.1.

14.3.1   Dataset Description

The dataset consist of 1,376 images belonging to two classes: masked and non-masked. Further, dataset is divided into training set and validation set with 1,104 and 272 images, respectively. Figures 14.2 and 14.3 show the distribution of dataset among training set and validation set.

14.3.2   Data Pre-Processing and Augmentation

Images are resized into $196 \times 196 \times 3$ and data augmentation is used to increase the amount and diversity of data. It is an integral process in which already presented data is randomly

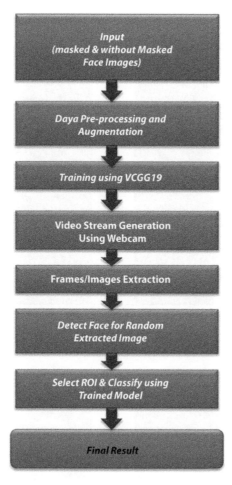

Figure 14.1 Block diagram for proposed work.

transformed instead of collecting new data. In this work, zoom range (0.2), rescale (1./255), horizontal flip (true), and shear range (0.2) are used as a data augmentation parameter.

14.3.3   VGG19 Architecture and Implementation

Images in the dataset are much less in number, so a neural network cannot be trained from scratch. Instead, a pre-trained network called VGG19 that is trained on the ImageNet data-set is fine-tuned. As an input to original VGG19 network, a fixed size (224 × 224) RGB image was given, which implies that the matrix was formed of shape (224, 224, 3). The only pre-processing that was conducted was that the average RGB value was subtracted from each pixel, measured over the entire training collection. 3 × 3 Kernels with a stride size of 1 pixel were used allowing them to cover the entire image notion and spatial padding was used to maintain the image's spatial resolution. Then, maxpooling with 2 × 2 pixels with stride 2 was performed followed by ReLu to provide non-linearity. At last, three fully

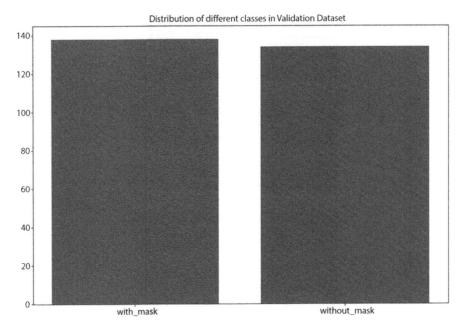

Figure 14.2 Dataset distribution in training set.

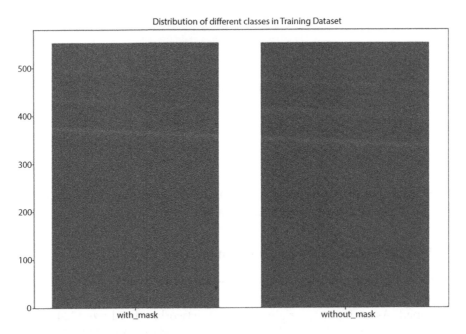

Figure 14.3 Dataset distribution in testing set.

connected layer of size 4,096, 4,096, and 1,000, respectively, followed by softmax function were implemented.

In this work, three fully connected layer of original VGG19 are replaced with two dense layers with 128 and 2 hidden nodes, respectively, as shown in Figure 14.4. Second dense

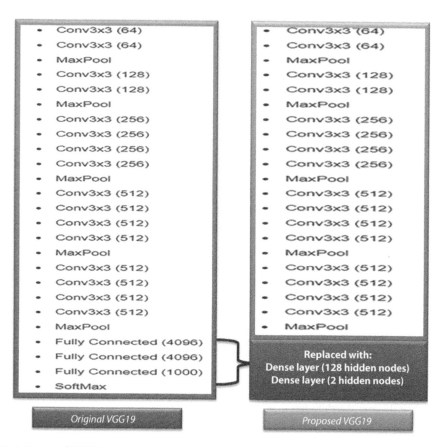

Figure 14.4 Proposed VGG19.

layer is used for the final output using softmax activation function. The detailed layered architecture of proposed VGG19 is shown in Figure 14.5.

14.3.4   Face Mask Detection From Real-Time Video Stream

For real-time face mask detection, video stream is captured using the webcam. Then, video frames are extracted from the video stream using OpenCV (cv2.VideoCapture(), video_capture.read()). OpenCV-based Haar cascade classifier developed by the Paul Viola and Michael Jones [13] is used for face detection on randomly selected images. Haar cascade classifier used a lot of positive and negative images for classifier training and it has the four steps.

- To collect the Haar features.
- Creation of the integral images.
- Training using AdaBoost
- Cascade classifier

Finally, trained VGG19 are applied on the detected faces for the output.

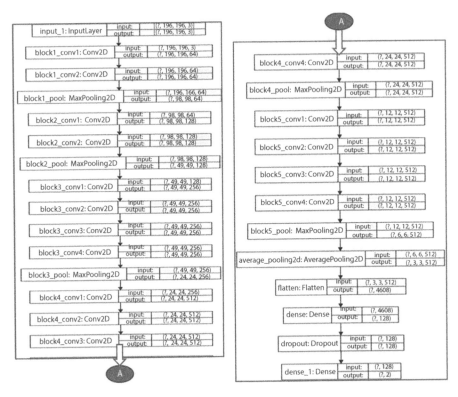

Figure 14.5 VGG19 layered architecture.

14.4   Results and Evaluation

This work is implemented in Google Colab using Python, Keras, and OpenCV. The experiments are performed for just 20 epochs using batch size of 16 and Adam optimizer. ReLu and softmax are used as the activation functions. During training, total parameters are recorded: 20,614,594 (590,210 trainable parameters and 20,024,384 non-trainable parameters). The performance matrices are calculated based on Equations (14.1), (14.2), (14.3), (14.4), (14.5), and (14.6) for accuracy, loss, precision, recall, F1-score, and specificity, respectively.

Accuracy calculates the ratio of correctly expected observations and total observations.

$$Accuracy = \frac{(TP+TN)}{(TP+TN+FP+FN)} \tag{14.1}$$

It is used to verify the model's performance, which penalizes false classifications, taking into account the likelihood of classification. The smaller the log loss, the better the model. The best model is said to be a model with 0 log loss.

$$logarithmic\ Loss = \frac{-1}{N} \sum_{i=1}^{N} \sum_{j=1}^{M} y_{ij} \times \log(p)_{ij} \tag{14.2}$$

Precision measures the ratio of correctly predicted positive observations to the predicted total positive observations. It assists when the cost of false positives is high.

$$Precision = \frac{TP}{TP + FP} \tag{14.3}$$

Recall calculates what proportion is correctly predicted as positive of the actual positive label. When the cost of false negatives is high, recall helps.

$$Recall = \frac{TP}{FN + TP} \tag{14.4}$$

The F1-score calculates the precision and recall weighted average.

$$f1\,score = 2 \times \frac{Precision \times Recall}{Precision + Recall} \tag{14.5}$$

Specificity is characterised as the percentage of real negatives that are expected to be negative.

$$Specificity = \frac{TN}{TN + FP} \tag{14.6}$$

where
  TP (true positive) is the number of positive instances that are corrected classified.
  TN (true negative) is the number of negative instances that are correctly classified.
  FP (false positive) is the number positive instances that are classified.
  FN (false negative) is the number of negative instances that are wrongly classified.

The detailed history for 20 epochs with accuracy and log loss score are shown in Figure 14.6.

The proposed work recorded overall 100% training accuracy with log loss of 0.00 and the validation accuracy of 99.63% with log loss of 0.01 in just 20 epochs. Accuracy and loss curve are shown in Figures 14.7 and 14.8.

Table 14.1 shows the precision, recall, F1-score, and support for individual class. The overall precision, recall, F1-score, and specificity are recorded 99.26%, 100%, 99.63%, and 99%, respectively, for the proposed work. Further, normalized and without normalized confusion matrices are drawn in Figures 14.9 and 14.10.

Figure 14.11 shows the sample image extracted from the real-time video stream (recorded using webcam) and the proposed VGG19 model prediction for the random selected images.

```
Epoch 1/20
69/69 [==============================] - 590s 9s/step - loss: 0.3119 - accuracy: 0.8741 - val_loss: 0.0469 - val_accuracy: 0.9926
Epoch 2/20
69/69 [==============================] - 17s 241ms/step - loss: 0.0600 - accuracy: 0.9810 - val_loss: 0.0285 - val_accuracy: 0.9926
Epoch 3/20
69/69 [==============================] - 17s 241ms/step - loss: 0.0548 - accuracy: 0.9755 - val_loss: 0.0273 - val_accuracy: 0.9816
Epoch 4/20
69/69 [==============================] - 17s 239ms/step - loss: 0.0450 - accuracy: 0.9828 - val_loss: 0.0205 - val_accuracy: 0.9926
Epoch 5/20
69/69 [==============================] - 16s 235ms/step - loss: 0.0298 - accuracy: 0.9891 - val_loss: 0.0276 - val_accuracy: 1.0000
Epoch 6/20
69/69 [==============================] - 16s 235ms/step - loss: 0.0374 - accuracy: 0.9873 - val_loss: 0.0212 - val_accuracy: 0.9890
Epoch 7/20
69/69 [==============================] - 16s 232ms/step - loss: 0.0213 - accuracy: 0.9928 - val_loss: 0.0153 - val_accuracy: 1.0000
Epoch 8/20
69/69 [==============================] - 16s 234ms/step - loss: 0.0150 - accuracy: 0.9964 - val_loss: 0.0080 - val_accuracy: 1.0000
Epoch 9/20
69/69 [==============================] - 16s 235ms/step - loss: 0.0191 - accuracy: 0.9937 - val_loss: 0.0348 - val_accuracy: 0.9890
Epoch 10/20
69/69 [==============================] - 16s 232ms/step - loss: 0.0269 - accuracy: 0.9909 - val_loss: 0.0064 - val_accuracy: 0.9963
Epoch 11/20
69/69 [==============================] - 17s 239ms/step - loss: 0.0380 - accuracy: 0.9882 - val_loss: 0.0312 - val_accuracy: 0.9890
Epoch 12/20
69/69 [==============================] - 16s 232ms/step - loss: 0.0360 - accuracy: 0.9864 - val_loss: 0.0058 - val_accuracy: 1.0000
Epoch 13/20
69/69 [==============================] - 16s 230ms/step - loss: 0.0192 - accuracy: 0.9955 - val_loss: 0.0100 - val_accuracy: 1.0000
Epoch 14/20
69/69 [==============================] - 16s 230ms/step - loss: 0.0273 - accuracy: 0.9918 - val_loss: 0.0218 - val_accuracy: 0.9963
Epoch 15/20
69/69 [==============================] - 16s 232ms/step - loss: 0.0205 - accuracy: 0.9928 - val_loss: 0.0038 - val_accuracy: 1.0000
Epoch 16/20
69/69 [==============================] - 16s 229ms/step - loss: 0.0085 - accuracy: 0.9982 - val_loss: 0.0317 - val_accuracy: 0.9890
Epoch 17/20
69/69 [==============================] - 16s 231ms/step - loss: 0.0135 - accuracy: 0.9955 - val_loss: 0.0048 - val_accuracy: 1.0000
Epoch 18/20
69/69 [==============================] - 16s 230ms/step - loss: 0.0247 - accuracy: 0.9909 - val_loss: 0.0092 - val_accuracy: 0.9963
Epoch 19/20
69/69 [==============================] - 16s 231ms/step - loss: 0.0138 - accuracy: 0.9937 - val_loss: 0.0298 - val_accuracy: 0.9890
Epoch 20/20
69/69 [==============================] - 16s 227ms/step - loss: 0.0198 - accuracy: 0.9928 - val_loss: 0.0081 - val_accuracy: 0.9963
```

Figure 14.6 Experiment history for each epoch.

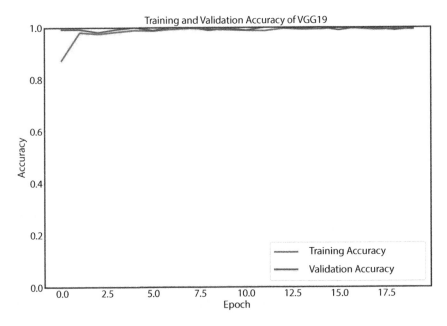

Figure 14.7 Accuracy curve.

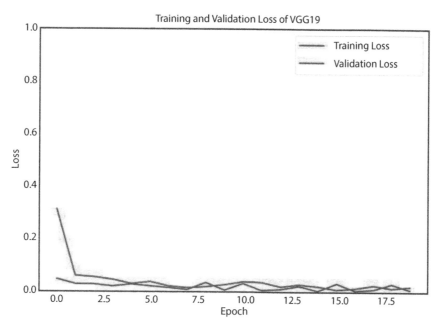

Figure 14.8 Loss curve.

Table 14.1 Classification report (in percent).

	Precision	**Recall**	**F1-score**	**Support**
with_mask	100	99	100	138
without_mask	99	100	100	134
macro avg	100	100	100	272
weighted avg	100	100	100	272

As described above, the proposed work recorded 100% training accuracy with log loss of 0.00 and the validation accuracy of 99.63% with log loss of 0.01 in just 20 epochs which are quite good but more experiment with the larger and standard dataset using advanced convolutional neural network can be performed for better analysis and comparisons with more complicated ones.

Although the aftermath of the COVID-19 global epidemic and also the recognition of face masks may be imperative to secure public safety, the usage of facial masks in public spaces has become a social duty. Studies have shown that wearing a face mask decreases the risk of viral transmission substantially as well as offers a sense of security. The use of face masks tends to be a way to restrict the spread of COVID-19. So, the proposed mechanism can be used as a preventive measure to fight with global pandemic COVID-19. This will help monitor security breaches, facilitate the use of face masks, and maintain a secure working atmosphere.

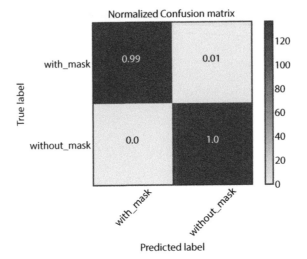

Figure 14.9 Normalized confusion matrix.

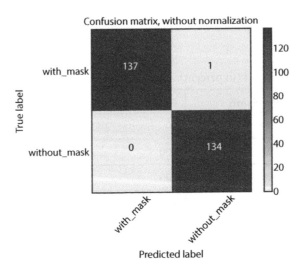

Figure 14.10 Confusion matrix without normalization.

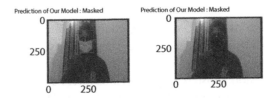

Figure 14.11 Model prediction for sample images extracted from video stream.

14.5 Conclusion

Implementation of the preventive measures is important steps to protect humanity from the spread of COVID-19. Several researchers and physicians are focusing on corona vaccination and treatment. WHO made wearing masks obligatory to defend against this lethal virus during the COVID-19 pandemic. It is really important to wear a mask when you go home, particularly in the crowded places along with marketplaces or hospitals, to keep from getting affected or sharing it. In this chapter, we proposed a real-time face mask detection approach using VGG19 from the video stream recorded using the webcam and achieved 100% training accuracy with log loss of 0.00 and the validation accuracy of 99.63% with log loss of 0.01 in just 20 epochs. The overall precision, recall, F1-score, and specificity are recorded as 99.26%, 100%, 99.63% and 99%, respectively. In order to fight with COVID-19 global pandemic, this technical approach will allow researchers to design the best solution.

References

1. Jagadeeswari, C. and Uday Theja, M., Performance Evaluation of Intelligent Face Mask Detection System with various Deep Learning Classifiers. *Int. J. Adv. Sci. Technol.*, 29, 11s, 3083–3087, 2020. Retrieved from http://sersc.org/journals/index.php/IJAST/article/view/23805.

2. Chavda, A., Dsouza, J., Badgujar, S., Damani, A., *Multi-Stage CNN Architecture for Face Mask Detection*, 2020, arXiv preprint arXiv:2009.07627.

3. Ejaz, M.S. and Islam, M.N., Masked Face Recognition Using Convolutional Neural Network, in: *2019 International Conference on Sustainable Technologies for Industry 4.0 (STI)*, pp. 1–6, 2019.

4. Guo, Y.R., Cao, Q.D., Hong, Z.S., Tan, Y.Y., Chen, S.D., Jin, H.J., Yan, Y., The origin, transmission and clinical therapies on coronavirus disease 2019 (COVID-19) outbreak–an update on the status. *Mil. Med. Res.*, 7, 1, 1–10, 2020.

5. Kumar, K. and Shrimankar, D.D., Deep event learning boost-up approach: Delta. *Multimed. Tools. Appl.*, 77, 20, 26635–26655, 2018.

6. Kumar, K. and Shrimankar, D.D., F-DES: Fast and deep event summarization. *IEEE Trans. Multimedia*, 20, 2, 323–334, 2017.

7. Kumar, K., Shrimankar, D.D., Singh, N., Event bagging: A novel event summarization approach in multiview surveillance videos, in: *2017 International Conference on Innovations in Electronics, Signal Processing and Communication (IESC)*, IEEE, pp. 106–111, April 2017.

8. Kumar, K., Shrimankar, D.D., Singh, N., Eratosthenes sieve based key-frame extraction technique for event summarization in videos. *Multimed. Tools. Appl.*, 77, 6, 7383–7404, 2018.

9. Li, L., Xia, Z., Jiang, X., Ma, Y., Roli, F., Feng, X., 3D face mask presentation attack detection based on intrinsic image analysis. *IET Biom.*, 9, 3, 100–108, 2020.

10. Loey, M., Manogaran, G., Taha, M.H.N., Khalifa, N.E.M., A hybrid deep transfer learning model with machine learning methods for face mask detection in the era of the COVID-19 pandemic. *Measurement*, 167, 108288, 2020.

11. Meenpal, T., Balakrishnan, A., Verma, A., Facial Mask Detection using Semantic Segmentation, in: *2019 4th International Conference on Computing, Communications and Security (ICCCS)*, IEEE, pp. 1–5, October 2019.

12. Rosebrok, A., *COVID-19: Face Mask Detector with OpenCV Keras/TensorFlow and Deep Learning*, 2020, [online] Available: https://www.pyimagesearch.com/2020/05/04/covid-19-face-maskdetector-with-opencv-keras-tensorflow-and-deep-learning/.

13. Viola, P. and Jones, M., Rapid object detection using a boosted cascade of simple features, in: *Proceedings of the 2001 IEEE computer society conference on computer vision and pattern recognition. CVPR 2001*, Vol. 1, IEEE, pp. I–I, December 2001.

A Computational Intelligence Approach for Skin Disease Identification Using Machine/Deep Learning Algorithms

Swathi Jamjala Narayanan*, Pranav Raj Jaiswal, Ariyan Chowdhury,
Amitha Maria Joseph and Saurabh Ambar

*School of Computer Science and Engineering, Vellore Institute of Technology, Vellore,
Tamil Nadu, India*

Abstract

Skin diseases are debilitating to a person's health and social life. Among skin diseases, the diagnosis of the most common epidermal diseases would be based on the morphological manifestations of the disease. The morphological manifestations play a key role as an indicator for disease diagnosis. Proper image capture of these symptoms is the first step to diagnosis via the remote process. These images need to undergo pre-processing, and then, the necessary features of the images need to be extracted. This data is then subsequently fed into a model implementation of a machine learning algorithm, which has to be trained to detect and label the skin disease. For this purpose, various algorithms have been implemented over the past decade in the detection of diseases that affect the human epidermis. These algorithms have been noted to achieve varying degrees of success with different epidermal diseases. The most commonly used techniques are Random Forest, Decision Trees, and Naïve Bayes, whereas in recent years, deep learning plays a major role to develop accurate models for skin disease detection. In this chapter, we compare the efficacy of different machine learning algorithm techniques and deep learning techniques that are used for the process of skin disease detection. The algorithms include Random Forest, KNN, Logistic Regression, Naïve Bayes, SVM, and CNN methods along with the performance measures used by the classifiers. To establish the highest accuracy rate possible for diagnosis, a comparison of the results obtained from each algorithm used is necessary. For this comparison, a common dataset with a variety of images is needed. Hence, we propose a novel dataset generated from various sources. The dataset needs to be properly delineated into training sets and testing sets. Here, we also present models that are built to accurately identify five of the most common epidermal diseases with a notably high accuracy rate.

Keywords: Skin disease classification, machine learning, Logistic Regression, SVM, RNN, Decision Trees, CNN, KNN, Random Forest

Corresponding author: jnswathi@vit.ac.in

Om Prakash Jena, Alok Ranjan Tripathy, Ahmed A. Elngar and Zdzislaw Polkowski (eds.) Computational Intelligence and Healthcare Informatics, (269–296) © 2021 Scrivener Publishing LLC

15.1 Introduction

The skin is the most critical piece of the human body. The skin shields the body from UV radiation diseases, wounds, heat, and destructive radiation and helps in the assembling of nutrient D. The skin assumes a significant function in controlling the internal heat level, so it is essential to keep up great wellbeing and shield the body from skin maladies. Dermatological maladies are the most predominant illnesses around the world. Despite being common, its finding is significantly exhausting and requires broad involvement with the area. Around an investigation, 24 levels of the populace counsel their overall expert (GP) with a skin pickle in a time of one year. There is a conflicting (and by and large repressed) tutoring in dermatology at the undergrad level which indicates that the learners ought to rethink their current aptitudes and information in this specific territory. Right now, around 90 levels of illnesses of the skin are overseen only by the Primary Care facility. This implicatively suggests the greater part of the skin disease issues can be tackled if care is taken at a beginning phase. Skin infections can affect essentially the personal satisfaction of patients. Skin ailment rates are expanding and results rely upon early analysis. GPs have a significant function in the early conclusion of skin illnesses.

There have been numerous undertakings to actualize conventional medication over the various pieces of the globe particularly in the nations which are not innovatively progressed; however, the endeavors have been met with difficulties, for example, the colossal expense of clinical instruments and types of gear and the absence of clinical skill. Skin illness regularly results from ecological factors alongside different causes. The vital instruments required for the early discovery of these illnesses are as yet not promptly accessible in many populaces worldwide. With the quick improvement of tech innovation in the present many years, the utilization of machine learning innovation assumes a pivotal function in the investigation of skin diseases. Scientists are continually creating different forecast techniques; however, the biggest analysts utilize just a couple of arrangement calculations. Different types of research work are already done by the different researchers and here are some works that are related to our work.

Paja [31] used Random Forest (RF) in the feature selection process. In this process, the feature selection process is used to find out the interesting feature from the dataset. The used datasets are benign nevus, suspicious melanoma, and malignant. The error rate is 22.40%. Das [8] proposed a support vector machine (SVM) algorithm for skin lesion classification. It works in three modules: Database preparation for the dataset, Extract feature from the database, and SVM is used to evaluate the feature. For feature extraction, DCT, DFT, GLCM, and Binary Pattern are used. It has 89.66% accuracy. Okuboyejo [30] followed five steps to develop an automated skin disease classifier. The researchers followed a sequence like an Image Formation and Pre-processing, Segmentation, Feature Extraction and Classification of the Lesion, and Diagnosis Accuracy Assessment. The classification is done based on ABCD rules. It provides an easier, effective, and fastest diagnosis model. Shrivastava [38] introduced the Automated Psoriasis-Aided Diagnosis (PCAD) system for skin lesions classification. The researchers used machine learning for generalization and training-based color image datasets and physician classified labels used for that. SVM framework helped to utilize the machine learning paradigm. The model provides 92.84% accuracy and 94.42% reliability for psoriasis skin image, 93.83% accuracy, and 97.39% reliability for psoriatic lesions, and skin accuracy was 93.99% and reliability was 96% for the melanoma diagnosis process.

Daniel [9] uses RF, Convolutional Neural network (CNN), and LRM algorithms. In the proposed model, the dataset dermoscopic images and the images are the concentration of pheomelanin and eumelanin. Kumar [21] introduced a rule-based web-supported system in the paper. It is a self-learning model. The datasets are collected from the data repository of the University of California. KNN algorithms and Maximum Entropy Mode are used in the model. The accuracy rate is 95%. For different kinds of eczema classification, Alam [4] proposed method that is color-based segmentation. It is based on K-Means clustering, and morphological image processing technique also used. The accuracy rate of the method is 91%. Shoieb [39] introduced and enhanced segmentation to identify the infected skin lesion. CNN was used as an extractor. SVM trained the images with CNN. The accuracy rate is 93%. Zaqout [48] developed a melanoma detection model by using ABCD rules. PH 2 datasets were used in the paper. ABCD rules were used for feature extraction, and the TDS system was used for classification. The model has 90% accuracy. Tan [44] used the SVM classifier for benign and malignant skin lesion classification. In the model, dull razors and median filters are used for removing hair and other noise. Pixel limitation is used for segmentation. Features were extracted by using ABCD rules and epiluminescence microscopy (ELM) criteria. The model provides 92% accuracy for benign and 84% for malignant skin diseases.

Zhou [49] proposed a novel method for dermoscopy image classification. In this model, different types of CNN are used like ResNet-50, VGG-16, GoogleNet, and ResNet-50. The novel method has 90% accuracy. Esteva [10] used a single CNN for skin lesion classification. The image will be trained end-to-end directly for that input. The input is pixel and disease label based. An open-source repository is used for dataset collection. For detecting skin diseases like angioma, basal cell carcinoma, and lentigo simplex, Chakraborty [7] proposed a model based on the Artificial Neural Network (ANN). For the model meta-heuristic supported ANN technique is used. For training purposes, the undominated Sorting Genetic Algorithm–II is employed, and it is a multi-objective optimization method. The proposed NSGA II trained ANN has an 87.92% accuracy rate. Zhang [50] used a deep learning algorithm based on the GoogleNet Inception v3 code package for developing a computer-based diagnosis system for skin diseases. There are two types of dermatologists experienced one is if the diagnosis matches, and another one is if not matched. If the matched image is annotated if not matched it is consulted. The maximum accuracy rate is 86.54%. Ge [12] proposed to use the transfer learning of deep residual networks. It is used for extracting the global features from a large number of datasets. The model also adopted DCNN for local feature extraction. Pooling layers feature combinations used for local feature extraction. The Rectified Linear Unit (ReLu) layer is kept after the bilinear pooling layer insertion in the training parameter. SVM was used for classification and got 80% accuracy from the model for the psoriasis classification process.

Pal [32] describes DCNN, rfgraph cut algorithms, super-pixel generation algorithms, SVM, SLIC algorithms, and optimization algorithms. Fully CNN is also used in the system. It is an automated segmentation. The Ratio of Correct Pixel Classification (RCPC) and Jaccard's Coefficient (JC) accuracy are used for evaluating the segmentation performance. Yang [47] proposed method; skin lesions had captured based on manifestations and dermatological criteria. It can also be used to improve the prediction percentage. The state-of-the art method uses for improving the percentage. The method is based on an uninterpretable feature. Here, KNN, ANN, and SVM algorithms are used to classify the skin lesion. Pal [33] used CNN algorithms to classify skin lesions. ResNet50, DenseNet 121, and MoBiNet are used as layers. Back propagating is used to prevent the data imbalance problem. It has 77.5% accuracy. In the nevus, malignant melanoma classification process, Harangi [15] used different types of CNN methods like AlexNet, VGGNet, and GoogleNet. The process is used to train large amounts of data. The data size is almost 1.28 million. Rezvantalab [36] used gradient descent algorithms and different types of CNN like DenseNet 201, ResNet 152, Inception v3, and Inception ResNet v2 for classification. The results show 98.79% accuracy. Hasija [16] designed the model that was divided into three-phrase data collection and augmentation, designing model, and prediction. For classification of image, the average accuracy rate is 95% but CNN provides 91% accuracy; on the other hand, SVM provides 95.3%. Patnaik [34] divided the whole classification model into three modules. The divided parts were the feature extraction module, training module, and validation/testing module. For feature extraction, Inception_v3, MobileNet, ResNet, and Xception were used. Deep learning algorithms, RF algorithms, and Logistic Regression (LR) were used for training and testing purposes. The accuracy is 88%. For warts, hemangiomas, and vitiligo classification, Nosseir [29] proposed to use KNN, Multi-SVM, Image adjustment algorithms, and ID3 learning algorithms. The method has 98.2% accuracy for dermoscopic image classification.

Purnama [35] used CNN in the teledermatology system. The classification is applied in two ways. Those are store-and-forward and live interactive mode. The model has 78% accuracy in the Inception V3 process but it only provides 58% accuracy on web classifier MobileNet. Bhavani [5] proposed a method that is based on computer vision. The technique is used to detect different kinds of skin diseases. In the detection process, three deep learning algorithms are used for the feature extraction process. Those are Inception_v3, MobileNet, and ResNet. For training and testing, LR is used. CNN layers combination helps to achieve efficiency. HAM10000 dataset is used. Murugan [25] worked on Melanoma classification for which KNN, SVM, and RF algorithms are used. The classification is done based on three methods: ABCD rules, GLCM, and shape. In the ABCD rule, the provided accuracies are 90% for SVM, 75% for RF, and 70% for KNN; on the other hand, the accuracies in GLCM are 85% for SVM, 75% for RF, and 65% for KNN. SVM provides 81%, RF provides 71%, and KNN provides 61% accuracy by the system based on shape. Alkolifi Alenezi [1] implemented the method in MATLAB 2018b. The researchers follow steps like Pre-Processing (Image Resizing), Feature Extraction, and Classification. For classification, CNN and multi-class SVM are used. The accuracy of the method is 100%.

Ibrahim [20] proposed method that is used for classifying malignant and benign. In the method, at first, the dataset is pre-processed, and secondly, the CNN model is used for training and testing purposes. Gaussian filtering is used for extraction. The paper is based on identifying the melanoma category's diseases. Melbin [26] proposed an optimization-based DNN for skin disease classification. The model can detect 14 diseases automatically. The datasets are collected from Google images. GLCM-based feature extraction, enhanced DNN based detection mode, and optimization-based Deep-RNN model are used. In addition, 98% accuracy is provided by the system. Local Binary Pattern (LBP) and CNN used by Akmalia [2] for skin lesion classification. LBP was used for image extraction and CNN was used for classification. The researchers introduced a new algorithm called LBP Feature Map. The new method has a 92% accuracy rate. Mahbod [27] used three deep learning methods for developing a skin lesion classifier. They used deep learning methods such as AlexNet, VGG16, and ResNet-18. All are used for feature extraction and pre-trained. The system has 90.68% accuracy. Hosseinzadeh Kassani [17] used DCNNs and Xception architecture along with VGGNet, ResNet, and

AlexNet architectures to extract the features. CNN is used for evaluating skin lesions. The researchers experimented with GPU to speed up the training, testing, and deployment of the process. The class skewness was addressed by the data augmentation method. The model has a 92.74% F-score and 92.08% accuracy. To develop the CNN model accuracy, Sriwong [40] proposed to increase the patient's background knowledge. By using the proposed model, the accuracy rate increased up to 1.10%. The used algorithms were deep learning (based on ANN concept), UPNS, RNN, and CNN. The accuracy of the model is 72.1% and the increase and decrease rate is 0.9% for three-way classification and 55.4%, and the increase and decrease rate is 1.7% for nine-way classification. Machine learning, kernel SVM, Naïve Bayes, LR, Random Forest, and CNN were used by Bhadula [6] to identify skin diseases like acne, planus, lichen, and SJS TEN. For classification, five machine learning classifiers were used.

Velasco [45] proposed the MobileNet model that was designed for identifying seven kinds of skin diseases. The model was used as a mobile application. The datasets are collected from publicly accessible repositories. Acne, eczema, pityriasis rosea, psoriasis, tinea corporis, varicella (chickenpox), and vitiligo are used as the dataset. CNN MobileNet model is used here and provided accuracy is 93.6%. Kumar [22] used a method that was pre-processing the image, flattening those images and getting the pixel intensities of images into an array, appending all such arrays into a database, training the SVM with labeled data using a suitable kernel, and using the trained data to classify the samples successfully. The accuracy of classification is about 90%. El Saleh [11] proposed an automated facial skin disease method using a deep CNN. At first, the images were regenerated using some pre-processing image techniques based on the size of our database. Then, the images are used for training and validation purposes. The model had successfully identified eight facial skin diseases, normal skin class, and no-face class. Deep CNN and CNN architectures such as LeNet, AlexNet, VGGNet, GoogleNet, and ResNet were used as algorithms. The accuracy rate is 88%. Junayed [43] proposed an approach called Deep Residual Neural Network. The approach was used to identify five different types of skin diseases like Closed Comedo, Cystic, Keloidalis, Open Comedo, and Pustular. CNN was used for skin lesion classification. The accuracy of the model is 95.89%.

Putra [13] used SVM, K-Means Clustering, DWT, and color moments to classify benign keratosis, melanoma, nevus, and vascular after processing the RGB image. The method has 97.1% accuracy. Rimi [37] proposed a skin disease classification method by using image processing and CNN. Here, eczema hand, eczema nummular, eczema subacute, lichen simplex chronicus, stasis dermatitis, and ulcers will be classified. The image is processed in three steps: image compression, picture upgrade, and reclamation; and measurement extraction is followed and CNN is used for classification. It provides 73% precision. Almeida [3] worked with medical image texture analysis for classifying the skin diseases lime melanoma and nevus, and for that, Gray Level Co-occurrence Matrix (GLCM) is used. The method has 95.04% to 97.46% accuracy. Goswami [14] used CNN to classify benign and malignant diseases. In this process, the image is extracted based on pixel-based, edge-based, and region-based. For identifying eczema, benign, malignant, and melanoma, Hameed [18] proposed a model that is based on multi-class multi-level classification. Here, the hybrid technique is used for K-Means Clustering capability. Color and texture categories are used for malignant and melanoma feature extraction. Two types of algorithms are used here: supervised and unsupervised learning algorithms. The model provides 89.35% accuracy in melanoma vs. eczema and 76.78% in benign vs. malignant metadata used by Li et al. [24] for improving the skin diseases diagnosis. A novel framework used in the model and the framework called Data-Fusion Framework. AlexNet, VGG, ResNet, DenseNet, or SENet, and 441 × 441 pixels for PNASNet were the backbone of CNN architecture. All of them were used to pre-train the image on imagenet and provides 87.71% accuracy. Computer vision–based system is proposed by Shanthi [41]. CNN used the model and it had 11 layers like fully connected pooling layer, convolution layer, and ReLu layer. The datasets were collected from the DermNet database. The model provides accuracies that were 85.7% for acne, 92.3% for keratosis, 93.3% for Eczema Herpeticum, and 92.8% for urticaria. The above writing has made critical accomplishments in the distinguishing proof of skin illnesses. Nonetheless, the proposed strategies chiefly focus on the distinguishing proof of one sort of skin sickness, which makes it hard to apply to the exact ID of multi-type skins. A dataset has been made for this and a similar report is proposed to distinguish five different sorts of skin illnesses and the part of AI in foreseeing the infection consequently. Hilton study on Boltzmann Machines can also be seen [19].

The structure of this chapter is as follows: Section 15.2: Problem Statement; Section 15.3: Methodology; Section 15.4: Dataset; Section 15.5: Experiment/Technique Used; Section 15.6: Conclusion; and Section 15.7: Future Work. In this chapter, an attempt is done to use different machine learning algorithm and deep learning algorithm, which are Classification and Regression Trees (CART), Decision Tree (DT), RF, and SVM. By comparing these three machine learning methods with deep learning, we construct a model to predict skin disease. The best of both the models are used and implemented. The obtained final prediction results show that the proposed method generates more efficient use of the dataset and gives more accurate results than other methods mentioned.

15.2 Research Problem Statements

Our skin-involved a few layers of the epidermis, for example, the furthest layer, dermis, that lies underneath the epidermis, and subcutaneous layer, skin being the biggest organ in the human framework. While it assumes a significant part by directing sweat, seeing the outer temperature, and securing the body and the inward organs from outside attacks that incorporate fake skin harm and synthetic harm. As of late, the intercession of computerized reasoning and software engineering in all fields has been demonstrated to be inescapable. Clinical science is one such field that relies upon man-made reasoning and PCs generally for the determination of different infections. Including machines to help the doctors encourages them to address more patients and helps in analysis with the least blunders. Dermatological sicknesses will in the general show in a morphologically comparable way, and the finding of these infections can end up being both time and cash burning-through. The ongoing pandemic has additionally demonstrated to us that specialists will most likely be unable to analyze their patients in person constantly and that the utilization of such indicative instruments would enormously profit such circumstances.

15.3 Dataset Description

The dataset is generated by downloading images from Google search. For ease of use, we have taken only five primitive skin diseases. We have collected a total of 2,500 images and divided in the category. We have chosen it because the dataset was rich enough to let us play with it and see some common phenomena for the research purpose.

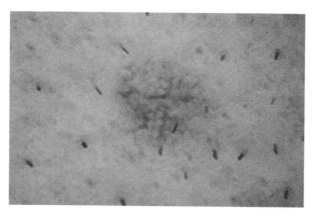

Figure 15.1 Actinic keratosis.

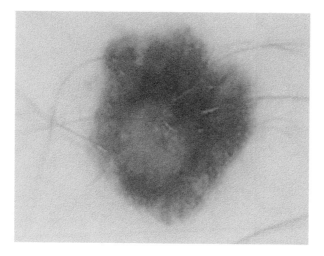

Figure 15.2 Melanoma.

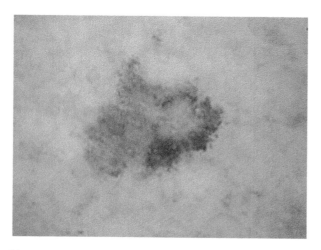

Figure 15.3 Pigmented keratosis.

15.4   Machine Learning Technique Used for Skin Disease Identification

In this section, we are discussing the different algorithms that are present around us. We have chosen the five diseases which can be seen in Figure 15.1, 15.2, 15.3, 15.4 and 15.5 and described how to use them for making the model. Later, we have discussed the results and accuracy of the algorithm.

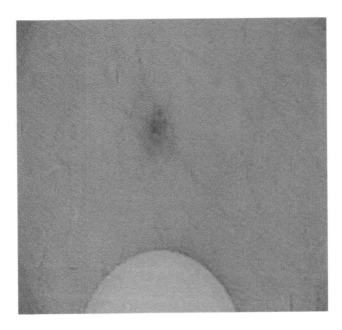

Figure 15.4 Nevus.

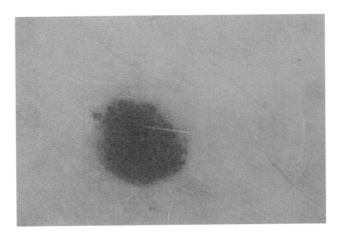

Figure 15.5 Vascular lesion.

15.4.1   Logistic Regression

LR is considered one of the best machine learning algorithms, used for the prediction when the dependent or input variable is categorical within the given set of independent variables. It is the supervised learning technique.

During the early 20th century, it was used in biological sciences and many social science applications. Even nowadays, LR models emphasis on medical research and its multivariable methods for modeling the relationship between multiple independent variables and categorical dependent variables.

It estimates the output of the categorical input variable. So, the result must be either categorical or discrete. The output can either be 0 or 1, "Yes" or "No", True or False, etc., but instead of giving value as 0 or 1, it provides the probabilistic value that lies between 1 and 0.

15.4.1.1   Logistic Regression Assumption

It assumes that there will be minimal or no multicollinearity with the independent variables.

It assumes that the independent variables are directly related to the log of odds.

The dependent variable must be categorical in nature.

Based on classification, LR can be divided into binary classification or multiclass classification. As in the chapter, we are predicting the five major diseases. This comes in the multiclass classification. The implementation and execution of multiclass classification are the same as binary classification. Each class will be treated as a binary classification problem. In the one vs. all class or one vs. rest classification algorithm, when working with a class, that class is marked as 1 and the other classes become 0.

For example, we have five classes: actinic keratosis, melanoma, nevus, pigmented benign keratosis, and vascular lesion. When we work on the actinic keratosis, we mark this as 1 and rest of the classes as 0.

Actinic keratosis	Melanoma	Nevus	Pigmented benign keratosis	Vascular lesion
1	0	0	0	0
0	1	0	0	0
0	0	1	0	0
0	0	0	0	1

15.4.1.2   Logistic Sigmoid Function

The mathematical function which is utilized to depict the probabilities of the predicted values is the sigmoid function. This function outputs any real value into the range of another value between 0 and 1 and as the value remains between 0 and 1, which means it cannot go beyond limits. The "S" shaped-curve is called the logistic function or the sigmoid function. The threshold value is used, which sets the limits of 0 or 1. As value crosses the threshold value, it tends toward 1, and if the value is below the threshold value, then it tends toward 0. Generally, the threshold value we take as 0.5, so if the sigmoid function or the logistic function returns a value greater than 0.5, consider it as 1, or if the sigmoid function returns, a value less than 0.5, take it as 0.

$$\log istic\ Regression : 0 \leq h_{\oslash}(x) \leq 1 \qquad (15.1)$$

$$h = \frac{1}{1 + e^{-z}} \qquad (15.2)$$

$$z = \Theta x \qquad (15.3)$$

z represents the input features/dependent variable multiplied by an arbitrary initialized value of theta (θ).

X represents the input feature. In most cases, there are multiple input features. So, the formula becomes large:

$$h = \oslash_0 + \oslash_1 X_1 + \oslash_2 X_2 + ... \qquad (15.4)$$

X_1, X_2, X_3, X_4 are input features or dependent variables and each input feature theta will be randomly initialized. The beginning theta, i.e., Θ_0 is the bias term. The main objective of this algorithm is to update the theta(θ) with each iteration to establish a relationship between the output label and the input feature.

15.4.1.3   Cost Function and Gradient Descent

The cost function represents the optimization objective, and it gives the estimate about how accurate the prediction is from the original output. The formula for that is

$$j = -\frac{1}{m}\left[\Sigma y^i \log h + (1 - y)\log(1 - h^i)\right] \qquad (15.5)$$

where m represents the number of training data or the number of training examples or y represents the original output label, and h represents the predicted output or the hypothesis.

The below equation is for the gradient descent. Using the below formula, in each iteration, theta value will be updated.

$$\oslash = \oslash - \beta\Sigma\left(h^i - y^i\right)X^i_{j}. \qquad (15.6)$$

Implementing the algorithm using the gradient descent approach.
Algorithm:

1. Input the dataset
   a. Import necessary packages like NumPy, pandas, and matplotlib.
   b. We will take out the dependent (input feature) and independent variables from the decided dataset.

    c. Dependent variable datasets have continuous feature-vectors (x_i's) of length K (no. of feature).

    d. Independent variable, the output for the dependent variable is represented by Y_i which holds values in the range from 1 to 5.

2. Computing the regression coefficient of the training data

    a. Make the hypothesis function that takes the input variables and theta and returns the calculated output.

    b. Create the cost function, it should take the input variables, output variable, and theta and give back the cost of the hypothesis. The cost of the hypothesis gives a rough idea about how far the prediction is from the original outputs.

3. Data pre-processing

    a. Add the bias column Θ_0 in the input variable. The length of the input variable and the output variable should be the same.

    b. The y column has values from 1 to 5, which means it has five classes.

    c. Make one column for every class with the same length as of y. When the class is 4, make a column that has 1 for the rows with 4 and 0 otherwise.

4. Gradient Descent

    a. In this function, put the input variable, alpha, output variable, theta, and the number of epochs as the parameter. The alpha represents the learning rate.

    b. Choose the learning rate as per the requirement. Too small or too big, a learning rate can make the algorithm slow. Run the algorithm with different learning rates, which helps in estimating the right learning rate.

    c. For each column in y, implement the binary classification.

    d. For example, on considering the actinic keratosis, it should return 1 for the disease actinic keratosis and 0 for the rest of the classes. So, as we have five classes, we need to run epoch (iteration) 5 times.

    e. Initialize the theta value.

       i. Implement LR for each class. For each class, there will be a series of theta (θ).

       ii. Choose the correct epochs for better accuracy.

5. The gradient descent function will return the updated theta. Use this theta for the step 2.a, which will return the calculated output value.

6. Now, we compare the calculated output value and original output value to calculate the accuracy of the model.

15.4.2   SVM

Initially, the help vector machine (SVM) was presented in the year 1992 and was portrayed as a directed learning calculation that was fit for unraveling both straight and non-direct order issues. According to neural organizations, SVM is portrayed as a feed-forward neural net that incorporates one shrouded layer.

The principle building squares of a SVM incorporate primary danger minimization, which was gotten from the measurable learning hypothesis created by Vapnik and Chervoneniks, non-direct advancement, duality, and piece prompted highlights spaces, which underlines the method that has been created with an accurate numerical structure.

The fundamental thought of grouping support vectors is in isolating models using a straight choice surface and to likewise work by augmenting the edge of various classes. This prompts the advancement of the raised quadratic programming issue.

Block Diagram

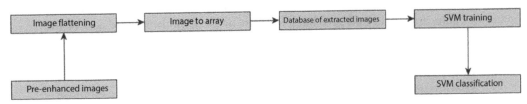

Figure 15.6 SVM block diagram.

Algorithm

To carry out the process of identifying skin diseases via SVM classifiers a block diagram is also given in Figure 15.6, the algorithm that is to be implemented includes steps as follows:

1. The statistical data to be analyzed is taken from an image database that is verified to be susceptible to a particular disease. This image is pre-enhanced, i.e., undergoes processes of softening, cantering of image, and hair removal.

2. These pre-processed images are furthermore converted into the RGB format and the pixel values of the resulting image in RGB format are converted into the 1D array. The intensities of the recorded pixels are scaled in between (0, 1).
   E.g.: In the case of a 64*64-pixel format, around 12,288 values for each image will be recorded.

3. These 1D arrays are further arranged into a database through the appending of all the resulting image pixel intensities of all the images.

4. Past this progression, the SVM should be prepared. A help vector machine is an AI calculation that arranges among at least two classes. This characterization happens because of various pieces, which are then utilized as hyperplanes to separate among the classes. The exactness and accuracy of this SVM primarily rely upon the sort of part being utilized and the limit esteems that are henceforth characterized. Besides, a proper bit must be picked to accomplish better outcomes. To separate among ailing and solid skin, a "straight part" is utilized. The previously mentioned direct bits are utilized in the situations when the classes to be isolated do not share numerous highlights practically speaking. A direct portion is one of the least difficult of the multitude of bits accessible. To arrange two classes, which share more highlights practically speaking, at that point different pieces like polynomial parts are to be utilized to accomplish better exactness and accuracy. Gamma portions are additionally utilized to characterize the limit estimations of the SVM. The direct bit's condition is as follows:

$$f(x,y) = x^T y + c \qquad (15.6)$$

The mentioned equation involves the calculation of the inner products of the new input vector (x) with all the support vectors included in the training data. These mentioned coefficients of "y" are the distance from the aforementioned hyperplane to the feature and "c" is an optional constant.

When unknown data is given to be analyzed by the SVM, it classifies the given sample based on the training samples. Hence, the SVM classifies the image whether it belongs to the category of fit or unfit skin. The "Enum" function is further used.

Pseudocode

Data: Dataset with p* variables and a binary outcome.
Output: Ranked list of variables according to their relevance.
Find the optimal values for the tuning parameters of the SVM model;
Train the SVM model;

$$p \leftarrow p *;$$

while $p \geq 2$ do

SVM$_p$ ← SVM with the optimized tuning parameters for the p variables and observations in Data;
Wp ← calculate weight vector of the SVM, ($w_{p1....} w_{pp}$);
rank. Criteria ← ($w_{p1....} w_{pp}$);
min. rank. criteria ← variable with the lowest value in rank. criteria vector;
Remove min. rank. criteria from Data:
Rank←min.rank.criteria;
p←p-1;
end
Rank← variable in Data
return (Ranks$_1$....Rank$_p$)

15.4.3   Recurrent Neural Networks

Recurrent neural networks (RNNs) [6, 46] are a robust and powerful kind of neural network and are one of the most favorable algorithms as it is the only algorithm containing internal memory. RNN architecture can be seen in the Figure 15.7.

As a result, having internal memory the RNN can memorize essential values of the input that would assist them in the accurate prediction of the result. Hence, this algorithm is highly favorable for processing sequential data like speech, text, time series, financial data, and many more.

In a RNN, the information is wound through a loop. While making decisions, it takes current input and the inputs it has received previously into respect. Usually, the RNN has a short-term memory.

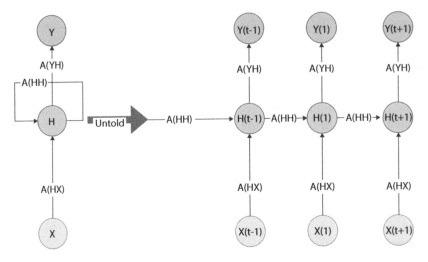

Figure 15.7 Recurrent neural network architecture.

RNN has two inputs i.e., the recent past and the present. This is essential because the order of data holds important information regarding what comes next, which is why the RNN can do things other algorithms cannot.

Algorithm:
Input: $x(t)$ is the input given to the network at time step t.
Hidden state: $h(t)$ represents a hidden state existing at time t and plays the role of "memory" of the network.
Output: $o(t)$ illustrates the output of the network.
RNN forward pass:

$$a^{(t)} = b + AH^{(t-1)} + UX^{(t)}$$

$$H^{(t)} = tan(a^{(t)})$$

$$O^{(t)} = c + Vh^{(t)}$$

$$Y^{(t)} = softmax(O^{(t)})$$

However, there are two crucial drawbacks RNN has to deal with, i.e.,

Exploding Gradient: When algorithm, without any specific reason assigns very high importance to weights.

Vanishing Gradient: When the value of the gradient becomes so small that the model stops learning.

To classify melanoma disease, a computer-aided diagnosis system is developed based on color and texture features that will be used for the extraction. GLCM and DRLBP will be used for texture extraction. Color, diameter detection, and symmetry detection are also used in the process. RNN is used as a classifier.

RNN Algorithm:

1. Input data.
2. Appy RGB or HSV color space for processing the color vision.
   - RGB represents the amount of red, green, and blue; on the other hand, HSV represents hue, saturation, and value.
3. Use descriptor local binary pattern (DRKBP) for comparing the pixel with neighbor pixels.
   - it helps to improve the robustness.
   3.1 Image divided into 3*3 blocks.
   3.2 Find LBP codes using gradient vector
   3.3 Find gradient magnitude
   3.4 Find RLBP
   3.5 Build DRLBP Histogram
4. Extract correlation, energy, homogeneity, entropy, and contract from the GLCM features.
5. Apply ABCD rules to assess the risk of malignity.
6. Find new data from unlabeled data by using K-means clustering
7. Apply RNN for classification
8. End of process.

15.4.4   Decision Tree Classification Algorithm

In the of a DT, a supervised machine learning model is used in the prediction of a target through the use of learning decision rules from the features of the given dataset. This algorithm is used in both classification as well as Regression problems. This algorithm continues to be preferred more for solving classification problems. Just as the name suggests, the model works by metaphorically breaking down our data into branches similar to tree, starting with the creation of a root node which further expands onto more branches, making a choice supported by asking a series of questions, overall constructing a structure like a tree. Decision Tree architecture can be seen in the Figure 15.8.

The DT separates the dataset into smaller units, and at the same moment, it steadily develops decision. The final tree will be the tree with leaf nodes and the DT. The classifier, structured like a tree, possesses internal nodes which describe the dataset features and branches which describe the decision rules and where each leaf node describes the outcome.

There are two types of nodes:

1. **Decision nodes**: These nodes are utilized to make any decision based on the dataset features and to possess multiple instances of branches.
2. **Leaf node**: These nodes are the result of the output of the aforementioned decisions and, thus, do not possess further branches.

The algorithm simply poses the question and, depending on the reply (Yes/No), further splits the given tree into subtrees as shown in the above diagram.

The reason that this algorithm is popularly used as a classifier due to its mimic human thinking ability while making a decision makes a good target to deal with the problem.

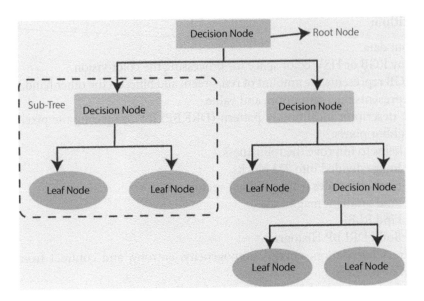

Figure 15.8 Decision tree architecture.

Decision Tree Terminologies

1. **Root Node:** It denotes the beginning of the given DT. It functions as a representation of the whole dataset, which is then further divided into two or more identical sets.
2. **Leaf Node:** These are the final nodes based on the output, and following this, the tree cannot be further divided beyond the leaf node.
3. **Splitting:** This is the term for the process of division of the root node/decision node into further sub-nodes/sub-trees as per the specified conditions.
4. **Branch/Sub Tree:** A DT that is formed through the splitting of the tree.
5. **Pruning:** This refers to the technique of data compression, which is used in the removal of unnecessary branches from the tree.
6. **Parent/Child Node:** The parent node refers to the root node of the specified tree whereas other nodes are referred to as the child nodes.

Algorithm

It begins from the root node of the tree for the prediction of the dataset class. This algorithm proceeds to compare these values of the given record/real dataset attribute with the root attribute, and based on correlation, it then proceeds to follow the branch and then jump to the next node. Again, when it comes across the next node, it continues to compare the attribute value with the neighboring sub-nodes and continues further. This process continues until it succeeds in reaching the leaf/final node of the tree. The procedure for induction of decision tree is given below:

Step 1: The process begins with the root node (e.g., T) which holds the entire dataset.

Step 2: Then, it finds the most suitable attribute within the dataset using the **ASM ("Attribute Selection Measure") technique.**

Step 3: T is then further divided into the subsets which contain a probable value for the finest attributes.

Step 4: The DT node is then generated which possesses the finest attribute.

Step 5: A new DT is then formed through recursion, through the use of the aforementioned subsets of the dataset, which were generated in step 3. This process is repeated till the stage where the further division of the node cannot occur and this node is termed as the leaf node/final node.

Attribute Selection Measures

When we implement the DTs, the main problem that arises is in selecting the best attribute in both the case of the root node and the sub-nodes. So, to resolve these issues, a technique named Attribute Selection Measure (ASM) is implemented. Through this measurement, the most suitable attribute for the nodes of the tree is chosen. These well-known techniques are Information Gain and Gini Index.

1. Information Gain: Here, changes in the entropy are measured after the process of segmentation of the dataset based on its attributes.
   a. The amount of information a feature can provide us about a class is calculated and based on this, the node is further split to build the DT.
   b. Each time the DT attempts to maximize the information gain value, the attribute possessing the highest gain of information will be the first to get split. This is calculated through the following formula:

$$\textbf{Information Gain} = \textbf{Entropy}(T) - \left[(\textbf{Weighted Avg.})^* \textbf{Entropy (each feature)} \right]$$

   c. Entropy: This is the metric used to measure the amount of impurity of a given attribute. It determines the scale of randomness within the data. It can be determined by:
   Entropy(s) = −P(yes)log2 P(yes) − P(no) log2 P(no), where, T stands for the total number of the samples, P(yes) stands for the probability of yes occurring, and P(no) stands for the probability of no occurring.
2. Gini Index: This index is also known as the Gini Impurity; it represents the calculation of the probability of the occurrence of a specific feature that may have been classified incorrectly while being selected randomly.
   a. The impurity or purity used during the creation of a DT via the Classification and Regression Tree algorithm is measured. The attribute possessing the least Gini Index is preferred more than the attribute with a higher Gini Index.
   b. It only creates binary splits, and the Gini Index (used in the CART method) proceeds to create the binary splits. It is calculated through the use of this formula.

Pseudocode

1. A node N is created.
2. If the tuples in set D (set of training tuples) are of the same class, C then
   a. Node N is designated as a leaf node and labeled with the class C;

3. in the case of attribute_list being empty then
   a. Node N is designated as a leaf node and then is labeled along with the majority class in D;   //majority voting
4. Attribute_selection_method (D, attribute_list) is applied to discover the "best" splitting_criterion;
5. Node N is labeled with the splitting_criterion;
6. if the aforementioned splitting_criterion is discrete-valued and
   a. multiway splits are permitted then // not restricted to binary tree
   b. attribute_list <- attribute_list – splitting_attribute; // remove splitting_attribute
7. for every outcome j of the step of splitting_criterion: //partition the tuples and grow subtrees for each partition
   a. let Dj be designated as the set of the data tuples in D which satisfy the outcome j;// a partition
   b. if Dj happens to be empty then
      i. Proceed with the attachment of a leaf labeled along with the majority class D to node N;
   c. else proceed with the attachment of the node returned by Generate_decision_tree (Dj, attribute_list) to the node N;
2. end for
3. return N;

15.4.5   CNN

CNN (additionally termed "CNN/ConvNets") is a kind of ANNs which happen to be immensely powerful in the Identification field as well as the image classification field.

Four principal tasks in the implementation of CNNs are as follows:

i.   Convolution: Here, the ultimate purpose of the convolution activity in the event of the implementation of a CNN is to recognize proper highlights of the picture which are a contribution to the main layer. Convolution keeps up the interrelation of the pixels in the spatial field. This step concludes via the establishment of picture highlights utilizing minuscule squares of the picture. CNN architecture can be seen in the Figure 15.9.

Convolution equation: $S(i,j) = (I * K)(i,j) = \Sigma\Sigma I(m,n)K(i-m,j-n)$

Each picture is visualized as a lattice of pixels, each possessing its worth. An arbitrary unit termed a pixel is the smallest unit that exists in this picture framework. It is to be noted that these pictures are by and large on the RGB scale with estimations of the pixels going from the range of 0 to 255 i.e., 256 pixels.

ii.   Non-linearity: ReLu is determined as a non-straight activity. ReLu follows up at a rudimentary level, and as such, it is an activity that is executed per

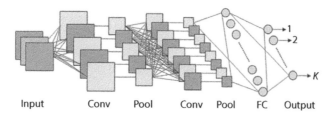

Figure 15.9 CNN architecture.

pixel and supplants all non-positive estimations of every pixel within the component map by zero. It is, by its fundamentals, a smooth guess

Equation: $f(x) = \ln(1 + e^x)$.

iii. Pooling or sub-testing: This process helps in the diminishing of the components of each element map while at the same time holding the most important data of the guide. After the process of pooling is complete, in the end, the 3D highlight map is transformed into a one-dimensional element vector.

iv. Grouping (fully connected layer): The resulting yield from these activities of convolution and pooling gives unmistakable highlights that are separated from the aforementioned picture. These highlights will then proceed to be used by the fully connected layer for consigning the information of the picture into the various classes that have been predicated on the preparation dataset.

The SoftMax classifier used in this process is the last layer of the network that will yield the actual probability of every label.

Pseudocode

Step 1. Importing libraries

Step 2. Initializing the model

Step 3. Adding all the required and hidden layers

Step 4. Pre-processing data

Step 5. Getting the training and testing data in batches of 18

Step 6. Fitting the model

Step 7. Prediction of model

Building the CNN model
# Layer 1: CONV => RELU => POOL
model = Sequential ()
model.add (Conv (20, 5,5, input_shape= (60, 60, 3))
model.add (Dropout (0.2))
model.add (Activation("relu"))   # Dropout to prevent overfitting
model.add (MaxPooling2D (pool_size= (2, 2), strides= (2, 2)))

Layer 2: CONV => RELU => POOL
model.add (Conv (50, 5, 5))
model.add (Dropout (0.2))
model.add (Activation("relu"))
model.add (MaxPooling2D (pool_size= (2, 2), strides= (2, 2)))

Layer 3: Fully Connected 1 => RELU layers
model.add (Flatten ())
model.add (Dense (500)) model
add (Dropout (0.2))
model.add (Activation("relu'))

Layer 4: SoftMax classifier
model.add (Dense (4))   # 4 output units denoting 4 classes
model.add (Dropout (0.2)
model add (Activation("SoftMax"))
model. Compile (loss='categorical cross entropy optimizer="Adam")

15.4.6   Random Forest

RF algorithm [23] uses data samples to build DTs and every DT helps to predict the class labels and finally selects the best class label through voting.

RF constructs multiple DTs combination to produce more accurate and stable predictions. The more trees within the forest, the higher the accuracy, and the problem of overfitting is avoided. RF process can be seen in the Figure 15.10.

RF is a supervised learning algorithm. The algorithms can be used for classification and regression, which constitutes most of the current machine learning systems.

The DT does the greedy selection of the best split point from the dataset at each step. Without pruning, RFs can make DTs vulnerable to high variance. By creating multiple trees using only different samples of the training dataset and mixing their predictions, this high variance can often be exploited and reduced.

This method is known as bootstrap aggregation or bagging. The limitation of bagging is that the equivalent greedy algorithm is used to make each tree, which means that equivalent or very similar split points are going to be selected in each tree so that the trees are very similar (trees are going to be correlated). This makes their predictions similar, thereby mitigating the differences that were originally sought.

We can force the choice trees by restricting the features (rows) that the greedy algorithm can find at each split point when creating the tree. This is referred to as the RF algorithm.

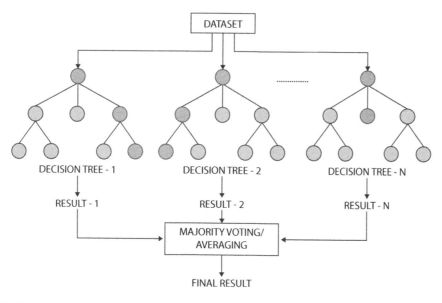

Figure 15.10 Random Forest.

Assumptions for Random Forest

The RF combines multiple trees to predict the category of the dataset, and sometimes, some DTs may predict the current output, while other DTs may not. There are some assumptions so that the tree predicts the correct output

1. The feature variable of the dataset must have some actual values so that the classifier can predict the exact results instead of guessed results.
2. The predictions from each tree must have very low correlations.

Pseudocode of Random Forest

1. Select K random data points from the training set.
2. Create a DT associated with the selected data points (Subset).
3. Select the number N for DTs to be created.
4. Repeat steps 1 and 2.
5. For new data points, find the predictions of each DT and assign the new data points to the category that won the majority votes.

Architecture

A RF is commonly known as a "meta-estimator" that is executed by fitting several DT classifiers on the various sub-samples of the dataset and use averaging to thus improve the predictive accuracy of the algorithm and control over-fitting. Within this algorithm, a low bias and low correlation factor are essential for accuracy. To get low bias, trees are grown to maximum depth. RF architecture can be seen in the Figure 15.11.

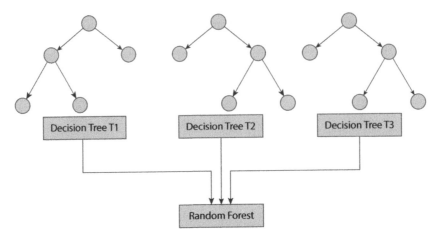

Figure 15.11 Random Forest architecture.

15.5   Result and Analysis

In the present work, we have considered the 1,400 training samples and 329 test samples for five different types of skin diseases likely actinic keratosis, melanoma, nevus, pigmented benign keratosis, and vascular lesion. We will compare the accuracy rate and find out the best algorithm among all.

Algorithm	Accuracy
CNN	94.0786%
SVM	75.22%
KNN	92.70%
DT	89.50%
RNN	95.45%
Random Forest	97.3%
Logistic Regression	73.76%

All the algorithms work well with the dataset and give and proper output as it can be seen in Figure 15.12. The accuracy score of the CNN algorithm was so far maxed in terms of output. In general, CNN is widely used for image classification.

CNN and SVM models were prepared by us on the dataset that we created and the accuracy is taken from that model, whereas for the rest of the algorithms, open-source tool was used and the result has been taken from a different user. The obtained results are compared with few machine learning algorithm in the literature [23, 28, 42, 46].

Analyzing all data, it is clear that CNN provides a better accuracy rate than the SVM in skin diseases identification. Also, based on various studies, it has been proven one of the

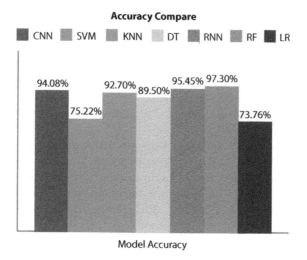

Figure 15.12 Accuracy rate.

best classification algorithms in practice. This review scarcely started to expose that CNNs, here, however, give a fundamental instinct on the above-expressed reality.

15.6   Conclusion

This research work is focused on different types of machine and deep learning algorithms like CNN and SVM for skin disease classification. The methods are very helpful to identify skin diseases very easily and in fewer periods. From the data analysis, we conclude that deep learning algorithms like CNN provides better accuracy the machine learning algorithms like SVM. CNN takes less period than SVM to classify skin diseases. In CNN, different types of layers like ReLu, Grouping, and Pooling are used that helps to provide better accuracy. It also helps to identification in less time. CNN needs lager dataset for training and testing to provide effective result in skin diseases classification.

References

1. Alkolifi Alenezi, N.S., A Method of Skin Disease Detection Using Image Processing and Machine Learning. *Proc. Comput. Sci.*, 163, 85–92, 2019, https://doi.org/10.1016/j.procs.2019.12.090.
2. Akmalia, N., Sihombing, P., Suherman, Skin Diseases Classification Using Local Binary Pattern and Convolutional Neural Network, in: *2019 3rd International Conference on Electrical, Telecommunication and Computer Engineering, ELTICOM 2019 - Proceedings*, pp. 168–173, 2019, https://doi.org/10.1109/ELTICOM47379.2019.8943892.
3. Almeida, M.A.M. and Santos, I.A.X., Classification Models for Skin Tumor Detection Using Texture Analysis in Medical Images. *J. Imaging*, 6, 6, 51, 2020, https://doi.org/10.3390/jimaging6060051.
4. Alam, M.N., Munia, T.T.K., Tavakolian, K., Vasefi, F., Mackinnon, N., Fazel-Rezai, R., Automatic detection and severity measurement of eczema using image processing. *Proceedings of the*

Annual International Conference of the IEEE Engineering in Medicine and Biology Society, EMBS, 2016-October, pp. 1365–1368, August 2016, https://doi.org/10.1109/IEMECON.2017.8079594.

5. Bhavani, R., Prakash, V., Kumaresh, R.V., Sundra Srinivasan, R., Vision-based skin disease identification using deep learning. *Int. J. Eng. Adv. Technol.*, 8, 6, 3784–3788, 2019, https://doi.org/10.35940/ijeat.F9391.088619.

6. Bhadula, S., Sharma, S., Juyal, P., Kulshrestha, C., Machine Learning Algorithms based Skin Disease Detection. *Int. J. Innov. Technol. Explor. Eng.*, 9, 2, 4044–4049, 2019, https://doi.org/10.35940/ijitee.b7686.129219.

7. Chakraborty, S., Mali, K., Chatterjee, S., Banerjee, S., Mazumdar, K.G., Debnath, M., Basu, P., Chakraborty, S., Mali, K., Chatterjee, S., Banerjee, S., Mazumdar, K.G., Debnath, M., Basu, P., Bose, S., Roy, K., Detection of skin disease using metaheuristic supported artificial neural networks, in: *2017 8th Industrial Automation and Electromechanical Engineering Conference*, IEMECON, pp. 224–229, 2017, https://doi.org/10.1109/IEMECON.2017.8079594.

8. Das, N., Pal, A., Mazumder, S., Sarkar, S., Gangopadhyay, D., Nasipuri, M., An SVM based skin disease identification using Local Binary Patterns, in: *Proceedings - 2013 3rd International Conference on Advances in Computing and Communications*, ICACC, pp. 208–211, 2013, https://doi.org/10.1109/ICACC.2013.48.

9. Daniel S. Cho, S.H., Physiological characterization of skin lesion using non-linear random forest regression model, in: *2014 36th Annual International Conference of the IEEE Engineering in Medicine and Biology Society*, IEEE, Chicago, IL, USA, 2014, https://doi.org/10.1109/embc.2014.6944340.

10. Esteva, A., Kuprel, B., Novoa, R.A., Ko, J., Swetter, S.M., Blau, H.M., Thrun, S., Dermatologist-level classification of skin cancer with deep neural networks. *Nature*, 542, 7639, 115–118, 2017, https://doi.org/10.1038/nature21056.

11. El Saleh, R., Bakhshi, S., Nait-Ali, A., Deep convolutional neural network for face skin diseases identification, in: *International Conference on Advances in Biomedical Engineering*, 2019-October, ICABME, pp. 1–4, 2019, https://doi.org/10.1109/ICABME47164.2019.8940336.

12. Ge, Z., Demyanov, S., Bozorgtabar, B., Abedini, M., Chakravorty, R., Bowling, A., Garnavi, R., Exploiting local and generic features for accurate skin lesions classification using clinical and dermoscopy imaging, in: *Proceedings - International Symposium on Biomedical Imaging*, pp. 986–990, 2017, https://doi.org/10.1109/ISBI.2017.7950681.

13. Gede, I.K., Putra, D., Putu, N., Oka, A., Wibawa, K.S., Suwija, I.M., Identification of Skin Disease Using K-Means Clustering, Discrete Wavelet Transform, Color Moments and Support Vector Machine. 10, 4, 542–548, 2020, https://doi.org/10.18178/ijmlc.2020.10.4.970.

14. Goswami, T., Dabhi, V.K., Prajapati, H.B., Skin Disease Classification from Image - A Survey, in: *2020 6th International Conference on Advanced Computing and Communication Systems*, ICACCS 2020, pp. 599–605, 2020, https://doi.org/10.1109/ICACCS48705.2020.9074232.

15. Harangi, B., Baran, A., Hajdu, A., Classification of Skin Lesions Using An Ensemble of Deep Neural Networks, in: *Proceedings of the Annual International Conference of the IEEE Engineering in Medicine and Biology Society*, 2018-July, EMBS, pp. 2575–2578, 2018, https://doi.org/10.1109/EMBC.2018.8512800.

16. Hasija, Y., Garg, N., Sourav, S., Automated detection of dermatological disorders through image-processing and machine learning, in: *Proceedings of the International Conference on Intelligent Sustainable Systems*, ICISS 2017, Iciss, pp. 1047–1051, 2018, https://doi.org/10.1109/ISS1.2017.8389340.

17. Hosseinzadeh Kassani, S. and Hosseinzadeh Kassani, P., A comparative study of deep learning architectures on melanoma detection. *Tissue Cell*, 58, April, 76–83, 2019, https://doi.org/10.1016/j.tice.2019.04.009.

18. Hameed, N., Shabut, A.M., Ghosh, M.K., Hossain, M.A., Multi-class multi-level classification algorithm for skin lesions classification using machine learning techniques. *Expert Syst. Appl.*, 141, 112961, 2020, https://doi.org/10.1016/j.eswa.2019.112961.

19. Hinton, G., Boltzmann Machines. *Encyclopedia Mach. Learn. Data Min.*, 1, 1–7, 2014, https://doi.org/10.1007/978-1-4899-7502-7_31-1.

20. Ibrahim, S.S., Clinical Image Analysis for Detection of Skin Cancer Using Convolution Neural Networks. *Theranostics Respir. Skin Dis.*, 1, 3, 61–64, 2019, https://doi.org/10.32474/trsd.2019.01.000111.

21. Kumar, V.B., Kumar, S.S., Saboo, V., Dermatological Disease Detection Using Image Processing and Machine Learning, in: *2016 3rd International Conference on Artificial Intelligence and Pattern Recognition*, AIPR 2016, pp. 88–93, 2016, https://doi.org/10.1109/ICAIPR.2016.7585217.

22. Kumar, N.V., Kumar, P.V., Pramodh, K., Karuna, Y., Classification of Skin diseases using Image processing and SVM, in: *Proceedings - International Conference on Vision Towards Emerging Trends in Communication and Networking*, ViTECoN 2019, pp. 1–5, 2019, https://doi.org/10.1109/ViTECoN.2019.8899449.

23. Kulshrestha, C., Bhadula, S., Sharma, S., Juyal, P., Machine Learning Algorithms based Skin Disease Detection. *Int. J. Innov. Technol. Explor. Eng.*, 9, 2, 4044–4049, https://doi.org/10.35940/ijitee.b7686.129219.

24. Li, W., Zhuang, J., Wang, R., Zhang, J., *Fusing Metadata and Dermoscopy Images for Skin Disease Diagnosis*, 2020, School of Data and Computer Science, Sun Yat-sen University, China Key Laboratory of Machine Intelligence and Advanced Computing, MOE, Guangzhou, China Department of Computer Science an. 1996–2000, http://www.isee-ai.cn/~wangruixuan/files/ISBI2020_2.pdf.

25. Murugan, A., Nair, S.A.H., Kumar, K.P.S., Detection of Skin Cancer Using SVM, Random Forest and kNN Classifiers. *J. Med. Syst.*, 43, 8, 269, 2019.

26. Melbin, K. and Raj, Y.J.V., *An Enhanced Model for Skin Disease Detection using Dragonfly Optimization Based Deep Neural Network*, 2019 Third International conference on I-SMAC (IoT in Social, Mobile, Analytics and Cloud) (I-SMAC), pp. 346–351, 2019.

27. Mahbod, A., Schaefer, G., Wang, C., Ecker, R., Ellinge, I., Skin Lesion Classification Using Hybrid Deep Neural Networks, in: *ICASSP, IEEE International Conference on Acoustics, Speech and Signal Processing - Proceedings*, 2019-May, pp. 1229–1233, 2019, https://doi.org/10.1109/ICASSP.2019.8683352.

28. Nandhini, S., Sofiyan, M.A., Kumar, S., Afridi, A., Skin Cancer Classification using Random Forest. *Int. J. Manage. Humanit.*, 4, 3, 39–42, 2019, https://doi.org/10.35940/ijmh.c0434.11431.

29. Nosseir, A. and Shawky, M.A., Automatic classifier for skin disease using k-NN and SVM, in: *ACM International Conference Proceeding Series*, pp. 259–262, 2019, https://doi.org/10.1145/3328833.3328862.

30. Okuboyejo, D.A., Olugbara, O.O., Odunaike, S.A., Automating skin disease diagnosis using image classification. *Lect. Notes Eng. Comput. Sci.*, 2, 850–854, 2013, https://doi.org/10.4172/2167-7964.S1.004.

31. Paja, W. and Wrzesien, M., Melanoma important features selection using random forest approach, in: *2013 6th International Conference on Human System Interactions*, 2013, HSI, pp. 415–418, 2013, https://doi.org/10.1109/HSI.2013.6577857.

32. Pal, A., Garain, U., Chandra, A., Chatterjee, R., Senapati, S., Psoriasis skin biopsy image segmentation using Deep Convolutional Neural Network. *Comput. Methods Programs Biomed.*, 159, 59–69, 2018, https://doi.org/10.1016/j.cmpb.2018.01.027.

33. Pal, A., Ray, S., Garain, U., *Skin disease identification from dermoscopy images using deep convolutional neural network*, pp. 9–10, 2018, http://arxiv.org/abs/1807.09163.

34. Patnaik, S.K., Sidhu, M.S., Gehlot, Y., Sharma, B., Muthu, P., Automated skin disease identification using deep learning algorithm. *Biomed. Pharmacol. J.*, 11, 3, 1429–1436, 2018.

35. Purnama, I.K.E., Hernanda, A.K., Ratna, A.A.P., Nurtanio, I., Hidayati, A.N., Purnomo, M.H., Nugroho, S.M.S., Rachmadi, R.F., Disease Classification based on Dermoscopic Skin Images Using Convolutional Neural Network in Teledermatology System, in: *2019 International Conference on Computer Engineering, Network, and Intelligent Multimedia, CENIM 2019 - Proceeding*, 2019-November, pp. 1–5, https://doi.org/10.1109/CENIM48368.2019.8973303.

36. Rezvantalab, A., Safigholi, H., Karimijeshni, S., *Dermatologist Level Dermoscopy Skin Cancer Classification Using Different Deep Learning Convolutional Neural Networks Algorithms*, 2018, http://arxiv.org/abs/1810.10348.

37. Rimi, T.A., Sultana, N., Ahmed Foysal, M.F., Derm-NN: Skin Diseases Detection Using Convolutional Neural Network, in: *Proceedings of the International Conference on Intelligent Computing and Control Systems, ICICCS 2020*, Iciccs, pp. 1205–1209, 2020, https://doi.org/10.1109/ICICCS48265.2020.9120925.

38. Shrivastava, V.K., Londhe, N.D., Sonawane, R.S., Suri, J.S., Exploring the color feature power for psoriasis risk stratification and classification: A data mining paradigm. *Comput. Biol. Med.*, 65, 54–68, 2015, https://doi.org/10.1016/j.compbiomed.2015.07.021.

39. Shoieb, D.A., Youssef, S.M., Aly, W.M., Computer-Aided Model for Skin Diagnosis Using Deep Learning. *J. Image Graph.*, 4, 2, 122–129, 2016, https://doi.org/10.18178/joig.4.2.122-129.

40. Sriwong, K., Bunrit, S., Kerdprasop, K., Kerdprasop, N., Dermatological classification using deep learning of skin image and patient background knowledge. *Int. J. Mach. Learn. Comput.*, 9, 6, 862–867, 2019, https://doi.org/10.18178/ijmlc.2019.9.6.884.

41. Shanthi, T., Sabeenian, R.S., Anand, R., Automatic diagnosis of skin diseases using convolution neural network. *Microprocess. Microsyst.*, 76, 103074, 2020, https://doi.org/10.1016/j.micpro.2020.103074.

42. S., R. D., P., A. C., Raghuraman, M., Classification of Skin Lesion using Pattern Features with Recurrent Neural Network (RNN). 9, 3, 20947–20949, 2019.

43. S.T., Neehal, Junayed, M.S., Jeny, A.A., Atik, N., Karim, A., Azam, S., Shanmugam, B., AcneNet - A deep CNN based classification approach for acne classes, in: *Proceedings of 2019 International Conference on Information and Communication Technology and Systems, ICTS 2019*, pp. 203–208, 2019, https://doi.org/10.1109/ICTS.2019.8850935.

44. Tan, T.Y., Zhang, L., Jiang, M., An intelligent decision support system for skin cancer detection from dermoscopic images, in: *2016 12th International Conference on Natural Computation, Fuzzy Systems and Knowledge Discovery, ICNC-FSKD 2016*, pp. 2194–2199, 2016, https://doi.org/10.1109/FSKD.2016.7603521.

45. Velasco, J., Pascion, C., Alberio, J.W., Apuang, J., Cruz, J.S., Gomez, A., Molina, B.J., Tuala, L., Thio-ac, A., Jorda, R.J., A Smartphone-Based Skin Disease Classification Using MobileNet CNN. *Int. J. Adv. Trends Comput. Sci. Eng.*, 2019, https://doi.org/10.30534/ijatcse/2019/116852019. Available Online at http://www.warse.org/IJATCSE/static/pdf/file/ijatcse116852019.pdf, 8, 5, September-October 2019.

46. Victor, A. and Ghalib, M.R., Automatic detection and classification of skin cancer. *Int. J. Intell. Eng. Syst.*, 10, 3, 444–451, 2017, https://doi.org/10.22266/ijies2017.0630.50.

47. Yang, J., Sun, X., Liang, J., Rosin, P.L., Clinical Skin Lesion Diagnosis Using Representations Inspired by Dermatologist Criteria, in: *Proceedings of the IEEE Computer Society Conference on Computer Vision and Pattern Recognition*, pp. 1258–1266, 2018, https://doi.org/10.1109/CVPR.2018.00137.

48. Zaqout, I.S., Diagnosis of Skin Lesions Based on Dermoscopic Images Using Image Processing Techniques. *Int. J. Signal Processing, Image Process. Pattern Recognition*, 9, 9, 189–204, 2016, https://doi.org/10.14257/ijsip.2016.9.9.18.

49. Zhou, H., Xie, F., Jiang, Z., Liu, J., Wang, S., Zhu, C., Multi-classification of skin diseases for dermoscopy images using deep learning, in: *IST 2017 - IEEE International Conference on Imaging Systems and Techniques, Proceedings*, 2018-January, pp. 1–5, 2017, https://doi.org/10.1109/IST.2017.8261543.

50. Zhang, X., Wang, S., Liu, J., Tao, C., Computer-aided diagnosis of four common cutaneous diseases using deep learning algorithm, in: *Proceedings - 2017 IEEE International Conference on Bioinformatics and Biomedicine*, 2017-January, BIBM 2017, pp. 1304–1306, 2017, https://doi.org/10.1109/BIBM.2017.8217850.

16

Asymptotic Patients' Healthcare Monitoring and Identification of Health Ailments in Post COVID-19 Scenario

Pushan K.R. Dutta*, Akshay Vinayak and Simran Kumari

Amity School of Engineering and Technology, Amity University Kolkata Major Arterial Road, Newtown, Kolkata, West Bengal, India

Abstract

COVID-19 patients have been admitted to hospitals based on the reports of clinical symptoms associated with pulmonary disease identification. Medical Informatics has attracted attention for past five decades; however, while working with this discipline with existing artificial intelligence techniques. In EMR and CDSS, focus is then directed to the knowledge-based method, which is a very low-cost option. Over the past two decades, CBDSS (Case-Based Decision Support System), knowledge-based systems in medicine, especially in EMR (Electronic Medical Recording) and CDSS (Clinical Decision Support System), have gained a lot of interest due to the possible benefits that can be derived at a low cost. In a medical context, they can promote increasing efficiency; help diagnosis, decision-making in the management of the illness, and any other form of medical decision-making; assist in the training of medical practitioners; assist in medical study, technique, data, and information; and can also perform some routine activities in a medical environment. In this proposed methodology, we will be keeping track of heartbeat, pulse rate, geographical inclination, the temperature of the body, and the location of the patients (GPS). These parameters will be under watch for abnormalities. Reducing human intervention as much as possible, we prepared this model that will be able to keep an eye on the parameters related to the symptoms of COVID-19. As per the guidelines of WHO, the common symptoms of COVID-19 are the rise in temperature of the body and time-to-time chills which are eminent and that can be observed with the help of the LM35 temperature sensor. Patients not quarantining and moving away from the prescribed place/location can be tracked using the NEO6mV2 GPS module. Around the same time, by moral judgments, it will enhance the quality of treatment and minimize the cost of care by disposing of the need for a parental figure to efficiently participate in data collection, examination, knowledge assortment, and analysis.

Keywords: Asymptotic, COVID detection, temperature evaluation, routine management

*Corresponding author: pkdutta@kol.amity.edu

Om Prakash Jena, Alok Ranjan Tripathy, Ahmed A. Elngar and Zdzislaw Polkowski (eds.) Computational Intelligence and Healthcare Informatics, (297–312) © 2021 Scrivener Publishing LLC

16.1 Introduction

In a developing country like India, where already established classic medical infrastructure is too little for the mass. Successful implementation of Telemedicine project "Telemedik" in the state of West Bengal for the first time in India has shown that application of Medical Informatics is the answer [1]. At the same time, we cannot afford wide research and implementation of expensive artificial intelligence techniques in all the cases. Knowledge-based EMR is low-cost and knowledge-intensive sector which can be easily applied with low budget and good group of clinician advisors [2]. The Internet of Things (IoT) has made us understand the dream of the more trendy future in practice and it has many application domains like healthcare. In smart healthcare, the confluence of IoT-cloud will play a notable role by providing deeper integration through healthcare content to promote reliable and quality patient care [3]. The goal of IoT in healthcare is to empower oneself to lead a healthier life by integrating wirelessly connected devices.

There, the number of doctoral ward members is short in hand and is facing a lot of trouble to help people who are exposed and have to observe patients in quarantine. The most relevant clinical predictors for the death of this illness are hypertension and cardiovascular diseases. In the later phase of this disease, infected individuals are characterized by continuous difficulty in breathing, tachypnoea, severe acute respiratory distress syndrome, or life-threatening complexities.

The uncommon symptoms of COVID-19 are tiredness and fatigue, headache, shortness of breath, chest pain, and diarrhea. All the unusual symptoms result in increased heart rate, pulse rate, and geographical inclination that is notifiable when compared to a healthy person. This elevation of heart rate and pulse rate and the inclination angle is recorded, with the help of respective sensors. The data values are generated [8–11], with the help of sensors. The data is next examined for any ambiguity of the patient. The thresholds of every sensor are calculated and accordingly are fixed. If any abnormalities found in the patient, then several necessary actions and precautions are followed. The overall system is designed, in such a way, that the doctors or the officials may append the made model to several quarantined patients. By this, they can examine the patients from a distance without any issue of involvement or exposing themselves. The output that is generated by the proposed system is transmitted to a web server then from the observer to a platform convenient for the doctors to examine their patients. In using IoT technology in the healthcare field, it not only provides changes and benefits to doctors and administrators in meeting a wide variety of data sources but also explores nuanced IoT data access, especially in the remote context of real-time IoT application methods.

16.1.1 Motivation

Several authors have exhibited their meaningful contributions to numerous healthcare fields from a diverse viewpoint. But still, there is much more technique that demands to be explored. There is a strong link between the medical healthcare field and the IoT, here are few techniques that few authors have used such as [31] information IoT telemedicine healthcare region by instant heart rate monitoring for the elderly living isolated network or alone. Authors in [4] demonstrate the evolving component of IoT in different domains in order to recognize its importance in healthcare. In [5], there is a great overseer to develop the other associated areas. Researchers in [6] expect developments in creative data transmission of digital mobile healthcare value. Another study shows that wearables [33] are used to monitor their patients and collect data for clinical examination tests and educational research studies that make health as a medical device wearable. Another author [34] measured a person's heart rate and calories consumed every day, and from that, it is expected that the entire patient's body should be tracked to facilitate a healthier standard of living [35]. The author presents a solution focused on how data is connected to IoT-based healthcare systems using a Raspberry Pi and docker. Raspberry Pi collects and collects the medicinal data through linked sensors. The received data can be transferred to the user through mobile apps which is then analyzed for improving the health of the patients [12–16].

16.1.2   Contributions

When we go to the physician and see him examining us, we do not realize that he/she is actually noting some value (describing the finding) against a given parameter. That value varies according to the parameter, again the parameter varies according to part of the body/ organ the physician is examining. The information generated by the customized application allows a significant reduction of operational costs in the Clinical Establishment. While working on this, we realized that a human readable knowledge base is the best option that I can work with, as creating an EMR was our target, not any decision to arrive at. Let us try to preserve healthy health by practises to improve health, upholding the "keeping healthy laws" and lifestyle of prevention [17]. Cases found were registered samples in the laboratories that were only being checked and may not correspond to the population's daily rate or real figures.

16.1.3   Paper Organization

Day by day, the number of patients infected by this virus is exponentially increasing which is giving a tough time to the administrators and the doctors [18, 19]. The medicinal service plot is centered around the estimation and checking different natural parameters of the patient's body like heart pulse, heart rate, and body temperature, the orientation of data at whatever point required from anyplace and need not physically present. If the threshold value crosses as measured by the scattered values that differ from the normal values, then the alarm is triggered and emergency contacts to the nearby quarantine centers are informed.

16.1.4   System Model Problem Formulation

In the current scenario, where the world is plagued by the deadly Corona Virus Disease (COVID-19) with the virus spreading rampantly, how fast the infection can spread is a gripping question on everyone's mind [20–24], and it is something that most of us do not have a good intuition for. In this paper, we aim to simulate a mathematical model for predicting the rate of spread of the infectious COVID-19 disease which would also be beneficial for the future analysis of the control of the disease. The vaccine would spur an immune response by inducing cells to create the antigen, allowing the body to develop antibodies that would protect against infection. Guidelines for utilizing an ECG system have been suggested.

A portion of the methodologies using heart rate monitoring in their device, the monitor using, continuously measures the patient's BPM. Temperature sensors were an essential fundamental technique for the examinations conducted in this specific subject, we also suggested a system that takes patients' temperature analysis by some amount of imagination period and also takes care of the customer's orientation while the customer is on the bed or in a particular role [25], and this has been spared potential references. Distributed computing has been used in recent years, where each of the patient's readings was transferred and protected on a remote server. Enabling clients to get to the recorded information over the web, moreover, can be seen by numerous partners of the framework. One-touch call alternative is a significant component of any patient checking framework; this strategy is under a prototyped phase.

16.1.5 Proposed Methodology

Reducing the human intervention as much as possible, this model is prepared which will be able to keep an eye on the parameters related to the symptoms of COVID-19. As per the guidelines of WHO, the common symptoms of COVID-19 are rise in temperature of the body and time-to-time chills which are eminent and that can be observed with the help of LM35 temperature sensor [26]. Patient not quarantining and moving away from the prescribed place/location can be tracked using NEO6mV2 GPS module. All the uncommon symptoms result in increased heart rate, pulse rate, and geographical inclination which can be notifiable when compared to a healthy person. The thresholds are set accordingly, and if found any abnormalities in the patient, certain necessary actions adhere [27]. The output that is generated by the proposed system is sent to a webserver from there to a platform convenient for the doctors. The overall working model can be illustrated in Figure 16.1.

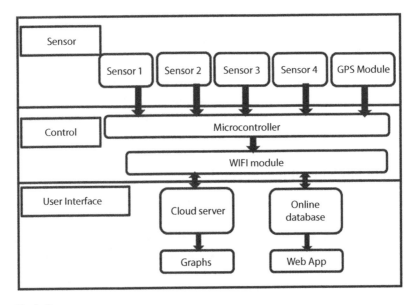

Figure 16.1 Block diagram.

16.2   Material Properties and Design Specifications

16.2.1   Hardware Components

16.2.1.1   *Microcontroller*

A microcontroller board with its open-source IoT and electronics project creation platform based on the Arduino Uno, also known as ATmega328. Arduino has both a programmable physical circuit board (often referred to as a microcontroller) and a piece of software consistent with operating on our devices or IDE (Integrated Programming Environment). You just need to mount it to a device with a USB cable or power it with an adapter or battery from AC to DC to get started, so it contains everything you need to support the microcontroller. The system operates within such a range of 1.8–5.5 V. By executing powerful instructions in one single clock cycle and by balancing power consumption and CPU usage, the device achieves throughputs exceeding 1 MIPS per MHz.

16.2.1.2   *ESP8266 Wi-Fi Shield*

The Wi-Fi shield commonly known as ESP8266 is a popular, low-cost, system-on-chip (SoC) Wi-Fi/microcontroller. While it can be used vital to establish a connection as it is easy to operate and comes with beautiful bandwidth connectivity, it can also be programmed easily like any microcontroller; the popularity of the ESP8266 has been gained as a simple, serially controlled Wi-Fi gateway. Using an AT command collection, it can be used to connect to Wi-Fi networks over TCP or UDP and to communicate with the rest of the Internet. It is a simple (and inexpensive!) way to get your Arduino online!

16.2.2   Sensors

16.2.2.1   *Temperature Sensor (LM 35)*

This is a small black colored precision integrated-circuit sensor that is used for taking temperature readings of our surroundings. The sensor operates on 3.3 V and has a heating point of 0.08°C in still air. This is a local sensor and can be found in any tech shops.

16.2.2.2   *ECG Sensor (AD8232)*

Electrocardiogram sensor is a test that measures the physical activity of the heart to show whether it is working fine or not. The AD232 sensor sends an electric signal of 5 V from the integrated chip to its pads which we are placing on our hand and chest. These electric signals check for heart pulse and revert to the output monitor.

16.2.2.3   *Pulse Sensor*

This sensor is much similar to the heart rate sensor, but instead of taking heart rate measures, it reads the heartbeat pulse in real time. This sensor is a plug and plays a sort of sensor which operates on 3.3 and 5 V, respectively. The sensor can be used easily by anyone like students for their projects, athletes, and so on. The microchip that is connected to the tip of the sensor helps in reading the heartbeat pulse.

16.2.2.4 GPS Module (NEO 6M V2)

This sensor is also known as GPS (Global Positioning Systems) module. This device consists of a chip that receives and transmits the GPS signal from the satellite that revolves around the earth and accordingly assists the user in drawing the longitude and latitude, such that one can track the position or area where this device is active. We have used this sensor to track the shipment of the fruit container so that we can easily find the location of the ship.

16.2.2.5 Gyroscope (GY-521)

This sensor is known as angular velocity or angular rate sensor which helps in determining the geographical orientation of the body. The sensor adds some additional information to the accelerometer that is by tracking rotation or twisting to the value. This sensor is operated on 3–5 V. All the sensors are graphically represented in Figure 16.2.

16.2.3 Software Components

16.2.3.1 Arduino Software

To get started with the Arduino UNO microcontroller, we need an IDE (Integrated Development Environment) to process the running state of the sensor. This software is open source and can work on Mac, Windows, and Linux. The environment of the system is scripted in java which makes it platform-independent. This software is independent of any Arduino board. The basic programming language or you call it the Arduino language is embedded C++ or C.

16.2.3.2 MySQL Database

Storing sensors extracted data to MySQL database and retrieving that data to the dashboard so that operations can be performed on them, which is discussed later in this report.

16.2.3.3 Wireless Communication

This is the establishment of remote connection with the server taking the help of TCP/IP and HTTP/HTTPS protocol, which is discussed later in this paper.

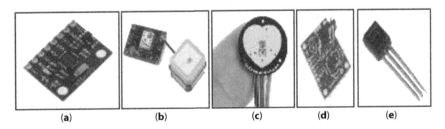

(a)   (b)   (c)   (d)   (e)

Figure 16.2 (a) LM-35 temperature sensor, (b) AD8232 heart rate sensor, (c) pulse rate sensor, (d) NEO 6M V2 GPS module, (e) GY-521 gyroscope sensor

16.3   Experimental Methods and Materials

16.3.1   Simulation Environment

Work process and procedures include the following components and is described in Figure 16.3.

16.3.1.1   System Hardware

Independent systems have different designs and are based on different functionalities. In this project, the design includes a single microcontroller, various types of sensors, internet connectivity for the prototype, and a laptop [28–30]. Apart from the server, the entire unit will be attached to the patients' bodies with the help of a band or some sort of attachments. In the current working process, the microcontroller is configured with some of the sensors, namely, Neo 6m gyroscope, ECG, and pulse sensor to get the readings of the patient. The system generates an output which is then sent to the remote server with the help of wireless connection, TCP/IP, and HTTPS and MQTT protocol. The server is connected to the cloud (database) and the data is stored in the cloud itself. This output is also reflected in the dashboard that is fetching the data from the database and helps the user to keep an eye on any kind of rise in values.

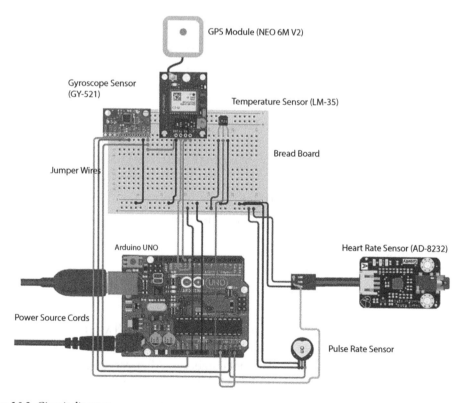

Figure 16.3 Circuit diagram.

16.3.1.2   *Connection and Circuitry*

NodeMCU Esp8266: To operate the microcontroller, power source needed is 3.3–4.7 V which is given through USB port via Laptop or with the help of batteries. The baud rate is set to 9,600–153,200 m/s; the port is selected as COM (Computer Monitor Output Screen).

16.3.1.2.1   Creation of Database and Website

16.3.1.2.1.1   HOSTING PHP APPLICATION AND CREATION OF MYSQL DATABASE

The goal here is to create a database along with the website for the project such that sensors data can be stored and analysed as per requirements. For this, we need to have the domain name of this project and hosting account which will allow the user to store sensor readings from the microcontroller, i.e., NODEMCU ESP8266 so that one can visualize the readings from anywhere in the world by accessing the server name and domain address.

16.3.1.2.1.2   CREATION OF API (APPLICATION PROGRAMMING INTERFACES) KEY

An API is a device that renders a machine digestible of data from a website. By loading pages with sensor data and submitting forms and many other things, a computer can view and edit data just like a person can. When systems connect through an API, we say they are integrated. One side is the server which supports the API, and the other side is the application which consumes and can control the API.

Here, API key value is generated from the GoDaddy developers' page and then used to link both the PHP code and ESP8266 code as well so that the data can be transferred from NODEMCU to the website.

    i.   API key value: Application Program Interface is a set of routines and some set of rules that are followed when developing software. API specifies how system software components should interact with each other.

Here, API key value is generated from Google's cloud platform for using maps services. Example:
$api_key_value= "3mM44UaC2DjFcV_63GZ14aWJcRDNmYBMsxceu"

16.3.1.2.1.3   PREPARING MySQL DATABASE

To prepare My SQL database, we need to follow these steps:

    i.   Creation of database
    ii.   Creation of user and username
    iii.   Creation of password and SQL table.

16.3.1.2.1.4   CREATION AND INSERTION OF VALUES IN SQL TABLE

Structured Query Language is a standard database language that is used in this project to create, maintain, and retrieve the relational databases. After creating database and user account info, with the help of cPanel and PhpMyAdmin, the creation of a database table is done. To create the table, the following code snipped is required.

CREATE TABLE Sensor Data (id INT (6) UNSIGNED AUTO_INCREMENT PRIMARY KEY,
value1 VARCHAR (10),
value2 VARCHAR (10),
value3 VARCHAR (10),
value4 VARCHAR (10),
value5 VARCHAR (10),
value6 VARCHAR (10),
reading-time TIMESTAMP DEFAULT CURRENT_TIMESTAMP ON UPDATE CURRENT_ TIMESTAMP

After the creation of table is done according to the values that we need to present, the value insertion process to the database is set with the help of following code snippet:

```
$sql = "INSERT INTO Sensor Data (id, value1, value2, value3, value4, value5, value6)
VALUES ('" . id . "', '" . $value1 . "', '" . $value2 . "', '" . $value3 . "', '" . $value4 . "', '" . $value5 . "', '" . $value6 . "')"
```

16.3.1.2.1.5 ADDING DYNAMIC GRAPH TO THE WEBSITE

Graphs are also added to the website such that the values can be easily be interpreted and certain estimations can be taken in short hand notice. Adding graph to the project is an essential part because it helps to take a record of the situation and further analysis can be done on the graph to suspect the condition of the patient. We are displaying graphs for temperature, heart rate, pulse rate, and geographic inclination. Code snippet of graph is as follows:

```
// function for creation of graphs.
function createTemperatureGraph () {
  const temperature = document.getElementById('temperature').getContext('2d');
temperaturemyChart = new Chart (temperature, {
 type: 'line',
 data: {
 labels: []
datasets: [
{
label: "Temperature (Celsius)",
data: [],
backgroundColor: "transparent",
borderColor: "orange"
}
]
};
options: {
 scales: {
   yAxes: [{
    ticks: {
```

```
    beginAtZero: false
  }
}
});
```

In the graph page and reading page itself, we have also added an option of downloading the data set. That is done so that the data that we take real time can be read carefully and predictions can be made on the condition of the keep of the particular victim. The data can be downloaded in (.)jason format and .txt format.

16.3.1.3   Protocols Used

16.3.1.3.1   TCP/IP
The *Transmission Control Protocol/ Internet Protocol* is a set of networking protocols that helps in inter-communication of several computers on a specific server-side client-side domain. The protocol provides end-to-end communication specifying how the data should be arranged, packetized, addressed, routed, transmitted, and received [31]. This protocol is a standardized protocol that is used in the project to make a server and client communication successful.

16.3.1.3.2   UART
The *Universal Asynchronous Receiver Transmitter Protocol* is used to establish a communication link between the system (laptop/PC) and the microcontroller. This protocol helps in receiving and transmitting the data packet that is sent by the microcontroller to the system. There is no clock as it tells its asynchronous and also receiver and transmitter need to be on the same baud rate and bit rate.

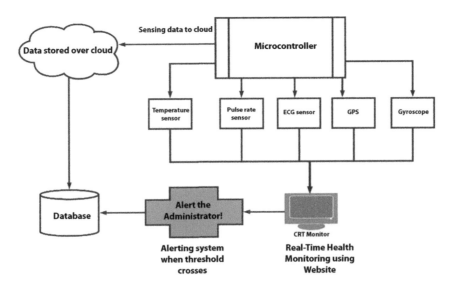

Figure 16.4 Data flow diagram.

16.3.1.3.3   I2C Protocol

The *Inter-Integrated Communication Protocol* is a master-slave communication protocol that is some set of rules and regulations that allow electronic devices to connect and communicate with one another. There are start bit, device address bits, read-write bits, and stop bits in the architecture of this protocol. The sole purpose of this protocol is to set communication between the microcontroller and the sensors.

16.3.1.3.4   MQTT

The *Message Queue Telemetry Transport Protocol* is a publish-subscribe messaging protocol that allows the device to publish the data on unique channels. There are a large overhead data and IoT devices and sensors containing limited processing capabilities and contained internet bandwidth, usage of HTTP and HTTPS cannot be feasible where the overhead of data is very much. Hence, the use of MQTT protocol is necessary.

16.3.1.4   Libraries Used

16.3.1.4.1   ESP8266WiFi.h

To run the module on internet connectivity, we require either GSM or Wi-Fi connectivity, for this server and client connection need to be established. This library helps in establishing the connection between the server and the client.

16.3.1.4.2   ESP8266HTTPClient.h

This library is similar to the above library; it identifies the client and helps in connection establishment.

16.3.1.4.3   Pulse-Sensor-Playground.h

This is the library used for the pulse sensor to help the sensor in taking readings more accurately.

16.3.1.4.4   Tinygpsplus.h

This is the library for the GPS Module, with the help of this gaining the latitudes and longitudes is much easier.

16.3.1.4.5   Adafruit-Sensor-Master

This library is used for the AD8232 heart rate sensor such that the heart pulse reading can be derived in the aesthetic state of the heart.

16.4   Simulation Results

The website that is developed will constantly update the data of the patients and the graphs will tell us about the condition of the patient if and when there are certain abnormalities reflected. The respective data of the patient can also be downloaded from the website so that further medication can be provided to the patient as required. The overall flow of working system suggested in Figure 16.4 and Figure 16.5 to 16.11 describe stepwise process, simulation and result of the proposed mehodology.

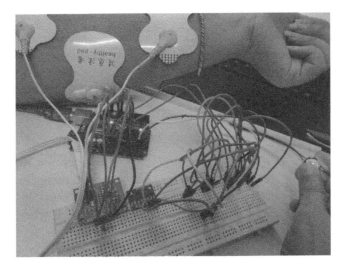

Figure 16.5 A working prototype.

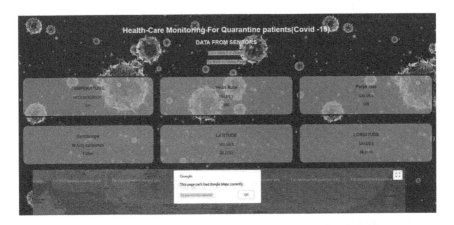

Figure 16.6 Reading on website.

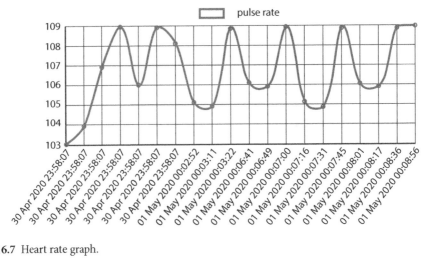

Figure 16.7 Heart rate graph.

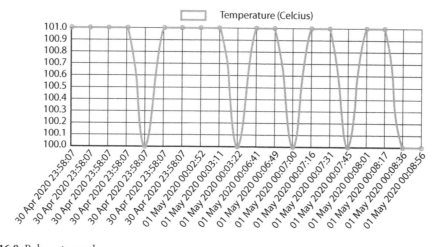

Figure 16.8 Pulse rate graph.

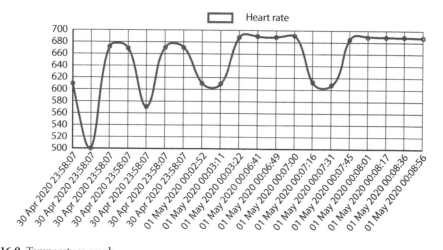

Figure 16.9 Temperature graph.

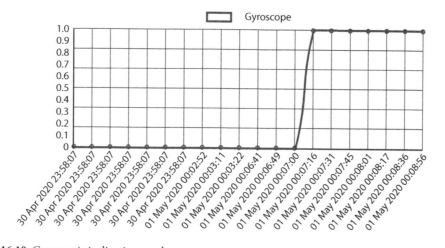

Figure 16.10 Gyroscopic inclination graph.

	id	value1	value2	value3	value4	value5	value6	reading_time
☐ 🖉 Edit ⬚ Copy ⊖ Delete	77	101	610	22.5703	88.5116	105	0	2020-05-01 00:02:52
☐ 🖉 Edit ⬚ Copy ⊖ Delete	78	101	610	22.5703	88.5116	105	0	2020-05-01 00:03:11
☐ 🖉 Edit ⬚ Copy ⊖ Delete	79	100	690	22.5703	88.5116	109	0	2020-05-01 00:03:22
☐ 🖉 Edit ⬚ Copy ⊖ Delete	80	101	690	22.5703	88.5116	106	0	2020-05-01 00:06:41
☐ 🖉 Edit ⬚ Copy ⊖ Delete	81	101	690	22.5703	88.5116	106	0	2020-05-01 00:06:49
☐ 🖉 Edit ⬚ Copy ⊖ Delete	82	100	690	22.5703	88.5116	109	0	2020-05-01 00:07:00
☐ 🖉 Edit ⬚ Copy ⊖ Delete	83	101	610	22.5703	88.5116	105	1	2020-05-01 00:07:16
☐ 🖉 Edit ⬚ Copy ⊖ Delete	84	101	610	22.5703	88.5116	105	1	2020-05-01 00:07:31
☐ 🖉 Edit ⬚ Copy ⊖ Delete	85	100	690	22.5703	88.5116	109	1	2020-05-01 00:07:45
☐ 🖉 Edit ⬚ Copy ⊖ Delete	86	101	690	22.5703	88.5116	106	1	2020-05-01 00:08:01
☐ 🖉 Edit ⬚ Copy ⊖ Delete	87	101	690	22.5703	88.5116	106	1	2020-05-01 00:08:17
☐ 🖉 Edit ⬚ Copy ⊖ Delete	88	100	690	22.5703	88.5116	109	1	2020-05-01 00:08:36
☐ 🖉 Edit ⬚ Copy ⊖ Delete	89	100	690	22.5703	88.5116	109	1	2020-05-01 00:08:56

Figure 16.11 Database entries: value1, temperature; value2, heart rate; value3, latitude; value4, longitude; value5, pulse rate; value6, geographic inclination.

16.5 Conclusion

We developed a program for collecting heart rhythm, pulse rate temperature, and inclination data from patients. With the support of the IoT devices sent to doctors and administrators to control, the program is able to get all the above mentioned parameter and method got data in a specific predefined form. This device has the power to transfer data to the webserver, too. Intelligent functions include reliable truthful data and operations; capture, process, interpret, and monitor information; and integrate all decision-making processes as the threshold for all sensors is given. Such functions help automate patient monitoring programs remotely and thereby enhance the quality of medical care and reducing costs [32]. Through this study, it is foreseen to track the whole body of the sufferer from a distant location and to expand the technology to the world widely for patient tracking through the delivery of customized care, which will provide a more true example of living.

16.6 Abbreviations and Acronyms

IoT   Internet of Things;
Wi-Fi   Wireless Fidelity
LCD   Liquid Crystal Display
USB   Universal Serial Bus;
PWM   Pulse Width Modulation
DC   Direct Current
LM35   Temperature sensor
ECG   Electrocardiogram
SoC   System-on-Chip
PDA   Personal Digital Assistant
UDP   User Datagram Protocol
SQL   Structured Query Language

References

1. Al-Fuqaha, A., Guizani, M., Mohammadi, M., Aledhari, M., Ayyash, M., Internet of things: A survey on enabling technologies, protocols, and applications. *IEEE Commun. Surv. Tutorials*, 17, 4, 2347–2376, 2015.

2. Perrier, E., *Positive disruption: Healthcare, ageing and participation in the age of technology*, The McKell Institute, Sydney, NSW, Australia, 2015.

3. Gheraibia, Y., Kabir, S. and Sikdar, B., A secure IoT-based modern healthcare system with fault-tolerant decision making process. *IEEE J. Biomed. Health Inf.*, 1–1, 2020. 10.1109/JBHI.2020.3007488.

4. Sodhro, A.H., Pirbhulal, S., Sangaiah, A.K., Convergence of IoT and product lifecycle management in medical healthcare. *Future Gener. Comput. Syst.*, 86, 380–391, 2018.

5. Pirbhulal, S., Wu, W., Mukhopadhyay, S.C., Li, G., A medical-IoT based framework for eHealthcare, in: *2018 International Symposium in Sensing and Instrumentation in IoT Era (ISSI)*, IEEE, pp. 1–4, 2018 September.

6. Zhu, N., Diethe, T., Camplani, M., Tao, L., Burrows, A., Twomey, N., Craddock, I., Bridging e-health and the internet of things: The sphere project. *IEEE Intell. Syst.*, 30, 4, 39–46, 2015.

7. Chang, S.H., Chiang, R.D., Wu, S.J., Chang, W.T., A context-aware, interactive M-health system for diabetics. *IT Prof.*, 18, 3, 14–22, 2016.

8. Pasluosta, C.F., Gassner, H., Winkler, J., Klucken, J., Eskofier, B.M., An emerging era in the management of Parkinson's disease: wearable technologies and the internet of things. *IEEE J. Biomed. Health Inf.*, 19, 6, 1873–1881, 2015.

9. Fan, Y.J., Yin, Y.H., Da Xu, L., Zeng, Y., Wu, F., IoT-based smart rehabilitation system. *IEEE Trans. Ind. Inf.*, 10, 2, 1568–1577, 2014.

10. Sarkar, S. and Misra, S., From micro to nano: The evolution of wireless sensor-based healthcare. *IEEE Pulse*, 7, 1, 21–25, 2016.

11. Yuehong, Y., II, Zeng, Y., Chen, X., Fan, Y., The internet of things in healthcare: An overview. *J. Ind. Inf. Integr.*, 1, 3–13, 2016.

12. Islam, S.R., Kwak, D., Kabir, M.H., Hossain, M., Kwak, K.S., The internet of things for healthcare: a comprehensive survey. *IEEE Access*, 3, 678–708, 2015.

13. Dimitrov, D.V., Medical internet of things and big data in healthcare. *Healthc. Inform. Res.*, 22, 3, 156–163, 2016.

14. Poon, C.C., Lo, B.P., Yuce, M.R., Alomainy, A., Hao, Y., Body sensor networks: In the era of big data and beyond. *IEEE Rev. Biomed. Eng.*, 8, 4–16, 2015.

15. Schwab, K., The Fourth Industrial Revolution: what it means, how to respond. *World Economic Forum*, 2016, Retrieved from https://www. weforum. org/agenda/2016/01/the-fourth-industrial-revolution-what-it-means-and-how-to-respond.

16. Smart Parking, *SmartEye, SmartRep, and RFID Technology*, Westminster City Council, London, 2017, [Online]. Available: www.smartparking.com/keep-up-to-date/case-studies/3-500-vehicle-detection-sensors-and-epermit-technologyin-the-city-of-westminster-london.

17. Catarinucci, L., De Donno, D., Mainetti, L., Palano, L., Patrono, L., Stefanizzi, M.L., Tarricone, L., An IoT-aware architecture for smart healthcare systems. *IEEE Internet Things J.*, 2, 6, 515–526, 2015.

18. Woo, M.W., Lee, J., Park, K., A reliable IoT system for personal healthcare devices. *Future Gener. Comput. Syst.*, 78, 626–640, 2018.

19. Farahani, B., Firouzi, F., Chang, V., Badaroglu, M., Constant, N., Mankodiya, K., Towards fog-driven IoT eHealth: Promises and challenges of IoT in medicine and healthcare. *Future Gener. Comput. Syst.*, 78, 659–676, 2018.

20. Firouzi, F., Rahmani, A.M., Mankodiya, K., Badaroglu, M., Merrett, G.V., Wong, P., Farahani, B., Internet-of-Things and big data for smarter healthcare: From device to architecture, applications and analytics, Future Generation Computer Systems, 78 (Part 2), 583–586, 2018.

21. Islam, S.R., Kwak, D., Kabir, M.H., Hossain, M., Kwak, K.S., The internet of things for healthcare: a comprehensive survey. *IEEE Access*, 3, 678–708, 2015.

22. Fourati, H., Khssibi, S., Val, T., Idoudi, H., Van Den Bossche, A., Saidane, L.A., Comparative study of IEEE 802.15. 4 and IEEE 802.15. 6 for WBAN-based CANet. International Journal of Engineering Research & Technology (IJERT) PEMWN – 2015, 4, 04, 1–7.

23. Machado, F.M., Koehler, I.M., Ferreira, M.S., Sovierzoski, M.A., An mHealth remote monitor system approach applied to MCC using ECG signal in an android application, in: *New Advances in Information Systems and Technologies*, pp. 43–49, Springer, Cham, 2016.

24. Maia, P., Batista, T., Cavalcante, E., Baffa, A., Delicato, F.C., Pires, P.F., Zomaya, A., A Web platform for interconnecting body sensors and improving healthcare. *Proc. Comput. Sci.*, 40, 135–142, 2014.

25. Serafim, E. and Motoyama, S., *Estrutura de rede baseadaemtecnologia IoT para atendimentomédicoemáreasurbanas e rurais*, Doctoral dissertation, Master's thesis, Programa de MestradoemCiência da Computação, Faculdade Campo LimpoPaulista, 2014.

26. Laine, T.H., Lee, C., Suk, H., Mobile gateway for ubiquitous healthcare system using zigbee and bluetooth, in: *2014 Eighth International Conference on Innovative Mobile and Internet Services in Ubiquitous Computing*, IEEE, pp. 139–145, 2014, July.

27. Rodrigues, J.J., Segundo, D.B.D.R., Junqueira, H.A., Sabino, M.H., Prince, R.M., Al-Muhtadi, J., De Albuquerque, V.H.C., Enabling technologies for the internet of health things. *IEEE Access*, 6, 13129–13141, 2018.

28. Rodrigues, J.J., Segundo, D.B.D.R., Junqueira, H.A., Sabino, M.H., Prince, R.M., Al-Muhtadi, J., De Albuquerque, V.H.C., Enabling technologies for the internet of health things. *IEEE Access*, 6, 13129–13141, 2018.

29. Matar, G., Lina, J.M., Carrier, J., Riley, A., Kaddoum, G., Internet of Things in sleep monitoring: An application for posture recognition using supervised learning, in: *2016 IEEE 18th International Conference on e-Health Networking, Applications and Services (Healthcom)*, IEEE, pp. 1–6, 2016.

30. Istepanian, R.S., Hu, S., Philip, N.Y., Sungoor, A., The potential of Internet of m-health Things "m-IoT" for non-invasive glucose level sensing, in: *2011 Annual International Conference of the IEEE Engineering in Medicine and Biology Society*, IEEE, pp. 5264–5266, 2011, August.

31. Senthilkumar, R., Ponmagal, R.S., Sujatha, K., Efficient healthcare monitoring and emergency management system using IoT. *Int. J. Control Theory Appl.*, 9, 4, 137–145, 2016.

32. Pirbhulal, S., Wu, W., Mukhopadhyay, S.C., Li, G., A medical-IoT based framework for eHealthcare, in: *2018 International Symposium in Sensing and Instrumentation in IoT Era (ISSI)*, IEEE, pp. 1–4, 2018.

33. Patel, S., Park, H., Bonato, P., Chan, L., Rodgers, M., A review of wearable sensors and systems with application in rehabilitation. *J. Neuroeng. Rehabil.*, 9, 1, 1–17, 2012.

34. Tripathi, V. and Shakeel, F., Monitoring healthcare system using internet of things-an immaculate pairing, in: *2017 International Conference on Next Generation Computing and Information Systems (ICNGCIS)*, IEEE, pp. 153–158, 2017.

35. Jaiswal, K., Sobhanayak, S., Mohanta, B.K., Jena, D., IoT-cloud based framework for patient's data collection in smart healthcare system using raspberry-pi, in: *2017 International conference on electrical and computing technologies and applications (ICECTA)*, IEEE, pp. 1–4, 2017.

17

COVID-19 Detection System Using Cellular Automata–Based Segmentation Techniques

Rupashri Barik[1*], M. Nazma B. J. Naskar[2] and Sarbajyoti Mallik[1]

[1]*Department of Information Technology JIS College of Engineering, Kalyani, W. B., India*
[2]*School of Computer Engineering, Kalinga Institute of Industrial Technology, Odisha, India*

Abstract

In this pandemic situation, human lives are in stake, and it is very urgent to detect the infection earliest to save the lives. X-ray is the most common test among medical imaging modalities. X-ray is cheaper and faster to carry out the Computed Tomography (CT). As COVID-19 causes pneumonia in massive sense, the chest X-ray can help to identify whether the person is infected by novel Coronavirus or not. In this paper, we have proposed one automatic COVID-19 detection system that can be used as an alternative diagnosis medium of COVID-19 detection. Applying filter quality of image has been enhanced first. It may help to get a better contrast image depending on chest X-ray image. To detect the growth of infection in lungs, it is required to segment the infected region of lungs from its background. Cellular automata (CA) are very much effective for bio-medical image processing in terms of computation time and clarity. Henceforth, applying CA segmentation rules, here, we perform the lung segmentation and the segmented images to be compared with the chest X-ray of non-infected persons as well as with the chest X-ray of pneumonia infected person to determine which kind of infection it is. This training leads the system to predict COVID-19 detection automated and the proposed system acquired 93% of accuracy for detecting novel Coronavirus in human being. This entire process will help the physicians to determine that what kind of infection is present in lungs and it will be done only analyzing the chest X-ray or analyzing the CT scan image of the chest.

Keywords: Coronavirus, convolutional neural network, artificial neural network, cellular automata, image segmentation

17.1 Introduction

The novel Coronavirus or COVID-19 [1] pandemic is originated in Wuhan city of China in December, 2019. Appearance of this virus caused a major health issue in human society worldwide. Due to this virus COVID-19 pandemic, situation has arisen and it leads the world at a stake. This pandemic disease is known as severe Acute Respiratory Syndrome–Corona Virus-2 (SARS-CoV-2) [2]. Coronaviruses belong to the group of viruses which are

---

Corresponding author: barikrupashri@gmail.com

Om Prakash Jena, Alok Ranjan Tripathy, Ahmed A. Elngar and Zdzislaw Polkowski (eds.) Computational Intelligence and Healthcare Informatics, (313–324) © 2021 Scrivener Publishing LLC

the reasons of severe diseases due to colds and it causes SARS-CoV. COVID-19 [3] is a kind of virus that has not been found earlier in humans. Due to contamination from animals to humans, this virus is of zoonotic type. It is presumed that coronavirus was contaminated from bats to humans. Coronavirus spreads rapidly from a person to person through respiratory transmission and so that this epidemic situation aroused. Nowadays, Coronavirus has no specific signs of infection. In some cases, it has been found asymptomatic. Still, most common symptoms are fever, cold, cough, dehydration, dyspnea, and moreover severe breathing issues. This infection may cause multi-organ failure, SARS, massive pneumonia, and moreover death.

Presently, detection of COVID-19 is a big challenge because of unavailability of proper diagnosis system. As the COVID-19 testing kits are not available in huge number in comparison to increasing number of infections, and it is one of the reasons of spreading the viruses rapidly. To reduce spreading of the viruses, isolation is a major solution and the necessary actions can be taken after detection of the infection. In this situation to detect the infection earliest, it is required to have an alternative diagnosis solution. Mainly, the epithelial cells which indicate the line of human respiratory tract are being attacked by COVID-19. For this reason, X-ray of chest can be used for analyzing the status of human lungs. X-ray images are frequently used to diagnose severe lungs issues like lung inflammation and pneumonia. X-ray is an easily available imaging modalities and it is comparatively less expensive than the other imaging modalities. Analyzing chest X-ray images, COVID-19 infection in lungs also can be detected. An automated system can make this detection faster by analyzing the X-ray images without the intervention of the radiologist and for performing this task the system required to be well trained with chest X-ray image set. It will save the time of the medical practitioners and with this early detection spreading of coronavirus can be reduced and will save the lives.

Medical image processing can play a major role to detect COVID-19 from X-ray image of chest and it takes less time than other testing methodologies. Medical images can be processed in better way using different transition rules of cellular automata (CA) [4]. CA are very much efficient for medical image processing due to its clarity and computation time. Image segmentation is a powerful technique for extracting the features of the object of interest as well as it helps to separate the region of interest from its background. Using image segmentation techniques, COVID-19 infection can be detected from chest X-ray. CA-based segmentation can help to distinguish the area of infection of the lungs effectively.

As it is required to get an automated system for reducing the rapid spreading of the coronavirus, the chest X-ray image set to be trained and machine learning plays a vital role in this field. The automated detection system will detect the infection automatically from the chest X-ray of the infectant. To make the detection system automated concept of convolutional neural networks (CNNs) to be applied first and the concept of artificial neural network (ANN) is also required for getting the final outcome. Hence, the patient can go for isolation to prevent the spreading of it as well as the person can take necessary action to save the life.

17.2   Literature Survey

In this section, the basic concept of CA, CA-based image segmentation, CNN, and ANN has been illustrated. In this proposed work, CA have been used for segmenting the infection area of lungs from its background and the automated part has been developed with the working principle of CNN and ANN.

17.2.1   Cellular Automata

CA was introduced by J. Von Neumann and Stan Ulam in early 1950s. A CA [5] is a discrete system that consists of an infinite array of cells. It is dynamic in nature. In CA [6], a set of finite states exist and each cell has a state. The cells change their states according to a local update rule that provides the new state based on the old states of the cell and its neighbors. Each cell is also called grid. Local rules are applied to the adjacent neighbors of a cell. CA can be universal.

One-dimensional (1D), two-dimensional (2D), and three-dimensional (3D) CA are used to solve different types of problems. One-dimensional CA are represented by an infinite horizontal array of cells. One-dimensional CA have two possible states, i.e., 0 or 1. Two-dimensional CA has rectangular or hexagonal grid of cells. A 2D CA is most suitable for representing a digital image. Each cell of a 2D CA [7] represents image pixel and the state of that cell is suitable for representing the intensity of the pixel. Using different neighborhood operations in a CA, an image can be transformed as per requirement. Von Neumann neighborhood CA consists of a central cell and four horizontally and vertically adjacent neighbors. It is also called as five neighborhood CA. One central cell and adjacent eight neighbors formed Moore neighborhood CA which is also known as nine neighborhood CA. CA have a major application in image processing due to its 2D matrix structure and transition rules. These transition rules can be used as transformation function for processing an image.

Figure 17.1 represents a linear 1D CA. Structure of a 2D CA has been shown in Figure 17.2. It also represents the neighborhood concept of a 2D CA. Figure 17.3 illustrates different neighborhood models, i.e., Von Neumann or 4-neighborhood models, Moore or 9-neighborhood models, and extended Moore or 25-neighborhood models [8].

Figure 17.1 Structure of 1D CA.

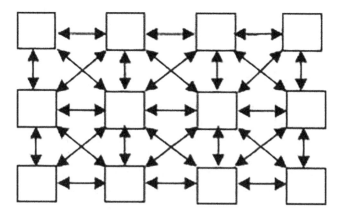

Figure 17.2 Structure of 2D CA [7].

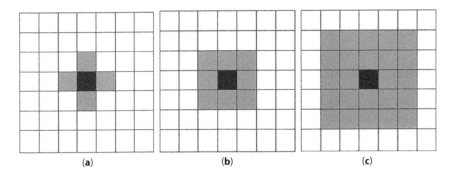

Figure 17.3 (a) Von Neumann neighborhood models, (b) Moore neighborhood models, (c) extended Moore neighborhood models [11].

17.2.2   Image Segmentation

Nowadays, different image processing techniques are widely used in several medical fields for detecting several diseases from different imaging modalities. Medical image processing [9] helps a lot for easy detection of COVID-19 infection also. In some of the cases, time factor is so important for diagnosing the disease in the patient as early as possible. It is very much applicable for various cancer tumors detection such as the brain tumor, breast tumor, and lung cancer. To detect tumors in different organs, image segmentation has a major role. Image segmentation [10] is an essential process for most image analysis subsequent tasks. Segmentation helps to divide the whole image into different components considering different regions or objects. The aim of image segmentation is simplified representation of the imaging modalities into some more significant transformed image which will be easy to analyse. Image segmentation is mainly used for detecting objects and its edges or boundaries of the images. As image segmentation also concentrates on boundary detection so it may use the concept of edge detection [11]. Thresholding is also very important in image segmentation as on basis of this threshold value segmentation would be more prominent depending on quality of input images. In terms of clarity and computation time CA rules produces better results in case of finding out the boundaries as well as the object of interest presents in the medical images. Applying CA-based segmentation techniques [12] region of interest can be segmented more effectively. Applying different transition rules features can be extracted from different imaging modalities which may help to detect the infection area in lungs [13].

17.2.3   Deep Learning Techniques

Deep learning is a part of machine learning which is based on concepts of neural networks. A CNN [14] belongs to a class of deep neural networks. It is mostly applicable for analyzing visual imagery aspect. A CNN [15] is one of the deep learning algorithms that can take image as input. For processing, it assigns biases and learnable weights to the different aspects present in the input image and it can differentiate each from the other. It is also represented as an ANN which is mostly used for analyzing different images. Deep learning algorithms are not only used for analyzing images, it is also used for data analysis as well as for classification problems. High accuracy can be acquired with the help of CNNs performing image

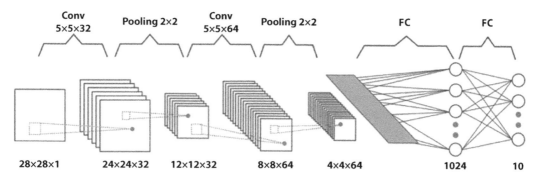

Conv 5×5×32 **Pooling 2×2** **Conv 5×5×64** **Pooling 2×2** **FC** **FC**

28×28×1   24×24×32   12×12×32   8×8×64   4×4×64   1024   10

Figure 17.4 CNN architecture.

classification and recognition. A CNN follows a hierarchical model for getting a network, and at last it produces a fully connected layer. Neurons of all these layers are fully connected with each other and finally output image is obtained. An ANN has one input and one output layer. It also consists of multiple hidden layers. These hidden layers consist of a series of convolutional layers which helps to convolve with a multiplication product.

Figure 17.4 illustrates the architecture of a CNN. Here, the entire convolution process has been described in terms of convolution layers to the hidden layer as well as describing the fully connected layer for obtaining the output layer.

Ali Narin *et al.* [16] proposed one automatic system for detecting COVID-19 infection from chest X-ray images using deep CNNs. In this work, a set of chest X-ray images has been pre-trained using ResNet50, InceptionV3, ResNet101, Inception-ResNetV2, and ResNet152. Next, the pre-trained images are being trained for three binary sets.

Faisal Muhammad Shah *et al.* [17] considered X-ray and CT scan images of chest for detecting COVID-19 infection. Applying deep learning methods to these two sets of data corona virus disease has been detected. Here, first pre-processing techniques have been applied, and next, using deep neural network, features have been extracted. Applying CNN with *softmax* layer, COVID-19 and normal chest have been identified with a good accuracy.

Boran Sekeroglu *et al.* [18] detected COVID-19 from chest X-ray using CNN. Here, the experiments were carried over with CNN and different machine learning models. Different percentages of specificity, sensitivity, and accuracy have been acquired here from the training data.

17.3 Proposed Methodology

In this section, one methodology has been proposed for detecting COVID-19 from chest X-ray. For detecting infection in lungs, chest X-ray of the infectant person is to be analyzed. Figure 17.5 illustrates the entire process of detecting coronavirus infection within a human body, analyzing the chest X-ray images. Proposed method involves machine learning techniques for detecting the infection automatically.

Analysis of chest X-ray helps to detect Coronavirus infection as it includes the details of lungs. As the X-ray images may have noise in it, first, the quality of image has to be enhanced using a filter. Here, bilateral filter has been used to improve the quality of the

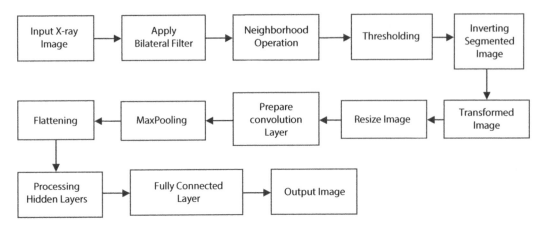

Figure 17.5 System flow diagram.

input image. Bilateral filter is a non-linear smoothing filter for images. It helps to reduce the noise of imaging modalities and also preserves the edge features of an image. Intensity of each pixel is being replaced with the weighted average of intensity values considering the nearby pixels. After improving the quality of the imaging modality, the resultant image is being padded with 0 as further neighborhood operations to be performed for segmenting the mass from the surrounding normal cells. Next, Moore neighborhood or nine neighborhood CA has been used as transition rules for transforming the image. Moore neighborhood CA includes one central cell and eight adjacent neighbors of it. One central cell has been taken in consideration and it is subtracted from all of its eight adjacent cells. Value of the reference cell to be replaced with 0 if all these differences are less than the chosen threshold otherwise the value of central cell will remain unchanged. Threshold value may be depending on the input image. Different threshold values may produce segmented images with different clarity. Applying this neighborhood operation, the affected part of the imaging modalities can be highlighted. In this way, the mass will be segmented from its background. To better understand the infected area, the segmented image is to be inverted. Inverse of an image implies negative image. In negative image, the dark areas of an image appear light and the light parts appear dark. Finally, the transformed image is being obtained for analyzing, and henceforth, it can be used for determining whether there are any infections in lungs or not.

Furthermore, for implementing an automated system for detecting COVID-19 automatically, a number of images have been trained after transforming the images with proposed method. Here, transformed images have been scaled with a size of 256×256 and have been multiplied with different feature detector with a stride of 1 and also with rectilinear activation function to get the best feature from the transformed image, and as a result, we get her two different feature maps. Next, taking 3×3 feature detector and multiplying it with huge matrix of 256×256 input image to reduce the size of the matrix of the image. After that, max pooling has been applied, and a box of 2×2 pixels has been taken and placed it in the top left corner. Now, it is required to find the maximum value in that box, and then, this value is being reduced. Next, the box is being moved to the right side with stride of two. Here, again, max pooling has been done to reduce the size of the 32 different feature maps, and as a result, we get 32 pooled feature maps. To get best accuracy in the train and test set, three more convolution layers have been added. First one with 3 × 3 matrix of 32 feature detector. Second one is with 3 × 3 matrix of 64 feature detector and third one is 3 × 3 matrix of 128 feature detectors. Henceforth, max pooling has been added with each of these convolution layer. Now, taking each and every pooled feature map and then flatten it into a column. Basically, just to take the number row by row from pooled feature map and put them into one long column to get a one huge vector of inputs for an ANN.

Figure 17.6 shows the involvement of convolutional neural network for implementing the automatic COVID-19 detection. Here, the transformed image set has been resized and then that has been taken as the input for the convolution layer.

Next, two fully connected layers with output_dim (dimension of dense embedding) of 128 have been prepared, and also with rectilinear activation function here, categorical cross entropy has been used to calculate the loss. So, the error is calculated in the output layer with *softmax* activation function and with *adam* optimizer is back propagated through the network again and again to adjust the network and to optimize the performance. After that, the dataset of normal, pneumonia, and COVID-19 has been trained with a target size of 256 × 256 and batch size of 10 and also the test set of normal, pneumonia and COVID-19 with a target size of 256 × 256, batch size of 2, and with 50 epochs.

Figure 17.7 illustrates the second part of training image set. Concept of ANN has been applied here. In this part, three hidden layers have been considered, and finally, from the fully connected layer, the output image has been obtained and it determines the detection of COVID-19 infections.

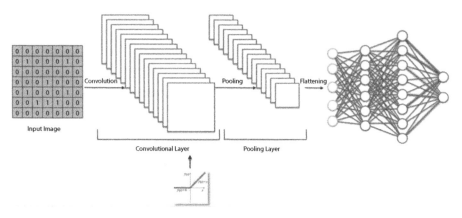

Figure 17.6 Schema of convolutional neural network part.

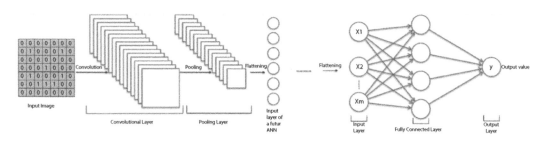

Figure 17.7 Schema of artificial neural network part.

17.4 Results and Discussion

For implementing automatic COVID-19 detection system, around 1,000 image set of normal chest X-ray and COVID-19 effected chest X-ray images have been trained here. All the image set has been collected from Kaggle [19, 20]. All the image set has been transformed first with the proposed CA-based imaged segmentation technique. Then, all the transformed images have been scaled and resized for training.

Figure 17.8 represents sample image set after transforming the original normal chest X-ray images with the proposed CA-based image segmentation technique. These X-ray images of normal chest have been trained for comparing with COVID-19 infected chest X-ray.

In Figure 17.9, COVID-19 infected sample chest X-ray images have been shown after transforming with the proposed CA-based image segmentation technique. Here, it can be observed that using this proposed segmentation technique some unwanted part of the

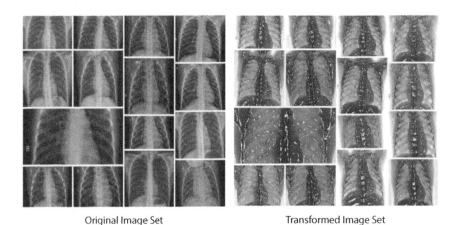

Original Image Set   Transformed Image Set

Figure 17.8 Normal chest X-ray [20].

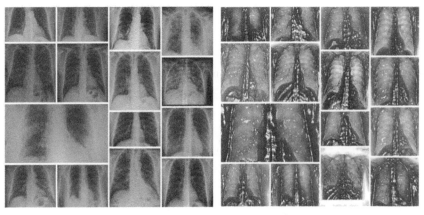

Original Image Set   Transformed Image Set

Figure 17.9 COVID-19 positive chest X-ray [19].

images has been removed. So, the infected areas are clearer which may help to identify the detection easily.

Figure 17.10 represents sample image set after transforming the original pneumonia affected chest X-ray images with the proposed CA-based image segmentation technique. These X-ray images are having pneumonia infection and have been trained to get the comparison with a normal lung which may help to predict the infection.

CNN has been applied to all these transformed images. In Figure 17.6, it has been shown that convolution layers have been prepared for these input images, and then, pooling layer has been created from which max pool has been considered. The nodes of this pool have been flattening then for feeding it to the next level of ANN. In ANN, three hidden layers have been considered. Figure 17.11 shows the nodes of one of the hidden layers.

Here, the images are representing the intermediate processed images of hidden layer 1 after flattening. Following same process, two more hidden layers are considered, and thereafter, all these nodes are being fully connected to get the ultimate output layer. After training, the transformed image set of three different class 93% accuracy has been acquired following this approach.

Henceforth, if a chest X-ray has been given as a input image to this system, so the X-ray image will be preprocessed, and then, applying CA-based segmentation rule the infected area of lungs will be segmented and this transformed image will be compared with the training image set for determining whether it is COVID-19 positive chest X-ray or whether it is normal lungs.

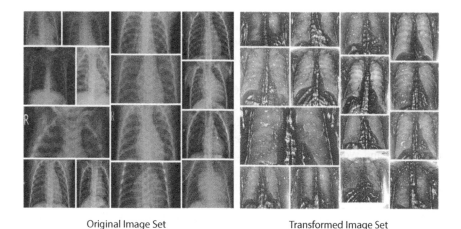

Original Image Set   Transformed Image Set

Figure 17.10 Pneumonia chest X-ray [20].

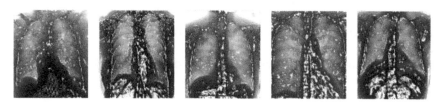

Figure 17.11 Sample images of hidden layer 1.

17.5   Conclusion

As the coronavirus infection is spreading rapidly, so it is very much required to detect it earliest. An early detection of this disease may slow down the spreading of it as the infected person can take necessary actions immediate after detection. Due to lack of test kits, it is hard to determine whether a person is COVID-19 positive or negative. Henceforth, analyzing different imaging modalities of chest or lungs, the coronavirus infection can be detected also. Computed Tomography or CT images are expensive than the X-ray images, so the people can be preferring X-ray images as the medium of detection. This proposed method produced 93% of accuracy in case of detecting coronavirus infection from the chest X-ray images. The same process also can be applied for the CT images for detecting COVID-19 infection.

References

1. https://www.webmd.com/lung/coronavirus
2. https://www.who.int/emergencies/diseases/novel-coronavirus-2019/global-research-on-novel-coronavirus-2019-ncov
3. https://www.pharmaceutical-journal.com/news-and-analysis/features/everything-you-should-know-about-the-coronavirus-outbreak/20207629.article?firstPass=false
4. Kari, J., Cellular Automata, Spring. *J. Cel. Atom., 5, 339,* 2013.
5. von Neumann, J., *The Theory of Self-Reproducing Automata,* A.W. Burks (Ed.), Univ. of Illinois Press, Urbana, 1966.
6. Wolfram, S., Statistical Mechanics of Cellular Automata, *Rev. Mod. Phys.,* 55, 601, 1983.
7. Nayak, D.R., Patra, P., Mahapatra, A., A Survey on Two Dimensional Cellular Automata and Its Application in Image Processing. *Int. J. Comput. Appl.,* 0975–8887, ETCC-2014, 78-87. arxiv.org/ 1407. 7626.
8. Nayak, D.R., Sahu, S.K., Mohammed, J., A Cellular Automata Based Optimal Edge Detection Technique using Twenty-Five Neighborhood Model. *IJCA,* 84, 10, 27–33, 2013.
9. Wongthanavasu, S., Cellular Automata for Medical Image Processing, in: *Cellular Automata - Innovative Modelling for Science and Engineering.*
10. Gonzalez, R.C. and Woods, R.E., *Digital Image Processing,* 2nd ed, Prentice Hall, Upper Saddle River, New Jersey, 2002.
11. Popovici, A. and Popovici, D., Cellular automata in image processing. *International Symposium on the Mathematical Theory of Networks and Systems,* 2002.
12. Safia, D. and Djidel, O., Image Segmentation Using Continuous Cellular Automata, in: *10th International Symposium on Programming and Systems (ISPS),* IEEE Xplore, May, 2011.
13. Senthil Kumar, K., Venkatalakshmi, K., Karthikeyan, K., Lung Cancer Detection Using Image Segmentation by means of Various Evolutionary Algorithms. *Hindawi Computational and Mathematical Methods in Medicine,* 2019, 1-17, Article ID 4909846, https://doi.org/10.1155/2019/4909846.
14. Kwak, N., *Introduction to Convolutional Neural Networks (CNNs),* LAMDA Group, China, 2016.
15. Albawi, S., Mohammed, T.A., Al-Zawi, S., Understanding of a Convolutional Neural Network. *ICET2017,* Antalya, Turkey.

16. Narin, A., Kaya, C., Pamuk, Z., *Automatic Detection of Coronavirus Disease (COVID-19) Using X-ray Images and Deep Convolutional Neural Networks.* Pattern Analysis and Applications, 1–14, Oct., 2020, DOI:10.1007/s10044-021-00984-y.

17. Shah, F.M., Joy, S.K.S., Ahmed, F., Humaira, M., Ami, A.S., Paul, S., Jim, Md A. R. K., A Comprehensive Survey of COVID-19 Detection Using Medical Images, Preprint: https://engrxiv.org/9fdyp/, August, 2020, Preprint DOI: 10.31224/osf.io/9fdyp.

18. Sekeroglu, B. and Ozsahin, I., Detection of COVID-19 from Chest X-Ray Images Using Convolutional Neural Networks. *SAGE Journals*, 25 6, 553–565, September, 2020.

19. https://www.kaggle.com/masumrefat/chest-xray-images-pneumonia-and-covid19

20. https://www.kaggle.com/paultimothymooney/chest-xray-pneumonia

18

Interesting Patterns From COVID-19 Dataset Using Graph-Based Statistical Analysis for Preventive Measures

Abhilash C. B.* and Kavi Mahesh

Indian Institute of Information Technology Dharwad, Karnataka, India

Abstract

The coronavirus disease (COVID-19) caused by the novel severe acute respiratory syndrome–coronavirus 2 (SARS-CoV-2) was declared a global pandemic on March 11, 2020, by WHO. Different countries adopted many interventions at different levels of the outbreak. The common one is social distancing and lockdown, which were opted to flatten the mortality curve [13].

The important aspect of data mining is knowledge discovery for interesting patterns. We propose an innovative approach for deriving interesting patterns using machine learning and graph database models to incorporate the preventive measures in an earlier state. We propose a graph-based statistical analysis (GSA) model to study the pandemic outbreak's impact and propose prevention and control strategies. We analyze the model using available data from the ministry of health and family welfare service, GOI. The study will explore the visual analytics for deriving the interesting patterns from the knowledge graph considering the attributes of infected COVID-19 patients, which will benefit the preventive measures. The pandemic's spread to the respective geographical population is predicted using the time series and statistical analysis with the statistical model. This method often requires sufficient data, but with the available data about the initial and mid-stages of an epidemic, the spread rate is predicted for preventive measures that the administrative levels should take. Our study uses Neo4j, a graph database tool for building the knowledge graph represented by RDF (Resource Descriptive Framework) for optimized query operations resulting in graph visualization. On the other hand, we also discuss the machine learning model to predict the trend and short-term transmission predictions through the COVID-19 outbreak. The results have potentially interesting insights on the effect of the pandemic.

Keywords: COVID-19, machine learning, graph database, RDF, statistical analysis, preventive measures

Corresponding author: abhilashcb@iiitdwd.ac.in

Om Prakash Jena, Alok Ranjan Tripathy, Ahmed A. Elngar and Zdzislaw Polkowski (eds.) Computational Intelligence and Healthcare Informatics, (325–358) © 2021 Scrivener Publishing LLC

18.1   Introduction

Data analytics is playing an important role in deriving interesting patterns from a large amount of data. There exist a wide range of methods starting from traditional statistical techniques to much visual analytics. Despite many exiting techniques, graph-based analysis plays an important role in defining data as a connected network. The graph-based analysis enables visual data processing and designs the knowledge graph for deriving interesting patterns [7].

The coronavirus pandemic across the world has unprecedented. It had made countries entirely under lockdown and millions of people in-home quarantine, which led to the global economic crash. Managing the status of the healthcare system with human resources and the necessary equipment was challenging. The most interesting fact is the impact of air pollution across the globe. There was a significant drop in air pollution in many parts of the world. This pandemic turned out to be the best thing for Venice's water canals, the United States air index is increased, and the Delhi, India air pollution index is down to a healthy level [16, 18].

In today's digital world, we are continuously surrounded by information, but not all are accurate. We mainly rely on data to gauge whether something is true or false, but we rarely see the data in its raw forms. You can imagine how rows and rows of numbers could be very confusing to interpret. We usually use a method called data visualization to represent patterns and trends in data more efficiently [3]. Data visualization translates data into visual representations like charts and graphs to communicate the data significance. However, this method simplifies understanding data [4].

In the world of data, we can look at things at more abstract individuals like person, accounts, and banks, but in the graph, we call these nodes, and the lines connecting them are relationship. The abstract data can be modeled as a graph using the nodes and relationships. We can model all abstract data in the real world with the nodes, relationships, and key value properties attached to the node. The knowledge representation is best done using graphs as it is flexible [2]. The representation power and flexibility is the main advantage of why researchers have adopted the graph-based representation model in different aspects of machine learning [1, 2].

18.2   Methods

18.2.1   Data

COVID-19 data of Karnataka state from Department of Health and Family Welfare Service, Karnataka, MoHFWS, news bulletin is recoded and cleaned by segregating and merging the required attributes. The mechanism and data description are shown in Figure 18.1. Additionally, we have considered the census data for district-wise population count and the centroid data for location tracking.

The MoHFWS, GoK maintains the media bulletin of Karnataka state COVID-19 dashboard. The data about the patients were made available till July 2020 [11, 12]. Considering

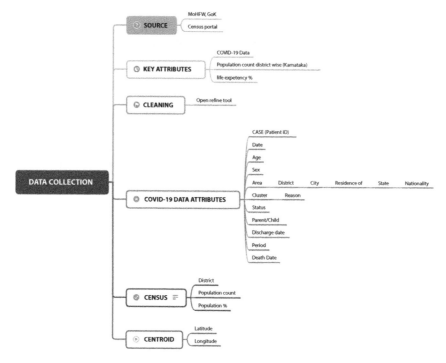

Figure 18.1 Data collection and cleaning mechanism.

the contact tracing data, we have added certain additional attributes for our study, as indicated in Table 18.1. The daily announcement of patient data, including the cumulative number of positive cases, the cumulative number of tests conducted, the cumulative number of discharges, and the cumulative number of deaths, helped aggregate the data over time.

18.3   GSA Model: Graph-Based Statistical Analysis

The county's central and state government has taken preventive measures after the pandemic outbreak, such as Lockdown, social distancing, and wearing the mask. People with symptoms were categorized, isolated, and quarantined over a while. Considering the total population in the knowledge graph of KaTrace, we can find the percentage of infects across different districts, which helps in the concerned authorities preventive measures. We tried to figure out the best possible way for prediction and preventive analysis with the available data. As per the study, the possible effective control measures are using a graph-based analytical system model for contact tracing and the control of the spread [7, 8].

Further, the statistical model can be used for finding insights and interesting patterns. Finally, we use machine learning techniques for deeper insights and propose a preventive measure for controlling the pandemic.

Table 18.1 COVID-19 dataset "KaTrace" description.

COVID-19 dataset description by MoHFWS, GoK	Additional attributes	Final version

A. **Case number** - As recognized by the Karnataka Government
B. **Date** - When they tested positive
C. **Age**
D. **Sex**
E. **City** - It contains both the city where a patient is held and the city of their residence.
F. **State**
G. **Cluster** - Divided according to the clusters we have in the Karnataka trace history.
H. **Reason** - This mentions the patient's place of travel or their relationship with the person they contracted the disease from.
I. **Nationality** - India for all the cases
J. **Status** is today - in terms of Cured(C)/ Deceased(D). If nothing is mentioned, they are currently hospitalized.
K. **Parent** - If the patient they contracted the virus from is known, this column mentions the case number of the "parent."
L. **Number of children** - The number of (known) people infected by this case.
M. **Relationship** - Their relationship with any other people infected is listed as the type of relationship and the case number of the other infected individual.
	1. The city is divided into Area, City, Residence, District
	2. The following attributes were added referring to the media bulletin of MoHFWS, GoK
	  a. Out date
	  b. Discharge date
	3. An integer value for status was assigned as follows: 0-deceased, 1- cured, 2-hospitalized
	4. The new attribute as "Survival Status" was added based on the integer value referred to in the previous point.
	5. Period attribute is computed based on the Admission date and out date
		KaTrace

This article mainly focuses on a dynamic model using graph and machine learning techniques for the COVID-19 pandemic and a statistical model based on time series analysis all put together named as GSA model as shown in Figure 18.2. The predictive result of our study indicates the precautionary measures required for the pandemic spread. Due to the outbreak and data availability from MoHFWS, the existing data is not relatively large sample data [17].

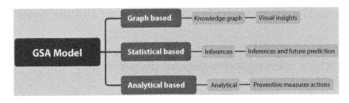

Figure 18.2 Proposed GSA model.

By a statistical approach, we are proposing a **mathematical model** for finding the healthy population count during a pandemic [10].

Considering the total population as Q_t, infected as I_n, not infected as H_d

Population exposed to I_n and got infected -> (E_i)

Population exposed to I_n but not infected -> ($E_{i\_}$)

Population not infected is computed as $H_d = Q_t - I_n - E_i + (E_{i\_})$

H_d includes a healthy population as they are not exposed to I_n and also, few are exposed but not in E_i, which adds they are resistant.

On day 1:

$$H_1 = Q_t - I_{n1} - E_{i1} + (E_{i1\_})$$

On day 2:

$$H_2 = Q_t - I_{n2} - E_{i2} + (E_{i2\_})$$

Change in day 1 and day 2 is $\Delta H_d = H_2 - H_1$

$$\Delta H_d = \{Q_t - I_{n2} - E_{i2} + (E_{i2\_})\} - \{Q_t - I_{n1} - E_{i1} + (E_{i1\_})\}$$

$$\Delta H_d = Q_t - I_{n2} - E_{i2} + (E_{i2\_}) - Q_t + I_{n1} + E_{i1} - (E_{i1\_})$$

$$\Delta H_d = I_{n1} - I_{n2} + E_{i1} - E_{i2} + (E_{i2\_}) - (E_{i1\_})$$

$$\Delta H_d = \Delta I_n + \Delta E_i + (\Delta E_{i\_})$$

ΔH_d decreases when ΔI_n and ΔE_i increases and $\Delta E_{i\_}$ decreases.

18.4   Graph-Based Analysis

A graph is a collection of nodes/vertices as points and edges as lines between those points.

Figure 18.3 indicates the property graph with relationships and properties for each node and edges. Here, the node P1281 has the property ID, location, and status with edge spread. The P1281 infects the P1356, and P1356, in turn, has infected to P1396. Our study considers the logical graph generated by the COVID data Katrace [9] where the nodes are represented by patient ID, and relationships concerning residence and symptoms are defined. The method of data modeling using graph helps to find new insight from the data [14].

18.4.1   Modeling Your Data as a Graph

Considering the COVID data KaTrace, a patient with basic demographic information is the node in the graph, and edges will be the relationship like primary and secondary

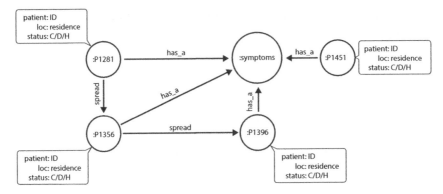

Figure 18.3 Graph representation of healthcare data.

contact information. Use this model in the neo4j graph database tool to create a graph database [6].

Syntax:

$ LOAD CSV WITH HEADERS FROM 'file:///KAtrace.csv' AS data
WITH data WHERE data.`Case` IS NOT NULL
WITH data, SPLIT(data.`Date`, '/') AS date
MERGE (patient:Patient {id: data.`Case`,sex: data.`Sex`,age: toInteger(data.`Age`),
children: toInteger(data.`Child`), status: coalesce(data.`Status`,"Hospitalized"),
period: coalesce(toInteger(data.`Period`), 'NA')})
SET patient.year = toInteger(date[2]),
patient.month = toInteger(date[1]),
patient.day = toInteger(date[0])
MERGE (residence:Residence {city: data.`City`, area: data.`Area`, district:
data.`District`, resident: coalesce(data.`ResidentOf`,'NA')})
MERGE (patient)-[:LIVES]->(residence)
MERGE (reason:Reason {place: data.`Cluster`, reason: coalesce(data.`Reason`,"NA")})
MERGE (patient)-[:REASON]->(reason)

$ CREATE CONSTRAINT ON (p: patient) ASSERT p.id IS UNIQUE

The above syntax will load the COVID dataset in CSV format and create the knowledge graph. The representation o the node is as shown in Table 18.2.

Table 18.2 Relationship established in neo2j tool.

Node label	Merge attributes
Patient	date, PID, sex, age, parent, child, status, period
Residence	city, area, district, resident
Reason	place, cluster, reason

18.4.2   RDF for Knowledge Graph

RDF triples are a way of describing information. Triples come from RDF, which is the resource description framework which was developed by W3C, the World Wide Web Consortium, as a way of describing resources on the web and we can see here that graph of simple triples, so triples are made up of three parts, the first part is the subject. The Neo4j tool can be used for a unique reasoning technology to deliver a very expressive and highly competitive reasoning engine for RDF [7, 8].

The regular analytical process cannot discover the complex pattern in the large data. The RDF knowledge graph is incorporated in the Neo4j tool using the neosemantics and Neo4j blooms plug-in. Querying by a systematic approach is enabled in the neosemantics for discovering the interesting patterns from the knowledge graph. The RDF of the PATIENT node with the relationship of FROM and LIVES is displayed on the query input, as shown in Figure 18.4.

18.4.3   Knowledge Graph Representation

The knowledge graph shown in Figure 18.5 is queried with the cipher queries to get different insights. The attributes like age, sex, residence, reason of infect, and primary and secondary contacts of patients are used to query the knowledge graph.

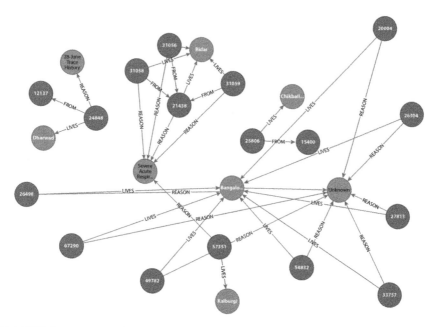

Figure 18.4 RDF data representation.

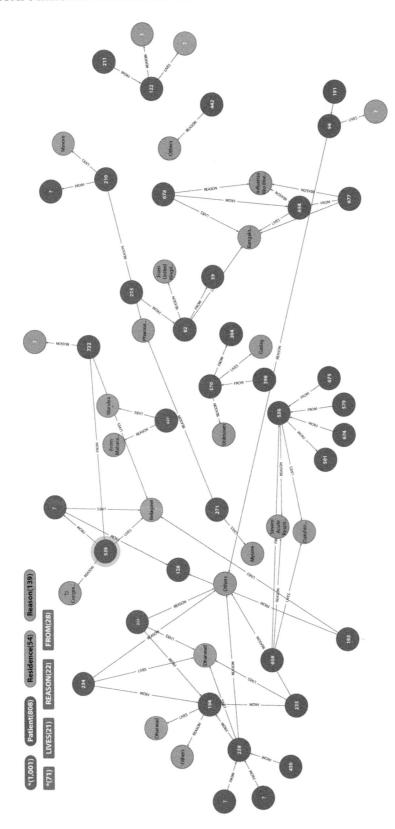

Figure 18.5 Knowledge representation of COVID, KaTrace dataset.

18.4.4   RDF Triple for KaTrace

The resource framework descriptor indicated in Figure 18.6 is generated based on the CODO ontology [19] for the attributes ID, residence, age, and gender. The graph based on the query is generated as shown in Figure 18.7, which indicated the different age group of patients from 30 districts of Karnataka state. Similarly, the graph representation can be drawn considering age as key attribute. The preventive measures based on these key attributes controls the pandemic spread.

```
@prefix ns1: <http://www.isibang.ac.in/ns/> .
@prefix xsd: <http://www.w3.org/2001/XMLSchema#> .

<http://example.org/people/1> a ns1:codopatientID,
        <http://xmlns.com/foaf/0.1/openid> ;
    ns1:codoCity "Bangalore-Urban"^^xsd:string ;
    ns1:codoage 41 ;
    ns1:codocurrentStatus "C"^^xsd:string ;
    ns1:codogender "Male"^^xsd:string .

<http://example.org/people/10> a ns1:codopatientID,
        <http://xmlns.com/foaf/0.1/openid> ;
    ns1:codoCity "Bangalore-Urban"^^xsd:string ;
    ns1:codoage 20 ;
    ns1:codocurrentStatus "C"^^xsd:string ;
    ns1:codogender "Female"^^xsd:string .

<http://example.org/people/100> a ns1:codopatientID,
        <http://xmlns.com/foaf/0.1/openid> ;
    ns1:codoCity "Bangalore-Urban"^^xsd:string ;
    ns1:codoage 40 ;
    ns1:codocurrentStatus "C"^^xsd:string ;
    ns1:codogender "Male"^^xsd:string .
```

Figure 18.6 RDF for KaTrace, initial data only.

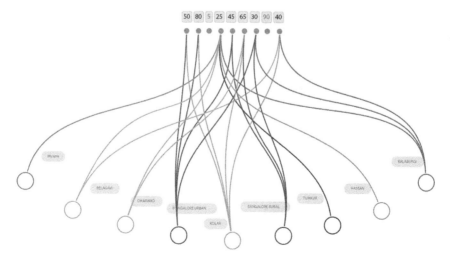

Figure 18.7 District-wise patient represented by age.

The graph centrality is experimented using the NEuler plug-in available in the Neo4j tool. Referring to Figure 18.8, the betweenness centrality of P43350 is 148, which indicates that the maximum spread is by the patient with ID P43350. Similarly, centrality measures like degree, betweenness, and PageRank can be derived from the knowledge graph generated by the KaTrace dataset [9].

Figure 18.9 represents the PageRank centrality for the knowledge graph of KaTrace. The residence node is considered for the PageRank centrality. The PageRank count of Bangalore urban is more based on the spread count. So, the influence node is Bangalore urban. So, the preventive measures can be taken considering these insights.

The knowledge graph visualization on neo4j blooms as shown in Figure 18.10 enables the query in natural language and visually checks the graph's interesting connections. We can also have a relationship combination, which builds the sub graph for extracting the interesting patterns from the connected graph, as shown in Figure 18.11. The generated graph can be further queried for hidden patterns in the data. For primary contact tracing of patient P52, the input query text can be in a natural language like "patient 52" or "P52" or "52" [6].

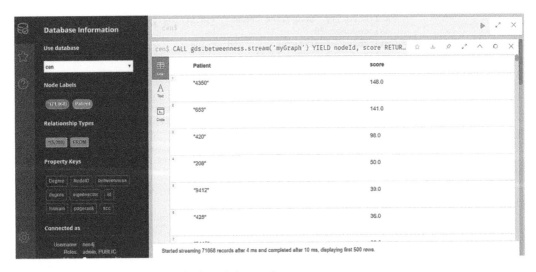

Figure 18.8 Betweenness centrality for knowledge graph.

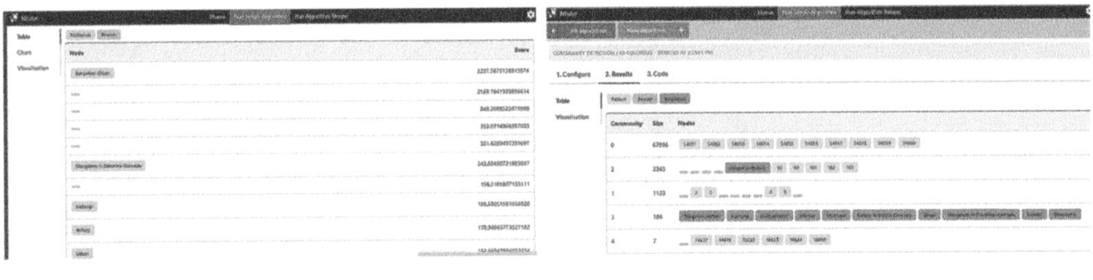

Figure 18.9 PageRank centrality for knowledge graph.

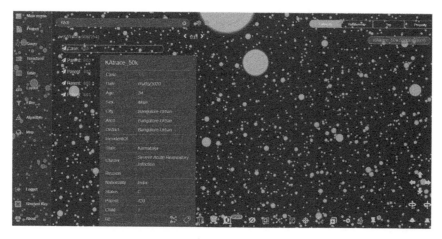

Figure 18.10   RDF query on the knowledge graph.

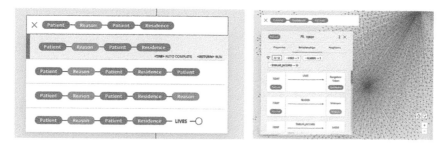

Figure 18.11   PageRank centrality for knowledge graph.

18.4.5   Cipher Query Operation on Knowledge Graph

Patient infected month-wise in Karnataka starting from March 2020.
   $ Match (n:Patient) return n.month, count(n)

Month	Count
March	101
April	464
May	2,656
June	12,021
July *	55,826

*The above output indicates the number of cases in Karnataka state. we can observe the increase in the number of cases over a time.

18.4.5.1   Inter-District Travel

In the KaTrace dataset of 71,000 patients, 338 patients (children nodes) have got infected by the inter-district travel patients (parent nodes). Insights from the data are during lockdown 1,

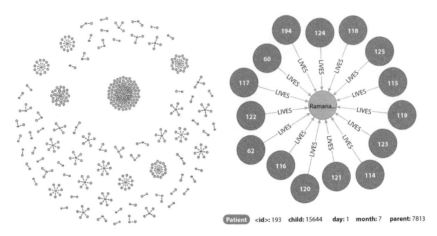

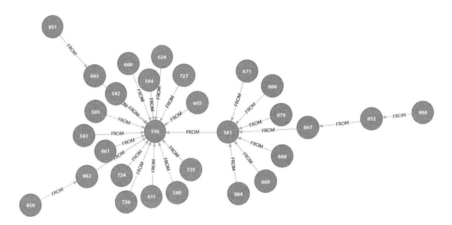

Figure 18.12 Overall inter-district graph.

Figure 18.13 Reference graph for P566.

the number of spread due to inter-district travel was significantly less, but it has been a very exponential trend in July and August that is post lockdown. Even the number 338 is less than the total 71,000 data, but these 338 are the parent nodes for many other child nodes in the dataset. In Figure 18.12, the inter-district graph shows all the inter-district travel details along with the parent and child nodes.

In Figure 18.13, P566 is the parent for 17 child nodes because of which total count of the spread is 28. If P566 has maintained the precautionary measures like social distancing and a proper self-quarantine, the this spread count could have been reduced or controlled.

18.4.5.2 Patient 653 Spread Analysis

```
$ match (n:Patient{id: '653'})-[:LIVES]->(m:Residence)
match (o:Patient {id: '653'})<-[:FROM]-(p:Patient)
match (n{id: '653'})-[:REASON]->(k:Reason) return n.id as PatientID, n.age
as Age, n.sex as Gender, m.district as Residence, count(p) as Infects, k.place as
Reason, n.status as Status
```

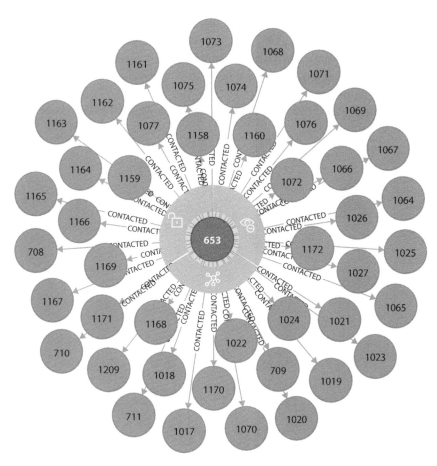

Figure 18.14 P653 spread to 45 nodes.

n.patientID	n.age	n.sex	m.district	Infects	K.place	n.status
653	34	Male	Bangalore-Urban	45	Severe acute respiratory infection	C

Figure 18.15 P653 infect details.

Patient P653 has infected to 45 people and his primary contact is patient P420. The spread details of P653 are indicated in Figure 18.14 and Figure 18.15 indicated the details pertaining to patient P653.

18.4.5.3   Spread Analysis Using Parent-Child Relationships

Using the parent and child relationship in neo4j, we have categorized the most speeded patient by cipher query, as indicated below.

➤ Match r=(n:Patient)<-[:FROM]-(m:Patient)<-[:FROM]-(o:Patient)<-[:FROM]-(p:Patient)<-[:FROM]-(k:Patient)<-[:FROM]-(s:Patient)<-[:FROM]-(t:Patient) return r

The above query indicates the six levels of spread by the patient with ID "P4184". He is 35-year-old male from Bellary, and he had traveled to Bangalore before he got infected. There is no trace of his parent node, and his spread has six levels of the parent-child relationship. He is identified as a direct parent node to 30 patients as per the KaTrace data as indicated in Figure 18.16.

The centrality measure considering degree, page-rank and betweenness centrality with age is indicated in Table 18.3.

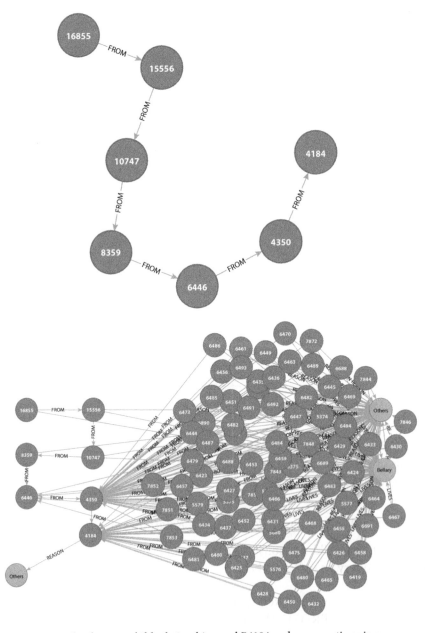

Figure 18.16 P4184, six-level parent-child relationships, and P4184 nodes connection view.

Table 18.3 Centrality for the knowledge graph.

Patient ID	Degree	Page rank	Betweenness	Age	Date
4184	30.0	12.53	0	35	4 June
4350	51.0	21.17	148.0	52	5 June
6446	4.0	2.237	14.0	25	5 June
8359	1.0	0.95	9.0	23	20 June
10747	1.0	1.02	8.0	22	26 June
15556	1.0	1.10	5.0	36	1 July
16855	0	0.61	0	29	2 July

18.4.5.4   Delhi Congregation Attended the Patient's Analysis

In the initial days of the pandemic, i.e., in March, a set of people had attended the congregation from 13 to 18 March in Delhi and returned to their respective states. A total of 97 patients tested positive, in which 27 patients were identified as parent nodes and 74 as child nodes. The part of the graph is represented in Figure 18.17.

match (n:Patient)-[:REASON]->(r:Reason)

return r.place, count(n)

Interestingly, as per the data, there is no interdistrict spread by the patients. The reason attributes values as "the Congregation from 13 to 18 March in Delhi" as they were quarantined when they returned to the Karnataka State. Also, all 97 were cured and discharged.

District-wise count of 97 patients, along with parent and child count is indicated in Table 18.4.

Referring to the table, the patients from Dakshina-Kannada, Bellary, and Bangalore-rural have a parent and child relationship with a very minimum spread count. The result is tabulated as shown in Table 18.5.

18.5   Machine Learning Techniques

Predictive data analytics consider the data source or the dataset, which contains the historical data. In our study, we consider COVID-19 Karnataka state data. The predictive analytics is applied to the dataset for preventive measures. The COVID-19 pandemic, which has encountered a global change in all domains, needs preventive measures for further actions [17].

18.5.1   Apriori Algorithm

This is normally used for the "market basket analysis" for finding an association between the different items. It figures out the frequent patterns and suggests interesting patterns for the business domain. In our study, the data is about specific ages with different gender in different areas, whether they are cured, hospitalized, and a different set of data for "died".

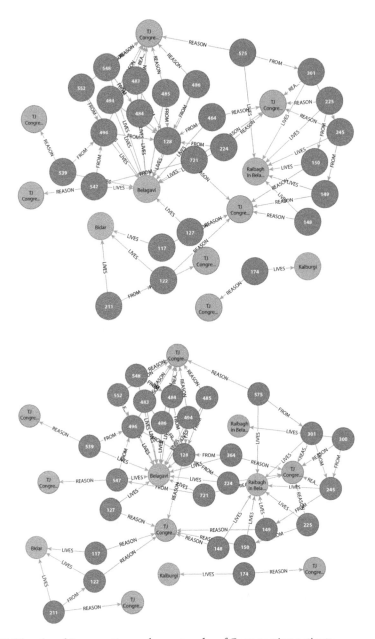

Figure 18.17 Child nodes of Congregation and parent nodes of Congregation patients.

The algorithm can predict whether a case will get cured or not. The graph in Figure 18.18 is an easier representation, which is a decision tree. Again, from this tree, we can analyze the data grouping for cured or died. We can pull out some facts from the tree leading either to cured or died. Each path from the root to the leaf is an association rule or fact.

The association rules with age, gender, and area are indicated in Figure 18.19. The rules with consequents as "c" can be used. Similarly, we can generate rules for status "d" as indicated in Figure 18.16. The association rule predicts the patient's status.

Table 18.4 District-wise parent and child count of patients attended congregation at Delhi.

District	Count	Parent	Child
Dakshina-Kannada	2	Nil	NIL
Belagavi	76	23	69
Bidar	14	3	4
Bellary	1	NIL	NIL
Bangalore-Rural	1	NIL	NIL
Kalburgi	3	1	1

Table 18.5 Comparing the death count of a few districts.

District	Count	Male	Female	Total cases		Percentage	
Bangalore Urban	688	466	222	21,880	13,083	2.12	1.69
Mysore	80	62	18	1,266	642	4.89	2.80
Dharwad	73	53	20	1,470	857	3.60	2.33
Dakshina-Kannada	74	48	26	2,545	1,294	1.88	2.00
Bangalore Rural	8	4	4	620	319	0.64	1.25
Bellary	57	34	23	1,890	965	1.798	2.384

The facts are as follows:

Fact 1: In June, the cases are mostly from travel history, whereas after June, the data distribution is different, which is more of contact transmission.

Fact 2: In the initial days, number of children varies and is traceable, whereas, in later days, the number of children is limited, which means there are two possibilities.

Interesting fact: Maybe, awareness is increased, or maybe, traceability is decreased.

18.5.2   Decision Tree Classifier

Various models are compared for the accuracy and relevance as shown in Figure 18.20.

The ROC for decision tree classifier indicated in Figure 18.21. The ROCs are used to see how well your classifier can separate positive and negative examples and to identify the best threshold for separating them. Generally, it shows the relationship between clinical sensitivity and specificity for every possible cutoff.

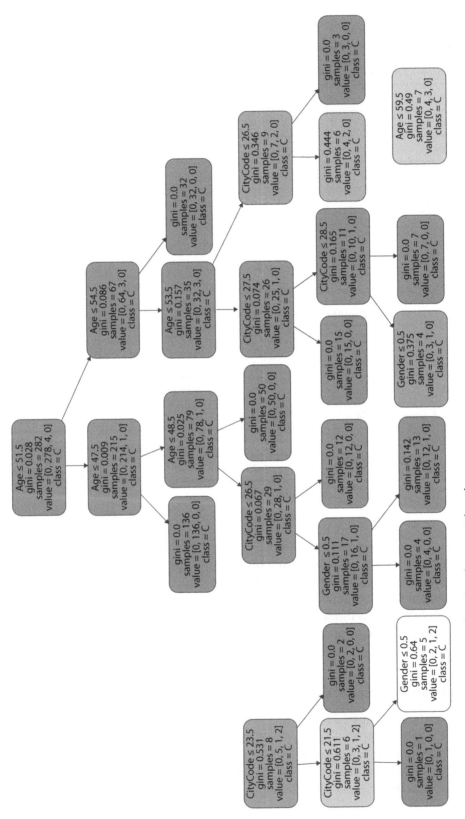

Figure 18.18 Part of the decision tree based on the apriori algorithm.

```
    antecedents      consequents    antecedent support      consequent support      support confidence
0   (Male, Teen)        (C)       0.0594  0.9694  0.0594  1.0000  1.0316  0.0018  inf
1   (Male, Yadgir)      (C)       0.0517  0.9694  0.0517  1.0000  1.0316  0.0016  inf
2   (Male, Udupi, MiddleAged)    (C)       0.0579  0.9694  0.0579  1.0000  1.0316  0.0018  inf
3   (Mandya)            (C)       0.0533  0.9694  0.0533  1.0000  1.0316  0.0016  inf
4   (Udupi, MiddleAged) (C)               0.0835  0.9694  0.0835  1.0000  1.0316  0.0026  inf
5   (Yadgir)            (C)       0.0904  0.9694  0.0902  0.9980  1.0296  0.0026  15.6410
6   (Udupi) (C)         0.1699    0.9694  0.1693  0.9969  1.0284  0.0047  9.7948
7   (Teen)  (C)         0.0978    0.9694  0.0975  0.9964  1.0278  0.0026  8.4633
8   (Male, Udupi)       (C)       0.1231  0.9694  0.1226  0.9957  1.0271  0.0032  7.1012
9   (Kid)   (C)         0.0950    0.9694  0.0945  0.9944  1.0258  0.0024  5.4789
10  (Elderly, Udupi)    (C)       0.0554  0.9694  0.0550  0.9936  1.0250  0.0013  4.7903
11  (Male, MiddleAged)  (C)       0.3144  0.9694  0.3123  0.9932  1.0246  0.0075  4.5326
12  (Male, Kid)         (C)       0.0524  0.9694  0.0520  0.9932  1.0246  0.0012  4.5301
13  (MiddleAged)        (C)       0.4910  0.9694  0.4874  0.9928  1.0241  0.0115  4.2469
14  (Female, MiddleAged)(C)       0.1766  0.9694  0.1752  0.9920  1.0233  0.0040  3.8184
15  (Kalburgi, MiddleAged)(C)     0.0632  0.9694  0.0621  0.9832  1.0142  0.0009  1.8212
16  (Male)  (C)         0.6373    0.9694  0.6185  0.9706  1.0012  0.0008  1.0401
17  (Female)            (C)       0.3627  0.9694  0.3508  0.9673  0.9979  -0.0008 0.9365
18  (Kalburgi, Female)  (C)       0.0534  0.9694  0.0515  0.9636  0.9940  -0.0003 0.8403
19  (Kalburgi)          (C)       0.1272  0.9694  0.1223  0.9611  0.9914  -0.0011 0.7860
20  (Kalburgi, Male)    (C)       0.0738  0.9694  0.0708  0.9592  0.9895  -0.0007 0.7508
21  (Elderly, Male) (C) 0.1635    0.9694  0.1564  0.9567  0.9869  -0.0021 0.7071
22  (Elderly)           (C)       0.2289  0.9694  0.2180  0.9521  0.9821  -0.0040 0.6388
23  (Bidar) (C)         0.0564    0.9694  0.0534  0.9467  0.9766  -0.0013 0.5744
24  (Elderly, Female)   (C)       0.0655  0.9694  0.0616  0.9405  0.9702  -0.0019 0.5148
25  (Bangalore-Urban)   (C)       0.0856  0.9694  0.0725  0.8471  0.8739  -0.0105 0.2002
26  (Udupi) (Male)      0.1699    0.6373  0.1231  0.7250  1.1376  0.0149  1.3189
27  (Udupi, C)      (Male) 0.1693  0.6373  0.1226  0.7241  1.1363  0.0147  1.3148
28  (Udupi) (Male, C)   0.1699    0.6185  0.1226  0.7219  1.1671  0.0176  1.3715
29  (Elderly, C)    (Male) 0.2180  0.6373  0.1564  0.7175  1.1259  0.0175  1.2841
30  (Elderly)       (Male) 0.2289  0.6373  0.1635  0.7141  1.1205  0.0176  1.2685
31  (Udupi, MiddleAged) (Male, C)         0.0835  0.6185  0.0579  0.6928  1.1200  0.0062  1.2417
32  (Udupi, MiddleAged, C)(Male) 0.0835   0.6373  0.0579  0.6928  1.0871  0.0046  1.1807
33  (Udupi, MiddleAged) (Male) 0.0835     0.6373  0.0579  0.6928  1.0871  0.0046  1.1807
```

Figure 18.19 Association rule of data.

	Model	Accuracy	AUC	Recall	Prec.	F1	Kappa
0	Extreme Gradient Boosting	0.980100	0.903000	0.997700	0.982300	0.989900	0.222700
1	Logistic Regression	0.979800	0.905900	0.997900	0.981800	0.989800	0.189700
2	CatBoost Classifier	0.979700	0.913500	0.996800	0.982700	0.989700	0.242400
3	Ridge Classifier	0.979300	0.000000	1.000000	0.979300	0.989600	0.000000
4	Gradient Boosting Classifier	0.979200	0.913200	0.995200	0.983800	0.989400	0.292600
5	Ada Boost Classifier	0.978200	0.875400	0.995300	0.982700	0.989000	0.226700
6	K Neighbors Classifier	0.977600	0.689200	0.998100	0.979500	0.988700	0.009000
7	Random Forest Classifier	0.977500	0.792300	0.995200	0.982100	0.988600	0.190600
8	Extra Trees Classifier	0.976700	0.872100	0.995000	0.981400	0.988200	0.146500
9	Light Gradient Boosting Machine	0.976500	0.890700	0.992800	0.983400	0.988100	0.251700
10	SVM - Linear Kernel	0.975400	0.000000	0.995800	0.979400	0.987500	0.006500
11	Decision Tree Classifier	0.970200	0.615000	0.985500	0.984100	0.984800	0.230700
12	Linear Discriminant Analysis	0.970000	0.897900	0.982500	0.986900	0.984700	0.327500
13	Naive Bayes	0.739900	0.833700	0.738400	0.994600	0.847500	0.078900
14	Quadratic Discriminant Analysis	0.241400	0.791900	0.227600	0.992100	0.365600	0.006200

Figure 18.20 Model comparison.

18.5.3 System Generated Facts on Pandas

1. In Figure 18.22, the graph below shows the age group with maximum infections, and the next image shows the gender proportion.
   Same way in Figure 18.23, in the month of June, the cases are mostly from travel to Maharashtra and travel to Mumbai.

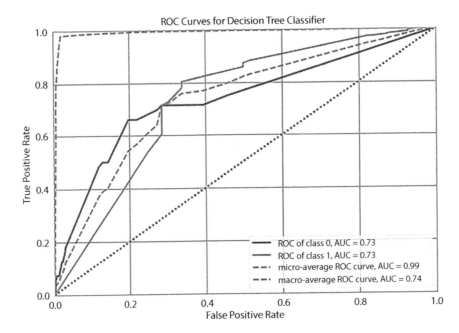

Figure 18.21 ROC for decision tree classifier.

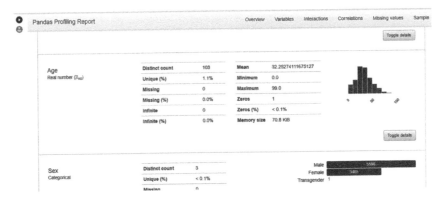

Figure 18.22 Age-wise case distribution.

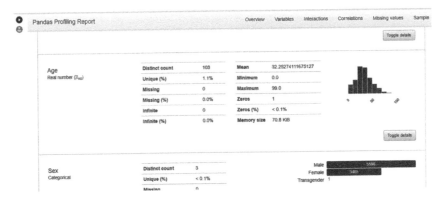

Figure 18.23 Cases from Maharashtra.

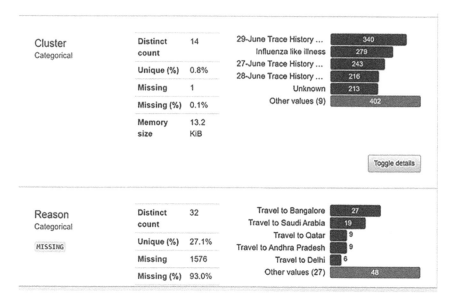

Figure 18.24 Indicating cluster and reason attribute.

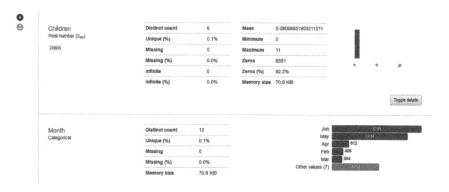

Figure 18.25 Primary contact tracing.

2. Where is after June the data distribution is different, which is more of contact transmission?
   As in Figures 18.24 and 18.25, in initial days, number of children varies and is also traceable.
3. Whereas in later days, the number of children is limited, which means there are two possibilities: Maybe, awareness is increased or maybe traceability is decreased.
4. This also means slowly moving to community transmission.

18.5.4   Time Series Model

The time series model predicts the trend and proposes a short-term prediction of the transmission of COVID-19, which will be favorable to take the preventive measures for COVID-19 by the respective authorities at all levels [15].

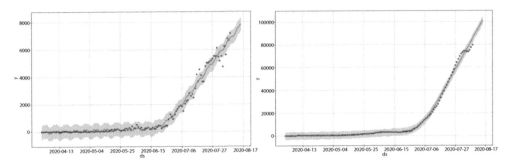

Figure 18.26 New cases forecast and active cases forecast.

Active cases forecast

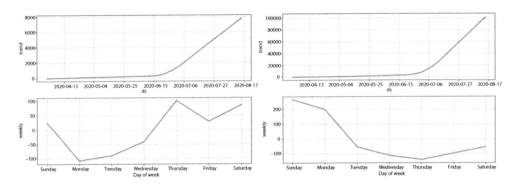

Figure 18.27 New cases trend and weekly curve and active cases trend and weekly curve.

Figure 18.26 shows the new cases forecast and active cases forecast using prophet model. Figure 18.27 shows the new cases trend and weekly curve and the active cases trend and weekly curve.

18.6 Exploratory Data Analysis

The exploratory analysis, referred to as EDA in short, for the KaTrace dataset is done to understand the current scenarios, conducts a future forecast for the betterment, and has a clear insight with interesting facts to handle the pandemic in a controlled manner. What caused the increase in virus spread count and the death counts over time despite the lockdown? Certain age groups are directly or indirectly responsible for the widespread which we currently face. Figure 18.28 indicated the new cases, active cases, and sample test conducted. The sample test has increased over a time, and the active case growth is exponential.

Karnataka COVID-19 Cases

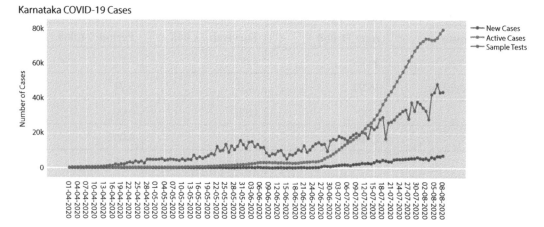

Figure 18.28 New, active, and sample test curve.

18.6.1 Statistical Inference

Detailed analysis and visualization of bivariate and multivariate statistics

The following attributes from KaTrace are considered age, surv_status, and period. The survival status was initially indicated as C for cured, H for hospitalized, and D for the deceased. For the computational purpose, we have modified the status as 0-death, 1-cured, 2-hospitalized indicated in Table 18.6.

Analysis of attribute relationships can be performed in two different ways: bivariate and multivariate statistics [5]. Whereas bivariate statistics only analyze the association of a chosen pair of attributes, the intersection of more than two variables is analyzed using multivariate statistics. As per Tufféry [5], bivariate analysis needs to be performed before multivariate analysis.

The dataset has 44,394 hospitalized with 25,254 cured patients and 1,420 deceased. Considering the attribute age, the patients' survival status has a normal distribution curve showing the maximum deceased age group is 60 as indicated in Figure 18.29. Also, Figure 18.30 indicated the distribution of days toward survival status. The statistical inference for the dataset is indicated in Table 18.7.

Table 18.6 Survival status and gender count.

Surv_status	Count	Gender count	Count
0 - death	1,420	0 - female	26,226
1 - cured	25,254	1 - male	44,840
2 - hospitalized	44,394	2 - transgender	2

Table 18.7 Statistical inference.

Attribute count	Age: 71,068	Survival: 71,068	Period: 71,068
Mean	38.69	1.60	3.77
Standard Deviation	16.91	0.52	5.91
Min	0.00	0.00	0.00
25%	27.00	1.00	0.00
50%	37.00	2.00	0.00
75%	50.00	2.00	8.00
Max	105.00	2.00	53.00

Insights from Figures 18.29 and 18.30

1. Age group in the range 20–40 has a high survival rate.
2. Age group in the range 45–65 has high chances of deceased and should be with proper medical care.
3. The hospitalized count is increasing over time, which is proportional to the cured rate.
4. Patients infected between mid of July and August have more survival rate.
5. The percentage of male in the total count is equal to the percentage of hospitalized, and the percentage of cured is equal to the percentage of female infects.

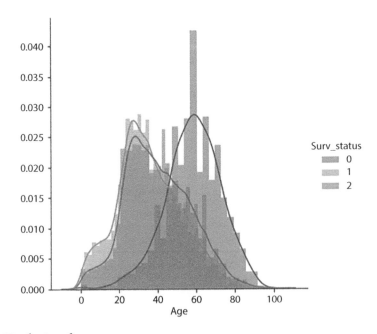

Figure 18.29 Distribution of age.

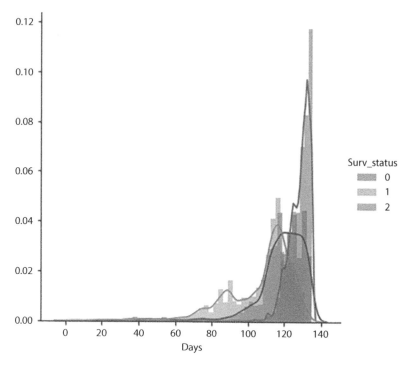

Figure 18.30 Distribution of days.

We are using the cumulative distributive function and probability density function with age as an attribute. The age attributes are counted based on the bin value set with the range 10.

Insights from Figures 18.31 and 18.32

1. If we draw a straight line from age value at 60, then it intersects the curve cumulative distribution function at a value approximately equal to 0.8, i.e., there are 80% people from the cumulative sum of 0 to 60 age group.
2. It is observed that people who had been infected with the age group of 0 to 50 survived.

Some of the general insights from the statistical data analytics are as follows:

1. P17121 is the patient with a widespread count in primary contact with 60 people, and P4350 is the second highest with 51 counts.
2. Over time, the primary spread count has exponentially decreased. This may be because of the increased resistive power or because of the awareness about the pandemic.

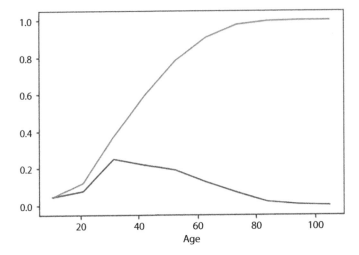

Figure 18.31 PDF and CDF.

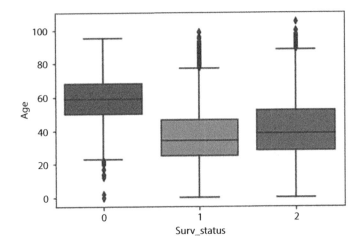

Figure 18.32 Box plot for survival rate.

The graph below represents the cumulative growth of confirmed COVID-19 cases starting from March to July 2020. To facilitate the comparison between districts, we have lined up the districts, so they are cases for one lakh population is indicated in Figure 18.31.

The total population count is higher, for which we have considered the spread count for one lakh population count. About nine districts have an upward trend in the cumulative graph represented in Figure 18.31.

These numbers give a sense of the relative impact of COVID-19 on these districts regarding total cases factoring in their population sizes. Also, the total confirmed, new cases, and growth rates are indicated in Figure 18.33. Also, the ratio of the total tests conducted daily over total confirmed cases is plotted. The date is used on the X-axis, and the ratio percentage is Y-axis. We have compared growth rates between total tests conducted and total positive cases, which shows the trend is upward.

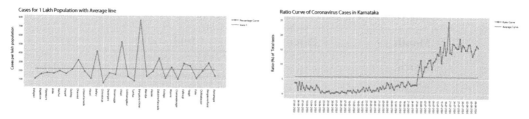

Figure 18.33 Cases for 1 lakh population and ratio curve for total test and confirmed cases.

The data used in the following analytical operation is extracted from the graph database of the KaTrace dataset using cipher queries.

In Figure 18.34, the higher the ratio lesser is the new cases count. Due to lockdown 1.0 in March and April, the new cases were in four digits, whereas in June and July, it drastically increased to five digits. If the ratio value increases in the coming months, then the number of new cases will be lesser. Also, comparing June and July, the pandemic looks contained as the number of tests increases, and the ratio is higher.

Using the moving average for September, we can see that the ratio value decreases, which implies that the new cases will increase. In COVID-19, Karnataka KaTrace dataset, patients are identified with the ID number assigned in sequential order. Patients are assigned with unique sequential ID along with parent and child relationship if available. The parent column indicates the source patient ID from whom the infection has occurred, and child columns have 0 or 1 with true and false meaning indicating the spread.

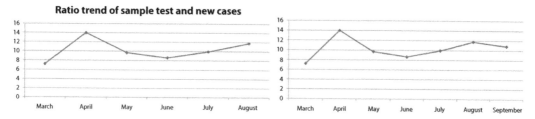

Figure 18.34 Ratio curve of sample tests over new cases and ratio curve prediction using moving average.

1. **New case compared with sample tested: Data from March to August 2020 August 2020 is indicated in Table 18.8. the ratio of test conducted and new case are compared.**

Table 18.8 Data values of tests conducted.

Month	New cases	Sample tests	Ratio
March	101	727	7.19802
April	464	6,492	13.99138
May	2,656	25,755	9.696913
June	12,021	103,817	8.636303
July	108,873	1,083,563	9.952541
August	140,431	1,650,494	11.75306

Table 18.9 Parent and child relationship count.

Month	Parent_count	Child_count
March	25	70
April	116	402
May	150	529
June	942	2,852
July	485	1,235

Parent: Patient who has a child node (have spread to others).

Child: Child who has a source/parent node. Table 18.9 indicates the parent and child count. We can clearly notice the ratio of spread that has occurred.

In the above plot, considering May, June, and July, we can say that the spread by parent and child relationship is controlled. Even after having an upward trend in the new cases, the spread is controlled at the parent and child level (primary contact level). The concerned authorities have controlled the spread at the primary contact level with good awareness and preventive measures.

With a more detailed view, see Table 18.10, indicating the patient with spread count considering the primary contact of parent and child relationship: Top six spreaders are listed.

Referring to Figure 18.35, the maximum spread age group is 20. But interesting is that the survival rate of this age group is also high. The age group in the range of 20–30 is well contained.

Table 18.10 Spread count of a few patients.

P_ID	Day	Month	Year	Spread count
17121	2	7	2020	60
4350	5	6	2020	51
653	5	5	2020	45
8300	20	6	2020	39
9546	23	6	2020	32
533	29	4	2020	30

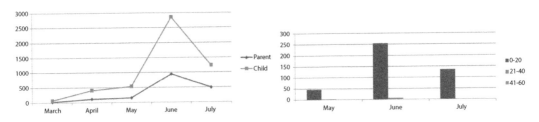

Figure 18.35 Parent-child spread curve and cases represented age-wise.

Insights from Figures 18.36–18.44:

- The age group with a high cure rate is 30.
- Analyzing the Bangalore urban patient's age, the maximum patient count is from the age group 30.

District-wise cases per one lakh population count: Data as of August 04.

Oversea Patients Analysis

The oversea patients, parent and child count with non-spreaders details is indicated in Table 18.11. The overall count of overseas patients in Karnataka during COVID-19, as reported by MoHFWS, GoK, is 672 distributed across twenty districts of Karnataka.

Patients From Maharashtra to Karnataka State

A total of 5,919 patients came to various Karnataka districts from Maharashtra, as shown in the below graph. Considering a total of 5,919 patients who traveled from Maharashtra, out of which 425 patients have parent-child relationships. Interesting is that only 117 patients have spread to 308 patients in total.

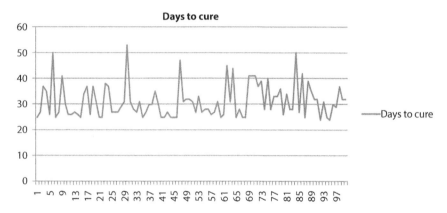

Figure 18.36 Day-wise cure status.

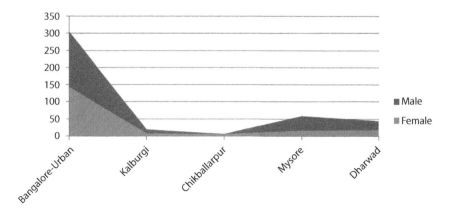

Figure 18.37 Gender-wise infection.

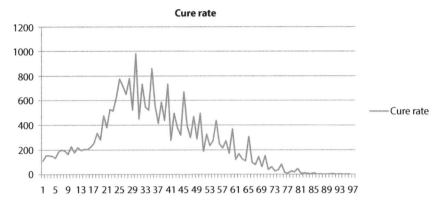

Figure 18.38 Curve rate over at a time.

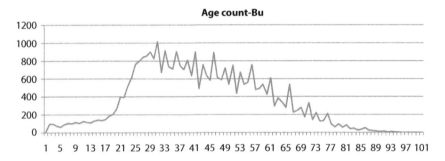

Figure 18.39 Bangalore urban age-wise spread.

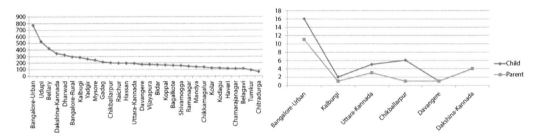

Figure 18.40 Cases for one lakh population and primary contact spread of major districts.

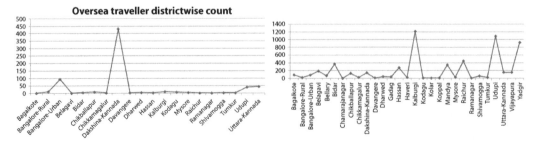

Figure 18.41 Oversea patient's district-wise count and patient from Maharashtra state.

Table 18.11 Oversea patient's details.

District	Child	Parent	Total	Non-spreaders
Bangalore-Urban	16	11	94	83
Kalburgi	2	1	10	9
Uttara-Kannada	5	3	44	41
Chikballarpur	6	1	8	7
Davangere	1	1	3	2
Dakshina-Kannada	4	4	431	427

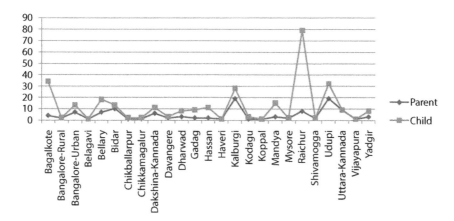

Figure 18.42 Parent-child of the patient from Maharashtra.

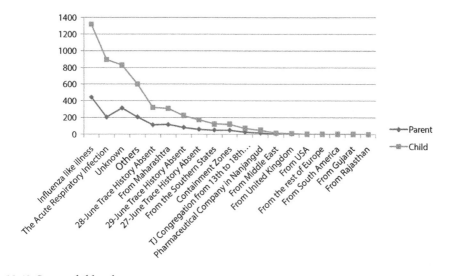

Figure 18.43 Parent-child with a reason.

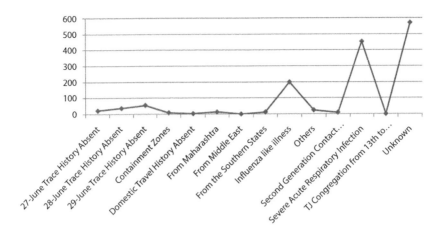

Figure 18.44 Death trend with reason.

18.7 Conclusion

Regarding COVID-19 pandemic situation in Karnataka, we proposed a GSA model incorporating preventive measures based on the results obtained. This study illustrates the GSA model's capabilities to identify the outbreak ratio and control the spread with preventive actions. In the proposed mathematical approach, the healthy population is computed to identify the population's susceptibility.

The proposed model shows that the control measures such as wearing masks, maintaining 6 feet of social distancing, washing hands frequently, and staying or working from home policies will reduce the spread. There is no efficient mathematical model that predicts pandemic conditions for preventive measures, but the preventive measures can be incorporated based on the results and predictions. The proposed GSA model was designed to analyze the pandemic's impact and predict the spread rate considering different dataset attributes. This model can make the contact tracing easier and suggest preventive measures for controlling the spread with primary and secondary contact. Graph-based analytics allows to naturally defining new relationships based on the attributes of the dataset, which discovers the interesting patterns. The graph centrality algorithm explores the interesting relationship, spread count of each node, and insights of the dataset.

18.8 Limitations

This proposed model was designed to look at epidemiological dynamics, and it does not illustrate the morbidity and mortality rate.

Acknowledgments

The authors appreciate the ample time given by their respective institutes toward this manuscript and thank the editor in chief of this special issue article for the opportunity and cooperation.

Abbreviations

COVID-19	Coronavirus disease 2019
MoHFWS	Ministry of Health and Family Welfare service
GoK	Government of Karnataka
GSA	Graph-based Statistical Analysis
EDA	Exploratory data analysis
WHO	World Health Organization
ROC	Receiver Operating Characteristic
PDF	Probability density function
CDF	Cumulative density function

References

1. Kuramochi, M. and Karypis, G., *An Efficient Algorithm for Discovering Frequent Subgraphs.* Tech. Report, Dept. of Computing Science, University of Minnesota, United States, June, 2002.
2. Cook, D.J. and Holder, L.B., Substructure discovery using minimum description length and background knowledge. *J. Artif. Intell. Res.*, 1, 231–255, 1994.
3. Mahesh, K. and Karanth, P., Organizing Knowledge to Facilitate Analytics, in: *Advances in Knowledge Organization*, vol. 15 - Knowledge Organization for a Sustainable World: Challenges and Perspectives for Cultural, Scientific, and Technological Sharing in a Connected Society, J.A.C. Guimaraes, S.O. Milani, V. Dodebei (Eds.), pp. 437–443, Ergon Verlag, Brazil, January 2016.
4. Hegde, L.V., Sreelakshmi, N., Mahesh, K., Visual Analytics of Terrorism Data. *2016 IEEE International Conference on Cloud Computing in Emerging Markets (CCEM)*, Bangalore, pp. 90–94, 2016.
5. Tufféry, S., *Data Mining and Statistics for Decision Making*, vol. 2, Wiley, Chichester, 2011.
6. Neo4j blogspot - https://neo4j.com/blog/neo4j-rdf-graph-database-reasoning-engine/.
7. Karanth, P. and Mahesh, K., From data to knowledge analytics: Capabilities and Limitations. *Information Studies*, 21, 4, 261–274, October 2015.
8. Moyano, L.G., Appel, A.P., de Santana, V.F., Ito, M., dos Santos, T.D., GraPhys: Understanding Healthcare Insurance Data through Graph Analytics, IBM Research, Brazil, ACM 978-1-4503-4144-8/16/04, April 2016, http://dx.doi.org/10.1145/2872518.2890544.
9. Yan, E. and Ding, Y., P-Rank: An indicator measuring prestige in heterogeneous scholarly networks. School of Library and Information Science, Indiana University, Bloomington, USA.
10. Li, Y., Wang, B., Peng, R., Zhou, C., Zhan, Y., Liu, Z. *et al.*, Mathematical Modeling and Epidemic Prediction of COVID-19 and its Significance to Epidemic Prevention and Control Measures. *Ann. Infect. Dis. Epidemiol.*, 5, 1, 1052, 2020.
11. *MoHFWS Media bulletin*, Government of Karnataka, Bangalore, March 2020.
12. Athreya, S., Srivatsa, B., Gadhiwala, N., Mishra, A., Nandi, S., Rathod, N., Sarath, A.Y., Sundaresan, R., Covid-19 States of India and Karnataka District Timeline 20-21, 2020. https://www.isibang.ac.in/~athreya/incovid19/data.html.
13. https://www.who.int/director-general/speeches/detail/who-director-general-s-opening-remarks-at-the-media-briefing-on-covid-19—11-march-2020.
14. Graph Algorithms - Combat-TB-NeoDB, 2020, https://combattb.org/combat-tb-neodb/graph-algorithms/.

15. Time Series Forecasting — ARIMA vs. Prophet | https://medium.com/analytics-vidhya/time-series-forecasting-arima-vs-prophet-5015928e402a, 2020.

16. https://www.nbcnews.com/science/environment/coronavirus-shutdowns-have-unintended-climate-benefits-n1161921.

17. https://towardsdatascience.com/which-python-data-science-package-should-i-use-when-e98c701364c.

18. Mwalili, S., Kimathi, M., Ojiambo, V., Gathungu, D., Mbogo, R., SEIR model for COVID-19 dynamics incorporating the environment and social distancing". *BMC Res. Notes*, 13, 352, 2020, Published online 2020 Jul 23.

19. Dutta, B. and DeBellis, M., CODO: CODO: An ontology for collection and analysis of COVID-19 data, in: *Proc. of 12th Int. Conf. on Knowledge Engineering and Ontology Development (KEOD)*, 2-4 November 2020 (accepted), 2020.

Part IV

PROSPECTIVE OF COMPUTATIONAL INTELLIGENCE IN HEALTHCARE

Conceptualizing Tomorrow's Healthcare Through Digitization

Riddhi Chatterjee[1], Ratula Ray[2], Satya Ranjan Dash[3]* and Om Prakash Jena[4]

[1]Department of Computer Science and Engineering, Heritage Institute of Technology, Kolkata, India
[2]School of Biotechnology, KIIT Deemed to be University, Bhubaneswar, India
[3]School of Computer Applications, KIIT Deemed to be University, Bhubaneswar, India
[4]Department of Computer Science, Ravenshaw University, Cuttack, India

Abstract

With an increasing demand of the world to catch up on newer and advanced technology options rapidly, the power of Internet of Medical Things (IoMT) combined with data science and biomedical informatics has become the need of the hour. From cutting down on unnecessary supply costs to bridging the gap between the caregiver and the patient, there is a plethora of options to explore currently. The world is heading toward a data-driven era, and hence, mining for these crucial biomedical data has become a thing of utmost importance. Using wearable technologies which can provide the caregiver with the information necessary to conduct a tailored diagnosis has become increasingly necessary, thus allowing the caregiver to stay updated with the health status of the patient. In this chapter, we are mainly focused toward exploring two different case studies: a) an integrated telemedicine platform in wake of the COVID-19 crisis and b) a smart sleep detection system to track the sleeping pattern in patients suffering from sleep apnea.

While designing the chapter, our attempt has been to put forward effective models which can be translated in real life to handle different biomedical scenarios and can act as a blueprint of an integrated platform to the biomedical community. Our aim has been to utilize the latest resources available at hand and use it to design the case studies.

Keywords: Internet of Medical Things, telemedicine, COVID-19, sleep apnea, big data, healthcare, neural network, machine learning

19.1 Introduction

Advancement of information technology has brought about a revolutionizing change in the context of medical sciences, which has changed the way we tackle the healthcare challenges. Digitization of the healthcare has brought so many options to the forefront, and the

---

Corresponding author: sdashfca@kiit.ac.in

Om Prakash Jena, Alok Ranjan Tripathy, Ahmed A. Elngar and Zdzislaw Polkowski (eds.) *Computational Intelligence and Healthcare Informatics*, (361–376) © 2021 Scrivener Publishing LLC

emergence of the concept of telemedicine has gained the maximum popularity. In the era of unprecedented health challenges posed by the ever-changing dynamics of the diseases, understanding the concept of Smart Healthcare has become more and more important, owing to the rise in demand for personally tailored healthcare facility. Also, tackling a large cluster of the population and tracking of the trend of some diseases need a randomized trial, which is only possible to be conducted by laying down an effective telemedicine platform, which is accessible to the scientific community for deriving conclusions, backed up by effective statistical evidences.

Bringing about these changes require an all-around transformation and introduction of technological advancements at multiple levels. The importance of telemedicine focused toward meeting of the needs of people at an individual level as well as at that community level is the main challenge that is faced in most of the cases. The true essence of the concept of Smart Healthcare lies in utilizing of the sensor technology to perceive and transmit information through Internet of Things (IoT) and IoMT (Internet of Medical Things), hybridized with the cloud storage capability. Also, Artificial Intelligence plays a very important role in creating of intelligent systems, which are efficient for prediction tasks. These platforms, backed up with the power of AI technology, make the whole system extremely user-friendly and allow for taking rational decisions with regard to the allocation of proper resources and making informed choices.

In our book chapter, we have primarily focused on two telemedicine platforms, which are becoming increasingly important and necessary. Monitoring of health also requires the aid of wearable technologies, which are gaining more mainstream popularity these days, with the accessibility of smart phones and smart watches. The data collected from these devices are to be stored in a common integrated information platform, which will be accessible to the healthcare professionals and scientists all over the globe, for carrying out informed and good quality research. This chapter mainly focuses on providing with novel ideas for a smart healthcare network to address different issues concerning the medical community.

19.2   Importance of IoMT in Healthcare

The IoMT is an infrastructure that links the traditional healthcare system with digital medical devices and software applications to synthesize various healthcare services. It has truly been transformative for the healthcare industry and profoundly benefits patients, care providers, and all other segments associated with the system. The simultaneous collection, processing, and analyzing of large volumes of data have been effective in managing the patient care workflow. The escalation of IoMT products has produced several opportunities, making this sector a veritable market for giant IT companies and startups. Microsoft Azure, a cloud computing service by Microsoft Corporation, enables the use of its AI tools to deliver healthcare services. Remote health monitoring via devices that use sensor technology has been instrumental in re-defining care delivery. According to a study conducted by researchers at Stanford University School of Medicine, wearable sensors that monitor vital signs and other clinical measurements coupled with algorithms can reveal the onset of infection, inflammation, and even insulin resistance in an individual.

19.3 Case Study I: An Integrated Telemedicine Platform in Wake of the COVID-19 Crisis

19.3.1 Introduction to the Case Study

Coronavirus disease (COVID-19) is a contagious disease that emerged to be a potentially fatal one, posing a global threat to public health in 2019. It is caused by zoonotic severe acute respiratory syndrome coronavirus 2 (SARS-CoV-2). An outbreak of the disease was first reported in Wuhan, the capital city of Hubei province in the People's Republic of China. The swift spread of the disease to several other countries with unprecedented high infection rates caused the outbreak to be formally declared as a *"Public Health Emergency of International Concern"* by the World Health Organization (WHO) on 30 January 2020. It gained the status of a pandemic on 11 March 2020.

The virus is primarily spread through direct contact via droplet transmission. Although the clinical manifestations of COVID-19 reflect heterogeneities, fever, dry cough, and fatigue are the most common ones. According to WHO, one in every five people are at risk of contracting serious illness and developing respiratory distress. Older adults and people with underlying chronic medical conditions like diabetes, hypertension, cancer, heart, and lung diseases are at an elevated risk of severe disease following infection. The outbreak management has been mainly preventive in nature, as no specific vaccines or antiviral treatments were immediately available.

19.3.2 Merits

The emergence of the Coronavirus pandemic has revolutionized the perception of telemedicine. Without the ready availability of vaccines for this infectious disease, social distancing had been enforced as a primary preventive method. Telemedicine has proven to be a boon as digital healthcare facilities are being increasingly utilized by masses during this time. Teleconsultations have risen significantly.

Telemedicine or telehealth is also actively being used during the pandemic to restrain vast patient displacement to healthcare facilities. This not only reduces the patient load on the hospitals but also *minimizes chances of exposure* of the virus to medical care personnel. Tyto Care, a telemedicine company, had partnered with hospitals in Israel to examine COVID-19 patients in isolated wards as well as monitor them in home isolation using their digital devices.

In our chapter, we have focused on building an integrated telemedicine platform with the help of IoMT and information technology in order to minimize contact between the patient and the healthcare providers, thus impeding the spread of infection. Our strategy involves breaking of the telemedicine model into three separate parts, so that we can provide a comprehensive case-by-case solution for individual stratum, as described in Figure 19.1.

19.3.3 Proposed Design

19.3.3.1 Homecare

The home-based module is at the grass-roots level as it connects and monitors the health of individuals in a country. It should be deployed as an application to connect to a broader

Figure 19.1 Our three-strata approach for building a strategic telemedicine platform to combat COVID-19.

population, incorporate device features, and provide a personalized experience. It is advised that the application be GPS-enabled to provide better services. Immediately after downloading the application, a digital personal health record (PHR) of the user is created. Examples of requested health-related data include name, age, gender, address, contacts, occupation, blood group, allergies, past medical conditions, and current medications. The PHR is shared with healthcare providers and public health authorities. The various components of the module are illustrated in Figure 19.2.

1. An AI-powered chatbot functioning as a healthcare assistant: A chatbot modeled on machine learning (ML) and natural language processing (NLP)

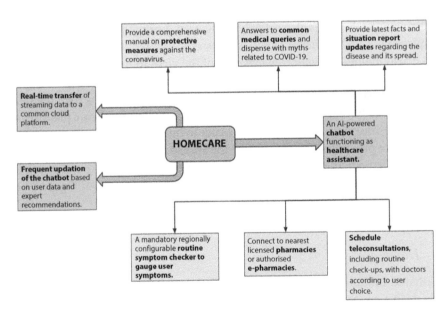

Figure 19.2 Depiction of the flowchart of the "Homecare" model for our suggested telemedicine platform.

can identify and train itself to perceive user needs better and optimize its services accordingly [6]. The functions of the chatbot are as follows:

a. Provide a comprehensive manual on protective measures against the coronavirus, including a guideline on the usage and utilization of different kinds of face masks and respirators.

b. A Frequently Asked Question (FAQ) section that will answer an exhaustive list of common medical queries and dispense with myths related to COVID-19.

c. Provide the latest facts and situation report updates regarding the disease and its spread. The updates should be of regional, state, national, and international level.

d. Schedule teleconsultations including routine checkups and follow-ups to previous appointments, with relevant medical professionals according to user choice. Integration of the national database of physicians is necessary. Third-party integrations can help the bot in the generation of e-prescription and assist in e-billing.

e. Connecting to nearest licensed pharmacies or authorized e-pharmacies to facilitate the online purchase of medicines.

f. A *regionally configurable* routine symptom checker that utilizes customized information and employs diagnostic support tools to gauge user symptoms. The usage of the symptom checker should be made mandatory, in the light of a pandemic. Users can either select their answers from a set of choices or write their responses. NLP solutions can be used to sense and analyze the responses to provide a better-recommended course of action. Integration of context into the system is of utmost need. Based on the user input and findings, risk factor detection is done. Risk ratio can be evaluated based on a number of risk factors. A recurrent neural network (RNN) model can be used to predict risk. The model learns from its previous results and inputs to increase the accuracy of predictions. Figure 19.3 shows the course of action that the system can take post risk evaluation. The symptom tracking tool is automatically activated if an individual is found to have "medium" risk status. Lab reports should automatically be uploaded in the user portal.

2. Real-time transfer of streaming data to a cloud platform to aid in data analysis and improve decision-making. The homecare database must be integrated with the community database.

3. Frequently updating the chatbot based on streaming user data and expert recommendations. Knowledge management is a vital function of the chatbot. ML techniques can be used to analyze the aggregated data and generate helpful insights to make the user experience more streamlined.

19.3.3.2   Healthcare Provider

This is the second component of the proposed design which has been put to place and is in fact one of the most important ones, as it forms the backbone of the healthcare ecosystem. Healthcare providers all across the globe are committed toward finding possible solutions to fight off the disease and telemedicine can play an important role in stimulating

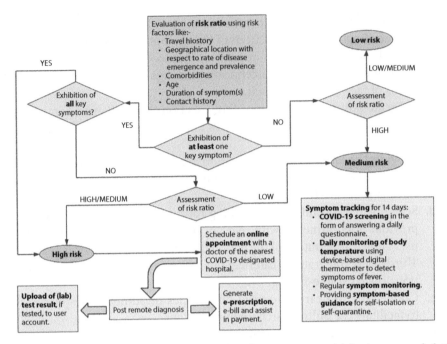

Figure 19.3 Modus operandi post risk evaluation based on the Homecare model for the proposed platform.

the process. Figure 19.4 demonstrates the workflow of the integrated network that furnish healthcare providers with important information needed to study the condition better and make prompt, informed decisions.

The individual components of the workflow are elaborated in the following points:

1. Access to the patient's digital health record at the beginning of teleconsultation.

2. Syncing of lab test reports with a patient's health history is vital. An AI tool that adopts NLP techniques to interpret lab reports should be integrated, thus helping physicians by making the process of diagnosis simpler. In 2017, an AI company, Doc.ai launched a software that used deep learning to interpret blood test reports.

3. An AI-powered radiology tool for automated medical image diagnosis can aid care experts in quicker diagnosis. Radiography scans have recently been proposed as an alternative COVID-19 screening. A Canadian startup, DarwinAI, had released an open-access convolutional neural network model, COVID-Net, that can detect COVID-19 from X-rays of individuals.

4. Integration of an AI system that makes the use of NLP techniques to provide clinical decision support to physicians. NLP techniques can extract structured data from unstructured patient-related documentation, which can then be analyzed by ML algorithms to augment structured medical data [6]. NLP algorithms identify a set of disease-relevant keywords in the medical notes. Based on its historical database, the vital keywords are selected and fed to classifiers to categorize into various clinical cases, thus reducing subjectivity in decision-making.

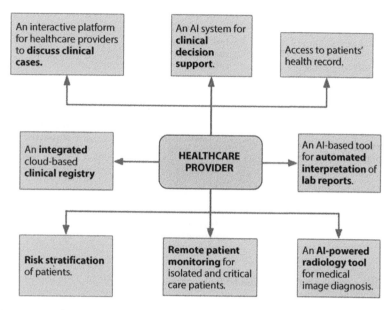

Figure 19.4 Integration of important components of the information flow that healthcare providers are being supplied with.

5. Remote interaction with patients to monitor and optimize care. In the face of COVID-19, contactless procedures of monitoring of patients in isolated wards have become essential to limit staff exposure to infection. Digital devices can be used to measure vital signs, integrated with automated systems that send alerts to care providers on detecting any abnormality. This method can also be used for routine monitoring of critical care patients or ones with chronic conditions. Clinical documentation and registry reporting of patients using NLP solutions are two aspects being extensively explored at present.

6. Establishment of a cloud-based clinical registry integrated across all healthcare facilities for aiding healthcare professionals in diagnosis.

7. An interactive platform for healthcare providers to discuss patient use cases in order to deliver superlative care.

8. Risk stratification of patients using AI solutions to optimize care management. This is extremely important to address public health management challenges effectively during outbreaks like that of COVID-19. Patients can be assigned a certain risk value and based on that value, the path of care can be determined. Predictive analytics tools can be used to build risk stratification models.

19.3.3.3 Community

The community-based module should be used by public health authorities and epidemiologists to guide planning and efficiently execute disease control programs. The most crucial points that stand out in this regard are shown in Figure 19.5.

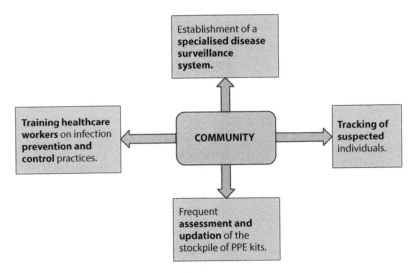

Figure 19.5 Workflow for the community model for the proposed design.

The various components of the model are described as follows:

1. Establishment of a robust categorical [5] disease surveillance system in the event of an outbreak to effectively curb the spread of the disease at every level. The field of *outbreak analytics*, an emerging data science, has gained momentum in the aftermath of the COVID-19 pandemic. It is touted to be a compact solution for accurate risk assessment, outbreak prediction, and analysis of outbreak responses. In any surveillance system, *continuous* surveillance is of paramount importance to improve response effectiveness. Figure 19.6 illustrates a suggested surveillance system and its objectives. Identification of appropriate, well-defined data variables for the specialized surveillance system should be followed by the periodic systematic collection of data. *Standardization* of data [12] is crucial for better performance of the AI model used for risk assessment. The data collection can be done through automated routine surveys and amalgamation of various registries and databases. Therefore, it is vital to have a secure cloud-based storage system that protects data integrity. The various kinds of data can include the following:
   - Maps of population densities and demographics. This can be created using spatial modeling approaches linked with the Global Information System (GIS) [10]. Standard gridded population datasets [13] can also be used.
   - Demographic surveys.
   - Human mobility data by integration of immigration database, airways, and railways databases of the country.
   - Available contact history of users.
   - COVID-19 test results and reports from clinical laboratories.

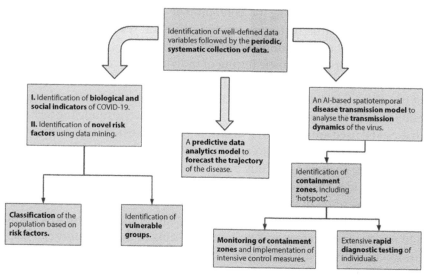

Figure 19.6 Depiction of the objectives of a possible surveillance system of the community model that can be put into place.

- Clinical data. NLP methods such as text mining [8] can be used to extract data from the records. The records are automatically grouped into a set of predefined classes. Data can be collected in two ways:
  - ○ Population-based health data [12] by the acquisition of users' personal health records (PHRs) and health surveys.
  - ○ Healthcare provider–based health data [12] by the accumulation of patient records from various medical registries. The presence of the COVID-19 will be the inclusion attribute.

Prevention and prediction constitute two fundamental units of an effective public health management system. Effective methods of prevention and prediction include the following:

a. Development of an AI-based spatiotemporal disease transmission model by the usage of various types of big data analytics to provide important precise insights into the transmission dynamics of the coronavirus. Descriptive analytics using statistical modeling techniques can be employed for analyzing the dynamics and planning targeted interventions by health officials. ML techniques can also be used. Incorporation of data visualization techniques [2] can aid in more sophisticated analysis. A thorough analysis of the spatial distribution of population is requisite for effective policy design as spatial heterogeneity impacts disease transmission [7, 11]. Identification of the different geospatial containment zones, including "hotspots", with respect to frequency of disease incidence and transmission efficiency must be carried out and the following steps should be taken.

- Continuous monitoring of containment zones for implementation of intensive control measures, optimization of resource allocation, and achievement of programmatic goals.
- Extensive rapid diagnostic testing of individuals in containment zones.

b. Development of a predictive data analytics model to forecast the trajectory of the disease, including peak infection rates and outcomes, thereby guiding public health response. Some of the common predictive modeling techniques that can be used are regression, decision trees, and neural networks.

c. Identification of the major biological and social indicators of COVID-19 and their further analysis for trends over time [12]. Data mining techniques can be used to identify and gain insights into novel risk factors [14] from the datasets. The result of the various kinds of analyses should be made available on public platforms to boost the advancement of epidemiological, clinical, and health service research. Regular monitoring of the indicators can help in the modification of the intervention programs [12]. This is done by analyzing the epidemiological patterns of the various indicators. This must include the following:

- Classification of the population based on the risk indicators. Some of the indicators can be age, comorbidities, gender, ethnicity, nutritional status, etc.
- Identification of the vulnerable groups [12] and examining the relationships between disease outcomes and these groups.

2. Tracking of suspected individuals through contact history and travel history (as depicted in Figure 19.7). Contact tracing should ideally be a voluntary opt-in service. According to the paper published by Chen *et al.* on a case study of SARS epidemic in Beijing in 2003, spatial-contact networks [3] for detecting spatial transmission risk proved to be beneficial. Contact tracing applications presently make the use of Bluetooth technology or Global Positioning System (GPS) or both and stored contact data to identify close contacts of the suspected or infected individual. The data should be encrypted locally and *only* public health officials should have access to location-based data.

3. Training healthcare workers on infection prevention and control practices by conducting periodic comprehensive training.

4. Frequent assessment and updation of the stockpile of Personal Protective Equipment (PPE) kits. This includes

- Contact manufacturers and distributors for timely production and distribution.
- Facilitate distribution of PPE kits to various healthcare facilities.

Our proposed integrated telemedicine platform is not confined to a particular use case of COVID-19 but can be translated for any outbreak of infectious disease that might occur in future. Effective implementation of the model depends on the geographic and socioeconomic profile of the target population so technologists and administrative bodies must customize the model accordingly. The use of the broadband network is suggested as it can tolerate greater data traffic. Easily adoptable low-cost technological solutions must be incorporated to make the model feasible to a greater population, especially the rural communities.

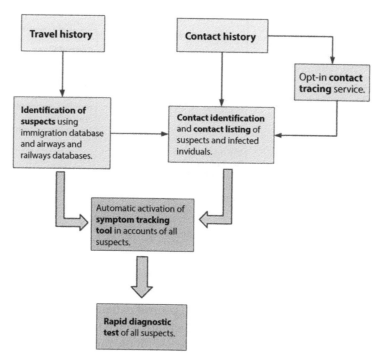

Figure 19.7 Illustration of a possible 'contact tracing' strategy for suspected individuals of COVID-19.

19.4   Case Study II: A Smart Sleep Detection System to Track the Sleeping Pattern in Patients Suffering From Sleep Apnea

19.4.1   Introduction to the Case Study

Sleep apnea [9] is classified as a sleeping disorder which can result in episodes causing stoppage of breathing at irregular intervals during sleep. Major warning signs of the patient suffering from this disorder include drowsiness and fatigue, even after getting an adequate amount of sleep per day. Sleep apnea [1] can be mainly classified into three major sub-types: obstructive sleep apnea (OSA), central sleep apnea, and complex sleep apnea. Out of the three, OSA is the most common one and it involves the throat muscles at the back of your mouth to become more relaxed than usual and collapse as a result during sleep. This results in blocking of the airway passage, which in some cases can prove to be fatal. Occurrence of five episodes per hour during sleep can result in cessation of breathing, which is the hallmark of OSA. Loud snoring combined with restlessness are major signs of OSA. Figure 19.8 describes the three types of sleep apnea in detail and how each one of them is separate from the other.

Apart from loud snoring, the glaring signs in day-to-day life, to prove that a person suffers from OSA can include irritability, heart burns, and dry mouth while waking up. Other physical complications can include storage of fat in the airway, which helps to relax and constrict the muscles involved in the breathing process. This narrows down the air passage, thereby blocking the entry of air during the breathing. Another physical obstruction that can contribute to OSA includes changes with respect to the changes in muscular activity

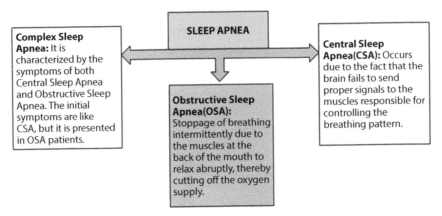

Figure 19.8 Classification of sleep apnea according to the different causes of occurrence.

controlling the air passageway. Understanding the different measures to be undertaken for estimating the low respiratory rate during OSA is critical for designing of the adaptive technologies, which is essential for categorizing the group of patients who are suffering from the disorder. Apnea-hypopnea index is one such measure which tracks the extremely low rate or cessation of respiration each hour during sleep. With the threshold value of the index set at 5, the people whose value exceeds greater than that can be categorized as the ones suffering from OSA. Interruptions ranging from 5 to 15 times per hour are generally recognized as "mild", 15–30 times as "moderate", and more than 30 times per hour as "severe", as per the categorization of the disease symptoms. Figure 19.9 shows the difference between the air passage of a person with and without OSA.

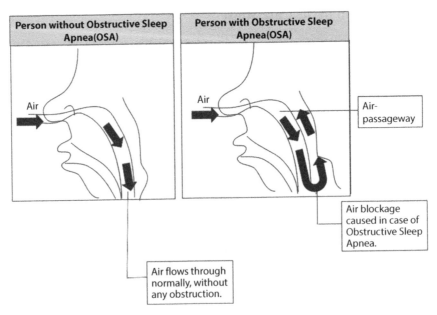

Figure 19.9 Illustration depicting how a person suffering from OSA different than that of a normal person without OSA.

Taking certain variables under consideration to predict whether a patient suffers from OSA is crucial for designing of the technologies that can help track and detect the symptoms. To be able to detect in the early stages is very crucial in order to prevent future complications, which can be quite serious and even prove to be fatal in certain cases. Along with these technologies helping to detect the symptoms for sleep apnea, certain lifestyle choices aimed at lowering the risks is also very important to be taken into account, such as cutting down on alcohol consumption and smoking, changing the posture of sleep and reducing weight.

19.4.2   Proposed Design

The power that Internet of Things (IoT) poses can be effectively harnessed into building a platform of interconnected devices, which can help in the timely detection of the disease. Along with it, with the advent of Big Data analytics in the technological scenario, the smart system detection methods have taken a giant leap, where most of the tracking systems have become automated. A person suffering from OSA can have a poor quality of life, which can include intellectual hindrance and decreased level of psychomotor abilities. The technology that aids in detection of the OSA episodes effectively can help in making a significant difference in improving the quality of life of such patients. The wireless technology to create an interconnected network is important in order to give the care to the patients from a distance, in places where a sleep clinic is often not available to track the different symptoms in patients occurring during sleep.

In our chapter, we have aimed at developing such an integrated platform which will help in detecting the episodes of OSA and track the different parameters related to the severity of the disease. Figure 19.10 gives a complete overview of the model being used for OSA detection.

Our model showcases a smart-watch embedded detection device, which is integrated with sensors to detect the physiological changes that are associated with OSA. The different components associated with the model are explained as follows:

- **Pulse oximeter:** It tracks the amount of oxygen level in the body while you are asleep. The recording in the pulse oximeter overnight helps in establishing the baseline, depending upon which the progress of the treatment is being tracked.

  The clip attached to your finger will give out a red light which basically penetrates through the surface of your fingertip and is further attached to sensor, which records the pulse rate and the oxygen level in the blood.

- **Movement tracking during sleep:** The three-axe accelerometer allows for the tracking of any movement during sleep. The displacement of the individual axis to detect the change in motion is referred to as the Signal Vector Magnitude (SVM) and can be quite effective in studying the motion intensity of the body. SVM gives the square root of the sum of the three accelerations and thus enables us to detect the changes in motion from all the three axes, rather than considering each one individually.

- **Microphone to track breathing pattern:** Our proposed smartwatch model typically will have a microphone embedded in it, in order to detect the duration

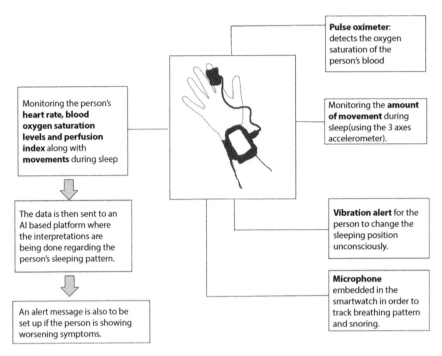

Pulse oximeter: detects the oxygen saturation of the person's blood

Monitoring the person's **heart rate, blood oxygen saturation levels and perfusion index** along with **movements** during sleep

Monitoring the **amount of movement** during sleep(using the 3 axes accelerometer).

The data is then sent to an AI based platform where the interpretations are being done regarding the person's sleeping pattern.

Vibration alert for the person to change the sleeping position unconsciously.

Microphone embedded in the smartwatch in order to track breathing pattern and snoring.

An alert message is also to be set up if the person is showing worsening symptoms.

Figure 19.10 Depiction of the proposed design to effectively work in detection of OSA.

and intensity of snoring patterns in the patients. Frequency of breathing can be well detected using this microphone. The results are recorded and passed into an AI-enabled platform, which is used for extraction of the important signals (which generally falls in between the range of 200–800 Hz), barring out the noise and other artifacts.

- **Vibration directed alert system:** The embedded vibration alert system in the smartwatch is used for stirring up the patient in case the oxygen saturation level falls below the threshold level.
- **AI-based platform to integrate the data:** All the information gathered are sent to an AI-enabled cloud platform, which critically analyzes the patterns and checks for the trends in the continuous data that is gathered. It then classifies the risk of the patient involved, depending on the Apnea-Hypopnea Index (AHI). AHI detects the severity associated with sleep apnea and measures the apnea and hypopnea events for every hour during sleep.

Future improvements in the devices tracking OSA could be integration of technologies which can detect the airflow in the patients suffering from this condition. Looking for developing unobtrusive wearable for detection of OSA should always be the goal as in most of the places, people do not have access to sleep clinics for getting the necessary treatment. Respiratory effort, also known as Continuous Positive Air Pressure (CPAP), is an important parameter which cannot be detected as of yet by the smart devices used at home for detecting sleep apnea. Technological advancements catering to these areas in particular should be an important component to be looked at while dealing with the future of OSA tracking wearable.

19.5   Future of Smart Healthcare

Emerging technologies are set to evolve the IoMT ecosystem. The collaboration of IoMT devices with mobile applications can ensure greater customization of services, a sector that is being widely developed by several technological solutions. The concept of ingestible sensors is still being immensely explored. Ability MyCite is the first digital pill to get approved by the U.S. Food and Drug Administration (FDA).

The promise of early diagnostics and optimized health management solutions is heavily dependent on technology. Malfunction of IoMT devices can prove to be disastrous. Ethical concerns regarding accumulation and storing of data must be addressed by stringent security and privacy regulations. For network protocol security, the Internet Protocol Version 6 (IPv6) is touted to be the next step to Internet Protocol Version 4 as it provides better security [4].

19.6   Conclusion

The prospect that Smart Healthcare entails is huge and, in future, will only penetrate deeper into the community. The major hurdles that it poses are mostly catered toward inaccessibility of technology to the lower socio-economic strata of the population. Digitizing healthcare is a concept which, if not made accessible to a certain chunk of the community, will render the whole idea of "medical information gathering" useless. If the information is not collected from people of different backgrounds suffering from a particular disease, it is not possible to draw a solid inference based on the evidences. Smart Healthcare options work tremendously in favor of reducing cost and time, thereby increasing the overall research efficiency of the scientists working toward a particular problem at hand. Increasing collaboration with the people of medical fraternities, research institutes, and information technology workers will enable in creating a strong web of network in the long run, which will further allow for better decision-making processes and in creating a platform supported by expert advisors, backed up with pure scientific evidences.

References

1. Al-Mardini, M., Aloul, F., Sagahyroon, A., Al-Husseini, L., Classifying obstructive sleep apnea using smartphones. *J. Biomed. Inf.*, 52, 251–259, 2014.
2. Cesario, M., Jervis, M., Luz, S., Masoodian, M., Rogers, B., Time-based geographical mapping of communicable diseases, in: *2012 16th International Conference on Information Visualisation*, 2012, July, IEEE, pp. 118–123.
3. Chen, H., Zeng, D., Buckeridge, D.L., Izadi, M.I., Verma, A., Okhmatovskaia, A., Zheng, X., AI for global disease surveillance. *IEEE Intell. Syst.*, 24, 6, 66–82, 2009.
4. Dey, N., Ashour, A.S., Bhatt, C., Internet of things driven connected healthcare, in: *Internet of things and big data technologies for next generation healthcare*, pp. 3–12, Springer, Cham, 2017.
5. Jamison, D.T., Breman, J.G., Measham, A.R., Alleyne, G., Claeson, M., Evans, D.B., Musgrove, P. (Eds.), *Disease control priorities in developing countries*, Washington (DC): The International

Bank for Reconstruction and Development/The World Bank; New York: Oxford University Press, 2006.

6. Jiang, F., Jiang, Y., Zhi, H., Dong, Y., Li, H., Ma, S., Wang, Y., Artificial intelligence in healthcare: past, present and future. *Stroke Vasc. Neurol.*, *2*, 4, 230–243, 2017.

7. Kubiak, R.J., Arinaminpathy, N., McLean, A.R., Insights into the evolution and emergence of a novel infectious disease. *PLoS Comput. Biol.*, *6*, 9, 1–9, 2010.

8. Küker, S., Faverjon, C., Furrer, L., Berezowski, J., Posthaus, H., Rinaldi, F., Vial, F., The value of necropsy reports for animal health surveillance. *BMC Vet. Res.*, *14*, 1, 191, 2018.

9. Motamedi, K.K., McClary, A.C., Amedee, R.G., Obstructive sleep apnea: a growing problem. *Ochsner J.*, *9*, 3, 149–153, 2009.

10. Musa, G.J., Chiang, P.H., Sylk, T., Bavley, R., Keating, W., Lakew, B., Hoven, C.W., Use of GIS mapping as a public health tool—from cholera to cancer. *Health Serv. Insights*, *6*, 111–116, 2013. HSI-S10471.

11. Riley, S., Large-scale spatial-transmission models of infectious disease. *Science*, *316*, 5829, 1298–1301, 2007.

12. Soucie, J.M., Public health surveillance and data collection: general principles and impact on hemophilia care. *Hematology*, *17*, sup1, s144–s146, 2012.

13. Tatem, A.J., Adamo, S., Bharti, N., Burgert, C.R., Castro, M., Dorelien, A., Montgomery, M.R., Mapping populations at risk: improving spatial demographic data for infectious disease modeling and metric derivation. *Popul. Health Metr.*, *10*, 1, 8, 2012.

14. VoPham, T., Hart, J.E., Laden, F., Chiang, Y.Y., Emerging trends in geospatial artificial intelligence (geoAI): potential applications for environmental epidemiology. *Environ. Health*, *17*, 1, 40, 2018.

20

Domain Adaptation of Parts of Speech Annotators in Hindi Biomedical Corpus: An NLP Approach

Pitambar Behera[1*] and Om Prakash Jena[2]

[1]Centre for Linguistics, SLL & CS, Jawaharlal Nehru University, New Delhi, India
[2]Department of Computer Science, Ravenshaw University, Cuttack, India

Abstract

The envisaged research demonstrates the development of bio-medically annotated Parts of Speech (POS) corpus in Hindi. The study presents the adaptation of POS tagger trained in general domain corpus to automatically annotate the corpus of health domain. The tagger is trained with 200,000 word tokens applied from the ILCI (Indian Languages Corpora Initiative) data of mixed domains (in addition to 50k newswire tokens of biomedical data) which provides a satisfactory accuracy of 92%. When adapted and tested with the fresh data of the biomedical domain, the tagger registers an accuracy of 86.5%. In addition, the paper also focuses light on the resource-poor scenario of Hindi and other Indian regional languages in general domain and biomedical corpus in particular. Furthermore, the study provides a detailed account of the issues and challenges encountered pertaining to inter-rater reliability, domain adaptation of corpus, linguistics, and NLP (Natural Language Processing).

Keywords: Parts of Speech Annotation, NLP, ILCI, biomedical text processing, Hindi, resource-poor, domain adaptation

20.1 Introduction

In the age of information revolution, the scientific research output of biomedical research is phenomenally and unprecedentedly developing in general and the knowledge base in particular is increasing and expanding rapidly [1]. The MEDLINE database in 2004 is one of the databases which contains 12.5 million records and receives 500k new and innovative citations each year [2]. Owing to the revolution of information, the biomedical research encounters information overload in the form of big data. To cater to this situation, NLP applications such as text mining, information retrieval, summarizing, and others have been developed. The boom in biomedical research in recent years has been excelled by the significant contribution of research and development in the fields of Artificial Intelligence (AI) and Natural Language Processing (NLP) in Computer Science. Therefore, one of the pivotal purposes of the text mining is to shift the responsibility of information overload from the

*Corresponding author: pitambarbehera2@gmail.com

Om Prakash Jena, Alok Ranjan Tripathy, Ahmed A. Elngar and Zdzislaw Polkowski (eds.) Computational Intelligence and Healthcare Informatics, (377–392) © 2021 Scrivener Publishing LLC

individual researchers to the computers with the application of NLP algorithms and statistical techniques, methods, and approaches. One of the objectives of the biomedical research is to search for knowledge and exploit that knowledge base in order to solve practical problems through diagnosis, prevention and treatment [1].

A large number of researches have already been conducted in biomedical NLP in major languages of the world such as English, French, Spanish, and Chinese considering various aspects. Contradictorily, Hindi and other Indian languages have witnessed a less number of research in clinical text processing so far which can be ascribed to the fact that there is a resource poor scenario of corpus even in the general domain corpus. There have been some corpus development activities by some major research institutions such as JNU New Delhi, IIIT Hyderabad, CIIL Mysore, and some others which include the corpus of health domain.

20.1.1 COVID-19 Pandemic Situation

The COVID-19 pandemic has supplied the arena of corpus with a huge amount of biomedical corpora which is ushering a new era in the domain of NLP in general and biomedical NLP in particular. This big data has to be pipelined through proper and systematic channel so as to cater to the demands of the discipline. This unprecedented situation has paved the way for not only major languages like English or Hindi corpus but also minor and regional languages such as Magahi [3] and Sambalpuri [4, 5], unlike the pre-COVID situation. Therefore, the discipline calls for serious attention from the academia and industry to focus on the application of big data or huge corpus to develop NLP applications to cater to the prevalent demands of the health system during the pandemic situation.

When the tagger is assigned to annotate the corpus of the other domains, the efficiency of the tagger registers a decreased rate of percentage [6]. Since there is the availability of the POS tagger in Hindi trained with the cross-domain corpora [7], the present study attempts at developing the efficiency, augmenting and adapting the tagger in order to annotate the corpus of the biomedical domain. The annotated output of the tagger proves to be having a fair amount efficient accuracy.

20.1.2 Salient Characteristics of Biomedical Corpus

Meystre and others [8] stated that biomedical texts have unique structural and linguistic characteristics because they are written by physicians and pertain to health domain. According to their opinion, they are specific informational categories, specific co-occurrence patterns and collocational words, paraphrastic patterns, deletion of context-related information, and telephonic or telegraphic or verbal statements recording, patterns of time, acronyms, and jargons. Some of the important features of the biomedical corpus are abbreviated words, section headers, undetected sentence boundary*, complex multi-words, date and time markers, names (generic and specific) of drugs, disease, alpha-numeric components, medical jargons, and so on.

---

*In some of the newswire sentences, it was really difficult to identify the sentence boundary detector.

20.2   Review of Related Literature

20.2.1   Biomedical NLP Research

AbGene [2] was one of the most successful NERs in biomedical corpus which worked extending the Brill POS tagger. It worked as the protein and gene names were included as one of the POS labels and incorporated in the manually annotated 7k sentences. It provided a precision of 85.7% and recall of 66.7%. GAPSCORE system was developed by Chang and others [9] in 2004 which used to assign labels on the words based on their appearance, morphology, and contextual features. It registered an accuracy rate of 74% on precision and 81% on recall measures with sloppy matches. Hanisch and others [10] in 2003 applied a large dictionary which encapsulated lexicons of gene and protein names and semantically specialized terms which provided an accuracy of 96% with specificity. Zhou and others [11] in 2004 have trained an HMM-based NER by selecting features such as word formation, morphology, semantic triggers, and intra-document name aliases. The application provided an accuracy of 66.5% and 66.6% on precision and recall measures, respectively. Chen and Friedman [12] have reported a system by adapting the MEDLEE system for the recognition of the phenotype information in the biomedical corpus. This system provided an accuracy of 64% of precision and 77.1% of recall. Tanabe and Wilbur have developed a gene and protein tagger applying the AbGene system which reportedly provided a higher accuracy than the previous reported research, i.e., 61% for exact matching and 88% for partial matching.

Text mining is one of the areas of biomedical NLP which initially received a great deal of attention. Yeh and others [13] have reported a system which applied figure options to curate a paper based on the presence of experimental information. Donaldson and others [14] have developed a system trained with words in MEDLINE abstracts for identifying the abstracts containing protein to protein information. The system provided an efficient accuracy of 96% and 84% on precision and recall, respectively. In an another study, Probabilistic Latent Categorizer (PLC) in combination with Kullback-Leiber (KL) divergence has been applied by Dobrokhotov, and others [15] for re-ranking documents as outputs provided by PubMed.

Cohen and others [1] in 2004 have provided an automatic strategy to extract synonyms of the names of the genes from biomedical corpus. Chen and Fiedman [12] have applied a large amount of MEDLINE abstracts to recognize co-located abbreviations and phrases and predicted 96.3% accurately. Chang and others [16] developed a logistic regression model on the abbreviated forms to predict their extended forms the accuracy of which ranges from 80% to 83%.

20.2.2   Domain Adaptation

Ferraro and others [17] in 2013 have reported an adapted tagger on clinical texts with an accuracy of 88.6%. They have taken two corpora of independent healthcare institutions, applied four leading POS annotators and trained them on general English data applying innovative models. Easy Adapt [18] is one of the taggers based on the perceptron supervised model which is modeled upon a method of domain adaptation that it produces superior results when evaluated against other augmentation approaches [19]. Smith and others [20] have developed an HMM-based POS tagger trained with bigram frequencies selected from

MEDLINE abstracts in the year 2004. They have registered a whopping and overwhelming accuracy of 97%. Campbell and Johnson [21] have applied the transformation-based POS tagger of Brill [22] which provides an overwhelming accuracy of 96.9%. Pakhomov and others [23] have developed an HMM-based TnT POS tagger applying a propriety corpus registering an accuracy of 94.7% trained on 100k tokens. This corpus is also known otherwise as the MED corpus later applied in another research by Savova and others [24] in 2010. The above-mentioned study evaluated the OpenNLP POS tagger which provided an accuracy of 93.6% on the MED corpus [25] when tested with progress notes registers an accuracy of 85%–88%.

20.2.3   POS Tagging in Hindi

Singh has proposed a POS tagger which applied a decision tree algorithm for learning on a modest size corpus of 15k words. The study was supported by manually crafted linguistic rules and efficiently produced an accuracy of 93.45%. Dalal and others [26] reported a POS tagger applying Maximum Entropy which reached an accuracy of 75% and started downgrading. Later, it registered an accuracy of 89.34%. Agarwal and Amni [27] in 2006 have proposed a CRF tagger with an efficiency of 82.67% making use of the morph analyzer. The training corpus also contained other information such as suffix length, word boundary and length, and special characters. Shrivastava and Bhattacharyya [28] have developed an HMM POS tagger which provided an accuracy of 93.12%. Mishra and Mishra [29] in 2011 have proposed a Hindi POS tagger which automatically extracted words and sentences from the concerned corpus. A Hindi POS tagger was reported by Ray and others [30] in 2003 the accuracy of which was not evaluated. Ojha and others [31] in 2015 have developed a Hindi POS tagger based on CRF++ which efficiently labeled the data between 82% and 86.7%. They also reported another tagger based on SVM which provided the range of accuracy from 88% to 93.7%.

20.3   Scope and Objectives

20.3.1   Research Questions

Will the domain adaptation be beneficial for a resource-poor language like Hindi?

Can the augmentation process be beneficial for other related low-resource languages?

How far does the tagger trained with a mixed domain corpus handle the specialized bio-medical data?

How well does the adapted tagger handle the specific issues of biomedical corpus?

20.3.2   Research Problem

In a low-resource scenario, domain adaptation of the NLP tools like POS tagger trained in a general domain corpus can be applied to partially annotate the specialized corpus of the same language or a language with the same script.

Hypothesis: Augmentation technique of Hindi mixed-domain POS tagger can be beneficial for a special domain biomedical corpus.

20.3.3   Objectives

Firstly, the undertaken study attempts at annotating a mixed-domain corpus of Hindi collected from the ILCI Corpora Project and some other web sources. Secondly, one of the purposes is to adapt the domain of biomedical corpus and get it annotated by the previous annotator. Thirdly, I wanted to oversee the performance and efficiency of the POS tagger of the mixed-domain corpus. Finally, I wanted to figure out whether the tagger could accommodate the corpus of other related languages having the same script, i.e., Devanagari.

20.4   Methodological Design

20.4.1   Method of Data Collection

The current study has applied the biomedical ILCI corpora belonging to the first and second phase which amounts to around 200,000 word tokens. In addition, the study has further incorporated 50k word tokens of newswire data of biomedical domain (considering present COVID-19 situation) crawled and sanitized by the IL (Indian Language) Crawler and Sanitizer. One of the most significant difficulties of dealing with the newswire data is that they have to be accommodated according to one's format unlike the corpora of the ILCI which is quite according to one's requirement beforehand.

20.4.2   Method of Data Annotation

The development POS tagger is really a mammoth task which involves the complicated processes of data collection to testing and error analysis of the outputs. There are some default and common stages of the development such as data collection, pre-processing, annotation, tokenization, normalization, training, testing, evaluation, and error analysis. The linear and chronological process may tend to become cyclic if one does not obtain satisfactory performance of the given tagger. The first stage is really painstaking as it involves either collection or creation of desired corpus in UTF-8 or ASCII encoding so as to make it machine-readable easily. In the second stage of pre-processing, one has to ensure that there are no glitches in the corpus which may hamper the performance of the model during training. Thereafter, the corpus has to be annotated following a specifically devised tagset. At the stage of tokenization, the data has to be tokenized according to the desired format for annotation either automatically or manually, although the former is followed. Even after the tokenization, one can observe that there are a few remaining glitches, errors, and encoding-related issues that need special attention and should be addressed. After these aforementioned stages, the corpus is now ready for the next pivotal stages: training, testing, and evaluation. One can go for the error analysis if they are not satisfied with the efficiency of the POS tagger in order to figure out the underlying issues and challenges.

20.4.2.1   *The BIS Tagset*

The Bureau of Indian Standards (BIS) tagset is a hierarchical set specifically designed by the POS Standardization Committee appointed by the DeitY, Government of India. It is a unique amalgamation of flat and hierarchical labels which covers 11 broader categories and

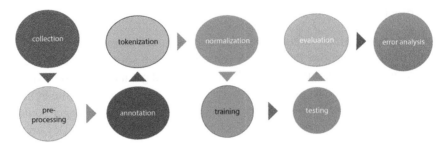

Figure 20.1 Systematic process of annotation (adapted from Behera, 2017).

39 sub-categorized tags for annotation. In the ILCI project, 50,000 corpora from the phase I have been annotated on the state-of-the-art web-based platform with the assistance of the annotators. A few other amounts of data have been annotated further by a semi-automated tool named ILCIANN App v2.0 [32] manually. The app provides a special feature of auto-edit tag list which provides a label automatically and by default so that no category goes un-annotated (Figure 20.1).

20.4.2.2 ILCI Semi-Automated Annotation Tool

The initial annotation of the ILCI corpus was conducted from the scratch having an IA agreement more than 85%. Later on, the agreement reached was more than 92% on the data of 150k word tokens. However, there was no IA conducted while incorporating the rest of the 100k word tokens accommodated later by the researcher himself. The application applied for the purpose of annotation is the ILCI ANN App V 2.0 developed by the ILCI Consortium. The annotation schema closely followed while dealing with the huge corpus is the BIS annotation schema developed by the some of the eminent NLP scientists of India.

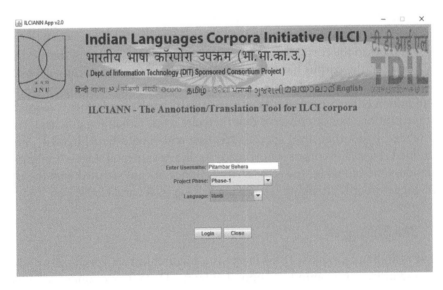

Figure 20.2 ILCI ANN App v. 2.0.

The ILCIANN App v 2.0 provides a special feature of auto-edit tag list which provides a label automatically and by default so that no category goes un-annotated (Figure 20.2).

20.4.2.3 IA Agreement

The tabulated representation of the data below demonstrates the average agreement among annotators, i.e., 91.15 (see Table 20.1). Furthermore, the total accuracy of the tokens where all the annotators agree is 89%, whereas the disagreement among them is 9.01%. Categories where all the annotators agree are symbols, punctuations, negative particle, and cardinal and ordinal quantifiers and disagree are proper nouns, foreign words, unknown words, and indefinite demonstratives. The reasons for disagreement could be ascribed to the fact that there are ambiguity issues in the categories like indefinite demonstratives. Categories such as proper nouns, foreign words and indefinite demonstratives are close-class categories where disagreement can be observed.

Table 20.1 IA agreement.

Annotators	ANN 1	ANN 2	ANN 3
accuracy	92.54	91.01	89.9
average	91.15		
all agree	89%		
all disagree	9.01%		

20.4.3 Method of Data Analysis

The following tabulated data (see Table 20.2) demonstrates the statistics of the corpora during the training and testing phases. The total corpus applied by the HMT during training and testing phases is 250k and 100k, respectively.

Table 20.2 Distribution of corpus in HMT and ABDT.

Domains	Training data (HMT)	Testing data (HMT)	Testing data (ABDT)
Health	66,400	24,345	Biomedical Domain Only 20,384
Tourism	30,122	15,329	
Sports	48,000	21,233	
Agriculture	24,036	17,540	
Literature	63,876	13,210	
Entertainment	17,450	10,210	
Total	249,884	100,459	20,384

20.4.3.1   The Theory of Support Vector Machines

The support vector machines (SVMs) by Vapnik [33] are the supervised learning algorithms which analyze data and recognize different patterns. If there is a set of data labeled as belonging to either of the categories of negative and positive and SVM algorithm develops a model which further assigns a label to a fed word based on its earlier learned model which makes it non-probabilistic and binary linear classifier in nature.

If we provide a set of data in N training examples {(x1, y1),..., (x_N, y_N)}, where each example x_i stands for a vector R^N and class label $y_i \in$ {−1, +1}, then an SVM learning model learns to classify the set of positive examples from their counterpart through a hyperplane with maximal margin[†]. The linear classifier or separator is defined by two components a weight vector w (with one component for each feature), and a bias b which stands for the distance of the hyperplane to the origin. The classification rule of an SVM is as follows:[‡]

$$\text{sgn} (f(x, w, b)) \tag{20.1}$$

$$f(x, w, b) = <w \cdot x> + b \tag{20.2}$$

being x the example to be classified. In the linearly separable case, learning the maximal margin hyperplane (w, b) can be stated as "a convex quadratic optimization problem with a unique solution": minimize $\|w\|$, subject to the constraints (one for each training example):

$$y_i (<w \cdot x_i> + b) \geq 1 \tag{20.3}[4]$$

Given some training data $\mathcal{D}$, a set of n points of the form

$$\mathcal{D} = \{(x_i, y_i) \mid x_i \in \mathbb{R}^p, y_i \in \{-1, 1\}\}_{i=1}^n \tag{20.4}$$

20.4.3.2   Experimental Setup

The below configuration (see Figure 20.3) file demonstrates the feature template selected during the modeling of the training through the SVM algorithm. As the figure suggests, the file encapsulates medium verbose (-V2), whereas the mode of learning and annotation for the automatic tagging is set the LRL method. The LRL method is left-right-left. The features of the corpus such as word, ambiguity level, probable tags, and the C parameter are set to the default setting. The other features such as dictionary look-up, prefixes, and suffixes have not considered for selection. However, the D ratio selected for the purpose has been taken as 0.005.

[†]the margin is defined as "the distance of the hyperplane to the nearest of the positive and negative examples" [34]
[‡]Ibid.

word features	$w_{-3}, w_{-2}, w_{-1}, w_0, w_{+1}, w_{+2}, w_{+3}$
POS features	$p_{-3}, p_{-2}, p_{-1}, p_0, p_{+1}, p_{+2}, p_{+3}$
ambiguity classes	a_0, a_1, a_2, a_3
may_be's	m_0, m_1, m_2, m_3

Figure 20.3 Feature template of the SVM POS tagger model.

20.5   Evaluation

The tabulated data in the following Table 20.3 demonstrates the category-wise accuracy rates of both the taggers HMT and ABDT in percentage. It has been observed that the categories such as foreign words, unknown words, proper nouns, gerundive verbs, adjective, and indefinite demonstrative are the lowest performing ones. While the categories such as punctuations, cardinal quantifiers, spatio-temporal nouns, coordinating conjunctions, negative particles, and a few others are the highest performing ones.

Table 20.3 Category-wise evaluation results of HMT and ABDT.

Id	Description	Tag	HMT accuracy (in %)	ABDT accuracy (in %)
1	Common Noun	N_NN	99.26	81.76
2	Proper Noun	N_NNP	81.71	73.82
3	Spatial-temporal Nouns	N_NST	96.43	97.48
5	Personal Pronoun	PR_PRP	92	87.18
6	Reflexive Pronoun	PR_PRF	96.83	94.08
7	Relative Pronoun	PR_PRL	93	93.19
8	Reciprocal Pronoun	PR_PRC	96	94.59
9	Interrogative Pronoun	PR_PRQ	92.12	93.34
10	Indefinite Pronoun	PR_PRI	98.32	91.44
11	Deictic Demonstrative	DM_DMD	99.12	89.21
12	Relative Demonstrative	DM_DMR	86.06	83.37
13	Interrogative Demonstrative	DM_DMQ	89.04	81.72
14	Indefinite Demonstrative	DM_DMI	81.39	80.79
15	Main Verb	V_VM	97.56	90.11
16	Finite Verb	V_VM_VF	94.32	87.07
17	Non-finite Verb	V_VM_VNF	92.66	88.03

(Continued)

Table 20.3 Category-wise Evaluation Results of HMT and ABDT. (*Continued*)

Id	Description	Tag	HMT accuracy (in %)	ABDT accuracy (in %)
18	Infinitive Verb	V_VM_VINF	96.79	92.72
19	Gerundive Verb	V_VM_VNG	82.66	77.89
20	Auxiliary Verb	V_VAUX	92.65	90.53
21	Adjective	JJ	88.87	80.02
22	Adverb	RB	94.92	84.3
23	Postposition	PSP	87.93	82.23
24	Coordinating Conjunction	CC_CCD	99.32	94.8
25	Subordinating Conjunction	CC_CCS	96.22	87.5
26	Default Particle	RP_RPD	99.01	92
27	Interjection	RP_INJ	96.22	91.22
28	Intensifier	RP_INTF	98.78	83.17
29	Negative Particle	RP_NEG	100	97.12
30	Foreign Words	RD_RDF	51.33	44.96
31	Symbols	RD_SYM	100	91.19
32	Punctuations	RD_PUNC	100	100
33	Unknown Words	RD_UNK	69.77	57.38
34	Echo-words	RD_ECH	89.59	84.4
35	Default Quantifier	QT_QTF	98.33	90.01
36	Cardinal Quantifier	QT_QTC	100	91.46
37	Ordinal Quantifier	QT_QTO	100	97.13
Total			92.45%	86.58%

20.5.1 Error Analysis

The following chart (see Figure 20.4) demonstrates nine categories of errors such as open-class category, unknown words, lexicon gap, difficult linguistics, under-specified labels, inconsistent gold data, wrong gold data, multi-word expressions, and plausibly correct. These are based on the discrepancies between the gold file and the evaluation file of the ABDT. The highest amount of errors can be observed in the plausibly correct section which suggests to categories annotated inconsistently by annotators even though they are correct. Contrarily, the less error-prone category of the nine is lexicon gap.

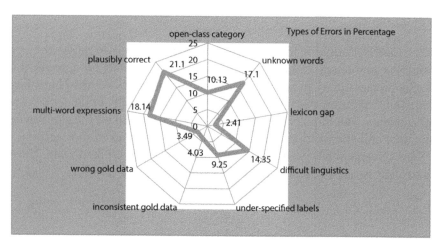

Figure 20.4 Typological statistics of errors.

The graphs (see Figure 20.5) demonstrated below exhibit a comparative analysis of error rates of various categories between HMT and ABDT. Categories such as foreign words, unknown words, proper noun, gerundive verb, adjective, and indefinite demonstrative have registered errors in both the taggers except interrogative demonstrative which is part of the ABDT. The highest error-prone common categories are foreign words, unknown words, and proper nouns for both the taggers. Out of these each seven error-prone categories, the less error-prone common categories are adjective, gerundive, and indefinite demonstrative. One of the observations that could be made here is that in both the taggers the highest amount of error is registered in categories which are open-class in nature. The open-class category refers to the parts of speeches which keep on changing according to the changing time.

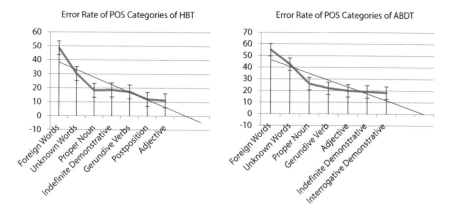

Figure 20.5 A comparison of error rates between HMT and ABDT.

20.5.2   Fleiss' Kappa

Fleiss (1971) has introduced a Kappa score measurement [35] to gauge the agreement between multiple annotators. Cohen's Kappa is applied on the data for agreement between two raters. Kappa measure is an advancement or improvement over the percentage agreement calculation. The automatic tagger output has been manually evaluated based on reliability and adequacy. The Kappa agreement has been performed on the agreement among three annotators and the word tokens of 2k data have been taken into account for that purpose. Their agreement has been rated based on the five-point Likert scale. The numeric 1 suggests strongly agree, whereas 0 stands for strongly disagree.

$$\kappa = \frac{\bar{P} - \bar{P}_e}{1 - \bar{P}_e}$$

Kappa can be defined as the degree of agreement among annotators that is obtainable above chance divided by the agreement actually achieved. The Kappa score for reliability is 0.81 while the score of adequacy is 0.78.

20.6   Issues

It is an established fact that even if we are at a stage of computing big data, IT revolution and NLP, we have not been able to gather abundant computational resources for our languages which are less-resourced already. The condition of the general domain corpus is grim; the situation in specialized domain such as health or biomedical domain is really inexplicable. One of the reasons that we need to focus on these resource-poor languages like Hindi and other regional languages is that sooner or later they are going to be the pivotal part of the IT and NLP market, as the population of India is 20% of the world's population and expected to rise in near future surpassing China. While focusing on the augmentation or adaptation of a specialized corpus, one of the obvious difficulties faced by researchers is the efficiency because of the nature of the application applied which is trained on general domain corpus. There are also issues pertaining to ambiguities and other discrepancies. For example, in the following instance /aʊr QT_QTF/ is a general quantifier but there is every possibility that it can also be annotated as a coordinating conjunction.

CC_CCD or QT_QTF: mʊɟʰko/P_PRP aʊr/QT_QTF d̪ə̪bai:ɟã /N_NN leni:/V_VM hai/V_VAUX

20.7   Conclusion and Future Work

Domain adaptation is one of the challenging tasks in POS annotation because a specialized corpus is at the focus of the issue. There is a probability that the POS annotator may perform or not based on the earlier domain of the data during the training phase of the developed

POS tagger. The study has provided a systematic procedure of the development of the POS tagger trained on general domain corpus and the development of biomedical corpus in Hindi. Furthermore, it has provided a detailed account of the adaptation of the biomedical corpus which provides a decent amount of accuracy. In addition, it delves deep into the underlying bottlenecks of the adapted POS annotation task with a detailed account of issues and challenges. One of the unique features of the analysis is its emphasis not only on the statistical evaluation but also on the qualitative evaluation of IA agreement and Kappa score. The former is conducted to figure out the consistency of the corpus annotation through qualitative agreement between human annotators. The latter suggests the agreement of the human annotators on the output of the automatic POS tagger. The present annotation work is at the basic level of morphological processing in the biomedical domain which can be extended to other domains and higher level of tasks such as chunking, parsing, semantic role labeling, and machine translation.

Acknowledgements

We acknowledge the ILCI Project led by JNU funded by the TDIL, DeitY, for providing the Hindi health corpus. We are further indebted to the ILCI Group for providing the ILCI ANN standalone semi-automated annotation tool.

References

1. Cohen, A.M. and Hersh, W.R., A Survey of Current Work in Biomedical Text Mining. *Briefings Bioinf.*, 6, I, 57–71, 2004.
2. Tanabe, L. and Wilbur, W.J., Tagging gene and protein names in biomedical text. *Bioinformatics*, 18, 8, 1124–1132, 2002.
3. Kumar, S., Behera, P., Jha, G.N., A classification-based approach to the identification of Multiword Expressions (MWEs) in Magahi Applying SVM. *Proc. Comput. Sci.*, 112, 594–603, 2017.
4. Behera, P., Ojha, A.K., Jha, G.N., Issues and Challenges in Developing Statistical POS Taggers for Sambalpuri, in: *Language and Technology Conference*, 2015, Nov, Springer, Cham, pp. 393–406.
5. Behera, P. and Dash, B., Documenting Sambalpuri-Kosli: The Case of a Less-resourced Language. *Indian J. Appl. Ling.*, Bahri Publications, 43, 1–2, 378, 2017.
6. Kübler, S. and Baucom, E., Fast domain adaptation for part of speech tagging for dialogues, in: *Proceedings of the International Conference Recent Advances in Natural Language Processing 2011*, pp. 41–48, 2011, September.
7. Ojha, A.K., Behera, P., Singh, S., Jha, G.N., Training & evaluation of POS taggers in Indo-Aryan languages: a case of Hindi, Odia and Bhojpuri, in: *the proceedings of 7th Language & Technology Conference: Human Language Technologies as a Challenge for Computer Science and Linguistics*, pp. 524–529, 2015.
8. Meystre, S.M., Savova, G.K., Kipper-Schuler, K.C., Hurdle, J.F., Extracting information from textual documents in the electronic health record: a review of recent research. *Yearb. Med. Inform.*, 17, 01, 128–144, 2008.
9. Chang, J.T., Schütze, H., Altman, R.B., GAPSCORE: finding gene and protein names one word at a time. *Bioinformatics*, 20, 2, 216–225, 2004.

10. Hanisch, D., Fluck, J., Mevissen, H.T., Zimmer, R., Playing biology's name game: identifying protein names in scientific text, in: *Biocomputing 2003*, pp. 403–414, 2002.
11. Zhou, G., Zhang, J., Su, J., Shen, D., Tan, C., Recognizing names in biomedical texts: a machine learning approach. *Bioinformatics, 20*, 7, 1178–1190, 2004.
12. Chen, L. and Friedman, C., Extracting phenotypic information from the literature via natural language processing, in: *Medinfo*, pp. 758–762, 2004, September.
13. Yeh, A.S., Hirschman, L., Morgan, A.A., Evaluation of text data mining for database curation: lessons learned from the KDD Challenge Cup. *Bioinformatics, 19*, suppl_1, i331–i339, 2003.
14. Donaldson, I., Martin, J., De Bruijn, B., Wolting, C., Lay, V., Tuekam, B., Hogue, C.W., PreBIND and Textomy–mining the biomedical literature for protein-protein interactions using a support vector machine. *BMC Bioinf., 4*, 1, 1–13, 2003.
15. Dobrokhotov, P.B., Goutte, C., Veuthey, A.L., Gaussier, E., Combining NLP and probabilistic categorisation for document and term selection for Swiss-Prot medical annotation. *Bioinformatics, 19*, suppl_1, i91–i94, 2003.
16. Chang, J.T., Schütze, H., Altman, R.B., Creating an online dictionary of abbreviations from MEDLINE. *J. Am. Med. Inf. Assoc., 9*, 6, 612–620, 2002.
17. Ferraro, J.P., Daume, H., Duvall, S.L., Chapman, W.W., Harkema, H., Haug, P.J., Improving Performance of Natural Language Processing Parts of Speech Tagging on Clinical Narratives through Domain Adaptation. *J. Am. Med. Inf. Assoc., 20*, 931–939, 2013.
18. Daumé, H. and Marcu, D., Learning as search optimization: approximate large margin methods for structured prediction. *Proceedings of the 22nd international conference on Machine Learning*, pp. 169–76, 2005.
19. Daumé, H., Frustratingly easy domain adaptation. *Proceedings of 45th Ann Meeting of the Assoc Computational Linguistics*, vol. 45, pp. 256–63, 2007.
20. Smith, L., Rindflesch, T., Wilbur, W.J., MedPost: a part-of-speech tagger for biomedical text. *Bioinformatics, 20*, 2320–1, 2004.
21. Campbell, D.A. and Johnson, S.B., Comparing syntactic complexity in medical and non-medical corpora, in: *Proceedings of the AMIA Symposium*, American Medical Informatics Association, p. 90, 2001.
22. Brill, E., Transformation-based error-driven learning and natural language processing: A case study in part-of-speech tagging. *Computat. Linguist., 21*, 4, 543–565, 1995.
23. Pakhomov, S.V., Coden, A., Chute, C.G., Developing a corpus of clinical notes manually annotated for part-of-speech. *Int. J. Med. Inf., 75*, 6, 418–429, 2006.
24. Savova, G.K., Masanz, J.J., Ogren, P.V. *et al.*, Mayo clinical Text Analysis and Knowledge Extraction System (cTAKES): architecture, component evaluation and applications. *J. Am. Med. Inf. Assoc., 17*, 507–13, 2010.
25. Fan, J.W., Prasad, R., Yabut, R.M., Loomis, R.M., Zisook, D.S., Mattison, J.E., Huang, Y., Part-of-speech tagging for clinical text: wall or bridge between institutions?, in: *AMIA Annual Symposium Proceedings*, vol. 2011, American Medical Informatics Association, p. 382, 2011.
26. Dalal, A., Nagaraj, K., Swant, U., Shelke, S., Bhattacharyya, P., Building feature rich pos tagger for morphologically rich languages: Experience in Hindi. *ICON*, 2007.
27. Agarwal, H. and Mani, A., Part of speech tagging and chunking with conditional random fields, in: *the Proceedings of NWAI workshop*, 2006.
28. Shrivastava, M. and Bhattacharyya, P., Hindi POS tagger using naive stemming: harnessing morphological information without extensive linguistic knowledge, in: *International Conference on NLP (ICON08)*, Pune, India, 2008, December.
29. Mishra, N. and Mishra, A., Part of speech tagging for Hindi corpus, in: *2011 International Conference on Communication Systems and Network Technologies*, 2011, June, IEEE, pp. 554–558.

30. Ray, P.R., Harish, V., Sarkar, S., Basu, A., Part of speech tagging and local word grouping techniques for natural language parsing in Hindi, in: *Proceedings of the 1st International Conference on Natural Language Processing (ICON 2003)*, 2003.

31. Ojha, A.K., Singh, S., Behera, P., Jha, G.N., A Hybrid Chunker for Hindi and Indian English, in: *Proceedings of the 3rd Workshop on Indian Language Data: Resources and Evaluation (under the 10th LREC2016*, pp. 93–99, 2016, May.

32. Kumar, R., Kaushik, S., Nainwani, P., Banerjee, E., Hadke, S., Jha, G.N., Using the ILCI annotation tool for pos annotation: A case of hindi, in: *13th International Conference on Intelligent Text Processing and Computational Linguistics (CICLing 2012)*, 2012, July.

33. Joachims, T., Making Large Scale SVM Learning Practical, in: *Advances in Kernel Methods-Support Vector Learning*, B. Schölkopf, C. Burges, A. Smola (Eds.), MIT Press, Cambridge, 1999.

34. Gimenenez, J. and Marquez., L., *SVMTool Technical Manual V1.3*, TALP Research Center, LSI Department, Univeritat Plotecnica de Cataluniya, Barcelona, 2006.

35. Fleiss, J.L., Measuring Nominal Scale Agreement among Many Raters. *Psychol. Bull.*, 76, 5, 378, 1971.

21

Application of Natural Language Processing in Healthcare

**Khushi Roy[1], Subhra Debdas[2], Sayantan Kundu[1]*, Shalini Chouhan[1],
Shivangi Mohanty[1] and Biswarup Biswas[3]**

*[1]School of Computer Science and Engineering, KIIT Deemed to be University, India
[2]School of Electrical Engineering, KIIT Deemed to be University, India
[3]School of Computer Science Engineering, KIIT Deemed to be University, India*

Abstract

The demand and recognition of Natural Language Processing(NLP) has been increasing in the clinical research field over the past few years. NLP is cost-efficient and it has been proven to be the best alternative to get the information in a structured manner. Research studies are assessed based on the patient-population grade; this is typically based on how a group of patients will respond or react to a particular therapy. Despite considering various predictions of NLP jobs at individual or on group of individuals, these assessments could not give the complete result. Because of the differences or inconsistency of the scientific assessments and discrepancy in the methodological assessments, it is quite tough to get the clear orientation. Various challenging issues involved in deciding the exact extrinsic and intrinsic assessment methods for NLP are discussed here, which can be used for the research of clinical outcomes. Mental health research is one of the main focuses of this study, because this area has not been explored by many of the NLP researcher's despite its significant relevance of NLP methods. For this, we are providing some suggestions like having a protocol which can be used while reporting NLP strategies/methods development and their assessments.

Keywords: Medical, data mining, task analysis, Natural Language Processing, optical character recognition software

21.1 Introduction

Health for all aims at ensuring good and proper healthcare facilities to be accessible to people from any of the smallest corners of the world. This becomes a major hurdle for the developing nations because the population of the people living in rural regions is quite large. There is a dearth of medical practitioners and diagnostic paraphernalia recognized in the remote regions which in overall points to paucity of proper healthcare facilities. A large number of the medical practitioners do not wish to officiate in the rural regions.

*Corresponding author: sayantan11kundu@gmail.com

Om Prakash Jena, Alok Ranjan Tripathy, Ahmed A. Elngar and Zdzislaw Polkowski (eds.) Computational Intelligence and Healthcare Informatics, (393–408) © 2021 Scrivener Publishing LLC

As its consequence, the already handful of care centers established in these regions lack largely in the number of medical staff members. It takes nearly a day for the population here to reach these health centers. For these daily wage earners, the regular check-ups come up as a hindrance to their livelihood. Even after the patients reach the care center, they suffer due to lack of proper examination time from the doctors owing to the high load of patients. Notwithstanding, owing to the injunction of networking systems, there prevails a divided framework which will be able to associate each and every smart device in automatic health centers [1]. This can be achieved with the help of the evolution of the narrowband IoT. Keeping the system as the backdrop, a framework to associate smart devices in automatic health centers established by using narrowband IoT and implement edge computing technology to be able to meet the requisite of dormancy in pharmaceutical proceedings can be brought to work.

ICT (Information and Communication Technology) has facilitated the use of various equipment like EMRs (Electronic Medical Records) and EHRs (Electronic Health Records). These tools are of very high importance for the healthcare system. These equipment increases the efficiency of healthcare system by decreasing the healthcare expenditure; it provides security to its users; it can also store large amount of data of patients related to medicines, treatments, diagnosis, result of the medical tests, radiology test results, and pathological test results; and with this, it can also store data which are unstructured. Because of the different natural languages used and various different ideologies used to discuss the same concept, it becomes little difficult for this healthcare system to understand [2] this information. Handling such type of unstructured information and timely treatment is a challenging task for the healthcare system because of its ambiguous nature. Because of these demerits, healthcare system was not considered to be so cost effective earlier. But now, Natural Language Processing (NLP) techniques are used to increase its efficiency and help the healthcare system by providing definite structure to the information. It does so by drawing out the necessary/relevant information from the data; thus, NLP effectively reduces the costs of the healthcare system. It is therefore against this background that this paper examines NLP techniques used in healthcare, their importance to the healthcare domain, as well as their limitations in healthcare.

The successful results of NLP techniques and its benefits in the healthcare system have resulted in the use of NLP to handle the complicated outcomes [3] of the clinical researches. Methods used for NLP appraisal are quite different from that used for the studies made from clinical researches. Clinical research studies depend on the NLP for data extraction. Software like open-source NLP has increased the demand for NLP as these are specifically made for Clinical texts. These software have the knowledge to analyze the clinical texts; these software also have extracting systems and the clinical language annotation, processing, and modeling, for text engineering, they have general architecture, they have SemEHR which is used for the retrieving information. Other initiatives like hNatural Language Processing (Health NLP) aim to improve the working of NLPs by providing transparency, reproducibility, and availability. In the past few years, the mental health related research field has also increased the use of NLP techniques. Some texts related to how the patients reacts socially or emotionally to different conditions and also how their system reacts to different clinical treatments are kept securely, these findings are collected through different social media and doctor-patient interactions [4]. Despite its broad possibilities, research is quite lesser in this field. Figure 21.1 shows the layout of NLP.

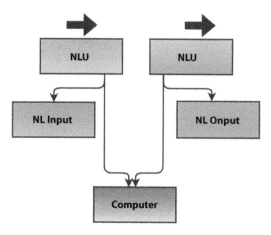

Figure 21.1 Layout of Natural Language Processing.

21.2   Evolution of Natural Language Processing

Natural Language in Symbolic Manner:

Era of the symbolic manner of the NLP started in the start of 1950 and continued till the end of the year 1090. Cause of symbolic NLP was summarized by John Searle.

1) Georgetown through his experiment/finding in 1954 infused the whole program explanation of a total of 60 Russian sentences into English sentences. The finders concluded that it would hardly take 4 to 6 years for the machine language to be a matter of interest for everyone. Unexpectedly, the technology was growing but the speed was slower than expectations; according to the report of ALPAC that was released in 1966, the technology could not fulfil the needs, and as a result, the financing of the technical idea of machine learning fell unexpectedly [5]. 1960: In 1960, two NLPs were found to be victorious: first one was SHRDLU and second one was ELIZA. SHRDLU basically worked [6] within narrowed "block words" with limited vocabulary. ELIZA was influenced by the idea of Joseph Weizenbaum. ELIZA, despite of being unaware of human sentiments, surprisingly showed some interactions like human; ELIZA provided responses which were generic like when the sufferer/patient said "my head is hurting", it replied "why did you say that your head is hurting?" 1970: Programmer in the early 1970s started writing the ideas of conceptual ontologies; it could convert language and information of actual world into the languages/data that could be understood by the computers. SAM, MARGIE, TaleSpin, PAM, and QUALM are some of the examples. 1980: Years of 1980 and 1990 are remarkable as they are remembered as the HEY-DAY in the field of symbolic methods of NLP. Parsing based on rules was the highlighted [7] field of research in that time. Examples are the progression of HPSG, two-level morphology, Lesk algorithm (semantic). Till 1980, NLP was basically influenced by the complicated set of the rules that are hand written. A little advancement was witnessed in the area of NLP after the involvement of algo of machine learning. 1990: Various considerable achievements were witnessed on statistical strategies of NLP in the area of translations through machines. 2000: Unannotated data was [8] available in the mid-year of 1990 because of advancement in the web technology; hence, the incompletely supervised and half supervised learning algos were the field of interest for the researchers [9]. This kind of study is more complicated and also it produces less efficient

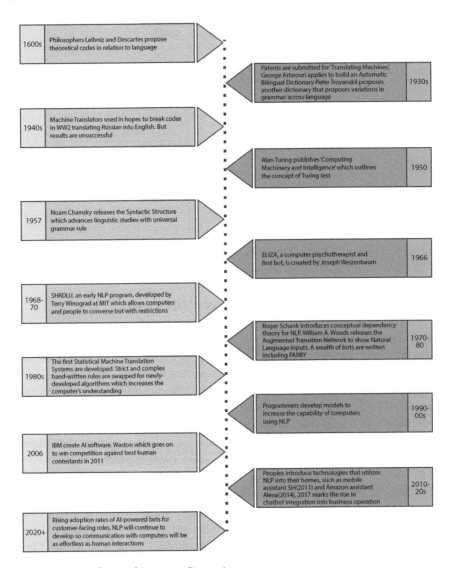

Figure 21.2 Chronology of Natural Language Processing.

results as compared to the completely supervised learning algo. Neural NLP or the present NLP: Deep Neural Network and NLP: presentation learning became adopted greatly in the whole world in the year 2010 for the NLP, because these methods could be proven to be successful in language modeling, parsing, etc. Figure 21.2 describes the archive of NLP.

21.3 Outline of NLP in Medical Management

The mode of communication which is used by all human beings is known as language. It can be verbal or written. These languages are composed of structured words, certain symbols, and some set of rules [10]. NLs or natural languages are the languages used by humans to communicate. Example of these languages can be English, French, German, Chinese,

ACRONYM	EXPANSION
IeCT	Information, Electronics and Communication Technology
EMR	Electronic Medical Record
EHR	Electronic Health Record
NLP	Natural Language Processing
hNLP	Healthcare Natural Language Processing
NL	Natural Language
ICT	Information and Communication technologies
NLU	Natural Language Understanding
NLG	Natural Language Generation
CRIS	Clinical Record Interactive Search

Figure 21.3 Abbreviation and its expansion used in the above article.

Japanese, and Arabic. There are many definitions. NLP is basically the use of computers for structuring/understanding natural languages that can also be described as a series of techniques (computational) used for understanding and equating/computing natural [11] texts which can be verbal or written that allows humans to communicate with the systems/computers in their natural languages, which is multidisciplinary, as it extracts its research links from AI (artificial intelligence), basically for the interaction of humans with computers or HCL (human-computer interaction). NLP can also be used in exploring various other fields like psychology, cognitive science, philosophy, and logical mathematics, which has two main tasks: one is natural language understanding (NLU) and another is natural language generation [12]. NLU is used for understanding/comprehending the natural language with the help of a computer; it also interprets the input language/text. Thus, NLU can comprehend the text and can also convert it to a language which can easily be understood by the computer. Natural language generation as the name suggests is used to generate the text. It structures the natural language in a specific sequence which can be understood. Figure 21.3 shows some abbreviations and its expansion that are used.

21.4 Levels of Natural Language Processing in Healthcare

Phonological Analysis: All the speech sounds organized in a language. For example, pop-up has two different sounds of p. There are three rules of phonology. First one is phonemic, second one is [13] phonetic, and the third one is prosodic. Phonemic is related to the various pronunciations; phonetic is concerned with the pronunciation of different sounds of words, whereas prosodic deals with the stresses on the words, their fluctuations, or frequencies.

Morphological Analysis: Morphology means the study of forms. Morphological study is used for identification, scientific study, analysis, and the explanation/description of the different forms of words and their structures and also their interrelation with each other [14]. Biomedical domain of healthcare has a very affluent use of morphological structure. Morphological study of words allows NLP to carry or handle such complex words with ease. These morphological analyses can be of two types: one is inflection and another is derivational. Inflectional analysis deals with the similar words having the same root, for example, eyes and eyes; both the words in this case have the same root word eye. Derivational morphology deals with the derivation or formation of new words from the pre-existing words, for instance, heart and burn are combined to form heartburn.

Lexical Analysis: The conversion of series of strings/characters into the definite sequence of tokens or group of characters with combined [15] meaning. Keywords, punctuation marks, white space, comments, or names are included in tokens. Thus, dividing/breaking the text into the tokens is known as tokenization. Any instance of token is said to be lexeme. In healthcare, examples of lexeme are DM and heart failure.

Syntactic Analysis: The process of conversion of the given input text into a definite shape/hierarchy which has certain meaning is known as synaptic parsing. This is of two types. Top-down and bottom-up parser. Top-down begins with the high-level sentence notation/symbol, which is said to be the root; it gradually [16] transforms into a tree, and the leaves of the tree consist of sentences of interest. The second one that is bottom-up parser establishes the relationship among the words in a sentence. Syntactic analysis basically deals with ordering of words in the sentences to get a meaningful conclusion. Figure 21.4 describes the various levels of NLP in the domain of healthcare.

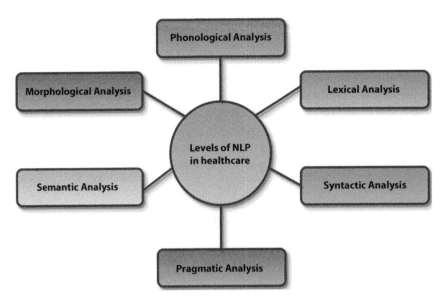

Figure 21.4 Levels of Natural Language Processing in healthcare.

Semantic Analysis: Semantic analysis focuses on the logical interrelation/interaction among the words of a sentence; the interaction should be meaningful [17]. Natural language is highly ambiguous or say heterogeneous in nature, which means a particular word can have different meaning in different sentences, for example, the word plant can be used to depict a living photosynthetic body or a manufacturing body. To overcome this confusion of polysemous words, this type of analysis requires a sensor which can differentiate among the words and can allow or pass only one sense/meaning of the ambiguous word. Lexicons like UMLS (Unified Medical Language System) are used to resolve the problem of this ambiguity or word sense disambiguation.

Pragmatic Analysis: This is related to the formation of paragraphs or documents by combining different sentences [18]; this type of analysis also deals with the use of particular sentences in different contexts. For example, mass in the religious/spiritual document denotes the ceremony/function and mass in the mammography denotes the breast cancer.

21.5 Opportunities and Challenges From a Clinical Perspective

NLP has a large scope in the clinical research field specifically in the field of mental health, as it is the least researched area. The advancement in the resources of clinical research or informatics has led to the advancement in the possibilities of accurate outcomes and has increased the effectiveness. Various types of data are required by the clinical informatics which are to be collected by social media, discussions, and interaction with the groups. EHR gives the exact value in less time provided the number of patients whose data is already collected or saved. Its coverage is more and also accurate than primary research cohorts.

21.5.1 Application of Natural Language Processing in the Field of Medical Health Records

The data is entered in the text formats and not in the form of pre-structured data; this is the most prominent problem with the EHR, approximately 70% of the data is entered in the text field. The CRIS (The Clinical record Interactive Search) System from the Maudsley Mental Health Trust and South London had approximately 30 million notes and letters with approximately three lakhs 22 thousand patients which produced about 90 journals/documents per patient. Mental healthcare does not rely on the structured format of the data completely, and this is the most important/salient feature of mental healthcare. These salient features include self-experienced reports, initial treatment determination and result/outcome evaluations/calculations, and some certain situations affecting prognoses and presentations, for instances, social support networks and complicated or stressful situations. Written information is always more reliable, accurate, and of more importance, thus, it helps more in the understanding the clinical situations. Well, these structured records are more beneficial for the researchers than the normal staffs of the clinics. Many researchers use clinical instruments like Positive and Negative Syndrome Scale and Beck Depression Inventory for keeping the structured data. This has helped in establishing a psychometric property for all the parameters [19] that they measure/estimate; these basically include concepts like severity level in the Schizophrenic patients (these symptoms include hallucinations and delusions). NLP can be used to get these ideas/concepts through EHR, though it requires careful methodology. For getting the desirable results from NLP, the process should focus on reliable measures, which requires a communication language which can easily be understood by all the related fields. Since medical practice requires utmost accuracy, converting the output of NLP into an understandable course/measure is important. It is very necessary to design the model of NLP in a way that it can easily resolve the particular problems of the clinic, for instance, it is very necessary to check the suicidal instinct or tendency in the patients through EHR though it is very difficult. Clinical construct increases the difficulty of this task. The tools or instruments that we have to measure this suicidal tendency are not efficient as such, and also the suicidal risk is quite rare. Data-driven methods provide us with the most appropriate approach to solve this problem by creating more accurate results. Application of NLP in mental health faces some other issues too, such as the shifting from simple/normal face or entity recognition to the high-profile recognition like socio-economic markers, and also detaching from temporary treatment [20] procedures/methods and switching to the permanent ones. Besides this, there are other problems related to computations such as shifting from single site application toward the broader multi-site applications and the use of translator for inter-nation uses must also be resolved. Some other challenges related to the data given by the patients have also to be resolved.

21.5.2   Using Natural Language Processing for Large-Sample Clinical Research

In large-sample studies, the NLP tries to extract or to pull the non-structured as well as some other additional information, which basically aims on finding the future predictors of possible result. In macroenvironment level which includes family or social issues and individual patient level, both the factors are included in the factors of large samples. Structured codes cannot hold the uncertainty of the diagnosis and it also does not allow the storing of other relevant clinical information such as mood and sleep which does not require any

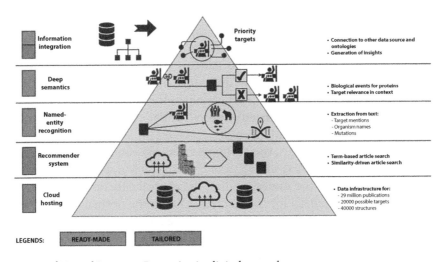

Figure 21.5 Use of Natural Language Processing in clinical research.

treatment but are useful for the treatment. So, NLP can improvise the identification of the case of the health record and it can also enrich the data as compared to the structured data. This rich data can result in the research transparency [21]. Before analysis, the clarification of the steps involved in the data collection is required for EHR study. For reusing the algorithms or structures developed by others, phenotypes are introduced in EHR. Introduction of the result of NLP with the phenotype makes it more difficult for the researchers who use EHR data for copying the result. Consider the example, when the data used to produce a NLP is used to pull/extract a phenotype like atrial fibrillation is particular to an EHR and geographical area. In this case, the NLP can give different results when we apply it on new or different data for the same task. If similar source documents are not available, their applications may be hindered despite sharing the NLP methods. Through the publication of study protocols, we can approach a reasonable solution to this problem. Figure 21.5 explains the process involved in it.

21.6   Openings and Difficulties From a Natural Language Processing Point of View

NLP has two major concepts: first is statistical which is based on the frequency of distribution and occurrence patterns and the other is symbolic which is based on the world knowledge and linguistic structure, and these are used rigorously in the development of clinical NLP. Development in the field of machine learning which includes neural network has considerable impact on applications of NLP, and thus, more developments are expected in this field. Developments in the field of network models require huge datasets (labeled), which are not available in the case of clinical study because the clinical [22] studies require the analysis/computation of EHR study. Another big challenge is the availability of the data, and ethical regulations and the privacy issues have to be resolved to use the reliable data of the EHR for the research; besides this, there are some other methods also available that can create a precise resource. Analysis of NLP systems is done using standard statistical metrics which are based on intrinsic criteria, it is not compulsorily optimal for the problems of the clinic. For resolving such problems, it is very necessary to identify what level of evaluation will suit.

21.6.1   Methods for Developing Shareable Data

Privacy or security issues becomes a concern when it comes to evaluating the texts from the health record which means the system fails to agree the similar authorities that all the data or information be it implicit or explicit has been de-identified (process used to hide the original identity of a person). Policies that deals with the safety issues make it complicated to store data, to use, and to interchange from one kind of study to another kind, and the limitations of the data exchange vary from countries to jurisdictions. A solution to this problem was developed in the form of synthetic clinical data. For instance, total of 301 cases of patients were taken which included recorded verbal handovers and annotated verbatim summarized record which is based on synthetic profiles of patients; it was shared and used in the year 2015 and 2016. In 2013–2014, synthetic data [23] was used in Japanese NLP in

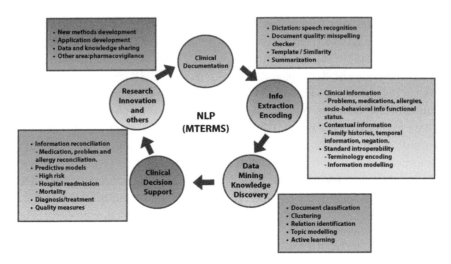

Figure 21.6 Solution to the challenges in Natural Language Processing.

shared tasks. For the generation of dialogue, synthetic record was proven to be successful. Figure 21.6 describes the solution to the challenges faced in NLP.

21.6.2   Intrinsic Evaluation and Representation Levels

While noticing both NLP strategies/methods and the outcomes of clinical research together, reducing the variations of grittiness is a tough task. NLP strategies are basically designed to point/identify the concepts of situations/phenomenon which are clinically relevant at a sub-document level. For instance, NLP strategies are used for retrieving the smoking status of patients, for example, whether the patient was a past smoker or present or a future smoker. While analyzing NLP methods, to check whether a NLP strategy perfectly points out or identifies the instances, Gold Standard Corpus having annotations is developed. For the evaluation score to be higher/greater, NLP systems must clearly classify the multiple or various annotations of Gold Standard Corpus. Whereas for the clinical research, only one of these can be correct. Having a higher number of irrelevant instances for a small group of patients can skew the NLP evaluation in regard to the questions of clinical research. For example, annotation of Gold Standard Corpus on suicidal info, for example, whether the patient is suicidal or not was used for developing a NLP system, and it has an accuracy of about ~91.9%. When this NLP system was used in the clinical research study to identify/point out the patients with suicidal tendency, applying a document and classification at patient level which was based on instance level annotations needed assumptions which were non-trivial because there were chances that the documents contain various positive and negative mentions [24]. It can now be concluded that there is a gap or difference between patient level and instance level evaluation of NLP. This gap has to be filled to resolve the differences among clinical outcomes and NLP evaluations. Before using NLP in clinical research outcomes, they have to be post-processed to filter out the instances. Post-processing can remove the instances which are irrelevant. Post-procedure is basically based on evidence which is available now, for example, the case identification of certain diseases such as asthma. This gap is not always present; these are not obvious and thus the post-processing is not necessarily required all the time. There might be some cases where NLP strategies/methods might be used for processing all the texts which are relevant and associated with a particular patient, for predicting a single/particular outcome or result for instance all the past texts can be used for assigning a diagnosis code. Patient level annotations, for example, reviewing the charts manually of a particular patient or patient-level clinical label, can prove to be more efficient/systematic for the development of Gold Standards and their solutions. The NLP system can more efficiently classify the groups as compared to the manual review and to measure the extent to which NLP is more efficient we can use evaluation metrics.

21.6.3   Beyond Electronic Health Record Data

Very emerging and positive results have been shown by working via computational language evaluation on transcription of speech for studying the disturbance and hindrance occurring in schizophrenic patients and also for predicting the chances of occurrence of psychosis. Advancement in psycholinguistics is also because of the presence of large datasets. NLP team has started modern levels of evaluation and metrics, for instance, judgment of present, future, and past mental health which is based on essays of shared tasks of early age or childhood longitudinal Cohort Data of 2018, CLPsych (Computational Linguistic and Clinical Psychology Workshop), but their direct application in clinical research has to be visualized. Tsakalidis *et al.* for the first time used both the languages and also the heterogeneous/diversified mobile photo data to detect the scores of mental well-being of the individuals with time marked against the psychological scales. This study got the promising result but their strategy or idea of evaluation included the training and testing of data from all the users, a condition which is faced more prominently while studying the predictions of mood score using data of mobile phones. If we want the evaluation to be more realistic, then we would use either predictions of some indicators with time for an anonymous user, provided an ideal model which can be created using the information's of other users or intra-user prediction with time, i.e., calculating the mood score and other health indicator provided earlier/previous data in row for the user over consecutive interval of time. New evaluation metrics should be introduced or inserted that focuses on the other aspects like time sensitivity and time-to-time predictions and longitudinal prediction of the indicators such as a score of a health indicator; all these should be done for the betterment of clinical utility. All these have to be forecasted with time and not like the predictions which are totally independent of time, because in the case of the classification approaches which are standardized, personalized data/model and intra-user sets are very helpful in monitoring the health issues.

21.7   Actionable Guidance and Directions for the Future

NLP strategy advancement for the medical area has arrived at full grown stages and has become a significant piece of propelling information driven medical services research. In equal, the medical network is progressively observing the worth and need of consolidating NLP in medical output contemplates, especially in areas, for example, psychological well-being, the place where story information holds key data. Notwithstanding, for medical

NLP strategy improvement to progress further worldwide and, for instance, become an indispensable piece of clinical results research or have a characteristic spot in medical practice, there are still difficulties ahead. In view of the conversations throughout the seminar, the fundamental difficulties incorporate information accessibility, assessment workbenches, and announcing guidelines. We sum up this underneath and give significant proposals to empower progress here.

Data Availability: The absence of adequately enormous arrangements of share able information is as yet an issue in the clinical NLP area. We support the expanded advancement of elective information sources, for example, manufactured clinical notes, which mitigates the complexities associated with administration structures. In any case, in equal, activities to make genuine information accessible to the examination network through elective administration models are likewise empowered, similar to the MIMIC-III information set. More noteworthy association between NLP analysts, essential information authorities, and learning members are vital. Further investigations in elective patient assent dummy (e.g., intelligent e-assent) could prompt bigger accessibility of true information, which thus could prompt generous promotion in NLP improvement and assessment. Working past EHR information, there is significant data likewise in available online information starting points, for example, web-based media that are of specific pertinence to the emotional well-being area and that could likewise be joined with EHR information. Endeavors to connect with clients in giving their public online media and sensor information for research are intriguing roads that could demonstrate truly important for NLP strategy improvement. Furthermore, notwithstanding composed documentation, there is guarantee in the utilization of discourse advances, explicitly for data passage at the bedside.

Evaluation Workbenches: Current medical NLP strategies are normally produced for explicit use-cases and assessed characteristically on restricted information sets. Utilizing such techniques off-the-rack on new use-cases and information sets prompts obscure execution [25]. For clinical NLP technique advancement to turn out to be more necessary in clinical results research, there is a need to create assessment workbenches that can be utilized by clinicians to more readily comprehend the fundamental pieces of a NLP framework and its effect on results. Work in the overall NLP area could be rousing for such turn of events, for example, incorporating strategies to investigate the impact of NLP pipeline steps in downstream undertakings (extraneous assessment, for example, the impact of reliance parsing approaches). On the other hand, techniques that empower examination of territories where a current NLP arrangement may require adjustment when applied on another issue, e.g., by back alignment, are a fascinating road of progress. In the event that medical NLP frameworks are created for non-NLP specialists, to be utilized in subsequent clinical results research, the NLP frameworks should be anything but difficult to utilize. Encouraging the mix of space information in NLP framework advancement should be possible by offering help for formalized information portrayals that can be utilized in ensuing NLP technique improvement.

Reporting Standards: In particular, guaranteeing straightforwardness and reproducibility of medical NLP techniques is critical to propel the area. In the medical exploration network, the matter of absence of logical proof for a lion's share of detailed medical examinations has been lifted. Many viewpoints ought to be steered to create conveyed examination revelations tentatively significant, among others replication culture and reproducibility practices. Typically, it is veritable moreover for clinical NLP procedure advancement. We propose an inconsequential tradition propelled by that charts the basic nuances of any clinical NLP ponder; by covering these, others can without a doubt recognize whether a disseminated technique can be fitting and important in another examination and for occasion [26], notwithstanding of whether changes may be imperative. This could energize further improvement of a far-reaching direction system for NLP, like what has been proposed for the announcing of observational investigations in the study of disease transmission in the STROBE proclamation, and different activities.

Rapid Growth of Incompatible Vocabularies in the Healthcare Domain: The restorative administration space is depicted by an exceptional improvement of vocabularies. From this time forward, various thoughts in these vocabularies can insinuate to a comparable thought. For case, mass implies bosom mass which may be a sort of bosom harmful development, whereas mass in a radio consistent report of the chest shows mass in the lung. Other than, the restorative administrations space comprises shortenings which may insinuate to a comparable thought. For occasion, the shortened form APC may cruel Enacted Protein C, Progressed Pancreatic Cancer, AlloPhyCocyanin, and Antibody Producing Cells, among others. Subsequently, equivocalness may be a test in restorative care as more thoughts are related with diverse resources. Along these lines, messages within the restorative care range have become difficult to dismember computationally.

Negation and Uncertainty in Clinical Texts: Most clinical ideas like indications, infections, analysis, and discoveries in clinical reports are invalidated and can be communicated with vulnerability. Invalidation in clinical reports alludes to the way toward recognizing if a named substance is available or missing. Nullification can be express or verifiable. Unequivocal nullification is portrayed by words like actually no, not, not one or the other, not just as their abbreviated structure like nt. Model incorporate the mediastinum isn't augmented which demonstrates the shortfall of Mediastnal broadening. Futhermore, the sentence "The patient isn't HIV (Human Immunodeficiency Virus) positive" suggests that the patient doesn't have HIV. Implied nullification includes lexico-semantic relations among etymological articulations. For example, lungs are clear upon auscultation, shows the shortfall of unusual lung sounds. Invalidations are typically semantically equivocal and subsequently may be hard to investigate computationally [27].

Presence of Spelling Errors: Medical records which contain spelling mistakes are hard to dissect utilizing NLP frameworks. This is on the grounds that the NLP framework may confound the data. For example, a spelling mistake "hypertension" might be alluded to as hypertension or hypotension and this would cause a deficiency of clinical data. Additionally, the medication Evista when spelt mistakenly as E-Vista alludes to an alternate medication. This mistake is anyway genuine and can be unfavorable to patients' well-being and would thus be able to prompt troublesome demise.

Heterogenous Formats: Clinical reports normally come up short on a uniform/standard structure [28]. Henceforth, clinical records are described by heterogeneous configurations.

For example, the titles and codes of the case reports vary in various clinics. Consequently, this absence of consistency is a test for NLP frameworks.

21.8 Conclusion

Clinical information is present in the form of narrative texts; thus, they are very unstructured, and hence, computers cannot understand the language, as a result, it becomes tough to access the health-related information. For retrieving meaning of these unstructured texts, NLP is used in the healthcare system; NLP helps in understanding the grammatical structures and also in the determination of the meaning of clinical terms, it also helps in translating the unstructured language so that computers could easily understand the language. Thus, NLP helps in accessing the necessary and valuable information easily. NLP can also decrease the amount/costs and increase the perfection of the healthcare system. Although NLP has many advantages, it also has some considerable challenges; these challenges are uncertainty, huge increase in number of words/vocabulary, lack/deficiency in the standard of the healthcare domains and also the lack of correct words in the reports. This paper studies the concepts of NLP used in the healthcare applications of NLP and examines the NLP system and also the resources which are used in healthcare; all the challenges of NLP are also studied in this paper. In this paper, different aspects of NLP as well as clinical methods have been studied, and thus, three basic challenges were figured out; these are evaluation, availability of data, and reporting standards and workbenches. After identifying the issues, solutions to each challenge were studied.

References

1. Vermesan, O., Friess, P., Guillemin, P., Serrano, M., IoT Digital Value Chain Connecting Research, Innovation and Deployment, 49, 15–128, 2016.
2. Das, J., Hammer, J., Leonard, K., The quality of medical advice in low-income countries. *J. Econ. Perspect.*, 22, 2, 93–114, 2008.
3. Zurn, P., Dal Poz, M.R., Stilwell, B., Adams, O., Imbalance in the health workforce. *Hum. Resour. Health*, 2, 1, 2–13, 2004.
4. Kaur, P., Kumar, R., Kumar, M., A healthcare monitoring system using random forest and Internet of Things (IoT). *Multimedia Tools and Applications*, 78, 14, 19905–19916, 2019.
5. Li, Q. and Cao, G., Providing Privacy-Aware Incentives in Mobile Sensing Systems. *IEE Trans. Mob. Comput.*, 15, 6, 1485–98, June, 2016.
6. Asabere, N.Y., Towards a viewpoint of context-aware recommender systems (CARS) and services. *Int. J. Comput. Sci. Telecomm.*, 4, 1, 10–29, 2013.
7. Catarinucci, L. *et al.*, An IoT-aware architecture for smart healthcare systems. *IEEE Internet Things J.*, 2, 6, 515–526, Dec. 2015.
8. Islam, S.M.R., Kwak, D., Kabir, M.H., Hossain, M., Kwak, K.S., The Internet of Things for healthcare: a comprehensive survey. *IEEE Access*, 3, 678–708, 2015.
9. Nasri, F. and Mtibaa, A., Smart Mobile Healthcare System based on WBSN and 5G. *International Journal of Advanced Computer Science and Applications (IJACSA)*, 8, 10, 147–156, 2017.
10. Catarinucci, L. *et al.*, An IoT-aware architecture for smart healthcare systems. *IEEE Internet Things J.*, 2, 6, 515–526, 2015.

11. Rajalakshmi, S., Deepika, N., Srivardhini, C.S., Vignesh, A.C., Vignesh, D.V., SDN controller for LTE networks. *Int. J. Comput. Appl.*, 133, 3, 31–36, 2016.

12. Kasem, E. and Prokopec, J., The evolution of LTE to LTEAdvanced and the corresponding changes in the uplink reference signals. *elektrorevue*, 3, 2, 1–5, 2012.

13. Chen, J. *et al.*, Narrowband Internet of Things: Implementations and applications. *IEEE Internet Things J.*, 4, 6, 2309–2314, 2017.

14. Mangalvedhe, N., Ratasuk, R., Ghosh, A., NB-IoT deployment study for low power wide area cellular IoT. *2016 IEEE 27th Annual International Symposium on Personal, Indoor, and Mobile Radio Communications*, 1–6, 2016.

15. Beyene, Y.D., Jantti, R., Ruttik, K., Iraji, S., On the performance of narrow-band Internet of Things (NB-IoT), *2017 IEEE wireless communications and networking conference (wcnc)*, 1–6, 2017.

16. Kindberg, T., People Places and Things: Web Presence of the Real World. *Mob. Netw. Appl.*, 7, 365–376, 2002.

17. Ji, S., Beyah, R., Li, Y., Continuous data collection capacity of wireless sensor networks under physical interference model. *2011 Eighth IEEE International Conference on Mobile Ad-Hoc and Sensor Systems*, 222–231, 2011.

18. Siau, K., Lim, E.P., Shen, Z., Mobile commerce: promises, challenges, and research agenda. *J. Database Manag. (JDM)*, 12, 3, 4–13, 2001.

19. Gioia, E., Passaro, P., Petracca, M., AMBER: An advanced gateway solution to support heterogeneous IoT technologies. *24th International Conference on Software, Telecommunications and Computer Networks (SoftCOM)*, 1–5, 2016.

20. Bound, J., Volz, B., Lemon, T., Perkins, C., Carney, M., Dynamic Host Configuration Protocol for IPv6 (DHCPv6), 85–113, 2003.

21. Lavric, A. and Popa, V., Performance evaluation of LoRaWAN communication scalability in large-scale wireless sensor networks, Journal title- *Wirel. Commun. Mob. Comput.*, 2018, 9, Article ID 6730719, 2018.

22. Chisholm, M., Kim, N., Ward, B.C., Otterness, N., Anderson, J., H. Smith, F.D., Reconciling the tension between hardware isolation and data sharing in mixed-criticality multicore systems, *IEEE Real-Time Systems Symposium (RTSS)*, 57–68, 2016.

23. Seshasayee, B., Schwan, K., Widener, P., SOAP-binQ: high-performance SOAP with continuous quality management, Georgia Tech. Library, 158–165, 2004.

24. Khanna, R., Liu, H., Rangarajan, T., Wireless Data Center Management Sensor Network Applications and Challenges. IEEE Microwave Magazine, 15, 45–60, 2014.

25. Liu, J., Zhang, S., Kato, N., Ujikawa, H., Suzuki, K., Device-to-device communications for enhancing quality of experience in software defined multi-tier LTE-A networks. *IEEE Network*, 29, 4, 46–52, 2015.

26. Chen, F.G., Wang, J.Y., Chen, S., Tu, S., Chen, K.Y., A hang-and-play intravenous infusion monitoring system. *Int. J. Eng. Tech. (IJET)*, 278–281, 2015.

27. Liu, J., Nishiyama, H., Kato, N., Guo, J., On the outage probability of device-to-device-communication-enabled multichannel cellular networks: An RSS-threshold-based perspective. *IEEE J. Sel. Areas Commun.*, 34, 1, 163–175, 2016.

28. Adamkó, A., Comprehensive healthcare interoperability framework integrating telemedicine consumer electronics with cloud architecture. *IEEE 15th International Symposium on Applied Machine Intelligence and Informatics (SAMI)*, 411–416, 2017.

Index

Printed and bound by CPI Group (UK) Ltd, Croydon, CR0 4YY

27/10/2024

14580181-0003